# THE DECLINE OF NAIR DOMINANCE

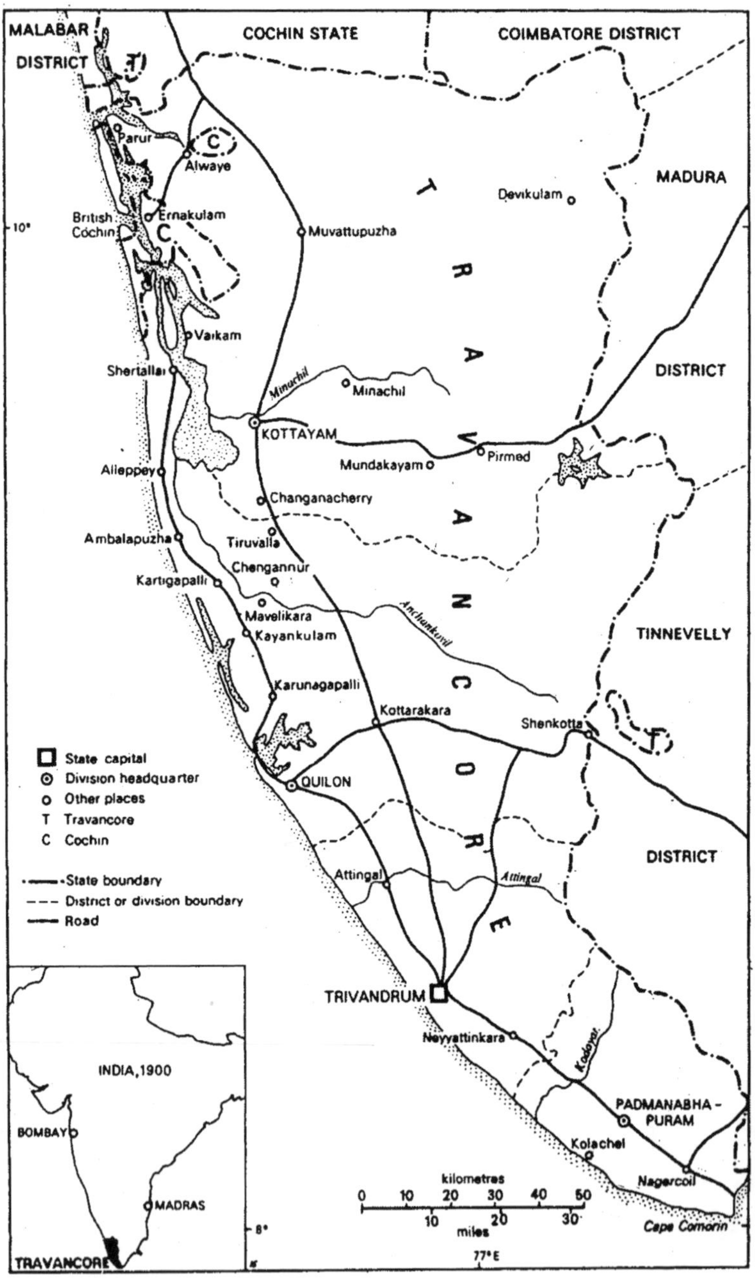


Travancore in 1900

# The Decline of Nair Dominance

*Society and Politics in Travancore*
*1847-1908*

ROBIN JEFFREY

MANOHAR
2026

First published 1976
Second edition 1994
Reprinted 2026



ISBN 978-93-5098-034-7

*Published by*
Ajay Kumar Jain *for*
Manohar Publishers & Distributors
4753/23 Ansari Road, Daryaganj
New Delhi 110 002

Printed and bound in India

To my mother and father
— guid gear's scarce

# Contents


| | |
|---|---|
| Abbreviations | xi |
| Preface to the Reprint of 2014 | xii |
| Preface to the Second Edition | xiv |
| Preface to the First Edition | xv |
| Introduction | xviii |
| 1. The Distribution of Resources, 1847: Nairs in Comfort | 1 |
| 2. Militant Missionaries: New Resources for Low Castes, 1847-60 | 34 |
| 3. Travancore Transformed: New Resources for All, 1860-72 | 63 |
| 4. Cash, Caste and Customs: The Effect of New Resources, 1872-91 | 93 |
| 5. The Malayali Sabha and the Malayali Memorial: Out of Change, Conflict, 1886-89 | 142 |
| 6. The Brahmin-Nair Official Elite and its Competitors, 1891-1904 | 161 |
| 7. 'Social Civil War': Nairs at Bay, 1902-08 | 195 |
| Epilogue: End of Matriliny: Beginning of Disillusion | 230 |
| Conclusion | 241 |
| Notes | 248 |
| Appendix | 326 |
| Glossary | 327 |
| Bibliography | 333 |
| Biographical Notes | 359 |
| Index | 377 |

*I would more especially call attention to the central point of interest ... in any descriptive and historical account of the Malayali race —the position, namely, which was occupied for centuries on centuries by the Nayar caste in the civil and military organization of the province, — a position so unique and so lasting that but for foreign intervention there seems no reason why it should not have continued to endure for centuries on centuries to come. Their functions in the body politic have been tersely described in their own traditions as* 'the eye', 'the hand', *and* 'the order', *and to the present day we find them spread throughout the length and breadth of the land, but no longer — I could say, alas! — 'preventing the rights (of all classes) from being curtailed or suffered to fall into disuse'.*

— *William Logan,* Malabar, *Vol. I, 1887, pp. v-vi.*

*O Who has not heard of that wonderful man,*
*Sir Gammon Row, the great Dewan,*
*Who has ruled for the last ten years or more,*
*The Protected State of Cocoanutcore?*
*This State, if judged from 'Reports' you read,*
*Is a very wonderful State indeed; —*
*A* 'Model State', *in which you may see*
*Everything* is *just as it should be,*
*Where dwells a worthy and well-oiled nation,*
*Blest with a faultless administration;*
*The brightest land, with the lightest tax,*
*And an annual surplus of fifty lacs;*
*Where happy ryots ne'er pestered by famines,*
*Till fields, in subjection to blessed Brahmins.*

.......................................

*In short, and I'm sure I cannot say more,*
*'Tis heaven on earth, this Cocoanutcore.*
*— R.C. Caldwell, 'The Good Sir Gammon Row',*
Chutney Lyrics, *1871.*

*While a Brahmin friend of mine was travelling on government duty in the Kottayam Division with a smart local officer, the latter said in reply to repeated questions about the country and people — 'Whenever you see a person that is strong in physique, smart and of good bearing, you may infer that he is either a Syrian Christian or an Ilavan; and if you see one that is weak in physique, pale and listless in bearing, your inference that he is a Nair will not often be mistaken. Similarly, if you see a garden land with a good hedge and first-rate cocoanut palms in it, you can infer that the owner is a Syrian or Ilavan — if hedgeless and unattended, you can be sure that the land belongs to a Nair'. My friend, the Brahmin official, found out subsequently by experience that all the local officer had said was true ... The same condition of things I have found to be true more or less in the South of Travancore also, if the world 'Native' is substituted for 'Syrian' and 'Shanar' for 'Ilavan'.*

— *Speech by P. Thanu Pillai, quoted in a letter to the* Madras Mail, *9 Oct. 1901.*

## ABBREVIATIONS

| | | |
|---|---|---|
| AP | - | Ampthill Papers |
| CCWM | - | Congregational Council for World Mission, London |
| Ch. Sec. | - | Chief Secretary to the Madras Government |
| CMS | - | Church Missionary Society |
| CMSA | - | Church Missionary Society Archives |
| CRR | - | Crown Representative Records |
| LD | - | Letters to the Dewan |
| LMG | - | Letters to the Madras Government |
| LMS | - | London Missionary Society |
| LMS, TDC | - | London Missionary Society, Travancore District Committee |
| *Mal. Mar. Com.* | - | *Report of the Malabar Marriage Commission, 1891* |
| *Maru. Report* | - | *Report of the Travancore Marumakkathayam Committee, 1908* |
| MML | - | Mannanam Monastery Library |
| MPP | - | Madras Political Proceedings |
| MRR | - | Madras Residency Records |
| NAI | - | National Archives of India |
| *RNNM* | - | *Reports on Native Newspapers, Madras* |
| *TAR* | - | *Travancore Administration Report* |
| TGER | - | Travancore Government English Records |
| *TGG* | - | Travancore Government Gazette |
| 'TLC Proc.' | - | 'Proceedings of the Travancore Legislative Council' |
| UTC | - | United Theological College, Bangalore |

# *Preface to the Reprint of 2014*

When I did the research for this book between 1970 and 1975, thousands of Malayalis had just begun to seek work in the Gulf, the Kerala tourist industry barely existed and Arundhati Roy was another one of thousands of middle-class children humming the hits from *The Sound of Music* that played non-stop from Kasargod to Kanyakumari.[1] In 2014, more than two million Malayalis work in West Asia, more than two million foreign tourists come to Kerala each year and Arundhati Roy is a household name. Kerala has changed a lot since this book was first published in 1976 and even since its last reprint in 1994.

The reason for a reprint in English is that the book is still in demand in Kerala where earlier editions are now hard to find even in libraries.[2] Though there has been much scholarly research on Kerala history and politics since 1976, this book still provides a readable account of an enthralling moment in modern Indian history. The period is the sixty years when practices implanted through British dominance hollowed out matrilineal institutions in the princely state of Travancore, which occupied the southern portion of today's Kerala.[3]

The book is not solely about matrilineal practices (i.e., descent and inheritance traced through women, not men) nor, in spite of the main title, about Nairs. When I wrote the book, I was trying to understand what happened when written legal codes, public works departments and such apparatus of a modern bureaucratic state were imposed in a corner of India. But as I began to investigate this line of inquiry, the dramatic story of the dissolving of matriliny emerged as a central aspect.

[1]My most trusted Malayali adviser points out that ordinary people at that time were captivated by the catchy tunes of Salil Chowdhary, sung by Hindi singers like Manna Dey and Lata Mangeshkar, from the film version of Thakazhi's *Chemmeen*.

[2]The present edition is a reprint using plates taken from the 1994 publication. D.C. Books in Kottayam published a Malayalam translation by Puthuppalli Raghavan and M.S. Chandrasekhara Warriar in 1979; rpt. 2003.

[3]G. Arunima, *There Comes Papa: Colonialism and the Transformation of Matriliny in Kerala. Malabar, c.1850-1940* (New Delhi: Orient Longman, 2003) has examined similar processes in the northern portion of today's Kerala.

Many people read the titles of books, but not so many read the books themselves. The title of this book needs a little explanation, because it has often been misunderstood. The Malayalam translation has not helped. *Nayar Medhavittvattinte Patanam* when translated back into English is sometimes rendered as 'the destruction of Nair rule.' I've sometimes been greeted by people who cheerily said, 'Oh, you are the person who wrote the book about the destruction of the Nairs.'[4] To paraphrase the disclaimers at the end of movies: no Nair is destroyed in this book. Indeed, people who identify as Nairs have fared at least as well as anyone else in Kerala over the past hundred years of head-spinning change. Perhaps the subtitle does a better job of capturing the scope of the book: 'society and politics in Travancore, 1847-1908.'

Anyone who visits the towns of southern Kerala will find vestiges of that time: the gravestone of the good-old, bad-old General William Cullen in the churchyard in Alleppey; CMS College in Kottayam; the Government Guest House on Ashtamudi Lake in Quilon; the Secretariat, General Hospital, Napier Museum and Victoria Jubilee Town Hall in Trivandrum.[5] And Trivandrum's favourite landmark – 'statue junction' – where Sir T. Madhava Rao, a leading figure of this book, stares sternly at the Secretariat. But though remnants of those days survive, much else has disappeared, just as most of the grand *taravad* houses have vanished. I suspect too that some of the records that I had the privilege of reading 40 years ago will by now have dissolved into dust.

In 1971 when I was researching this book, there were 21 million Keralites; in 2011, there were 33 million. New generations may find something of interest in a foreigner's attempt to understand their forebears.

I am grateful to Ramesh and Ajay Jain at Manohar for agreeing to reprint the book and to bring out an affordable paperback. And I am forever grateful to Malayalis for the kindnesses I have received from them and the immense pleasure I have derived from puzzling over their history.

Robin Jeffrey
Institute of South Asian Studies
National University of Singapore
October 2013

[4]'Naayar' is a better transliteration of the way in which the word is written and pronounced in Malayalam. 'Nair', however, has become a favoured spelling, partly, I think, to differentiate Malayalis from the Punjabi name 'Nayar' (as in Kuldip Nayar or Baldev Raj Nayar). Mystification arises when non-Malayalis make 'Nair' rhyme with 'hair'.

[5]I am using the old-fashioned spellings of place names, since they are the ones used in the book.

# *Preface to the Second Edition*

Only a few hundred copies of this book reached in India, and even in Britain, where it was originally published, it has been out of print for more than ten years. I am especially glad therefore to be able to bring out a new Indian edition.

I have not attempted to revise the manuscript in the light of work published since 1976. I believe that the overall argument still stands and that the narrative still holds some interest. To get an idea of subsequent scholarship on Kerala in this period, readers may wish to consult, for example, J.W. Gladstone, *Protestant Christianity and People's Movements in Kerala, 1850-1936* (Trivandrum: Seminary Publications, 1984) and Dick Kooiman, *Conversion and Social Equality in India: The London Missionary Society in South Travancore in the 19th Century* (New Delhi: Manohar, 1989). If readers want to know what (in my opinion) happened next, they may wish to look at my *Politics, Women and Well-Being: How Kerala Became 'a Model'* (London: Macmillan, 1992/New Delhi: Oxford University Press, 1993).

The most noticeable change in this edition is to the spelling of 'Nayar' — here, it appears as 'Nair'. This results from the insistence of Indian friends that such a style is more appropriate and intelligible for an Indian edition. Similarly, we have changed the transliteration of a few names of people and places. For example, S. Shungarasoobyer of the first edition becomes S. Sankara Subbaiyer in this one.

I have retained most of the original preface, partly because of its remarks about the study of Kerala and the location of sources in 1971.

Robin Jeffrey
La Trobe University
Melbourne
April 1994

# *Preface to the First Edition*

My reasons for choosing to attempt a study of a Malayalam-speaking area of India were initially unscholarly. The beauty of the area, the Malayalis' passion for newspapers and a tale about one of my dead relatives fascinated me when I first visited Kerala state as a tourist. I soon discovered, moreover, that in spite of the excellent articles of a few social anthropologists and the passing interest generated by the election of a Communist government in 1957, scholars had scarcely begun to examine the modern history of Kerala. A large part of the reason was the uncertainty of source materials. Because Travancore, the southern portion of modern Kerala was obviously a most unusual princely state — a 'model state' as early as 1867, according to one Secretary of State for India — and because the possibility of sources in Trivandrum seemed promising, I decided to concentrate my efforts there.

In Britain, the Madras Political Proceedings in the India Office Library and Records, London, contain most of the correspondence between the Madras Government and the Resident in Travancore for the first 60 years of the nineteenth century. From the 1860s, however, the Political Proceedings become less fruitful, and one must turn to the Madras Residency Records in the National Archives of India, New Delhi, for Residents' reports which were not forwarded to Britain. In Trivandrum, the Government of Kerala generously allowed me to look at nearly 20,000 unindexed files of the old Travancore government for the 1820-1904 period; these were stored in 1971 in the cellar of the Secretariat. I was also able to see the *Travancore Government Gazette* in the Kerala State Archives. To the custodians of all these materials, I am obviously greatly indebted.

The archives of the Church Missionary Society and the London Missionary Society (now the Congregational Council for World Mission) in London were highly rewarding. Both societies have large collections of letters from their agents in Travancore. Men like Samuel Mateer, John Cox, Arthur Painter and Joseph Peet were caught up in local politics and deeply interested in social customs. Their biases, because they are generally so glaring, rarely detract from the usefulness of their accounts of events. I have not, however, attempted to use the archives of the southern European Roman Catholic orders which worked in Travancore and Cochin.

Many of the periodicals and newspapers published in south India before the turn of the century have been lost or destroyed. The New York Public Library is said to hold a few years of the *Western Star* for the 1860s, but of the newspaper's 80 years of publication this is apparently all that remains; the back numbers of the *Cochin Argus* have vanished completely. Nor was I able to find the *Madras Standard* after 1889 or the originals of any of G. Parameswaran Pillai's pamphlets. However, through efforts of the Rt. Rev. S.A. Gnanadason, Bishop of Kanyakumari, I was able to see four valuable years of the *Travancore Times* for the 1880s, and John Mampilli of Cochin kindly made available the back numbers of the *Malabar Herald* which his father started in 1905. I am grateful to the British Museum Newspaper Archives, Colindale, London, and the library of the University of Western Australia for allowing me to read the *Madras Mail* and *The Hindu* respectively.

Other printed sources in south India are to be found in many places. The small, businesslike library at Scott Christian College, Nagercoil, preserved almost a complete run of the annual reports of the Travancore District Committee of the London Missionary Society. The proprietors of the Vivekananda Press, Jagathi, Trivandrum, allowed me to use the fine library of the late Ulloor S. Parameswara Aiyar. Among other things, the library had every issue of the *Malabar Quarterly Review*. I was also able to use the Theosophical Society Library, Adyar, Madras, the Connemara Public Library, Madras, the Univiersity of Kerala Library, Trivandrum, the Trivandrum Public Library, the Kerala High Court Library, Cochin, and the Mannanam Monastery Library near Kottayam. A number of individuals who own old books or periodicals allowed me to look at them. K. Prabhakaran, the son of N. Kumaran Asan, and P.C. Joseph, former principal of CMS College, Kottayam, were particularly helpful in this regard — and in many other things.

For the period before 1910, most source material is in English. C.V. Raman Pillai and his friends among the first generation of college-educated Nairs conducted their correspondence in English. Indeed, the letters which P.K. Parameswaran Nair uses in his Malayalam biography of Raman Pillai have been translated from English to Malayalam. The original letters unfortunately have now been lost or destroyed. Similarly, *Malayala Manorama* until at least 1910 published editorials in English when it was intent on attracting the attention of British governments and important officials. The back numbers of *Manorama* are well-preserved in its offices in Kottayam where I was able to look at them. Except for *Nasrani Deepika*, the Romo-Syrian newspaper, I was unable to find other early Malayalam periodicals.

I began my study of Malayalam in Kerala under the conscientious and good-humoured guidance of V.K. Narayanan, then a sub-editor of the *Malayalam Encyclopaedia*. I was extremely fortunate when I returned to England to be able to continue my study with Miss Dorothy Taylor of Saltdean, Sussex, who was more than 30 years in Trivandrum with the Church of England Zenana Missionary Society. I am very grateful to both my teachers who enabled me to use a number of Malayalam published sources. Transliteration is always a problem in Indian studies. I have followed a policy of consistent inconsistency. In the text I have spelled Malayalam words roughly as they would be pronounced. Most have been underlined, but a few — like taravad, karanavan, etc. — which recur frequently, have not.

The reader may find that a bafflingly large number of men with the title 'Pillai' appear in the story which follows. I have always referred to them with a prename — thus, Parameswaran Pillai, Raman Pillai, etc. There are about 60 names included in the Biographical Notes at the end, and these have been ordered on the basis of the prename — for example, Raman Pillai, C.V. Generally, I have spelled proper names in the way in which they usually appeared in documents and newspapers of the time.

I have incurred many debts to many people in the course of this project. Under the auspices of the Canadian University Service Overseas (CUSO), I was first able to go to India; the friends I made in those two years awakened my interest in India and have sustained it. Canada Council fellowships financed two years of the project, including another year in India. The manuscript was revised while I was holding a research fellowship in the Research

School of Pacific Studies, Australian National University. My mother and father saved me days of work by typing drafts or helping with indexing. Friends in Kerala and elsewhere — A.J. Tampi, K.R. Elenkath, K. Karunakaran Nair, P.K. Parameswaran Nair, Fr. Joseph James, Abraham M. Nidhiry, Dr. P.E. Thomas, Dr. K.M. George, to name a few whom I have not already mentioned — talked about the project, made suggestions and sent me in turn to their friends. In London, Mike and Jenny Gadsby provided the nicest of succour and shelter. David Arnold, Susan Lewandowski, James Manor, Christopher May, Dick Rooksby and Elizabeth Whitcombe took time and trouble to read and comment on the manuscript in its various incarnations. Hans Gunther of the Research School of Pacific Studies, Australian National University, drew the two excellent maps. Anthony Low and Peter Reeves had the doubtful privilege of following the project from beginning to end; their advice, encouragement and humour were perhaps most valuable of all. However, the responsibility for the interpretations and the faults in what follows is obviously mine alone.

# Introduction

This is a study of social and political change resulting from the impact of a cash economy, western-style education, improved communications and a British-inspired system of law on the complex social structure of an Indian princely state. Specifically, this study deals with the breakdown of the matrilineal social system which prevailed in Travancore among a large section of high-caste Hindus, and with the growth of social assertiveness and political aspirations among low-caste Hindus and Christians. It is the story of a 'dominant caste' being brought down from comfortable supremacy over its neighbours to keen competition with them in 60 years.

In every region of India the period from about 1850 to 1910 was one of striking change. To describe the processes at work, one turns to words like 'anglicization', 'modernization', 'secularization'. There are also impressive illustrations. In 1849, the uneducated great-grand-uncle of Prakash Tandon fought with the Sikh army against the British at the Battle of Chilianwala in the Punjab; by 1910 Tandon's father was a senior engineer in British service.[1] Perhaps nowhere in India, however, were the changes of these years so dramatic or so little known as in the Malayalam-speaking region of Kerala on the southwestern coast. In 1859 it took six weeks to travel by bullock cart from Madras to Travancore; in 1903 the railway journey to Quilon took thirty hours.[2] In the 1850s the Travancore government enforced caste laws which required most women to go bare-breasted; in 1915 a Travancore woman on a government scholarship graduated in medicine from the University of London.[3]

The modern linguistic state of Kerala, created in 1956, was formed from areas which were under three distinct governments yet shared a common language and culture when the British ruled India. The northern portion of the present state was the British Indian district of Malabar, a part of the Madras Presidency. South of Malabar was the small princely state of Cochin, and to its south again, the princely state of Travancore, covering an area of about 7,600 square miles, stretching from Cochin to Cape Comorin.[4]

Although Vasco da Gama found Kerala divided into dozens of rival principalities when he landed at Calicut in 1498, the region had an ancient cultural unity. According to the Brahminical tradition, the creation of Kerala resulted from the banishment from India of the god Parasurama. Having nowhere to live, he won the permission of Varuna, the god of the sea, to reclaim all the land within a throw of his axe. Parasurama threw his axe from Cape Comorin to Gokarnam, the sea receded and Kerala was formed. To populate the new area, Parasurama introduced a special race of Brahmins, the Nambudiris, and gave to them ownership of all the land and unique customs which prevented their return to the India on the other side of the Western Ghats. Next, he brought Sudras — the Nairs — to act as the servants and bodyguards of the Nambudiris. He bestowed on the Nairs the marumakkattayam or matrilineal system of family and inheritance, and decreed that Nairs should have no formal marriage and that their women should always be available to satisfy the desires of the Nambudiris.[5]

The legend, which is thought to date from the seventeenth century,[6] constitutes an attempt to justify some of the most important features of traditional society in Kerala: the hold of high-caste Hindus on the land, the matrilineal system of the Nairs, their close relationship with the Nambudiris, and the Nairs' military role. By inference the legend also sought to justify the debasing subservience which Nairs extracted from their caste inferiors. Ritual pollution, which in the rest of India was transmitted only by touch, could in Kerala be communicated over distance. A Nambudiri, seeing a man of the slave castes a hundred yards away, would consider himself polluted and undergo a series of purificatory ceremonies.

Travancore fell under British suzerainty and received a British Resident in 1800, but it was fifty years before the effects of the British connection began to show upon the dominance of high-caste Hindus, particularly Nairs. What was the extent of that dominance in the mid-19th century? In most villages or *desams* of Travancore,[7] Nairs, or their much less numerous Nambudiri or Kshatriya patrons, were the chief landholders. To be sure, in north and central Travancore there were *desams* in which the biggest landholders were Syrian

Christians, but in most of Travancore they were Nairs. Nairs, moreover, held slaves, and in the pre-British period had been responsible for maintaining order. In the administration of Travancore, they held more than sixty percent of the posts; their only rivals were non-Malayali Brahmins. Their hypergamous, matrilineal system of marriage meant that the wives of the Maharajas of Travancore and of local Kshatriyas were Nairs. The younger sons of Nambudiris and some non-Malayali Brahmins also entered into marriage alliances with Nairs. In a state dedicated to a Hindu deity, such as Travancore, Nairs enjoyed the privileges and power of being by far the most numerous 'clean' Hindu caste. Syrian Christians they could largely ignore, while from their caste inferiors — artisan castes, Shanars, Iravas and slave castes — they could compel the most exaggerated forms of submission and subservience.

The position of Nairs, therefore, squared fairly closely with the definition of a 'dominant caste' given by a modern anthropologist. A 'dominant caste' has 'relatively eminent right over the land; ... power to grant land and to employ other castes ... [and thereby] to build up a large clientele, not [to] say an armed force; power of justice ...; generally speaking monopoly of authority ...; ... the dominant caste is often a royal caste, [or] a caste allied to royal castes ...'[8] This is what is meant by 'Nair dominance' in the chapters which follow: not that Nairs were the largest landholders in every *desam* in Travancore, but that they were in most; not that every village officer and government official was a Nair, but that the great majority were; not that Nairs had the highest ritual status, but that their privileges far out-weighed their disabilities. This is not, therefore, the strictly defined village 'dominant caste' of some social anthropologists.[9] All that is argued here is that in Travancore in the mid-nineteenth century about one-fifth of the population were people known as Nairs — 'the' Nairs suggests too much homogeneity[10] — who had a number of common attributes and who were easily identified by non-Nairs; that these Nairs held most of the land in most of the *desams*, as well as most of the appointments under government; that they had a fairly high ritual status which gave them great advantages over low-caste people and non-Hindus in a traditional Hindu kingdom; that they enjoyed close relationships through their women with the small portion of the population who were their ritual superiors; and that this was 'Nair dominance'.

From the 1850s, however, the balance of the political and social system was increasingly disturbed as new resources became available for which all men, regardless of caste or religion, could compete on fairly equal terms. The commercial or menial occupations of many Christians and low-caste Hindus, and their association with European missionaries, gave them advantages in this competition which Nairs did not share. Indeed, the economic pressures, changing values and rigorous legal system, which were the concomitant of the new resources, seriously weakened the Nair matrilineal joint-family and hastened its disintegration. As the bonds of the matrilineal family loosened, so did the hold of Nairs on the land.

In 1847 European missionaries in Travancore began a campaign to end slavery. Since the system of slavery was inextricably connected with caste, the missionaries' campaign developed into a challenge to the principles of Travancore society and to the ramshackle administration. Slavery was abolished in 1855, and by the 1860s the Travancore government, responding to British pressure, had embarked on a vigorous programme of administrative and commercial reform. These reforms encouraged education and helped to extend a cash economy throughout the state.

Throughout the 1870s and 1880s different groups responded to these changes in different ways. The importance of ritual status began to decline. The idea grew that a man should no longer be accorded deference on the basis of his caste but on the basis of his academic qualifications, his industry or his wealth. Educated Nairs were the first to use such new ideas politically. Nair officials increasingly questioned the right of non-Malayali Brahmins to hold many of the most lucrative posts in the government service. After a petition and agitation against such non-Malayali Brahmin officials in 1891, these Brahmins and the first generation of college-educated Nair government servants reached a brief understanding over patronage in the administration. However, Christians and low-caste Hindus, modestly prospering in the new economic climate, could apply the new ideas about 'qualifications' and achievement against their chief rivals — Nairs. The latter, moreover, were increasingly aware of the chaotic conditions of the matrilineal joint-family and increasingly sensitive to charges that Nairs, unlike caste Hindus in the rest of India, had no formal, legal marriage.

Travancore's extraordinary rate of literacy facilitated communication between educated men in the towns and their castemen in rural areas. New ideas, aspirations and conflicts were not confined to an urban elite. The rate of male literacy in 1901 was 22 per cent, the highest in India, and in Travancore's nine small towns, it reached 36 per cent, higher than that of Calcutta.[11] By 1905 there were more than 20 Malayalam and English newspapers, and among most castes in most *desams* there were men able to read the newspapers aloud in coffee shops and by the roadside.

By 1908 educated members of various castes and religions were competing vigorously, and often bitterly, for positions in the government service. Many of the most important posts in that service were still reserved for high-caste Hindus, much to the anger and frustration of Christsians and low castes. Members of the first generation of college-educated Nairs had become deeply involved in palace politics in Trivandrum. Their aim, they asserted, was to win control of the highest posts in the government service from non-Malayali Brahmins and thus protect the interests of their castemen. By this time, however, the economic position of Nair joint-families having only modest holdings of land was obviously critical. The politics of the palace smacked of self-interest and delusions of grandeur. The report of a government committee set up in 1908 to investigate the matrilineal joint-family produced statistics which showed an alarming rate of land transfer from Nairs to Christians and low castes. The committee, composed entirely of matrilineal high-caste Hindus, took such a serious view of the situation that it advocated drastic changes in the law relating to the matrilineal joint-family. Yet it was this joint-family, according to the glorifiers of the Nair past, which had been the basis of Nairs' way of life in prosperous, powerful days of yore.

To be sure, Nairs in 1908 had not lost all their advantages or been swept from power. They still held more land than any other group; but they were alienating it steadily. They still preponderated in the government service; but their dominance, based partly as it was on ritual status, was constantly questioned. They were, indeed, like a retreating army, trying to rectify internal problems of administration and supply while counterattacking in some areas and defending others. In the years after 1908 they painfully succeeded in resolving the problems of the matrilineal joint-family and in checking the erosion of their power. Yet in having to cling to what they had, Nairs were in sharp contrast to 'dominant castes' in other areas of India. Elsewhere, the 'dominant caste' in the twentieth century displaced the elite 'service' castes — generally Brahmins — and grew powerful.[12] For Nairs, the unquestioned dominance which they enjoyed in traditional society vanished; the plural and competitive nature of Travancore society in the twentieth century made it impossible to achieve the political influence available to 'dominant castes' in other areas. To exercise power in future, men would have to rely on their skill in mobilizing increasingly wide popular support. The fusion of Nair sub-castes and the creation of a Nair political 'community', which some Nairs saw as the solution to the new problems of political power, were partially negated by the growing importance of class divisions among Nairs. All this was a far cry from the days of their idealized traditional glory, or, indeed, from the secure position which most Nairs held in 1847 when this story begins.

## NOTES

1. Prakash Tandon, *Punjabi Century, 1857-1947* (Berkeley: University of California Press, 1968), pp.11 and 29-31.
2. London Missionary Society [hereafter LMS], Travancore District Committee [hereafter TDC], *Annual Report* [hereafter *Report]*, 1908, p.10, quoting Rev. James Duthie who arrived in Travancore in 1859. The trip from Madras to Quilon by ship in the 1850s could be made in four or five days if a ship was available. The railway reached Quilon in 1903.
3. The woman was Mary Poonen (later Mrs. Mary Poonen Lukose) who became the director of the Travancore medical department in 1924. See the *Madras Mail*, 26 Oct.1915, p. 3 and 24 Sept. 1924, p. 4. She was the first Malayali woman to take a BA degree in 1909. *Madras Mail*, 6 March 1909, p. 5.
4. The area around Cape Comorin was Tamil-speaking. These Tamil taluks were transferred to Tamil Nadu (then Madras state) during the reorganization of the Indian states on a linguistic basis in 1956.
5. *Keralolpatti*, discussed in William Logan, *Malabar*, Vol. I (Madras: Government Press, 1951; first published 1887), pp. 221-4.
6. *Ibid.*, p. 224n. See also A. Sreedhara Menon, *A Survey of Kerala History* (Kottayam: National Book Stall, 1970), pp. 10-11, which suggests that the *keralolpatti* dates from the eighteenth or nineteenth century.
7. To talk of a 'village' in Kerala is to suggest a misleading picture. Settlement is dispersed. One house and cocoanut garden merges with another, and to a stranger it is impossible to discern where one *desam* ends and another begins.
8. Louis Dumont, *Homo Hierarchicus* (London: Paladin, 1972), p. 207.
9. For discussions of the 'dominant caste' see Dumont, *Hierarchicus*, pp. 205, 207 and 333 (note 34b); M.N. Srinivas, 'The Social System of a Mysore Village', in McKim Marriott, ed., *Village India* (Chicago: Chicago University Press, 1955), p. 17 and 'The Dominant Caste in Rampura', *American Anthropologist*, vol. XIV, 1958, pp. 416, 420 and 426; Kathleen Gough, 'The Hindu Jajmani System', *Economic Development and Cultural Change*, Vol.IX, No. 1, Oct.1960, p. 91; Peter M. Gardner, 'Dominance in India: A Reappraisal', *Contributions to Indian Sociology*, New Series, No. II, Dec. 1968, pp. 82-97; F.G. Bailey, *Tribe, Caste and Nation* (Manchester: Manchester University Press, 1960), pp.

257-63. For criticisms of the concept of the 'dominant caste' which stress the importance of factionalism among so-called 'dominant castes', see T.K. Oommen, 'The Concept of Dominant Caste: Some Queries', *Contributions to Indian Sociology*, New Series, No, II. Dec. 1968, pp. 58-81. See also E.E. Evans-Pritchard, 'The Nuer of the Southern Sudan' in M. Fortes and Evans-Pritchard, eds., *African Political Systems* (Oxford: University Press, 1962; first published, 1940), pp. 281-2 for a discussion of 'segmentary opposition' which I think strengthens the arguments of those who stress the importance of the 'dominant caste'.

10. Nairs were divided into a number of subcastes. These will be discussed later.
11. *Census of India*, 1901, Vol. I, Part 1 pp. 168-75. *Travancore Census Report* [hereafter *Census*], 1901, Vol. I, p. 208.
12. For discussions of dominant rural castes enhancing their political importance in the twentieth century, see Maureen L.P. Patterson, 'Caste and Political Leadership in Maharashtra. A Review and Current Appraisal', *Economic Weekly*, Bombay, 25 Sept. 1954, pp. 1065-7; John G. Leonard, 'Politics and Social Change in South India: A Study of the Andhra Movement', *Journal of Commonwealth Political Studies*, Vol. V, No.1, March 1967, pp. 60-77; Dagmar Bernstorff, 'Eclipse of "Reddy-Raj"? The Attempted Restructuring of the Congress Party Leadership in Andhra Pradesh', *Asian Survey*, Vol. XIII, No. 10, Oct. 1973, pp. 959-79; James Manor, *Political Change in an Indian State: Mysore, 1917-55* (Canberra: Monographs on South Asia, Australian National University, 1977); David Hardiman, *Peasant Nationalists of Gujarat: Kheda District, 1917-34* (New Delhi: Oxford University Press, 1981).

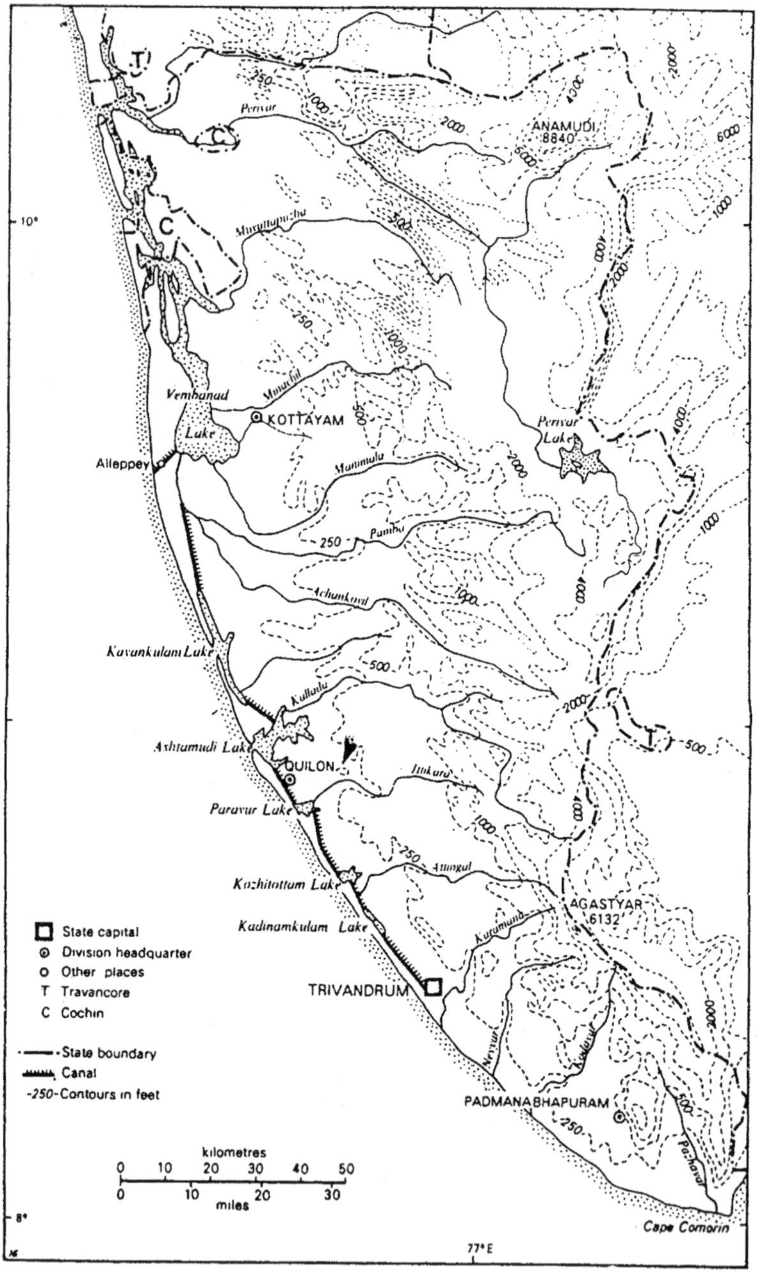


Travancore: Physical Features, showing 250, 500, 1,000, 2,000, 4,000 and 6,000-foot contours

# 1

# *The Distribution of Resources, 1847: Nairs in Comfort*

## *THE GOVERNMENT OF TRAVANCORE*

The Chera Empire, which appears to have survived in various forms from about 130 A.D. to 1100, occasionally brought a modicum of unity to the region of Kerala. In the course of a hundred-year war in the eleventh century with the Chola dynasty which ruled the country to the east, the Chera Empire disintegrated. Its local chiefs, deprived of a central loyalty, set themselves up as independent rulers.[1] For the next six or seven hundred years, dozens of petty chiefs waged intermittent wars. The largest and most successful of these rulers claimed Kshatriya status, but it seems likely that they were Nairs who as a result of political and military success were able to engineer a promotion in ritual status.[2]

Kerala lies on a narrow shelf of land, never more than seventy or eighty miles wide, between the Western Ghats and the Arabian Sea. In places the Ghats rise to 8,800 feet, and to cross them—except at the three major passes, Palghat, Shenkotta and Aruvamozhi—is a tortuous journey. Within Kerala, the country is hilly and intersected by thirty major rivers flowing from the Ghats to the sea. After the dissolution of the Chera Empire, the isolation imposed by the Ghats allowed the development of a political system largely undisturbed by events in the rest of India. At the same time, Kerala's difficult internal communications produced hereditary rulers of the smallest portions of land. They were linked by a loose system of vassalage to district and regional chiefs. These in turn were subject to the theoretical sovereignty of self-styled princes who might claim to be the regents of the last Chera emperor.[3]

At the lowest level of the administration of the land was the *desam* or village, varying between about one and ten square miles, depending on population, and presided over by an hereditary Nair headman.[4] These owed allegiance to the ruler of the district or *nad*, 'a territorial organisation of the ruling Nairs';[5] the *naduvazhi* was theoretically subject to Kshatriya or Samanthan princes. Conflicts over expansion and allegiance were recurring at various levels, but were played out under recognised rules. A conquered *naduvazhi* was left in control of his *desams*, although he paid tribute to his conqueror and became his subject—at least until the next war.[6]

Parallel with the *desam*, though not necessarily following the same geographic boundary, were local caste bodies. Nambudiris were said to have been organised into sixty-four *gramams* by Parasurama, and it was the *gramam* which was vital for them in matters of caste. Similarly, Nairs in Travancore were organised in *karas* (*tara* in north Kerala) and Ezhavas in *cheris*. For Nairs and Ezhavas, however, by the mid-ninteenth century, the caste organisations seem to have been of declining importance.[7]

Under the pre-British polity Nairs had privileges and power although they probably never accounted for more than 20 or 25 percent of the population. They were, moreover, recognised only as Sudras, inferior in ritual status to the small numbers of Nambudiri Brahmins, non-Malayali Brahmins, Kshatriyas and Ambalavasis (temple servants) who lived in Kerala. But Nairs provided the soldiers and officials who carried out the wishes of the higher castes, conducted the endless gentlemanly wars and kept the lower castes in order. William Logan, an Indian Civil Servant and the leading British student of Kerala, glorified their role:

> From the earliest times...down to the end of the eighteenth century the *tara* and *nad* organisation kept the country from oppression and tyranny on the part of the rulers...
>
> But besides protection the Nairs had originally another

> most important function in the body politic... they were also *supervisors or overseers*... Parasu Raman [the legendary creator of Kerala] (so the tradition in the Keralolpatti runs) 'separated the Nairs into Taras and ordered that to them belonged the duty of supervision (*lit. kan*=the eye), the executive power (*lit. kai* = the hand, as the emblem of power), and the giving of orders (*lit. kalpana* = order, command) so as to prevent the rights from being curtailed or suffered to fall into disuse'. The Nairs were originally the overseers or supervisors of the *nad*...[8]

Certainly Nairs ruled, but one may wonder whether the Kerala they governed was idyllic as Logan often represents. Of the Nairs at the beginning of the sixteenth century, Duarte Barbosa wrote: 'When they walk along a street or road, they shout to the low caste folk to get out of their way; this they do, and if one will not, the Nair may kill him without punishment...'[9]

When in 1729 Martanda Varma became Raja of Venad, reduced from former glories to a small principality centred around the village of Tiruvidamkod in what is now Tamil Nadu, he faced war, refractory chiefs and near-anarchy. Martanda Varma cast aside the rules of traditional Kerala warfare. Having captured the recalcitrant chiefs of eight leading Nair families, he had them executed and their women and dependents sold to low-caste fishermen.[10] He conquered and absorbed neighbouring principalities; he entered into treaties with the Nayaks of Madura and the British East India Company; and through Rama Aiyar, his minister, he introduced dependent, dependable Tamil Brahmins to administer his new territories in the place of the defeated local chiefs who were pensioned, imprisoned or killed.[11] A European soldier, Eustace de Lannoy, captured when a Dutch raid was defeated at Kolachel in 1741, reorganized the military and changed it from a feudal force, rallied by local chiefs, to a salaried, drilled and uniformed army. Its composition was overwhelmingly Nair, and the Nair militia was not abolished; but the new army represented a further incursion on the independence of local Nair leaders.

By the time Martanda Varma died in 1758, the borders of Travancore, as the expanding state came to be called, stood roughly where they remained until 1949: from Cochin in the north to Kanyakumari (Cape Comorin) in the south, from eight to ten degrees north latitude. The state was about 175 miles long, pressed between the Ghats and the sea, and had an area of about 7,600 square miles. This was slightly smaller than Wales, and about the same size as a number of districts in the Madras Presidency.

The expansion of Travancore from a tiny area near Nagercoil to the backwaters of Cochin brought loss and discomfort to some and put Martanda Varma and his state in debt to others. The new system of administration curtailed the power of Nair chiefs—many of whom, to be sure, moved effortlessly into Martanda Varma's organisation–and made it necessary to retain the goodwill of the numerous Tamil Brahmins brought into the sirkar service. Towards the latter end, dozens of *uttupuras*, free feeding houses for Brahmins, were opened throughout Travancore. At the same time, attempts were made to conciliate the Malayali Brahmins–Nambudiris and Pottis–who had been roughly handled in the course of Martanda Varma's consolidation. The state was dedicated to Padmanabha, the deity of the great temple of Trivandrum, and a sexennial ceremony, *murajapam*, 'a political "At-home" to the disaffected Nambudiris', was inaugurated, at which Brahmins were feasted for fifty-six days in return for offering prayers for the state.[12]

All this, however, marked a swing away from the Nairs and created around the ruler of Travancore non-Nair influences and institutions. Martanda Varma 'cared nothing whatever for Kerala ideals', a well-known Nair historian and diplomat has written with some pique. He elaborated:

> The Travancore state was in fact a Tamilian conception and its advancement towards the north was the victory of Tamilian over Kerala culture. Martanda Varma in the interest of his dynastic ambition surrounded himself with scheming Tamilians of whom Rammayyan was the supreme type and with ambitious adventurers like de Lannoy.[13]

Yet Nairs were merely brought to heel; they were not dispossessed. Under Martanda Varma's long-lived successor, the chief minister for most of the reign was Keshava Das, a Nair. Local Nair chiefs may have lost some of their independence, but the army was still composed of Nairs, and, with Tamil Brahmins, they carried on the administration of the state. Their relation to the ruler had changed, but not their relation to other sections of society.

The British imposed the next limitation on Nair dominance. Having fulfilled a treaty obligation and gone to war with Tipu Sultan when he attacked Travancore in December 1789, they extracted a treaty of subsidiary alliannce from Travancore in 1795.[14] It was not until 1800, however, after the death of Maharaja Rama Varma and the final defeat of Tipu, that the state received the doubtful blessing of a British political Resident. He was Major Colin Macaulay (Resident 1800-09), who had been four years a prisoner of Tipu in Seringapatam.[15] Macaulay was stubborn and abrasive; the Travancore sirkar, uncooperative and incompetent. The subsidy fell into arrears, and official suggestions to reduce the allowances to the Nair soldiery and militia provoked a rebellion in 1804. The following year a new treaty was imposed, the subsidy set at eight lakhs of rupees, and Travancore absolved of the obligation to aid its British ally with troops.

In 1809 Velu Thampi, the Nair Dewan who had been appointed on Macaulay's recommendation, became exasperated with the Resident's interference and appalled at the direction it appeared to be taking. He led a conservative rebellion against the British, who, he warned, intended to

> ...put their own guards in the palaces, Sircar buildings, and the fort gates, destroy the royal seal, do away with honorific palanquins and other distinguishing marks, suppress the Brahmanical communities and worship in pagodas, make monopolies of salt and of waste lands, impose exorbitant taxes on paddy lands, coconut trees, etc., get low-caste people to inflict heavy punishment for slight faults, put up crosses and Christian flags in pagodas, compel intermarriages with Brahman women without reference to caste or creed, and practise all the unjust and unlawful things which characterise Kaliyuga.[16]

Within months the rebellion was crushed, Velu Thampi driven to suicide, and the Nair soldiery disarmed and disbanded. Its last fight was ignominious: 'I never beheld a more dastardly crew', wrote James Welsh, 'nor did they deserve the name of soldiers, although neatly clothed in military uniforms, furnished with capital arms, and in a country, every inch of which might have been defended'.[17]

Velu Thampi's rebellion left the British suspicious of Nair leaders. The arrival of the new Resident, Major John Munro (Resident, 1810-19), coincided with the death of the weak Maharaja and the accession of a young Maharani. After a brief experiment with a Nair Dewan, whose dismissal led to another small revolt,[18] Munro himself took over the Dewanship from 1811 to 1814. Three Nair Dewans, who appear to have been no more than glorified clerks to the Resident, were tried from 1814 to 1817. In the latter year Munro fell back on Reddy Rao, a Desastha Brahmin, 'with a tolerable knowledge of the English language', who had come to Travancore in the Resident's entourage. Non-Malayali Brahmins held the Dewanship continuously until 1877, and only one Travancore Nair was ever to be Dewan again.[19]

Munro carried out a number of reforms intended to lessen still further the power of local officers and leaders, to centralise the administration and to bring it more into line with that of British India. He withdrew the judicial function from taluk officials, who had hitherto been 'military and civilian governors' whose investiture 'was given by the Rajah with a sword'; Munro renamed the officers tahsildars.[20] He had erring sirkar servants flogged, and established a system of courts with places reserved on the bench for Brahmins, Nairs and Christians.[21]

During Munro's time, Christians, who numbered at this stage perhaps fifteen per cent of the population, enjoyed a brief period of favour which they had not known before. Syrian Christians, as we shall see, had long enjoyed wealth and status but only rarely executive power. Munro, however, saw the encouragement of the Syrian Christians as a means of evangelising Travancore Hindus. This was desirable, he wrote, because 'the diffusion of genuine Christianity in India [is] a measure equally important to the intrests of humanity and to the stability of our power'. Given 'moderate assistance and encouragement from the British Government', Syrian Christians 'will firmly attach themselves to its interests, and may prove of material service in supporting its power'.[22] Munro appointed a Christian judge to each of his half-dozen new courts, and for about a year, two European missionaries also acted as judges. The provision of Christian judges, he wrote, 'is also agreeable to the Brahmins and Nairs, who find in the integrity of Christian judges, a check on the venality and corruption of the Nair judges'.[23] At the same time, 'more than 200'[24] Syrians were taken into the sirkar service. By 1818 these measures had led to 'the gradual subversion of the tyranny exercised heretofore by the Brahmins and Nairs'.[25]

However, when Munro left the state--he became a vice-patron of the Church Missionary Society from 1820 until his death in 1857--the old situation soon reasserted itself. A few Christian judges remained, but other Christians in the administration disappeared.[26] By 1847 Nair numerical dominance of the sirkar service was overwhelming, and probably at least a third of Nair matrilineal joint-families had a relative employed there in some capacity.[27]

The administration in the 1840s was lax, ramshackle, ill-paid, yet numerically extensive. There were 240 pravrattis in the state, each with its pravrattikaran and a small staff. Some of these offices were hereditary and were coveted 'by the bulk of our Nair population..., more on account of the dignity which they conferred than their gain... '[28] There was also a question of power, for the pravrattikar supervised land revenue, registration and assessment. The pravrattis were organised into thirty-two taluks, each presided over by a tahsildar and a larger staff. There were fifty-three sirkar post offices, forty-five warehouses for government monopolies, one hundred and thirty-four excise stations, thirty-seven customs houses and forty-one feeding houses for Brahmins.[29] In Trivandrum the Nair Brigade, the state's army, provided employment for 1,500 Nairs.[30] Of eleven posts in the huzur kutcherry in 1850, including the Dewanship, Nairs held five. They also filled eight of the twelve important positions in the palace.[31]

While Syrian Christians had been edged out of the sirkar service after Munro's departure, non-Malayali Brahmins--the Smarthas who had made themselves available to Martanda Varma and the Desasthas who came with British Residents--remained ensconced in many of the cosiest niches the administration had to offer. As we have seen, the Dewans from 1817 to 1872 were Desasthas. Their hold became so tight that a Marathi department was formed in the huzur kutcherry, and 'the Dewans generally performed a great portion of the work in Marathi'.[32] It was an effective way of closing part of the administration to rivals. In 1850 the Dewan, V. Krishna Rao, was a Brahmin from the Telugu country, a Smartha Brahmin was police sheristadar in the huzur kutcherry, and four Raos, very likely Desasthas, held judgeships.[33]

As well as being useful to the Resident because they often knew something of English and British administration, non-Malayali Brahmins had other functions in a state ruled in trust for a Hindu deity. Hundreds of temples were under sirkar supervision, and the Maharaja himself was required to perform numerous temple ceremonies during a year. Nairs were Sudras and carried a degree of pollution to Brahmin priests, to the Kshatriya Maharaja and to areas of some temples. Brahmins, on the other hand, could move with freedom and convenience. When a new Dewan was needed in 1857, a Brahmin was chosen, partly because 'a Soodra could not have conducted the great religious festival (*murajapam*) then celebrating at Trivandrum'.[34]

In the middle of the nineteenth century, the government of Travancore in Trivandrum had a number of superficial characteristics of a bureaucracy; but the full impact of British ideas of administration was still to come. The government was carried on by non-Malayali Brahmins and Nairs, with a sprinkling of Tamil Sudras and a handful of Christians, Kshatriyas and Ambalavasis. At the highest levels, Nairs and non-Malayali Brahmins were in muted competition: the Dewanship, which was in the gift of the Resident who had usurped many of the functions of the Maharaja, had become the preserve of non-Malayali Brahmins. Yet at lower levels, where the majority of the population was directly concerned, Nairs were the principal office holders, many of them passing on their pravrattikarships from uncle to nephew. A large number of Nair joint-families, perhaps a third, had members working for the sirkar. Syrian Christians, although some were landed and wealthy, were virtually excluded from jobs in the administration; their brief interlude of preferment had ended with the departure of John Munro. To polluting castes, like Ezhavas and Shanars, the sirkar service was expressly closed and, indeed, took upon itself the task of keeping polluting members of society in their place. What that place was, we shall now see.

## *CASTES: THEIR STATUS AND CUSTOMS*

The ritual status of a caste, carried privileges or disabilities which we may regard as 'resources' of a kind. Similarly, in the changing economic and social situation which developed in Travancore from the 1850s, a caste's traditional customs and occupations could be an advantage or a drawback. To this extent, they too may be seen as 'resources'.

In Kerala the concept of pollution was refined to a unique complexity, and pollution was capable of being transmitted not merely on touch, but from a distance.[35] The wife of a Church Missionary Society missionary wrote in 1860:

> ... a Nair may approach but not touch a Nambudiri Brahmin; a Chogan [Irava]] must remain thirty-six paces off, and a Poolayen slave ninety-six steps distant. A Chogan must remain twelve steps away from a Nair, and a Poolayen sixty-six steps off, and a Pariar some distance farther still. A Syrian Christian may touch a Nair (though this is not allowed in some parts of the country) but the latter may not eat with each other. Poolians and Pariars, who are the lowest of all, may approach but not touch, much less may they eat with each other.[36]

This is not the only version of the appropriate distances. Others varied by a yard or two,[37] but the important fact is the concrete form which distance pollution gave to abstract ritual status; the separateness of various groups was thus reinforced in the minds of Travancoreans.

For such a system to work, the caste of individuals had to be identifiable from a distance. 'Anyone after living a little while in the country' wrote a CMS missionary in 1884, 'can at first glance tell to what caste a stranger belongs by the way he or she wears the hair or their garments'.[38] It is worth giving two examples to emphasise Travancoreans' recognition of, and response to, other groups. The Rev. Jacob Chandy, Sr. was one of the first generation of English educated Syrian Christians. As a travelling pastor for the Church Missionary Society, he looked like the traditional Syrian Christian kathanar or priest who had been known to Malayalis for hundreds of years. His behaviour, however, was different. His journal entry for 15 August 1855 is revealing: 'A Nair who wanted to come near where I was sitting in a house shouted that the Chegons [Ezhavas] who were standing near me should get away...' When Chandy told the Nair that it would be wrong for a kathanar to send the Ezhavas away, the Nair shouted that 'if it was wrong in me as a kathanar to turn them away, I should take no notice of their being turned out by others; ...he...sat down at a distance from us'. Fifteen months later Chandy recorded a similar incident:

> One of the [Ezhava] converts said that a Syrian a few days ago pointed out to a Nair who passed by him, calling out to the Nair, 'You are defiled, the man whom you passed by is a convert from Chegons'. The Nair got very angry and used abusive language to him for not giving notice to the Nair that he was a Chegon and for not getting out of the road as Chegons do when they see a Nair. The Syrian was the cause of the disturbance; he acted as if he was in duty bound to see that the higher castes be not defiled by the approach of the lower castes.[39]

Such examples could be multiplied.[40] Towards the end of the nineteenth century when western-educated men increasingly claimed to speak for 'the Nairs' or for 'the Syrians', they were not manufacturing grand constituencies for themselves from questionable census statistics. Their right to act as spokesmen might be denied, but the 'communities' they claimed to represent had a reality which Malayalis had long acknowledged.

## *SAVARNA*[41]

### *Malayali Brahmins*

At the summit of this system sat in comfort the Nambudiri Brahmins. Although Nambudiris, and the Pottis of south Travancore who were said to be slightly inferior, probably never amounted to more than one per cent of the population of Travancore, their place in traditional society was supreme. Describing a Nambudiri, Nagam Aiya wrote in his 1875 census report:

> His tenants...bow down to him not simply as a landlord but as their royal liege and benefactor, their suzerain master, their household deity, their very God on earth... His person is holy; his directions are commands; his movements are processions; his meal is nectar. He is the holiest of human beings. He is the representative of God on earth.[42]

According to the legend, Parasurama peopled Kerala with the Nambudiris. Sankaracharya, the ninth century ascetic and reformer, was one, and Nambudiris were sought after as priests for the holiest temples in India, even in the Himalyas.[43]

In Travancore, Nambudiris were concentrated in the north, Pottis in the south. (Pottis, although Malayali Brahmins, were said to have come to Kerala after the Nambudiris).[44] They were primarily large landholders who often had an absolute tax free proprietorship of the soil. In Travancore in the mid-nineteenth century they were nearly all prosperous, and some, vastly wealthy.

Their style of life was calculated to prevent fragmentation of their family estates. They were patrilineal and practised primogeniture. Only the eldest son in a Nambudiri family married formally in his own caste. Nair families, which were matrilineal, welcomed the other males as evening visitors--arriving after supper and leaving before breakfast--to have liaisons with their women. Some families took pride in giving their women only to Malayali Brahmins.[45] The children of such unions were Nairs, they polluted their fathers--as, indeed, did their mothers--and were the complete responsibility of the Nair matrilineal joint-family. The legend of Parasurama was invoked to explain the relationship: Sudras were brought to Kerala to serve the Malayali Brahmins. The Nair girl was taught to bare her breasts as a mark of respect before such incarnate deities; her greatest pleasure should be giving pleasure to them. Perhaps it was. On the other hand, only a few Malayali Brahmin women could marry. The chastity of the rest was jealously guarded by their male relatives, and they were expected to live as spinsters and die virgins.[46]

The Nambudiri house was called an *illam*. Set well away from roads to prevent pollution, surrounded by a high wall, it had its own well and tank and a number of outbuildings. It was rambling and grand, and symbolised the exclusiveness of Malayali Brahmins. With their estates farmed by slaves or tenants and managed by Nairs or non-Malayali Brahmins, they rarely appeared in public, eschewed government service, and passed their time in religious observances and visiting their Nair women.[47] Their system of marriage and inheritance meant that their population remained almost static, while their wealth and ritual status placed them above and beyond the common problems of other Malayalis. Nambudiris could afford to ignore the changed conditions of the late nineteenth century much longer, for example, than Nairs. Not until 1863 did one of them enter a Travancore school to learn English, and in 1906 they were still characterised by 'their credulousness, simplicity and innocence...' Another writer in 1900 exclaimed: 'Long may they remain as they are, untouched by what we here called "progress"... '[48] It is for these reasons that Malayali Brahmins make only fleeting appearances in the following chapters. It was in the years after 1908 that 'progress' began to catch up with them.[49]

## *Non-Malayali Brahmins*

Credulousness, simplicity and innocence were not the attributes which Malayalis assigned to Travancore's non-Malayali Brahmins. We have already seen how their influence waxed under Martanda Varma and how they controlled certain sections of the sirkar service about 1850. In crossing the Ghats to Travancore, they took advantage of 'the high veneration experienced by the Brahmin caste in Travancore...'.[50] Even before Martanda Varma, their ritual status, which gave them extra-territorial rights in the old Kerala polity, coupled with their pragmatic attitude to pollution, made them useful as spies and emissaries.[51] Moreover, because they were Brahmins, Nairs grudgingly accorded them the right of liaisons with Nair women. A proverb advised: 'If there is none (to wed), then a Pattar [Tamil Brahmin], if there is nothing (to eat), then greens'.[52] Even in pre-British days they were not particularly loved by Nairs. The poet Kunjan Nambiar (1705-c. 1770), who satirised most of the groups in Kerala, gave Pattars 'a more vigorous and unrelieved trouncing' than the rest.

Of their displays in the free feedinghouses, he wrote:

> Rice and curd and plantain fruit
> Are mashed into a pulpy mess.
> With this they stoke themselves
> In a squelchy, slimy, ghastly way.[53]

Their population in Travancore in the 1850s was about 25,000 or a little more than one per cent of the total. However, their privileges, their established influence, and their connections on the eastern side of the Ghats gave them an importance far exceeding their numbers. When English education became widely available in Travancore after about 1860, many of them quickly added academic qualifications to their ritual advantages.

*Nairs*

Beneath Brahmins in the hierarchy of ritual status came a few thousand Kshatriyas and Ambalavasis (temple servants). According to the early imperfect censuses, however, by far the largest category was that of Nairs, who were nominally Sudras. The censuses of 1816, 1836 and 1854 reckoned Nairs at about 30 per cent of the population (see Appendix). The first 'scientific' census in 1875 put them at about twenty per cent. The earlier enumerations are interesting, however, because they were conducted chiefly by Nairs and reflect their view that Nairs *were* the largest, most important section of society. What was the place of Nairs in Kerala? One of them answered:

> The bulk of its inhabitants are Nairs... the lords of the country...guardians of the public weal; they wielded the distinctive privileges of the Kshatriya... These distinctive privileges...added to their close bond of union...with the Nambudiri Brahmin...point to their unmistakeable pre-eminence.[54]

The eye, the hand and the order–all depended on Nairs.

Nairs, however, were by no means a monolithic egalitarian group. There were among them a number of subcastes or lineages: those of 'royalty', of local chiefs, of village headmen and of 'commoners' who acted as retainers of the first three or of the Nambudiris.[55] Some menials, notably washermen and oilmongers, who worked only for Nairs and higher castes, claimed also to be 'Nairs'.[56] Nor were all Nairs equally wealthy. From very large landlords, they ranged through moderate landholders down to 'the poorest of them [who] are day labourers'.[57]

Yet the internal divisions into subcastes[58] were not readily apparent to other castes or groups who accorded all Nairs the same deference and respect. As a Syrian Christian newspaper complained at the end of the nineteenth century:

> ...there are Nairs and Nairs. From Kiriathu Nair who, in social status, is second only to Brahmins, we pass on through several intermediate stages to oilmongers, potters, barbers, washermen and several other sub-sections... Still, all of them pass off as Nairs and enjoy privileges refused to all others.[59]

All Nairs in Travancore in 1847 shared some customs. All, for example, wore their *kudumi* or tuft of hair at the front of the head; Tamilians wore it at the back. Nair men were entitled to carry umbrellas and to wear a shoulder cloth. Nair women could cover their breasts with a particular style of cloth–which they were expected to remove before temple idols and caste superiors–and wear gold and silver jewellery of special designs. Like the men, women tied their hair at the front of the head.[60]

More important, however, all Nairs followed the matrilineal marumakkattayam system of inheritance, based on the matrilocal joint-family called the taravad. All members of a taravad were descended from a common female ancestor, but the management of taravad affairs was vested in the eldest male member, the karanavan; the system was matrilineal, not matriarchal. The property and assets of the taravad were held in common by all members, and no individual could claim his or her share of the joint property.

The taravad house was originally built to be defended. It was surrounded by a walled garden, and was itself built as a rectangle around an inner courtyard.[61] A single house might sometimes contain a hundred people, spanning three or four generations.[62] Each woman had her own room where her young children slept and where at night she was visited by her husbands, who might be Nambudiris, Kshatriyas, Nairs of the same or a higher subcaste, or even non-Malayali Brahmins. The male members of her own taravad similarly went out at night to visit their wives.

Marriages were contracted and ended with considerable ease. A man negotiated with a woman's karanavan, obtained the woman's agreement and presented her with a cloth. This was called sambandham, and a woman might have sambandham with a number of men at the same time. They had no rights over her or her children, but were expected to provide her with small presents of luxury items like bath oil and to pay her expenses when she had a child.[63] Either the man or woman could end the sambandham union with little formality. Pre-pubescent Nair girls also underwent an expensive 'mock-marriage' ceremony called *talikettukalyanam*.[64]

Most Nair joint-families held land. As we shall see, more Nairs were returned as 'cultivators' in the 1875 census than any other social category in the state. As long as a spirit of 'communality' continued to pervade the taravad, Nairs had a family system calculated to preserve their holdings and their place as the leisured gentry of Travancore. Slaves tilled the soil, taxes were paid largely in kind, and land was not easily alienable. To dissipate a taravad's wealth would have been difficult even for incompetent managers. However, when slavery was abolished, when cash and salaries gained wider use, when land was made more easily transferable, when western-style education became more necessary, Nair customs ceased to be an aid to the maintenance of Nairs' position in society.

By the 1840s changes were apparent in the attitude of Nairs. Even if their military role in old Kerala was not the direct cause of their matrilineal system,[65] the removal of military activities may well have lengthened life expectancy and certainly left many Nair youths in idleness. They were guaranteed adequate food and shelter in their taravad house, but--depending on their relationship to and with the karanavan--probably little more. Had life been harder for Nairs, such young men might have turned to robbery and dacoity in the years after 1810. Instead, something like the reverse happened. In the space of a generation, one observer noted in 1838, 'that warlike, refractory and turbulent temper for which the Nairs of Travancore were once so remarkable... has totally disappeared...'[66] If the 'turbulent temper' disappeared in public, perhaps it turned inward, for as we shall see, taravads came to be riven with feuds and factions.

### *Syrian Christians*

In Travancore in 1847 only one other section of the population had a position roughly approximating that of Nairs in terms of numbers and status–Syrian Christians. Syrians amounted to about twelve per cent of the population, perhaps 150,000 people, in 1854.[67] Latin Catholics, converts of St. Francis Xavier in the sixteenth century, comprised perhaps six per cent of the population; but they were concentrated on the coast and were recognised by all as vastly inferior to Syrians who carefully avoided them.

Like Nairs, Syrian Christians were an identifiable group to other sections of the population, but within, they were scarcely homogeneous. According to one account, Syrian Christians were the descendants of high-caste converts made by St. Thomas the Apostle in the first century A.D.[68] Another version traced Syrian origins to Thomas of Cana, a merchant from west Asia, who settled in Kerala with his followers and made converts in the fourth century. Among Syrians there were two endogamous groups: Suddists, who claimed to be direct descendants of the early west Asian missionaries and racially pure; and Nordists, said to be descendants of early high-caste converts. Nordists were much more numerous.[69]

Until the coming of Vasco da Gama and the Portuguese, Syrian Christians maintained tenuous connections with the various patriarchs of orthodox churches in west Asia. The Portuguese, however, soon brought the spirit of the inquisition to bear, and by 1600 the Malabar church was in submission to Rome.[70] Unchallenged Roman dominance survived only until 1653 when outraged Syrians took an oath around the stone cross in a churchyard near Cochin to resist European bishops and European control.[71] The links with west Asia were again sought.

The oath of the Coonen Cross split Syrians into two sects: Romo-Syrians, and those who again sought the tenuous links with Jacobite Patriarchs in west Asia. There were Nordists and

Suddists in both sects. Feuds and schisms continued throughout the eighteenth century.[72] After the revision of the East India Company's charter in 1813 removing restrictions against missionaries, John Munro, the Resident in Travancore, asked for Anglican missionaries to be sent to Travancore to work for the reformation of the Jacobite Syrians and ultimately the conversion of the Romo-Syrians.[73] This 'mission of help' began in 1816 and lasted until 1836 when Jacobites, angered at the interference in their affairs of arrogant missionaries like the Rev. Joseph Peet, broke off the association.[74] But a few thousand Syrians remained loyal to the Church Missionary Society, and a third sect, the Anglican Syrians, was thus established.

Regardless of their sect, Syrians had a strong and respected position in Malayali society. At the time of their origin in Kerala, they had received patronage from local chiefs and converts from 'respectable' castes.[75] Like Nairs, Syrians trained their male heirs in the use of arms, and it was said that 'a native prince was respected or feared by his neighbours according to the number of Syrians in his dominions'.[76] Both high and low castes accorded Syrians a status similar to Nairs. Syrians walked where they pleased and carried only a minimum of pollution according to caste Hindus. Some Syrians, indeed, claimed to be socially superior to Nairs.[77]

Unlike Nairs, Syrian men wore their hair close cut, but they assumed the dignity of the shoulder cloth and the umbrella. Syrian women wore a long-sleeved blouse which they were not expected to doff before high-caste Hindus. Their lower cloth was tucked in at the back with a distinctive fan-shaped pleat; in the top part of the ear, they wore large gold rings. Syrians were strict about commensality, and regarded low-caste Hindus as unclean, if not ritually polluting. They were ostentatiously careful not to carry pollution to high castes through fraternisation with the low.[78]

Syrian families were extended, but they were patrilineal and patrilocal. In contrast to Nairs, marriage was monogamous and divorce almost impossible.

According to the legend, Thomas of Cana came to Kerala as a merchant, and from the earliest times Syrians were associated with trade.[79] They also held considerable areas of land.

Having been associated with the English missionaries from 1816, Syrians had the earliest and widest contacts with the new rulers of India. From the 1820s the missionaries made available English education, Malayalam printed books and a wide circle of connections.[80]

In 1847 Syrians derived considerable benefit from their customs and their traditional position in society. Although they did not have a leading role in the political system, they had an acknowledged and respected place in the total, Hindu-dominated society. This allowed them to move freely and placed few limitations on their enjoyment of what material comfort they could acquire. Their domestic arrangements, unlike those of Nairs, were neither unwieldy nor likely to invite ridicule in a 'westernising' society. As old established Christians, they had a fascination for, and a useful introduction to, the new ruling race.

### *Muslims*

Muslims in Kerala were concentrated in Malabar district of British India. In Travancore they comprised only about five or six per cent of the population in 1847. Like Syrian Christians, they were also generally accorded 'respectable' status by Hindus. However, their interests were primarily commercial, and questions of land and government did not necessarily involve them. Nor were they quick to take up English education. It was not until 1894 that a Kerala Muslim took a Bachelor of Arts degree, and he was a Malabar man.[81] For these reasons, Muslims make only rare appearances in this story.

### *AVARNA*

If one looks at the 1854 census (see Appendix), one finds roughly fifty-seven per cent of the population (about 715,000) among the 'respectable classes', people whose presence or touch was not offensively polluting. These mainly included Brahmins of all kinds, Nairs, Syrian Christians, Muslims and a variety of less numerous Hindu castes like Ambalavasis, Tamil Vellalas, Chettis and Konkanis.

In these early censuses, however, low-caste Hindus were probably grossly underenumerated. Indeed, rough calculations based on the 1875 census would put the 'offensively polluting' castes at about fifty-seven per cent of the population. The near presence of such men or women was offensive to caste Hindus, Syrians and even Muslims. Yet all low castes were not equally polluting, either in their own, or in high-caste, estimation. Even among the low castes the code of distance pollution was carefully refined.

We shall look at three broad categories which together made up more than thirty per cent of the total population. These were Ezhavas, Shanars and the slave castes.

### *Ezhavas*

Ezhavas were the tappers and tenders of the cocoanut palm, and the largest single category among the polluting castes, amounting to about fifteen per cent of the total population of Travancore. Ezhavas recognised subcaste distinctions among themselves,[82] but like Nairs, Ezhavas' dress and appearance readily identified them to other Malayalis. They were forbidden the dignity of an umbrella or a shoulder cloth, but they wore a tuft of hair at the front of the head. Their women were prohibited from covering their breasts and from wearing certain types of jewellery. Prohibitions were enforced against their keeping milk cows, using oil mills and metal vessels, and wearing sandals and finely woven cloth.[83] They often had about them the implements of their defiling, toddy-tapping trade. They were said to pollute a Nambudiri from thirty-six paces and a Nair from twelve. Public offices and roads close to temples or high castes' houses were closed to them.[84] In short, wrote Dr. Francis Day, they were 'a people despised by the higher castes... '[85]

Yet there were certain aspects of Ezhava customs which were to prove advantageous in the period of change which lay ahead. By tradition Ezhavas climbed the cocoanut palm to tap the bud at the top for sap which could be fermented into toddy or distilled into arrack. By soaking the husk of the cocoanut in the backwaters, they extracted the rot-resistant coir fibre which they spun into rope or thread and wove into mats. They plucked cocoanuts, opened them and set the kernel in the sun to dry into copra which was then pressed into oil. Ezhavas, however, were forbidden to extract the oil themselves. While cash was little used and the products of the cocoanut palm were not in great demand outside of Kerala, these traditional occupations held little promise but drudgery. However, when the demand for cocoanut products in Europe and America increased towards the end of the nineteenth century, Ezhavas were able to take advantage of a cash economy, and their labour became indispensable to the merchants established in towns like Alleppey. This is not to say that Ezhavas made fortunes overnight; but they were to experience a great improvement in their economic bargaining position, and some were to become prosperous.

In 1847, however, most Ezhava families were extremely poor. Those not directly involved with the cocoanut palm might be tenants or subtenants on the land of Nambudiris, Nairs or Syrian Christians; others might be labourers, weavers or ayurvedic doctors. Although Ezhavas of north Travancore, like Nairs, followed a pure matrilineal system, there were no grand houses, unwieldy taravads or large areas of ancestral property. Generally, a girl lived and worked with her mother, aunts, uncles and siblings until a household became too large for its limited resources. At that time, one branch would move to a new location. A girl received her husband or husbands where it was convenient, and in some cases went to live with her husband. Indeed, in the areas south of Quilon, a mixed system of inheritance was followed. The girl lived with her husband, and she and her children were entitled to half of his self-acquired property on his death, the other half passing to his nephews.[86] When the matrilineal system became burdensome, Ezhavas had little difficulty in casting it aside.

### *Shanars*

In the Tamil areas south of Trivandrum, Shanars occupied a position similar to that of Ezhavas. Enumerated at about six per cent of the population in 1854 (4.6 per cent in 1875 after extensive conversions to Christianity), Shanars were Tamil-speaking, patrilineal agriculturalists and labourers. They were primarily tappers of the palmyra, 'a palm inferior only to the cocoanut,'[87] which begins to flourish in the drier climate south of Neyyattinkara. A common occupation, however, promoted no fellow-feeling between Ezhavas and Shanars: in areas where they overlapped, there were 'constant contests ... about pre-eminence'.[88]

Unlike Nanjanad Vellalas, a respected caste of Sudras which had adopted Malayali ways, including the matrilineal system, when it found itself in a Malayali-dominated state,[89] Shanars remained Tamils, and, more important, dependent on Nair or Nanjanad Vellala landlords. In a number of ways the Tamil taluks of south Travancore were a Malayali colony. Nairs held much of the land, and Malayalam was 'the language of the courts, and of the domestic circle among Sudras and Brahmins. Tamil is the language of the Bazaar and of the lower castes'.[90]

The civil disabilities which applied to Ezhavas applied also to Shanars. They were offensively polluting to higher castes; their women were forbidden to cover their breasts.

Since 1806, however, conversion to Christianity had enabled more than 7,000 Shanars to escape from some of the worst disabilities imposed on them by their traditional status and occupation. In that year Tobias Ringeltaube, a Prussian, affiliated with the London Missionary Society, had entered the state and made the first Shanar converts around Nagercoil. Ringeltaube was succeeded by two English missionaries in 1816. One of them, Rev. Charles Mead, became a belligerent champion of the converts, and after disturbances with the high castes in the 1820s, he extracted from the sirkar the right for Shanar Christian women to cover their breasts with a distinctive jacket. By the 1850s the LMS had about 15,000 adherents in the area south of Trivandrum; most were Shanars.[91] (This was in contrast to north Travancore where the CMS did not begin to proselytise until after its rupture with the Jacobites became final in 1840.) Shanars' position of despised semi-aliens gave them little stake in Travancore society, and helps to account for their readiness to convert to a new religion which promised protection and opportunity for material improvement.

### *Slave Castes*

Despised and oppressed though Shanars and Ezhavas were, other castes suffered from graver disabilities–which Shanars and Ezhavas were fastidious about enforcing. The slave castes, principally composed of Pulayas, Parayas and Kuravas, were fairly accurately enumerated in the 1854 census at about thirteen per cent of the population. After thousands of conversions to Christianity, they still amounted to thirteen per cent in 1881.[92]

Pulayas were the largest section, Malayalam-speaking, and concentrated in the areas from Trivandrum north. In Paraya dominated regions south of Trivandrum, Pulayas were said to be the lowest of castes; but the same was claimed of Parayas who lived in central and north Travancore.[93] Although Kuravas shared some of the characteristics of the hill tribes, they had been bound to the land for generations; they were concentrated in Trivandrum district.

Within each slave caste there were endogamous subdivisions, but these were unimportant to their ritual superiors. Brahmins and Nairs considered themselves polluted if a slave approached within fifty or hundred yards, while 'none of the Shanars...will approach them within a distance of five or six yards'.[94] Slaves cried out as they walked along the edges of roads to warn high castes of their approach; if a high-caste man or woman approached, the slave took to the fields. The condition of the slave castes in 1847 could have been only slightly worse than Samuel Mateer found it in 1884:

> The men are in wretched filthy clothes. There is much suffering from sickness, the dirt of the house produces vermin and itch, which deprives them of rest by day and sleep by night. A respectable native must cover his nostrils with his cloth when he enters amongst them, for the stench and the filth. The aged, if there are any, suffer from debility, and may lie helpless day after day until they die; infants suffer from sores, diarrhoea, worms and want of food; adults from headache and indigestion, ague, dysentry, and intermittent fever.[95]

In 1847 slaves carried out all the most arduous agricultural labour, in return for which they received food. The sirkar owned about 15,000 whom it leased to private landholders. They were expected to pay the sirkar and feed the slaves.[96] Disobedient slaves could be beaten and murdered with impunity, and all slaves could be legally sold. '...Almost every market day', at

Changanacherry, wrote the Rev. Henry Baker, Jr., '*children* are brought by their parents or near relations for sale'. The going price was between six and eighteen rupees.[97]

The only advantage which slave castes derived from their traditional position was the horror and revulsion which they engendered in high castes. As late as the eighteenth century there had been months of the year when Pulayas were entitled to abduct or pollute high-caste women; women so polluted either followed their polluter or were sold into slavery.[98] Slave caste festivals were tolerated, which brought together more than 3,000 people 'armed with swords, slings, pointed sticks and other weapons... ' A fight usually followed 'which almost invariably ends in serious injuries or loss of life'. The same slave castes were noted for 'robberies and outrages' and 'attacks...on the Resident's baggage'.[99] Because they were so offensive, they were generally left alone.

At the same time, not all slave holders were cruel, and even a cruel master had an interest in keeping his slaves alive. He depended on their labour just as they depended on his patronage. As late as 1943 an Ezhava anthropologist claimed that members of former slave castes who were not tied to a high caste farmer felt 'handicapped that they have no protector and lord'.[100]

The position of the slave castes was in fact so debased that they were little touched by the rapid changes of the late nineteenth century which affected most other sections of Travancore society. In the 1890s accusations about slave holding were still made, and in 1918 a leading Nair could refer unconsciously to 'Pulaya slaves' and conclude that 'the Pulayas...have mostly remained serfs...'[101]

Conversion to Christianity was their only road to improvement; but they had so little to offer–their resources both of status and of material things were non-existent–that some missionaries were reluctant to accept them. They saw that slave-caste converts would lower the prestige of the mission and make it more difficult for them to retain Syrian Christians or to convert members of higher castes. For the following chapters, however, the slave castes are important because their plight first roused LMS and CMS agents to united protest to the sirkar and the Madras government. The missionaries' campaign for the abolition of slavery which began in 1847 soon broadened into a much wider challenge to some of the principles of Travancore society. The reforms which the sirkar was forced–and later encouraged–to make impelled decisive changes in that society.

Their traditional customs, status and occupations gave castes–and let us include Syrian Christians as a caste for the moment–different advantages and potential in 1847. Malayali Brahmins, a tiny fraction of the population, were so venerated, so wealthy and so removed from the everyday world that until the twentieth century they were to carry on unconscious of, and unresponsive to, the changes taking place around them. On the other hand, the slave castes were so badly placed in traditional society that there was little they could do to take advantage of change.

Between these two extremes, however, non-Malayali Brahmins, Nairs, Syrians, Ezhavas and Shanars were to be helped or handicapped after 1847 by their customs and ritual status. On the face of it, Nairs held the best cards. The largest identifiable group, they were the traditional keepers of the social order, closely linked through hypergamy to the Malayali Brahmins and Kshatriya princes. Moreover, as we shall see, much of the land was theirs, and their marumakkattayam system of inheritance was calculated to preserve their estates. Yet the marumakkattayam system was to prove unsuitable to new economic conditions and to the values imparted through an expanding system of English-style education. Nair pride in their traditional status was also to prevent them from taking advantage of new commercial opportunities.

Non-Malayali Brahmins, on the other hand, were able to use their high ritual status and scholarly traditions to retain their influence around the Maharajas of Travancore and their hold on some of the sirkar's most powerful posts.

Perhaps, however, Syrian Christians in 1847 were in the best position to exploit changes to come. Already enjoying a respectable ritual status, they were not handicapped by a single-minded view of their role in society, nor by a matrilineal system. They had diversified interests in trade and the land, and the advantage of connections with the ruling race through the missionaries.

Ezhavas and Shanars, despised though they might be, were not the lowest castes in ritual status. Moreover, like Syrians, they had occupational traditions which were to prove advantageous. Ezhavas, although matrilineal or partially matrilineal, were not rivetted to the system by affluence as Nairs were. For both castes, the interest in their disabilities, which they could evoke from conversion-minded missionaries, was to give them a useful relationship with the British and a certain leverage.

## *LAND*

In a state like Travancore in 1847, where agriculture was the main activity, where most labour was rewarded in kind, and where the population lived largely on what it grew, land was the primary resource. Possession of land complemented ritual status and brought power. There were three broad categories of rights in the land: (i) janmam, or absolute, tax-free, proprietorship; (ii) 'impure' janmam, absolute proprietorship but subject to a small tax; and (iii) various tenures in which the sirkar was recognised either as the proprietor of the land or as entitled to a full share of the produce.[102]

The legend of the origin of janmam illustrates the relationship between ritual status and land. Having created Kerala, Parasurama divided it among the Nambudiri Brahmins who acquired absolute right to the soil (janmam means 'birth, nativity'). Their ownership of the land preceded the political sovereignty of local Kshatriya chiefs. The land was supervised by Nairs and farmed by low-caste subtenants and slaves. In time, the power of the petty political rulers grew, and the land of extinct Nambudiri families began to escheat to the state.[103] Some Pottis, Kshatriyas and Nair chiefs were also eventually accepted as janmis, who held 'the supreme, absolute unqualified proprietorship to the soil, ... the highest and most complete type of private property in land'.[104] The advantages of janmam, however, attached only to its hereditary owners: if the land was alienated to other castes, it became 'impure' janmam and subject to a tax. By 1847 perhaps a few dozen families in Travancore were pure janmis,[105] and a few thousand 'impure'janmis.

The large majority of Travancoreans, however, held their land on some kind of sirkar tenure. This had come about as a result of Martanda Varma's expansion in the eighteenth century. He had little hesitation in dispossessing troublesome janmis and putting the sirkar in their place.[106] This new tenure, with the sirkar in the janmi's role, was known as sirkar pattam, and by

1847, 200,000 acres–nearly half of the cultivated rice land in the state–were thus held.[107] In theory the sirkar had the right of any janmi to evict tenants almost at will, but in practice this was seldom done. Sirkar pattam land, however, could not be sold or mortgaged, nor would a tenant get compensation for his improvements if he surrendered the land or was evicted. The tenure was restrictive and irksome, and involved thousands of families, the majority of them Nairs. By discouraging transfers of land, it supported the status quo. If one's taravad held sirkar pattam land, all one could do was live on it; it had no money value to the taravad beyond the crop it produced.

There were many other kinds of sirkar tenures, but they do not need to be detailed.[108] The important question is: who held land in 1847? Although the source material leaves much to be desired, probably a fairly accurate picture can be pieced together from various observers and their reports. 'The Nairs constitute the largest body of farmers', wrote Ward and Conner in 1820, 'the [Syrian] Christians also possess a good deal...[but] not one-twelfth of the Shovans [Ezhavas] (it was only within later years that they were permitted to hold them under any of the better tenures) have lands...'[109]

Ward and Conner's conclusion was reinforced by the census in 1875 which attempted to record occupations. It enumerated 218,000 Nair males and described 98,000 of them (forty-five per cent) as 'cultivators', that is men who owned or leased land to cultivate it or have it cultivated for them. (See Table 1.1). The next largest category comprised Christians of all kinds; 55,000 'cultivators' (twenty-three per cent of Christian males).

More interesting, however, under the heading of 'men of rank and property', 56,800 were enumerated. (See Table 1.2) A man qualified for inclusion merely by asserting to the census-taker's satisfaction that he was 'of rank and property'. Malayali Brahmins, whose total population was only 10,000, returned 2,000 'men of rank and property'; non-Malayali Brahmins, 2,900. But in absolute terms the most numerous category was that of Nairs: 15,700. There were 11,200 Christians and 7,400 Ezhavas. One should obviously not overstate the Nair hold on the land. It there were more than 15,000 Nair 'men of rank and property', there were also more than 12,000 Nair 'labourers'. Among Nairs there was not only the division into subcastes but disparities of wealth. Over the years as the importance of the subcastes declined, that of economic disparities—class—was to increase.

TABLE 1.1 [110]

*'Cultivators' and 'Labourers' according to the 1875 Census*
'Cultivators' owned or leased land

| | A<br>*No. of Males* | B<br>*Cultivators* | *B as %-age of A* | C<br>*Labourers* | *C as %-age of A* |
|---|---|---|---|---|---|
| Nairs | 218,030 | 98,330 | 45% | 12,490 | 6% |
| All Christians | 233,860 | 54,770 | 23% | 29,570 | 13% |
| Ezhavas | 188,400 | 26,890 | 14% | 40,400 | 21% |
| Shanars | 48,220 | 6,370 | 13% | 8,450 | 18% |
| Non-Malayali Brahmins | 14,520 | 2,536 | 18% | None | — |
| Malayali Brahmins | 5,840 | 527 | 9% | None | — |
| Pulayas | 94,790 | 2,280 | 2% | 55,040 | 58% |

In the case of 'labourers' a number of women may be included, but this does not detract from the interest of the percentages.

TABLE 1.2[111]

*'Men of Rank and Property' according to the 1875 census*
(A man qualified by convincing the enumerator that he was a man of rank and property)

| | A<br>*No. of Males* | B<br>*Men of Rank and Property* | B<br>*as %-age of A* |
|---|---|---|---|
| Nairs | 218,030 | 15,680 | 7% |
| Christians | 233,860 | 11,680 | 5% |
| Ezhavas | 188,400 | 7,390 | 4% |
| Shanars | 48,220 | 1,350 | 3% |
| Non-Malayali Brahmins | 14,520 | 2,910 | 20% |
| Malayali Brahmins | 5,840 | 1,950 | 33% |
| Pulayas | 94,790 | 2,520 | 3% |

In 1847, however, Nairs and their Nambudiri Brahmin patrons, did exercise widespread control of the land. From this control, the Nair taravad derived power, and a dominance which was complemented by its ritual status and preponderance in the sirkar service. Yet inseparable from this hold of the land was a dependence both on the land and on the conditions which allowed Nairs to control it. With almost half the cultivated wet land held on sirkar pattam, a tenure which precluded sale or mortgage, and with most rent and tax still paid in kind, the taravad had little experience of a cash economy. The difficulty of subdividing scattered parcels of land–how much easier to divide money–strengthened the 'communality' of interest which was vital to the taravad.

A taravad grew enough to feed itself, sold its pepper to the sirkar monopoly and purchased bathing and cooking oil, tobacco and cloth. If a man wished to leave the joint-family, waste land was free and abundant. (An estimated 1,000 square miles of paddy land was uncultivated in the 1830s.)[112] Slaves carried out the actual cultivation, and most Nairs could afford to bask in 'the most exalted notions of their own nobility'.[113] Commenting on Nairs' view of themselves and their lack of interest in money-grubbing pursuits, Ward and Conner wrote:

> However poor the Nair, his pride makes him unwilling to work for anyone of an inferior caste; he may perhaps act as an overseer to an opulent Christian farmer, but invariably smooths the concession by receiving a certain extent of land, not pay, as remuneration.[114]

For the future, however, such an attitude was fraught with hazards.

In terms of numbers, only 'Christians' rivalled Nairs as 'cultivators' and 'men of rank and property'. Probably 90 per cent of Christians of the latter category were Syrians, who also undoubtedly constituted the majority of 'cultivators'. Even among Syrians there were no pure janmis, and the English missionaries in 1822 regretted that 'very few' had property worth five thousand rupees.[115]

It is not difficult, however, to find examples of wealthy Syrians, especially Romanists, at this time. The father of the Romo-Syrian priest, Emmanuel Nidhiry, added to the family's already extensive lands in the 1830s and 1840s. The grand father of Fr. Mathew Palakkunnel (1831-1900) was said to have owned 1,000 acres, and the priest himself held ninety acres of cocoanut garden land and eighty paras (one acre equals about seven paras) of paddy land. Oomen Mamen, later a CMS archdeacon, received sixty-one paras of paddy land and some gardens as his share of family property in 1840. And the Rev. Jacob Chandy, Sr., an indefatigable CMS evangelist, was sometimes upbraided during his travels in the 1850s by indignant Syrians who told him that the education of the slaves by the CMS was 'the ruin of [the] country', for educated slaves were difficult to control.[116]

Syrians had a considerable interest in the land in 1847, but they were not wedded to it and dependent on it to the same extent as Nairs. Syrians also followed commercial pursuits, were more widely accustomed to dealing with money and had fewer reservations about what constituted a respectable occupation. Moreover, with each man responsible for his own family, Syrians were encouraged to take up waste land and to extend their holdings, which as early as 1820 were said to be 'gradually increasing'.[117] Syrians had a useful share of the land, they valued it and wanted more for the prestige and profit it could be made to bring; but they did not view ownership of land as the only satisfactory occupation.

Nor could low castes afford such an affectation. A few Ezhavas and Shanars did own land, but as late as 1925 it was estimated that fewer than 5,000 Ezhavas had more than an acre.[118] The 1875 census classifed only fourteen per cent of Ezhava men, and thirteen per cent of Shanar men as 'cultivators'. Of Ezhava men, twenty-one per cent were 'labourers'; of Shanars, eighteen per cent. Yet they wanted land, and when a few did acquire money, they 'invariably [used it] in the purchase of land'.[119] They were obviously not so deprived as Pulayas, nor had they any scruples about the kind of work they were prepared to tackle. These were to be advantages of a sort.

In 1847, however, the real enjoyment of the land lay with Malayali Brahmins, Kshatriyas, Nairs and, to a lesser extent, Syrian Christians. They had most of it, and for the first three categories, landholding was indisputably the best way for a man to live. But such an attitude, coupled with the family system under which Nairs held their property, was eventually to put their possession of the land in jeopardy.

## *TRADE*

From at least 1,000 B.C. western Asia had traded with Kerala.[120] Indeed, it was the search for spices that drew da Gama to Calicut in 1498. But although the export trade had long flourished and the pepper monopoly had provided the funds for Martanda Varma to reward his soldiers and officials,[121] internal trade in Travancore in 1847 was limited to a few articles. The sirkar maintained the old monopolies of pepper, cardamoms and other spices, which ryots were expected to sell to sirkar agents at fixed prices. The whole crop was then auctioned to foreign merchants at Alleppey. By 1847 the system was rotted by corruption and inefficiency, and the export of pepper had fallen from 15,100 candies (one candy equals about 500 lbs.) in 1833 to 5,000 candies in 1842. Enterprising smugglers, taking advantage of an increase in the price of pepper on the world market, accounted for much of the decline.[122] The sirkar also carried on a monopoly in salt and tobacco, which was one of the few 'luxury items' widely used.

In the port towns of Alleppey and Quilon there were Muslim, Jewish, non-Malayali Brahmin, Chetti, Konkani and Parsee merchants, but in the interior villages of north and central Travancore, the shopkeeping trade was largely in the hands of Muslims and Syrian Christians. 'Bazaars are not common', wrote Ward and Conner in about 1820; 'those seen are inhabited by Mauplays [Muslims] or Christians, or if kept by Nairs (a low order of this rank sometimes thus employ themselves), all other castes are excluded from having shops in the same place' Later they wrote:

> The languid habits of the higher orders...throws the trade into the hands of Lubbees, Konkanies, Vauniens, Christians and Vellaula Chetties, who are chiefly engaged... with the provinces of Tinnevelly, Madura and Coimbatoor, from whence is imported cloth of every description...tobacco and iron...[123]

Of the categories mentioned, only Christians were natives of Travancore.

Even before the investigation of Ward and Conner, Francis Buchanan had recognised Syrians as the only people likely to bring trade to the interior villages of Malabar:

> Everywhere in the interior of Malabar a prodigious inconvenience is felt from the want of bazaars or markets. A little encouragement given to the Nazareens (*Christians*) might induce that industrious class of men to settle in small villages...where they might keep shops, greatly to the advantage of the natives.[124]

Little changed in the next fifty or sixty years, and in 1860 the wife of the Rev. John Hawksworth of the CMS was describing Syrians as 'chiefly traders in rice, cloth, country produce, tobacco, etc. ... the beautiful rivers which intersect this province are often thickly dotted with their small canoes, laden with fish, salt, yams, plantains, and various kinds of vegetables and fruit... '[125]

Some writers see Syrians as filling the role of Vaisyas in the classical four-varna Hindu system.[126] Caste Hindus not only accorded Syrians respectable status but endowed them with the power to cleanse polluted food and objects. Whether this resulted from Syrians' position as petty traders and middlemen is open to question; but as late as 1900 'it was no unusual occurrence for a Brahmin, when he had reason to consider that an article...had been polluted..., to solicit the friendly assistance of a passing Syrian Christian to remove the blemish by his touch'.[127]

About 1847 Syrians had a large share of what local trade there was in central and north Travancore. But trade was not extensive, and they had by no means a monopoly. Muslims and non-Malayali Brahmins also engaged in such commerce. Indeed, Ward and Conner had written of non-Malayali Brahmins in 1820 that 'nearly half are merchants trading in cloth (of which they once had exclusive privilege), and grain'.[128] By the middle of the century a few Shanars and Ezhavas had 'turned their attention to traffic in the produce of the country...'[129] By 1875 Ezhavas had a higher percentage of 'traders' among them (fourteen per cent) than any other Malayali Hindu caste.[130]

But in 1847 when cash was little used, land was difficult to transfer and the sirkar was attempting to operate the most lucrative trades as monopolies, commercial pursuits did not bring telling advantages. They did, however, impart skills which were to be useful later. With the increasing substitution of cash for kind which was given impetus by the reform of the administration and the beginning of a widespread plantation industry in the 1860s, the scope for merchant activities widened. At the same time, the sirkar surrendered most of its monopolies, and the demand for cocoanut products in Europe and America grew. The opening of the Suez Canal in 1869 increased the flow to India of cheap manufactured goods suitable for the bazaar trade.[131] Those who were first in the field were to benefit from such developments.

In 1847 when the English missionaries made their first concerted effort to persuade the sirkar to modify some of the harsher aspects of Travancore society, the resources which determined a group's power could be placed under four general headings.

First, there was the government itself, presided over in theory by a Kshatriya Maharaja and a Brahmin Dewan, but subject to the continuous supervision, interference and instruction of the British Resident. With only a few hundred exceptions, the eight or nine thousand sirkar servants were Nairs or non-Malayali Brahmins. The tumbledown administration rarely managed to impair their ability to do much as they pleased in local matters; they therefore had considerable power.

Second was the ritual status, traditional customs and occupations of various groups. Thus some men were gods on earth and others were so vile that they polluted public buildings. Ritual status justified the possession of large tracts of land, enslavement, and the exclusion of some groups from the sirkar service. For those whose ritual status was high, some occupations were inconceivable. At the same time, traditional customs–the best example is the matriliny of Nairs–affected the way in which a group could retain or develop its concrete resources.

Third was the land, and in a largely subsistence economy, where cash did not play a great part, land was the most prized possession. Malayali Brahmins and Nairs had the largest share.

Finally, trade gave to some groups, notably Syrians, non-Malayali Brahmins and some Ezhavas and Shanars, an expertise which was to be an advantage in the period of change ahead.

In that period of change, the majority of Nairs, whose position in 1847 was one of comfortable dominance, were to experience a crisis in their matrilineal system which was to contribute vitally to the decline of their power. The matrilineal joint-family was to prove ill-suited to the demands of a cash economy and to the increasing individualism which reform in education and the administration were to foster. The decay of the Nair taravad will be central to the later chapters of this story. Other groups, not so encumbered, were better able to cope with change.

In Travancore in 1847, it was as if the various groups were seated at a table with stacks of poker chips in front of them. Nairs had more than most others, while Malayali Brahmins had so many that the ensuing 'game' lacked interest, and they disdained to play at all. For others, however, there was no option but to play. In the course of the game, new rules were made, new chips came into play and the value of some of the old chips was drastically reduced. By 1908 when the players looked up to take stock, they found that the chips had in many cases been redistributed. Some groups had gained from others or had won some of the new counters. Other groups found that, not only had they lost chips, but some of those they still held were either worthless, or, indeed, carried a penalty. At that point, even Malayali Brahmins were forced to join the game. The following chapters trace the progress of the game until 1908.

2

# Militant Missionaries: New Resources for Low Castes, 1847-60

The government of Travancore in the mid-nineteenth century was staunchly Hindu and thoroughly conservative. The Maharajas claimed to be Kshatriya princes, the regents on earth of the god Padmanabhan; their duties, especially after the imposition of British Residents, were more religious than secular. They saw themselves as entrusted with the preservation of the society they had inherited, a society in which agriculture, carried on by debased slaves and low-caste subtenants, was virtually the only activity. By the standards of the nineteenth-century Englishman, the system was neither just nor humane; but without external help, the low castes were unlikely to change it, nor were the high castes likely to want to. More humane relationships between landlords and labourers, the Travancore sirkar could argue, would endanger the interests of agriculture and ultimately, the production of food. To 'modernise' the administration would upset the social balance: a man's efficiency was far less important than his ritual status.

Until 1840s, the challenges to the sirkar were slight, but with the build-up to more than a dozen English missionaries, low-church men heaven-bent on soul-saving and conversion, low castes were offered new alternatives. The conservative, repressive, inept theocracy of the sirkar offered an opportunity to the missionaries, for it drove growing numbers of low-caste men to seek their protection and adopt their faith. Under pressure from the missionaries and eventually from the Madras government, the sirkar was forced to risk both the so-called interests of agriculture (by abolishing slavery), and the balance of society (by removing some low-caste disabilities and 'modernising' the administration). In doing so, it eventually lessened the need of low castes for missionary help and protection.

The low castes of Travancore society–primarily Ezhavas, Shanars, Pulayas and Parayas–accepted their station because they had no alternative. Physical and spiritual power were in the hands of higher castes; even the movement of low-caste people was restricted in order to make escape difficult.[1] The missionaries, however, were prepared to challenge the principles of Malayali society–the hierarchy of ritual status, the privileges of the high castes and the disabilities of the low–and to call on British governments to force the Travancore sirkar to change some of its discriminatory laws. The missionaries were also able to offer their adherents protection, English education, jobs and a widespread network of connections. But for higher castes, the conversion of Ezhavas, Shanars, Pulayas and Parayas was something to be resisted; it was a betrayal of Malayali Hinduism and a challenge to their own ritual supremacy and authority. Brahmins, wrote the Rev. John Abbs in 1855, 'look on, with unavailing regret', at mission work, 'and blame their immediate ancestors for not arresting the evil, by patronising the lower castes and thus preventing them from seeking the friendship and counsel of the missionaries'.[2]

Did the European missionaries come to Travancore with the intention of uplifting the low castes? The answer is emphatically no. They came to make converts and save souls. But like strangers at a party where they were snubbed by half the guests, they were too bewildered to offer much resistance when the other half took them by the arm and led them into a corner. The missionaries were spurned by the high castes and monopolised by the low. The CMS reported in 1857 that it had 'probably ... not more than ten Nairs' among its five or six thousand adherents.[3] The situation of the LMS in the south was similar: the vast majority of its converts were Shanars and Parayas. The missionaries were aware that in a sense they were being used. In 1847 Rev. Henry Baker, Jr. of the CMS wrote of the low castes in north Travancore: 'Every one that is in debt or in difficulty ... professes a desire to join the army of Xt [Christ]'. Rev. Charles Leitch of the LMS 'soon learned that secular motives rather than any appreciation of the truth and excellence of our holy religion had induced the great proportion to assume the Christian name ...' Rev. Ebenezer Lewis wrote:

> The poor, oppressed and trodden down natives, who can not afford large sums of money as bribes to those set over them, find that their grievances are more speedily, effectually and cheaply redressed by making the missionary their friend than in any other way. This at once furnishes the Shanars with a strong motive to become professing Christians and it is this motive alone which keeps many in connection with the mission.

Rev. J.O. Whitehouse concurred: 'They will sacrifice nothing by joining a church, rather the contrary, for it is ... by some looked upon as a step to employment...'[4] Rev. Joseph Peet of the CMS concluded that

> We have rushed needlessly into the arms of the lower classes ... fraternising with a despised race is just the way to raise prejudice and prevent the extention [sic] of our influence upward.[5]

Yet what could a missionary do?

> The addition of these low caste people [Pulayas] adds nothing to our importance and dignity in the eyes of the higher castes, and is in some respect a stumbling block to their reception of our Gospel; yet if the despised and forsaken gladly seek the words of eternal life, who shall say them nay?[6]

Most missionaries were prevented by humanity and circumstances from adopting so calculating a code as Peet's. The plight of the low castes genuinely moved them; in England, moreover, missionary committees judged their performance by the number of their converts.

A campaign for the abolition of slavery brought the CMS and LMS agents to concerted action and had wide repercussions.

It provoked the sirkar and the high castes to increased repression in an effort to defeat low-caste pretensions and maintain the status quo. At the same time, the open and pugnacious role of the missionaries encouraged low castes to an assertiveness which they would not otherwise have dared to show.

In the first section of this chapter we shall look at the campaign against slavery. In the second we shall see how the missionaries worked for their adherents' 'improvement' and in so doing, provided them with new resources and encouraged a new assertiveness. Then we shall look at the way in which low-caste adherents were able to seek the protection of their missionaries in disputes over what the missionaries called 'civil rights'. Finally, we shall see how the undeniable incompetence of the sirkar, publicised eagerly by the missionaries, led the Madras government, which was responsible for relations with Travancore, to demand reforms in the administration and in some of the customs prevalent in the state. These reforms, which are discussed in the next chapter, were to have important effects on most of Travancore society.

The Dewan and Resident who presided over Travancore at this crucial period were a fascinating pair who enjoyed a strange official and personal relationship. The Resident was Lieutenant-General William Cullen, who belonged to an older, merrier, more tolerant generation of Anglo-Indians. He held the Residency longer than any other man, from 1840 to 1860. The Dewan was V. Krishna Rao, a Brahmin from Masulipatam, whom Cullen, then Commissary General of the Madras Army, had met, liked and taken on his staff in 1835.

Cullen was the last of a long line of Scottish Residents, but by no means the last Scot to be attracted to the hills, rivers and women of Kerala. He came to India in 1805 at about eighteen and never married or returned to Britain. His amorous adventures were notorious. They were discussed in the *Madras Athenaeum*, reported to the Madras government and passed on as legend to succeeding generations.[7] In his youth he was said to have been known as 'the handsome adjutant' of the Madras Artillery,[8] but service in the artillery left him deaf, and by the time he came to Travancore he was bald. To the younger generation of missionaries whose contempt and intolerance provoked the break with the Syrians, he was 'our antiquated Brahminised

Resident'–'thoroughly "Hinduised"'–'more associated with "native friends" than European society'.[9]

Nor was Cullen an admirer of the missionaries. As a youth he had arrived in Madras at the time of the Vellore mutiny, which many of the Company's servants blamed on vociferous Christians.[10] The memory probably stayed with him. In the 1850s when a variety of troubles disturbed the Travancore sirkar, the Madras government and the even tenor of his ways, he laid much of the blame on the missionaries. Until 1833, he wrote, there were only seven European missionaries in the state. But in the next ten years the number doubled, seven new stations were opened, 'and to this sudden increase in numbers and extension of their operations to perfectly new localities may in some measure be ascribed many of the local disputes which have occurred'. In the same period he pointed out later, there had been six Residents.[11] The implication was clear: a firm hand was necessary to keep missionaries from causing trouble.

Yet Cullen was not a philistine devoted to debauchery. He dabbled in the sciences, patronised the Rev. Benjamin Bailey's *Malayalam-English Dictionary* and encouraged education through personal charity.[12] He lived in an exile's splendour,[13] an Ochterlony in the age of muscular Christians. Events in Travancore in the 1850s might have taken a different turn if the Resident had been John Nicholson or Herbert Edwardes.

Krishna Rao, who was to the missionaries 'the fountainhead of corruption' and 'notoriously corrupt and cruel',[14] was born in 1811, and at fifteen entered the collector's kutcherry in Masulipatam as a volunteer. His father had been employed by the Nawab of Kondapilli, and many of his cousins and brothers-in-law were in British service around Masulipatam. He worked for a year as the private writer of the chaplain of Masulipatam, and in January 1833 was appointed as a minor sheristadar by C.P. Brown, the acting collector of Guntur district. Guntur was poor preparation for a career of selfless probity.[15] He resigned within a year because of 'family affairs', but in 1835 Cullen employed him, and he soon rose to be deputy accountant in the Commissary General's department, where he 'was perfectly master of the whole complicated system'. On Cullen's appointment to Travancore, Krishna Rao asked to accompany him, 'and as an intelligent, confidential servant was necessary', Cullen wrote,

'I allowed him to attend me'.

The pair arrived in Trivandrum late in 1840, and although Cullen claimed that he made Krishna Rao learn Malayalam before approving him for a sirkar appointment, by March 1841 the stranger was a deputy peshkar, the third rung on the administrative ladder.[16] According to all accounts except Cullen's, the Resident pushed his protege forward, bullied the weak Maharaja, Swati Tirunal, who was more interested in musical composition than administration, and succeeded in 1842 in ousting the old Dewan and getting Krishna Rao temporarily appointed.[17] But when Cullen sought to have Krishna Rao's appointment made permanent, Swati Tirunal wrote to the Marquis of Tweeddale, the governor of Madras, to beg for relief from his acting Dewan.[18] Two months later Krishna Rao was dismissed. He did not leave Travancore, however, and in 1846 when Swati Tirunal was dying, he was taken back into service and appointed permanently as Dewan by Uttaram Tirunal, the new Maharaja, in 1847. 'Although he had only a limited knowledge of English', wrote Shankunni Menon, 'he wrote a good hand, and was a very fast writer and intelligent and active in his habits'. Cullen told the Madras government that Krishna Rao 'understands English perfectly'.[19] But perhaps it was the good handwriting which impressed the Resident who himself had difficulty in getting a dozen words of wildly sprawling script on a five-by-eight page.

Between Cullen and Krishna Rao, a curious, almost father-son relationship existed. Throughout the ten-year Dewanship, Cullen never failed to defend his protege to the Madras government and against the missionaries. Yet Cullen himself was constantly chiding the Dewan for his untidy work, his crumbling stationery and his tardiness.[20] In the official sphere the Maharaja had been pushed into the background completely, and Cullen's authority was absolute--when it was invoked. The Resident's approval was required for all sirkar appointments, and his instructions extended even to the use of sirkar elephants.[21] In Cullen's eyes the Dewan was intended to be the Resident's assistant. But in Travancore in the 1850s it was one thing to issue orders and another to have them carried out. Cullen's orders were continually frustrated, either by Krishna Rao's machinations or impotence. The latter is the more likely explanation. Regardless of what Resident or Dewan ordered, sirkar servants did much as they pleased. 'Fining is useless', Cullen complained. 'I shall be obliged to insist on the suspension or dismissal of sirkar officials who...wilfully neglect the Dewan's orders, known to be on the requisition of the Resident'.[22] As a member of the Madras government later observed, 'the degree of interference exercised by the representative of the British government has now become so large as...to fix the credit or discredit of the administration principally on the British government'.[23] Such a system of unproductive meddling offered no advantages, and as we shall see, was finally discarded after the breast-cloth disturbances in favour of greater power for the Maharaja and Dewan. At least then, the argument was to run, British governments would not have to take the blame.

The best summation of Krishna Rao was that of Vishakham Tirunal, Maharaja from 1880 to 1885, who as a boy knew the Dewan. 'Amiable but feeble',[24] Vishakham concluded, and it seems that Cullen, the lonely exile, valued the Dewan's amiability. For his part, Krishna Rao leaned heavily on Cullen. When the Senior Rani died in October 1857, the Dewan informed the Resident in an urgent official letter, to which he added a hurried postscript in his own hand: 'General should come immediately. I cannot keep the princes and His Highness hearty'.[25] Cullen and Krishna Rao were not the ideal pair to preside over a ramshackle administration under pressure from a changing society.

### *SLAVERY*

There was no great cordiality between the LMS and the CMS missionaries,[26] but the issue of slavery so much affected and offended the members of both societies that they joined in 1847 to present a joint petition to the new Maharaja. Uttaram Tirunal (Martanda Varma)[27] was installed in February of that year, two months after the death of his brother, Swati Tirunal. Both brothers knew English, although Uttaram was more fluent and gregarious,[28] which helped to explain the missionaries' eagerness to approach him. Their petition, dated 19 March 1847, was signed by twelve missionaries (four CMS, eight LMS), and pleaded for the abolition of all slavery or, at the very least, the emancipation of sirkar slaves, which the government could carry out without antagonising landholders.[29] The new Maharaja's urbanity, however, was deceptive, and in June, Krishna Rao informed the Resident that His Highness was willing to ameliorate the slaves' condition but that emancipation was 'too important to be entered upon at present...'[30]

Speedy administration was characteristic neither of Cullen nor the Travancore sirkar, and the correspondence with the missionaries over the slavery issue continued at a leisurely pace. In March 1848 the missionaries again petitioned, pointing out that legal recognition of slavery in British India had been withdrawn by Act V of 1843 and praying that Travancore might fall in line with the paramount power.[31] In August Cullen wrote to the Dewan that 'we ought...to do something on the subject–you know that my attention has long been directed to it'.[32] In March 1849 Cullen prepared a memorandum in which he concluded that slaves in Travancore were generally 'in a more degraded and miserable condition than in any other country' and suggested that the childern of sirkar slaves should be freed and laws enacted to protect slaves' welfare.[33] In May 1850 the Madras government, instructed by the Court of Directors, called on Cullen to provide information about slavery in Travancore; in July 1853 the inquiries remained unanswered.[34]

But while negotiations on the high plateau of the administration flowed gently, there were rocks and rapids lower down. By 1847 the missionaries had been closely involved with the slaves for eight or nine years. The CMS had become involved after its break with the Jacobites, while the LMS, strengthened by five new missionaries in 1828, found its agents increasingly appealed to by slaves. Advocacy of the slaves' cause did not stem from remote concern for an abstract principle. The slaves eagerly turned to the missionaries for help. One freed slave asked the Rev. Henry Baker, Jr. for money to buy his sweetheart. Baker gave him seven rupees with which he bought the girl and her brother. The whole family then asked to join the mission. 'Had I the means I might free many more from this horrid bondage', wrote Baker, who proposed to start an orphanage to prevent children being sold into slavery.[35] In the south, slaves similarly approached the LMS. 'As the slaves chiefly reside in my district', wrote Rev. Charles Mault,

> I have to fight their battles for them, for poor creatures they are so degraded and oppressed that they can do

> nothing to withstand their oppressors. In most instances the slaves are influenced by worldly motives to join us, but nevertheless they are brought under Christian instruction, and I greatly rejoice, for there is no other hope of their bettering their condition.[36]

Both societies opened schools for the slaves, and these brought the missions into increasing conflict with slave owners and sirkar officials. 'The owners of the slaves are much opposed to having them taught', wrote Rev. Henry Baker, Sr., 'and are constantly calling them away to their work and sometimes beating them'.[37] A CMS Syrian found in his evangelising tours that 'strong fears exist among all classes of people, that the enlightenment of slaves will be followed by their liberation, and the consequent ruin of the interests of agriculture. We are therefore being regarded as enemies to the best interests of the country...'[38]

Opposition and oppression, however, were the most likely things to bind the missionaries to the slaves, for most missionaries had a stubborn streak and a background of Christian martyrs. Nor had they any doubt of the righteousness of their cause, and in 1852 they began to publicise the plight of the Travancore slaves throughout India and in Britain. They were in touch with the *Friend of India* in Calcutta and the *Madras Athenaeum*; in the latter Rev. John Cox, using the pseudonym 'Not the Last', was to flay the Travancore sirkar until the early 1860s.[39]

Missionary interference with the slaves aroused the high castes, while at the same time missionaries themselves became less willing to accommodate Travancore custom. Physical clashes followed. In February 1853 Charles Mault and Ebenezer Lewis refused to take their palanquins down an embankment to avoid polluting an idol procession near the Suchindram temple. Lewis was pushed down a bank into a river bed and Mault was pelted with sand and dirt. The angry crowd also abused their wives. The missionaries concluded that now the outrageous prejudices of Travancore had been directed against Englishmen, reform must follow. 'It is not so much I as a man, but I as an Engishman that have been publicly dishonoured...', Lewis wrote to Cullen. To Lewis at least, the Resident's duty was clear: it was 'not so much to avenge my personal wrongs, as to defend our common national honour...'[40]

The slavery issue thus became embraced in a wider confrontation with the sirkar, and for the first time the Madras government examined missionary charges. The misfortune of Lewis and Mault in the south coincided with the discussion in the Madras Council of a CMS complaint about oppression in central Travancore, where missionaries' attitude towards slavery had provoked sirkar officers and caste-Hindu non-officials into making a stand in support of custom and caste law. Early in 1851 high-caste Hindus of Tiruvalla complained to the Dewan that Christian converts from the Ezhavas, and even Pulaya mission adherents–the CMS did not baptise a Pulaya until 1854–were using paths within pollution distance of the Tiruvalla temple and were refusing to move off roads and paths at the appproach of high castes. When the converts were abused by the high castes–and especially one convert, a former Ezhava named Cherian–the local pastor asked the pravrattikkaran and tahsildar for protection for his flock. He explained that the converts 'have now embraced the true religion and have become Christian Maplays, and that they will no longer follow the custom of the Illeivens [Ezhavas]...'[41] The tahsildar appealed to the Dewan for a ruling, and Krishna Rao handed down what the missionaries chose to call the 'Tiruvalla Edict':

> It is unnecessary to examine the complaint at the Huzzoor--you (the tahsildar) must settle it according to the Regulations, but though an Illeivan becomes a Christian, he must never cease to be an Illeivan, therefore you must not allow Cherian and other converts to the Christian religion to pass through the Public highway by the temple, but must compel them to go round through the fields.[42]

The CMS missionaries protested vigorously to the Madras government, and it was this case which Major-General Sir Henry Pottinger, the governor, considered in Council in January 1853. The Council called on Cullen for a report, and Cullen in turn called on Krishna Rao. The Dewan dwelt on the advantages low-caste converts were seeking to obtain through their connection with the European missionaries. 'The missionaries', he wrote, 'have been lately claiming privileges for their converts, which are perfect innovations and which the sirkar cannot, consistently with the feeling of the high-caste Hindoos, entertain'.[43]

When Cullen finally replied to the Madras government in August, he attacked the missionaries in a guarded way for allowing themselves to be used by their adherents and for thus rocking the Travancore ship of state. The missionaries were 'much in the habit of taking up the petty disputes of their converts...'[44] Such an excuse suggests that the appeal which the missionary alternative had for low castes was widely apparent and that high castes were aware that a new weight had been placed on the social balances in Travancore.

Before the Madras government could examine Cullen's reply, the Travancore sirkar made a small and grudging concession to missionary pressure. This was a proclamation which primarily emancipated the children, born after 15 September 1853, of sirkar slaves. Since sirkar slaves were thought to number only 6,000 (in fact, as we have seen, there were 15,000) of the 130,000 slaves in the state the measure was hardly radical.[45] Moreover, the second clause of the proclamation warned that 'the liberty conferred...does not authorise the infringement of the standing religious usages and customs of the different classes of our subjects'.[46] About this, even the Madras government, which was generally disposed to back Cullen and the sirkar, had some misgivings,[47] and Cullen later reprimanded Krishna Rao for the sharp practice which had enabled him to include the paragraph against Cullen's wishes.[48]

Token emancipation such as this could not of course satisfy the missionaries. They found themselves holding a large umbrella of protection under which growing numbers of low castes, especially slaves, were seeking shelter. The sirkar, meanwhile, doing its best to drive the low castes back into the traditional hail of abuse where they belonged, was in fact achieving the opposite end: its repression drove more to huddle under the umbrella. In February 1854 Pottinger's government in Madras came down heavily against the missionaries in the case of the 'Tiruvalla Edict' and forbade them to take up the causes of their converts.[49] But in the same month the missionaries extended their agitation with the publication in the *Madras Church Missionary Record* of a long and harrowing article based on questions put to adult slaves attending a mission school near Kottayam. Later reprinted in England–it was obviously aimed at the English audience from the start—it painted a picture of privation and cruelty. Slaves were granted a daily measure of rice only when they worked: 'no food is given during sickness...', and 'when old age disables from work, no wages or support of any kind is given by masters'. Although children worked, they were not given the rice because, 'not having proper food', they were 'weak and unable to do hard work'. Slaves were sold and beaten; families were divided.[50]

Such propaganda was well-timed, for in mid-1854 the unsympathetic Pottinger retired. He was replaced by Lord Harris, a practising Christian and devoted anti-slaver who had been governor of Trinidad and who came to India 'eager to stamp out slavery completely'.[51] By October the Madras government had passed a resolution calling for virtual emancipation of all slaves in Travancore.[52] Both Cullen and Krishna Rao now saw the necessity of falling in with the new governor's programme, and in November Cullen wrote to say that the sirkar would issue a proclamation similar to the Government of India's Act V of 1843.[53] A good deal of vacillation on the part of the Maharaja and Krishna Rao remained. The Cochin sirkar issued a suitable proclamation in April 1855, and Cullen lamented that 'the credit which I wished to obtain for Travancore from early publication is now lost...'[54] But on 24 June the proclamation was finally issued, although not widely circulated.[55] It emancipated all sirkar slaves and withdrew legal recognition from all aspects of slavery. Thus a slave-owner might keep his slaves if they chose to stay or were unaware of their rights, but he had no legal way of compelling them to remain with him.

Low castes who heard of the proclamation probably connected it with missionary influence, and even if they did not, Rev. Henry Baker, Sr. made the connection for them. As soon as the proclamation was issued, he had copies printed, and 'adding a few passages from the epistles on the duties of masters and servants respectively', had them passed out among the slaves. 'Slave-owners beg my people not to distribute them...'[56] Low castes were also undoubtedly struck by the same moral that Baker saw: slavery had been abolished--'pressure from without having effected it'.[57] For Baker, 'pressure from without' meant Madras and London, but for low castes the external agents were the missionaries. Low castes could look to a new resource:

effective political support. Even those who did not convert to Christianity were encouraged to greater assertiveness. The abolition of slavery caused low castes to magnify the missionaries' reputation as 'fixers' and increased the anxiety of high castes at the disruption and betrayal of traditional Malayali society.

*IMPROVEMENT*

But to reduce the high castes to the level of the low by bringing the social system crashing down was by no means the missionaries' chief aim. A few, like Joseph Peet--'to effect the regeneration of India is no child's play'[58]—may have seen their task in such apocalyptic terms, but for most, the elevation of their adherents was a far more important goal. In working towards it, the missionaries complemented their political leadership by making available an additional 'package' of resources to low castes. Rev. Frederic Baylis, analysing the causes of the breastcloth disturbances of 1859, pointed to the assistance which low castes had been able to obtain from the missionaries:

> I am inclined to think that the growing intelligence, wealth and influence of the Shanars (especially those of them who are Christians) owing to the efforts that have been made to educate them, to many of them going often to Ceylon where some are employed in situations of trust and responsibility (some of our people having situations of from 50 to 70 Rs. per mensem as conductors, etc.), and to their engaging to a much greater extent than formerly in trading in jaggery, tamarind, cotton, etc. have had much more to do in causing the present irritated and excited state of the Sudras here than the wearing of the upper cloth by their females.[59]

How were Shanars, especially Shanar Christians, able to get education, to go to Ceylon and to become successful petty traders? A large part of the answer was bound up with activities of the missionaries. Shanars were educated in mission schools. The skills which they learned there enabled them to carry on small businesses and to seek employment outside Travancore. When they left Travancore they carried letters of introduction from their missionaries to Englishmen in Ceylon or Tinnevelly or Madras. For example, Benjamin Bailey's brother, Joseph, was a CMS agent in Ceylon, and Charles Mead's second wife was the daughter of a missonary in Tanjore.

Literacy, especially in English, was coming to have an obvious commercial value by the 1850s. The missionaries had introduced English education to Travancore; CMS College, Kottayam, dated from John Munro's Residency, and the Nagercoil Seminary, from the 1820s. Although Syrian Christians tried to exclude converts from CMS College, many low-caste adherents of the CMS acquired basic literacy. Its usefulness was clear. In 1855 Rev. Henry Baker, Sr. reported a fall in enrolment in the higher classes at CMS College. This resulted from 'the very great demand among the mercantile gentlemen lately settled at Cochin for writers, domestic servants and workers...'[60] The CMS found difficulty in retaining the services of its educated youths because of 'the great temptation offered...by lucrative situations at Cochin...', and even considered eliminating English from the curriculum to make boys less employable elsewhere.[61] The LMS, on the other hand, encouraged its youths to seek work outside the state, for its Shanar converts did not have the wealth or the status of the Syrian adherents of the CMS. The LMS realised that only prosperous Christians could make a prosperous mission. One of its most successful adherents, P.D. Devasagaim, went to Ceylon for the first time in 1840. When Rev. John Russel visited Ceylon on his way back to England in 1856, he spoke of the educated Christians of South Travancore who were eager to escape to new opportunities, and urged merchants, planters and landlords in Ceylon to encourage them.[62]

The Syrian adherents of the CMS already enjoyed moderate prosperity and a respectable position in society. They objected to missionary attempts to raise low-caste converts to equality with Syrians; the missionaries were forced to proceed cautiously. In south Travancore, however, LMS agents did more for their converts because they had to. They formed saving banks whose directors, who had to be Christian landowners, were 'elected annually by the depositors'. They organised village councils for Christians 'for the promotion of peace and good order in the village... We try to keep our people as far as possible from the injustice, bribery and corruption that prevail in the police and other Courts'.[63] Their village school system expanded to provide respected employment for educated, baptised Christians who came to be regarded as village spokesmen. A modest economic system, which generated dozens of low-salaried–but nevertheless, *salaried*–jobs, grew up around the missions. At the head of a mission station was a European missionary; beneath him were his native pastors, their itinerating evangelists and the numerous catechists, one of whom lived among each congregation.[64]

By the 1850s the CMS had produced a generation of well-educated, English-speaking Syrian clergy who were constantly on the move throughout north and central Travancore. Because they were known to be Syrians and dressed like the traditional kathanar, they excited no fears about pollution and found ready audiences. The journals of Oomen Mamen, Jacob Chandy, Sr., and K. Koshi chronicle many encounters with high castes on paths, in paddy fields and under wayside trees. In the course of such conversations the clergymen would condemn idol worship, ridicule Nair marriage customs, distribute tracts, emphasise the exploitive nature of Brahmins and offer a few words about the hellfire to come.[65] On 13 June 1850, for example, Chandy talked to a 'respectable' Nair, and when 'the cunning of the Brahmins in imposing upon the Nairs laws that are favourable to the Brahmins and disadvantageous to the Nairs was alluded to, the man readily consented to the remarks...' One of Chandy's favourite themes when speaking to Nairs was 'the filthy character of the Brahmins';[66] he seems to have found willing listeners.

High castes could not ignore such a widespread mission network, and what they learned from catechists and evangelists was often disquieting. One of the Rev. Oomen Mamen's anecdotes illustrates the point. A Syrian friend had opened a school for slave children and was seen eating with the slaves. The Nair tahsildar was horrified and asked Mamen's friend why anyone would bother to educate slaves. Mamen's friend answered jocularly, 'they are taught to be qualified to the places of Proverthicaren, Goomastan and Tahsildar'. To this the tahsildar enquired seriously, 'Is it so?' Mamen's friend replied, 'Yes, in the north the Tiars (Tiyyas) and slaves hold places under government'.[67]

But missionary influence on the high castes could be more subtle and constructive. The public meetings, Sunday services and social functions of the CMS congregations were noted by caste Hindus. Oomen Mamen, who was to work for the CMS for fifty years, told how he had begun regular monthly meetings in some of his parishes around Mavelikara. Eventually, Nairs of the same villages began to import Tamil Brahmins twice a month to cook for Nair feasts, which Mamen felt were a social reply to the meetings of his parishioners.[68] Some caste Hindus also took advantage of mission schools. Two future Dewans, N. Nanu Pillai (Dewan, 1877-80) and T. Rama Rao (Dewan, 1887-92), were educated at the Nagercoil Seminary, where the 'day-scholars are of various castes, and among them are found Protestants, Roman Catholics, Mohammedans, and heathens'.[69] As early as 1827, the top boy in one of the classes at CMS College, Kottayam, was a Nair.[70]

High castes were aware of the activities of the missionaries, and the facilities they were offering to low castes. Indeed, some Brahmins and Nairs attended mission schools, listened to evangelists and read tracts. But the majority were hostile and suspicious. Even among low castes, for whom missionary patronage could be of great advantage, enthusiasm for the purely religious aspects of Christianity was lukewarm. In 1857 K. Koshi 'spoke a few words against the worshipping of idols' to a group of Ezhavas and Pulayas, but 'as soon as they heard their gods called wood and stone they began to clamour out...'[71] Most low castes joined the missions for the this-worldly benefits that were obviously there. Higher castes generally had no such need, but they knew enough of mission activities to be apprehensive.

## *CIVIL RIGHTS*

Krishna Rao's 'Tiruvalla Edict' declared that 'though an Illeivan becomes a Christian, he must never cease to be an Illeivan...' But the aim of conversion for low castes was escape from their old disabilities, and missionaries were not prepared to admit that their morally regenerated adherents were inferior to caste Hindus. Although Pottinger's Madras government upheld the 'Edict', Pottinger soon retired, and in 1855 the Court of Directors in the Ecclesiastical Department recognised the missionary 'as the natural protector of his flock under persecution'.[72] The missionaries had never regarded themselves as anything else.

As converts became better educated and slightly more prosperous, they became increasingly resentful of the traditional marks of inferiority which they were still legally required to observe. They flouted the sirkar-enforced caste law and turned to the European missionaries for support. This was usually provided. Alarmed and appalled at such illegal pretensions, high-caste sirkar officials intensified their repression; this further outraged the missionaries and committed them to the low-caste cause. The conflict between Travancore law and low-caste pretensions reached a climax in the breastcloth disturbance of 1859.

*Political Missionaries*

The plight of the low castes incited the pity, sympathy and anger of the missionaries who were unshakably convinced of where their duty lay. 'Those...were days of tyranny in Travancore', the Rev. John Abbs later wrote of the 1850s. 'We could at the time overcome injustice successfully only by disobeying the laws of the land and setting the government at defiance'.[73] Converts and mission adherents were increasingly able to count on missionary aid, and this led to more conversions and greater assertiveness even among the unconverted castemen of new Christians. 'I do not think we should be too much afraid of being called political missionaries', wrote the third medical missionary to come to Travancore. 'As men, no less than as Christians, and Christian Ministers, we are bound to protest against the corruption and oppression which abound'.[74]

Converts often found it possible to interpose the missionary between themselves and corrupt, oppressive sirkar officials. Some of the missionaries engaged in local politics with skill and enthusiasm. When sirkar officials at Trivandrum beat one of John Cox's readers who had sheltered a Christian wanted for forced labour, Cox went immediately to the Dewan's kutcherry and succeeded, he said, in having the oppressive officials imprisoned. Later, he wrote:

> I am sure I could never have obtained justice or even the rescue of the Reader and others from prison and punishment under false charges but by personal attendance at the cutcherry of the Dewan, not even writing would have sufficed. It was only my going and addressing him, not in English and aside, as he wished, but in the native language before his crowded cutcherry... [75]

Ostentatious, personal intervention, the power implicit in a white skin, knowing whom to bully and whom to conciliate—these were the counters which missionaries like Cox and Joseph Peet played cunningly to get quick and satisfactory settlements of their converts' grievances. When one of Peet's Ezhava converts carrying nine bushels of wet salt was badly beaten by the retainers of the Mavelikara raja for not moving off the road, Peet went to the local tahsildar, a young, educated Nair. The tahsildar hoped for a reference from Peet, and after initial unwillingness, he finally agreed to hear a case of assault. The raja then sent a relative–'with just a dash of snake slime', Peet wrote with characteristic charity–to tell Peet that the raja was willing, as a special favour, to let the matter drop. Peet replied that the case must go on or he would write to the Maharaja of Travancore. Within hours the relative returned with an apology which Peet refused. Finally, the missionary went to the worried tahsildar and agreed not to press the matter–if the tahsildar would fine the raja one rupee in open court. This was done accordingly the next day, and Peet was jubilant. He did not seek involvement in local politics, he explained, but '...here I am and will remain, only to advance by fair means the progress of the Gospel–that is–simply to uphold my people's civil rights'.[76]

### *Forced Labour*

Chief among what Peet and other missionaries regarded as 'civil rights' were the exemption from *uriyam* or forced labour, and the freedom to use roads, appear in public buildings and speak and dress like the high castes. Such disabilities were enforced by sirkar officials. Syrian Christians, however, were accorded high status and moved freely, and CMS agents were led to claim for their converts the same privileges as Syrians. Eventually missionary tenacity and influence began to make high castes less ready to challenge converts on the roads, and even Cullen was disposed to support converts' rights to appear in 'courts of justice or cutcherries'.[77] The missionaries also tried to keep their slave-caste adherents out of unnecessary confrontations. Peet sent them to stations where they were not known.[78]

Perhaps the most persistent source of grievance was *uriyam* which fell primarily on the low castes. In a state like Travancore where there had never been a public works department or commissariat, some method had to be found to repair roads and public buildings and to acquire provisions for festivals and touring officials. *Uriyam* had traditionally filled the void. When something needed to be done, sirkar officials co-opted all the available labour, including poorer Nairs and Syrians. In 1838, for example, the Resident pressed for construction of a north-south trunk road, but the Dewan explained that because the *murajapam* festival was approaching, 'there will unavoidably be a want of labourers to execute the work as the services of the inhabitants of almost all the Districts of Travancore will be required for a long time for collecting and furnishing provisions...'[79]

*Uriyam* was burdensome, and mission adherents made the missionaries aware of it from the first. As early as 1815 John Munro had arranged for Syrians and other Christians to be exempted from performing *uriyam* for temples, and six years later Charles Mead won for his Shanar converts the right of not having to do *uriyam* on Sundays. But sirkar proclamations mattered little to officials in the countryside, and whenever they needed labour, they continued to draft the nearest low castes, regardless of their religion or the day of the week. In 1851 Peet succeeded in getting the exemption proclamations reissued,[80] and from that time converts asserted their rights with increasing success. Some began to avoid *uriyam* completely. Nor was the effect of the missionaries' pressures confined to their adherents. Seeing their converted castemen protected by the missionaries, low-caste Hindus also avoided doing *uriyam*, and the inept, apprehensive sirkar under Krishna Rao had neither the confidence nor the ability to coerce them systematically. By 1857 *uriyam* had fallen into disuse in some areas, although the sirkar had issued no proclamation of abolition. When T. Madhava Rao, newly appointed as district officer of the southern division, inquired about the sirkar's right to demand forced labour to maintain roads, Cullen was somewhat bewildered. He wrote to the Dewan that formerly *uriyam* was 'customary' and that 'very material aid' had been 'apparently cheerfully afforded'. In recent years, however, customs had changed--'but it would be very desirable to re-establish the system quietly'.[81] The creation of a public works department in the 1860s introduced salaried labour and ended *uriyam* for good.

## *The Breastcloth Disturbances*

Winning exemption from *uriyam*, however, was only one way in which converts and aspiring low-caste Hindus sought to take advantage of missionary involvement to improve their comfort and status. We have already seen how dress restrictions were important to distinguish castes and thus preserve distinctions of ritual status. The most tangible assertion of social advance was the adoption of high-caste styles of dress, and in this question low-castes were able to harness missionary zeal for decency to their own ideas of prestige. Castes below Nairs were forbidden sandals, umbrellas and some types of jewellery, but what most offended the missionaries–and most clearly marked a woman as low-caste–was the custom which prohibited low-caste women from covering their breasts. This was not completely unfair, for Nair women, although they had the right to wear a scanty upper cloth, were required to bare their breasts before temple deities and caste superiors. Moreover, in north Travancore where the CMS worked, Nair woman generally went bare-breasted by choice; in the southern districts Tamil influence was stronger and the distinctive upper cloth was worn.[82] Syrian Christian women traditionally wore a long-sleeved blouse. In the north then, the CMS could put its converts into costumes similar to the Syrians'; the style of dress was long established, and for women, a covered torso brought little status anyway. But in the south the right to cover the breasts was regarded as a great social privilege, and the sirkar punished those low-caste women who assumed the dignity.[83]

After some rioting in 1829 Mead achieved confirmation of an earlier proclamation allowing Shanar converts to wear a jacket (*kuppayam*), but they were still forbidden to wear the upper cloth of the Nairs or the blouse of Tamil Brahmins. Hindu Shanars were to go bare-breasted as before.[84] But it was status, not decency, that Shanars sought. The *kuppayam* did not become fairly general among Christian woman until the slight improvement in the financial condition of Shanars in the 1850s, and even then the missionaries had to resort to subsidies and gentle coercion to popularise it. 'Those who can afford it invariably wear them', wrote the Rev. Ebenezer Lewis, 'and even those who cannot afford to purchase such always cover themselves in the house of God'. But local cloth was too rough to be satisfactory, and he appealed for old dresses from England which could be remade into *kuppayam*.[85] About a year later, in 1856, the missionaries began an organised campaign to clothe their female adherents. '...It has been exceedingly difficult', confessed the Rev. Frederic Baylis, 'to introduce what to them is a strange custom ... the women generally have been content with putting their cloth over their heads and folding it in front, when they come to service, which is not sufficient covering even then, and on other occasions going about as the heathen women'. In the previous year, however, about five hundred jackets were made by the girls in the boarding school in Nagercoil; one hundred and fifty were distributed free and the rest sold for the cost of the material. 'At our last celebration of the Lord's Supper, *for the first time*, every one of the female members, old women as well as young (and the old generally have a great objection to these new-fangled customs) had on the jacket and were thus decently clothed'.[86]

But there was more enthusiasm for the flimsy upper cloth than for the thoroughly decent *kuppayam*. In 1855 a group of Shanar converts, not content with the *kuppayam*, petitioned the sirkar for permission to dress their woman as they pleased.[87] Their request was rejected, but perceiving the weakness of the sirkar and encouraged by the missionaries' contempt for Krishna Rao's government,[88] Christian women began increasingly to wear the forbidden upper cloth, often on top of the *kuppayam*. Hindu Shanars followed their example.

In December 1858, after a few earlier disturbances, P. Shankunni Menon, the Nair dewan peshkar of the southern division, heard charges against a Christian Shanar woman who had worn the upper cloth in violation of the terms of the proclamation which Mead had extracted in 1829. Shankunni Menon accused the Hindu and Christian Shanars of 'mutual consultation' to overturn the laws of the state, and reported that if a decision was given against the accused woman 'it is their intention to assemble in a multitude and create disturbances...' The crux of the matter was that 'the Shanar women wearing different kinds of cloth [sic] like the Soodras and other high caste people, and frequenting the public roads, cannot be distinguished as Shanars... When the disloyal conduct of the Christian Shanars is properly dealt with, the Hindu Shanars would behave [sic] themselves as they ought to do'.[89] On 3 January 1859, after the circulation of a sirkar notification reiterating the laws of dress, he reported that a Shanar mob had attacked the tobacco shop and some merchants in Kottar, near Nagercoil.[90] Shankunni Menon's sympathies obviously lay with the Nair and Vellala landlords of his district who were being plagued by aggressive Shanars and recalcitrant Paraya slaves.

Christian and Hindu Shanars, however, had the support of the missionaries, who told a different story. They agreed that the trouble began in Kottar on 4 January, but it was Nairs and Vellalas who beat Shanars and tore off upper cloths.[91] Bypassing Shankunni Menon and the Dewan, the missionaries wrote directly to Cullen. They accused four aristocratic Nairs of having organised the attacks, but Cullen was sceptical. 'These Thumbies are probably men of respectability, two of the four more especially', he wrote to the Dewan, who was by this time T. Madhava Rao. 'I should be cautious therefore of implicating them without the strongest evidence'.[92]

Throughout January there were scattered clashes and stealthy incendiarism directed against mission property. A detachment of a hundred men of the Nair Brigade was sent to Nagercoil under a European officer. But as Cullen pointed out, the men were all Nairs, many with relatives and property in the south; and they therefore 'could hardly be expected to afford much aid'.[93]

Yet a picture of a district ravaged by fire and sword is hardly accurate. To be sure there were reports of Shanars in Tinnevelly in British India preparing to invade Travancore and of Travancore Shanars seeking refuge in Tinnevelly.[94] But by the beginning of February all was again quiet. No one was killed in the disturbances, and the damage to mission property amounted to Rs. 128 by the sirkar's estimate or Rs. 1,105 by John Cox's. Cullen regretted 'these little contretemps' at the close of his Residency and Lord Harris's governorship.[95] He traced the disturbances to a number of causes: 'a growing feeling of disquietude on the part of the Soodras, at the innovations of the Shanar, both Christian and Heathen'; the strong feelings of slaveholders against the missionaries since the emancipation proclamation of 1855; the belief of Nairs that Queen Victoria's proclamation of November 1858 had 'annulled all previous innovations' in caste.[96]

Although Hindu and Christian Shanars outnumbered Nairs and Vellalas, the latter were better organised and armed, and could count on the support of their relatives and castemen employed by the sirkar and of their dependent ex-slaves and tenants. When it came to open violence, Shanars gained no advantage from their connections with the missionaries. But even while the disturbances were going on, the usefulness of missionary support was apparent in the letters to Cullen and appeals to the Madras government. The missionaries ensured that the battle was noisily lost, and this did much to win the war. With the Rebellion of 1857 still not completely crushed in north India, the Madras government could not ignore conflict in habitually delinquent Travancore.

## *MAKING THE SIRKAR MEND ITS WAYS*

For the Madras government, the breastcloth disturbances were the last straw. Since 1852 there had been a steady stream of petitions and complaints from Travancore, and little response from the Travancore sirkar except excuses and vacillation. Not all the complaints had come from missionaries, but missionary protests received greatest credence. The missionaries made no distinction between the oppression, corruption and incompetence of the sirkar and its discriminatory laws. At first, the Madras government was inclined to condemn the former and shrug its shoulders at the latter. But over the years missionary propaganda succeeded in blurring the distinction, and by 1859 the missionaries had made the issue of inequitable laws inseparable from that of administrative chaos.

### *Misgovernment*

To be on the side of the administrative angels as far as the Madras government was concerned, one had to produce budgetary surpluses; the road to hell was paved with deficits and the signposts were written in red ink. By such standards the Travancore sirkar was on the way to damnation when Krishna Rao took office, for he inherited a debt of six lakhs of rupees.[97] He scarcely tried to moderate the expenditure. In his first year in office, a lakh of rupees was spent on ceremonies connected with the Maharaja's death and the thread ceremonies of one of the princes. In the next four years, Rs. 2.13 lakhs were spent on the Maharaja's weighing-in-gold ceremony and Rs. 2 lakhs on the *murajapam* festival. By 1851 expenditure on *uttupuras*, the Brahmin feedinghouses, had climbed to a new high of Rs. 3.36 lakhs. Palace and temple expenses hovered around Rs. 3 lakhs each.[98] The sirkar's attitude to expenditure was well illustrated in 1838 when the Dewan rejected the Resident's proposal for construction of a north-south road:

> ... independent of certain important repairs and additions which are now being made to the Shri Padmanabha Pagoda at Trivandrum, two new palaces ... are under construction for the use of His Highness the Rajah and the various Pagodas, Palaces and other public buildings from Suchindram to the North of Travancore having fallen into a state of decay and ruin are also undergoing considerable repairs now, and all the above-mentioned works would necessarily require a very large outlay of public funds.[99]

Remunerative public works were not within the sirkar's ken. When Krishna Rao proudly reported economies of Rs. 75,000 in 1852, the Madras government was dismayed to find that they had been effected by discontinuing the engineering office, dismissing 200 pioneers, reducing the number of munsiffs and cutting the price of pepper paid to the ryots.[100]

The early 1850s were replete with deficits and signs of inefficiency. The accounts for 1851-52, for example, did not reach the Madras government until Februuary 1854, and in October 1852 some Travancore public servants embarrassed the sirkar by petitioning Madras about their salary arrears.[101] Cullen assured the Madras government that 'none but the most ordinary arrears of two or three months exists',[102] but later wrote to Krishna Rao to warn of impending 'most dangerous consequences'. He pointed out that a European employee at Quilon was seven months in arrears and that all the court officials at Alleppey and Parur were unpaid.[103]

The operation of the pepper monopoly increasingly brought the sirkar into disrepute. In the ten years, 1849-58, Travancore pepper sales had averaged only 5,000 candies annually (1 candy equals 500 lbs.) while Malabar district, with the same climate and area, had averaged 18,600 candies.[104] From the early 1850s, the Travancore ryots had not been paid for the pepper which they turned over to the sirkar's pepper stations. The payment which rightfully belonged to them was kept by the local officials. Pepper smuggling to British Cochin in exchange for contraband tobacco became a major traffic, while some poorer farmers were said to have destroyed their vines to escape to attentions of the tahsildars and the pepper department. The shortage of pepper, and the subterfuge involved in getting it, occasioned memorials to the Madras government from the Chambers of Commerce of Madras, Bombay and Ceylon and the merchants of Pondicherry; all called for the abolition of the Travancore monopoly.[105]

The corruption and incompetence of local officials, which the pepper problem underlined for the Madras government, was clear even to Cullen. He tried to exert greater control over tahsildars and other officials by appointing district officers, one of them T. Madhava Rao, in 1855. Hitherto tahsildars had no supervision except from the huzur kutcherry.[106] But the quality of the existing tahsildars made improvement difficult. Their chief qualification was that they were Brahmins or Nairs and that they could, according to one petitioner, afford to purchase their appointments from the Dewan.[107] 'The ignorance of a large proportion of tahsildars' was well known, as was the obsolescence of many offices. 'The salt department', Cullen wrote on discovering gross wastage, 'is under Ananda Row...who should be more careful that he does not by such neglects hasten the abolition of a useless appointment'.[108] But Cullen's admonitions did little good. Krishna Rao had neither the ability nor the inclination to wrestle with such problems. Cullen had not the will, nor the heart, to compel him.

### *Towards Annexation*

By almost all admissions, Travancore was misgoverned, and the concrete manifestations of misrule, which the Madras government noted, were complemented by the petitions of missionaries and others. Between 1853 and 1856 the missionaries petitioned six times, and in 1857 John Cox published much of the correspondence in *Travancore Its Present Ruin Shown and the Remedy Sought in A Correspondence with the Government of Madras in the Years 1855-57.* During the same period there were eight other lengthy petitions to which the Madras government chose to attach little significance because they came from Indians, Eurasians or disreputable Europeans. The catalogue of crimes and injustices in each petition is of no great interest. What was important was the cumulative effect on a sympathetic governor like Harris, who, as well as pressing for the abolition of slavery, had been responsible for the appointment of the Torture Commission in Madras. By the middle of 1855, Harris was beginning to favour some form of direct interference in Travancore's internal affairs. To prepare the way, the Madras government in August forwarded a long LMS petition, containing detailed charges, to the Governor-General. Contrary to his reputation as an eager annexationist, Dalhousie pointed out that Travancore's payment of the subsidy of eight lakhs of rupees was not endangered, and he therefore declined to interfere.[109] The sirkar escaped with another warning. However, when the Court of Directors received the the same papers, it authorised the Madras government to establish a commission to inquire into Travancore affairs. Confronted by this contradiction of instructions, the Madras government submitted all the papers to Calcutta for a definitive ruling in August 1856. They were still circulating when the great revolt began in May 1857.

But while the files revolved, in Curzon's words, stately, solemn, sure and slow, in Calcutta, events in Travancore and Madras were moving more rapidly. Another missionary petition was taken up by the Madras government in March 1856,[110] and the *Madras Athenaeum* continued to inveigh against the Travancore sirkar. In October of the same year, the *Athenaeum* published 'A Political Sketch of Travancore', by 'A Native'. The writer was in fact the nineteen-year-old second prince, Vishakham Tirunal. The article indicated opposition within the palace to the weak Maharaja and the bad old ways of Cullen and Krishna Rao. It concluded that Travancore was in a most 'perilous position'.

> Native States are every day all around fast falling victim to the all-grasping policy of the paramount power. The prelude in Travancore is already sung... Those who ought most to feel, and endeavour to avert it [the threat of annexation] are least aware and mindful of it. The only way of saving the state is to place its management in the hands of a resolute and vigorous minister like Salar Jung of Hyderabad.[111]

External forces, however, began to benefit Travancore. The outbreak of the revolt removed the immediate threat of annexation, and death removed Krishna Rao, on 26 November 1857, ten days after the second relief of Lucknow. His successor as Dewan was the twenty-nine-year-old T. Madhava Rao, a Desastha Brahmin, dewan peshkar and formerly tutor of the two princes, Ayilyam and Vishakham Tirunal. Both Madhava Rao's father and uncle had been Dewans of Travancore (respectively, Ranga Rao, Dewan 1837-38; Venkata Rao, Dewan 1822-30, 1838-39). Since 1855, as a result of Cullen's insistence, Madhava Rao had been working as district officer in the southern division, where even the missionaries applauded 'the integrity, energy and impartiality with which you have fulfilled the duties of your office'.[112] His appointment was probationary for a year, but in that time he battled against the chaotic administration and won the confidence of both Cullen and the Madras government. Harris exonerated him from blame for the breastcloth disturbances. 'The fire was smouldering', the Governor explained, when Madhava Rao took office.[113]

### *The Aftermath of the Disturbances*

Travancore now had a Dewan who appeared able to put the administration in order and produce surpluses. Such success would have satisfied the Madras government five years earlier, but in the aftermath of the breastcloth disturbances and of the revolt, the relationship between the Maharaja, the Dewan and the Resident, and the social issues in Travancore, could not be ignored. In three tortuous despatches, the home government tried to explain the policy which it wished to see implemented in Travancore.[114] Generally, its conclusions were that Residents had exercised too great an interference in internal affairs, that the Maharaja had become a cipher, that he must be made to take greater responsibility in the governing of the state and that Cullen's resignation would be helpful if a new policy were to be followed. In September 1859, Cullen announced his intention to resign.

Meanwhile, on the social front, the sirkar in July issued a proclamation granting Hindu Shanar women the same rights to cover their breasts as Christian Shanars--i.e., in any manner except that of the high castes. But no similar rights were granted to Ezhavas or other low-caste Hindus. About August 1859 the LMS agents petitioned the Madras government for what proved to be the last time for many years. They conceded Madhava Rao's achievements, but complained at the omissions in the proclamation, Cullen's retention, and the continued bondage of many ex-slaves.[115] They received a sympathetic hearing from the new governor, Sir Charles Trevelyan. Trevelyan had already in May expressed his horror at the laws which required women to go bare-breasted,[116] and now with Cullen's resignation to come into effect on 1 January 1860, he took the opportunity to instruct a new Resident in the kinds of social changes which ought to be instigated in Travancore.[117]

As the new Resident, he chose F.N. Maltby, a former member of the Madras committee of the Church Missionary Society, brother of a later acting governor of Madras, nephew of a former Biship of Durham and 'a good Christian, Church of England man'.[118] Instead of giving Maltby written instructions, Trevelyan called him for an interview, after which Maltby prepared a memorandum of what Trevelyan had said. The chief subjects were the abolition of the Travancore monopolies and the dress restrictions imposed on Shanar women. To effect the latter, Trevelyan told Maltby, 'even if the use of cold steel is necessary, this will be afforded'.[119]

Although the reference to 'cold steel' understandably upset Trevelyan's council, Maltby can have had few doubts of what was expected of him. Within a few months of taking up his appointment he had become, to at least one missionary, 'our present excellent Resident', who visited mission stations, distributed Bibles and encouraged the propagation of Christian truth. 'Surely', wrote the same missionary, 'we have the dawning of a better day'.[120]

From the arrival of English missionaries in Travancore, their adherents had looked to them for protection. Moreover, in the later 1830s and early 1840s the number of missionaries doubled, and their protection became more widely available. At the same time, the CMS in north Travancore broke with the Jacobites, and began to proselytise for a new Anglican church. The missionaries did not seek the low castes; the low castes sought them. Indeed, some missionaries had grave misgivings about accepting low-caste adherents, especially Pulayas and Parayas. It was difficult, however, for most missionaries to deny the call on their humanity, and in 1847 the LMS and CMS jointly petitioned the Travancore sirkar for the abolition of slavery. Their plea was rejected, but their work among the slaves, their newspaper campaigns and their petitions were instrumental in forcing abolition in 1855. As more and more slaves turned to the missionaries, however, high castes became alarmed and resentful. Their efforts at repression only strengthened the bonds between low-caste adherents and missionaries. Meanwhile, low-caste adherents were benefiting from mission education, which not only gave them an enhanced idea of their own status but the skills to carry on trade or seek salaried work outside Travancore. But the new assertiveness on the part of mission adherents--and to some extent of their unconverted castemen--was bitterly resisted by high castes, and the missionaries found themselves forced to provide political leadership to help secure what they regarded as the 'civil rights' of their regenerated adherents. The Madras government, which was continually confronted with missionary petitions, had other grounds for displeasure with the Travancore sirkar. It was moving towards an inquiry into the whole Travancore administration when it was deflected by bureaucratic delay and the outbreak of the revolt of 1857. However, the breastcloth disturbances, which amounted to a direct clash between missionary-inspired, low-caste assertiveness and high-caste conservatism, forced the Madras government to turn its attention again to Travancore. Its decisions enhanced the prestige of the missions. It virtually ordered concessions on dress restrictions and sent to Travancore a devout Resident instructed to reform the administration and work for the abolition of all restrictions on dress. In the wake of the breastcloth disturbances, 3,000 Shanars joined the missions; for them, the lessons and advantages were obvious.[121] In effect, the missionaries in Travancore offered low castes resources which had not previously been available to them. High castes were suspicious, resentful and angry. However, the reforms carried out by the sirkar in the 1860s were to bring a number of new resources within comfortable reach of the high castes.

3

# *Travancore Transformed: New Resources for All, 1860-72*

In the 1860s Madhava Rao set out to remodel the administration and win a good name with British governments for himself and the Travancore sirkar. He established a successful system of fee-paying, government English and vernacular schools. He began to insist on the need for academic qualifications for admission to certain jobs in the sirkar service. He created and provided the finance for a large public works department. He reformed land tenures, commercial laws and the sirkar's policy–on paper at least–regarding caste disabilities.

The express intention of this multifarious government activity was the administrative 'modernisation' of Travancore. The goal of the reforming sirkar was to lift the whole of Travancore society a few notches on some abstract scale of civilisation–without altering the relative positions of the various groups.

To foresee the consequences of such wide-reaching changes was impossible. Just as the activities of the missionaries in the 1850s offered new resources to low castes, the efforts of the sirkar in the 1860s presented a broad range of new resources for all groups in Travancore to compete for or cope with. Some measures which aimed to benefit the 'respectable classes' in fact harmed them in the long run. We shall see this especially in Chapter 4 in the case of Nairs and land reform. The general trend of the sirkar's activities in the 1860s, and this was certainly not appreciated at the time, was to advance the interests of those able to grapple with a cash economy; some groups, notaby Christians and, to a certain extent, Ezhavas, were more able than others.

Yet it would be wrong to suggest that the sirkar's initiatives brought no benefits to Nairs. Indeed, over the short term, Nairs were enabled to maintain their dominance of many aspects of Travancore life. With non-Malayali Brahmins, they quickly responded to the new educational opportunities and thereby continued their overwhelming numerical control of the sirkar service. This in turn allowed them to frustrate the sirkar's proclamations granting certain civil rights to low castes. Ritual distances–literal and figurative–were generally preserved in spite of formal enactments; so too was the fairly exalted social position of Nairs.

In this chapter we shall look at the reforms and innovations of Madhava Rao's time; in Chapter 4 we shall see how various groups responded in the twenty years after Madhava Rao left Travancore in 1872.

## *WHY REFORM?*

After the breastcloth disturbances the Madras government was determined to improve the efficiency of the Travancore administration and to reform caste disabilities and the state's commercial laws. Indeed, as one writer has observed of the post-revolt period, 'intervention in native states to cure their administrations' became 'a moral imperative of British policy...'[1] Certainly Sir Charles Trevelyan would have agreed. Yet as Cullen's experience showed, there were many ways for an unwilling sirkar to destroy, or avoid, policies which it disliked. A Resident could not be everywhere or see everything. However, in Travancore in the 1860s, the Dewan, the Maharaja and the royal family showed a positive enthusiasm for certain aspects of administrative 'modernisation'–for the sorts of measures which could be proudly described in annual reports–and pursued new programmes with determination and zeal. The backgrounds of the leading figures help to explain their attitudes.

Francis Maltby had been Resident in Travancore only eight months when the Maharaja, Uttaram Tirunal, died in August

1860 at the age of forty-six. Because his eldest nephew was mentally retarded, he was succeeded by his second nephew, the twenty-nine year old Ayilyam Tirunal. Thus within three years the state had a new Dewan, Resident and Maharaja.

From 1849 to 1853 Ayilyam Tirunal and his younger brother Vishakham Tirunal, had been pupils of Madhava Rao, now the Dewan. Madhava Rao himself was one of the earliest products of the Madras High School, founded in 1841 under E.B. Powell, a Cambridge graduate and later the first director of public instruction for the Madras Presidency. From the Madras High School Madhava Rao received 'a Certificate of the highest grade', and from Powell, a testimonial which described his attainments as 'far more extensive than those of most native young men: his aptitude for pure Mathematics and Physics is decidedly great, and ... would secure him an honourable position even in the University of Cambridge'. His English was perfect; his prose, majestic; his favourite author, Gibbon.[2] He educated the princes in the subjects which he had studied under Powell: Goldsmith, Shakespeare and Pope; John Locke; Euclid and Newton's *Principia;* history, geography, astronomy, chemistry and 'elements of electricity'.[3] His success delighted Cullen. All the princes, the Resident wrote in 1853, 'express themselves in English with the greatest propriety and fluency, and the third or youngest prince [Vishakham] especially has exhibited an intelligence and a desire to acquire knowledge that has been quite remarkable'. Ayilyam, too, although he had a slight stammer, had improved under Madhava Rao 'and has acquired much general knowledge and information on a variety of subjects'. For his part, Madhava Rao wrote that Ayilyam had 'honoured me with his intimate friendship'.[4]

From the education which they received from Madhava Rao, the princes acquired a keen insight into the kind of administration which would win the approval and applause of British governments. As we have seen, as early as 1856 Vishakham Tirunal was invoking the name of Salar Jang, the widely praised Dewan of Hyderabad, to illustrate the ministerial needs of Travancore. The princes recognised 'cheerfully, and cordially', according to a speech of Ayilyam delivered for him at his installation by Madhava Rao, that 'the great object of a good government is the promotion of the well-being of its subjects...' Ayilyam

Tirunal's stated aim was 'that education should permeate all parts of this community' to create 'a wholesome discontent with a state of stagnation and a desire for progress'.[5] Had discontent been his only goal, his success would be unchallengeable. For his part, Vishakham Tirunal was compared by sycophants to Peter the Great, and when he wrote his epitaph on Madhava Rao's administration, he chose to do so in terms familiar to nineteenth century English public schoolboys: 'What Pericles did for Athens, what Cromwell did for England, that Madhava Rao did for Travancore'.[6]

Yet the brothers were by no means radicals. Vishakham may have regarded his uncle, the late Maharaja, as 'an ultraconservative'[7] and Ayilyam may have been prepared to take the wife of the governor of Madras to dinner on his arm; but neither brother was prepared to eat in the same room with Englishmen. The brothers conscientiously performed the many costly religious ceremonies of their theocratic state and received their European guests in the early morning before their purificatory bath. When Vishakham Tirunal lay dying in 1885, his Nair wife and children were forbidden to come near him and were not 'allowed (by his own order) to see him for days...nor indeed had any doctor a fair chance, as no examination of the patient could be made'.[8] Only Brahmins were permitted to touch him. This was the same man who once described Travancore as 'the most priest-ridden native state in the whole of India'.[9]

Both brothers felt a tension between what they knew British governments expected of them and what they expected of themselves. They were deeply attached to their own exalted position in Travancore and the customs and traditions which maintained it. They could enthuse over, and perhaps believe in, the British Empire and the physical manifestations of 'modernisation'; but they were reluctant indeed to tamper with the social order. A family anecdote recounts that in 1869 Ayilyam Tirunal, having laid the foundation stone for the Maharaja's College, returned to the palace and addressed his brother-in-law: 'Well, Thampi, I have just laid the foundation stone for anarchy'.[10] The brothers wanted the approbation of British governments, and they knew how to win it.

Not surprisingly, their mentor, Madhava Rao, was even more adept. As well as having great ability, he understood the art of self-advertisement. Although he undoubtedly appreciated the administrative usefulness of well-printed, punctual annual reports and of elegant memoranda on important issues, he also recognised the immense personal value of having such documents connected with his name. He, too, knew what the British wanted, and he was able to give it to them; he played them succesfully at their own game. Successive governors of Madras paid tribute to the 'liberal English education' of Madhava Rao and the princes, and even Joseph Peet, no lover of Brahmins, was impressed. What did Madhava Rao want? He told Peet 'plainly and in confidence that his personal object was not money, for he had much, but Fame'. Peet added: 'He was working for a good name, and I honour him much for his honesty'.[11]

With the death of Uttaram Tirunal in August 1860, the last obstacle to an enthusiastic modernising programme was removed. British governments had demanded a modest programme on these lines and would have tried to force it on the sirkar regardless of the Maharaja's wishes or the Dewan's abilities. But without the co-operation of the Indians in charge of the state, the interference and importunity of Residents would have had little effect. Now, however, the Dewan and the Maharaja were prepared to go farther in some directions than British governments would have ever asked. That indeed was the trick: only by exceeding expectations could one win a reputation for truly enlightened rule. The Dewan and the Maharaja pleased the British government so successfully that in 1866 the minister was knighted and the ruler was officially recognised as a 'Maharaja', a title his subjects had always accorded him. But in this 'modernisation' the ruler and his minister intended no attempt at social engineering; they sought to 'improve' society as a whole, not to adjust relationships among its members. In this, of course, they failed, as we shall see. But if their intentions now seem naive, in the 1860s they did not.

## *EDUCATION AND THE SIRKAR SERVICE*

When he was Resident, Cullen had bemoaned the poor quality of subordinate officials in the sirkar service. Madhava Rao, as a product of the Madras High School, placed great value on education. To have an efficient administration one must have educated officers. Education, too, had intrinsic benefits for the whole populace, although some sections required more than others. One of the aims of the new administration was to spread western-style education, especially among the 'respectable classes', and to this end the sirkar began to spend considerable sums of money.

It has been suggested that the high rate of literacy in modern Kerala results largely from the fact that 'Kerala had an unusually high proportion of literate people in the traditional period', and that among Nairs, 'virtually all the men and most women were literate'. The argument continues that 'there was "an alarming increase of illiteracy" early in the British period', and implies that the tradition of literacy finally began to reassert itself towards the end of the nineteenth century.[12] Such contentions are as difficult to disprove as to prove. The Travancore census of 1875, which was reasonably accurate, arrived at a literacy rate of 5.74 per cent, only slightly better than that for the whole Madras Presidency. Among Nairs, twenty-one per cent of men and one per cent of women were returned as literate.[13] This is far indeed from 'virtually all men and most women', and suggests that the reassertion of 'traditional literacy' must have been powerfully encouraged.

This is not to deny the importance of the old village schools. 'The country abounds with indigenous schools', Madhava Rao wrote in 1867, but as late as 1903 the sirkar was still lamenting the difficulties of bringing the local schools up to useful standards.[14] One may doubt whether in 1860 the local schools were teaching even basic literacy. Their curriculum was said to be 'astrology, vocal singing and poetry, didactic and religious'.[15] Paper was scarcely known outside the huzur kutcherry, children were taught to write on sand and later on strips of palm leaf, and even if a child did learn to read, he had little scope to exercise his new talent. The sirkar began to change this situation.

The Travancore government had maintained the Raja's Free School in Trivandrum since 1836, and had briefly and reluctantly established a few English district schools at the same time. The latter, however, were abandoned at the first opportunity--during the quick succession of Residents which preceded Cullen's appointment.[16] When Madhava Rao became Dewan, the sirkar had only the Trivandrum school and a small branch establishment in Quilon. The principle from the start had been that 'preference be given to those who have a prospect of employment in the sirkar'.[17] But to encourage was not enough. Madhava Rao set out to compel the education of youths likely to enter the government service. This meant primarily non-Malayali Brahmins and Nairs. He spelled out his message clearly in a speech in 1866 when he assured his audience that:

> ...apart from the intrinsic worth of Education it would be the chief passport to honour and preferment, and so far as the sirkar was concerned, all important posts under it would be filled by educated men, and by educated men alone, as soon as they became available.[18]

This was no idle speech-making. The sirkar department of vernacular education was begun in conjunction with 'a general test to be passed as a condition of employment in the sirkar service in any capacity above that of peon. Such procedure will act as a powerful stimulus to vernacular education'.[19] To those Nair families which had traditionally filled posts in the administration, the sirkar was saying: educate your dependents in the new schools or we will find others whose education meets our standards. Indeed, Ayilyam Tirunal said as much when he told Travancoreans to 'answer the demand of your country for cultivated intelligence'.[20]

The message was reinforced by the influx of non-Malayalis into Travancore. The new chief engineer wrote that most of his establishment would have to come from outside the state, while Madhava Rao regretted that the lack of educated Nairs made it necessary to employ many non-Travancoreans as judges.[21] Under cover of the need for outside expertise, a number of the Dewan's relatives and castemen became established in the sirkar service.[22]

Such lessons, coupled with the traditional willingness of Malayalis, especially Nairs, to send their dependents to the village schools, produced striking results. In 1861, after Ayilyam Tirunal had ruled for about a year, there were 269 boys in the Free School, Trivandrum. A year later their numbers had nearly doubled to 517, which included 171 Nairs, 123 Brahmins and 119 Tamil Sudras.[23]

More important, however, was the new system of English district schools, which originated from the British government's decision in 1859 to abolish the export duty on Tinnevelly tobacco entering Travancore. The Acting Resident suggested that the sirkar, which ran the monopoly, should cut the price of tobacco. Madhava Rao, however, replied that 'his highness is of opinion that the people should enjoy the benefit of this remission of duty in some more palpable shape'. He asked permission to apply it to education.[24] English schools were established in eight chief towns, and by 1864 there were 1,000 students in the mofussil. Including those in the Free School, Trivandrum, the distribution by categories was as follows:[25]

| | |
|---|---|
| Tamil Sudras | 517 |
| Malayali Sudras, (i.e. Nairs) | 424 |
| Christians | 315 |
| Non-Malayali Brahmins | 266 |
| Muslims | 37 |
| Nambudiris | 1 |
| Other Hindus | 19 |
| | 1,579 |

The numbers of Tamil Sudras were probably swollen by the children of sirkar servants from Madras. At any rate they remained static over the next few years while those of Nairs and non-Malayali Brahmins increased dramatically. Even the imposition of fees in the Trivandrum school in 1864—which then became known as the Maharaja's High School—resulted in a fall of enrolment of only two, and by 1866 the school had more than seven hundred boys.[26] By 1869 the district schools had grown to sixteen and the High School was receiving more applications than it had places.[27]

In 1866 the High School had been reorganised by John Ross, an Edinburgh graduate, hired as principal. He was joined two years later by another Edinburgh man, Robert Harvey. The two were to direct the educational affairs of Travancore for the next twenty years. The modern Travancore administrative service, it was later said, was their creation.[28]

Madhava Rao made certain that no one missed the connection between education and sirkar preferment. In 1863 P.K. Palpanabha Pillai, sent to Madras at sirkar expense, became the first Travancore Nair to take a B.A. and was immediately taken into government service. In the administration reports of succeeeding years, Travancore graduates and their employment under the sirkar were often mentioned; by 1869 nine were in sirkar service.[29] The message was also heard in north Travancore. 'There is a great idea prevalent here', wrote the Rev. Henry Baker, Jr. from Kottayam in 1869, 'of the necessity of English education and the high pay to be got for it'.[30] By 1872 Travancore schools had turned out nearly two hundred matriculates, about half of whom were non-Malayali Brahmins, and fourteen Bachelors of Arts--ten non-Malayali Brahmins, three Nairs and a CMS Syrian.[31]

English education was less than half of the story. As we have seen, when Madhava Rao outlined his plans for vernacular education in 1866, he stipulated that for a man to be selected for any post 'above that of peon' he must have passed 'a general test'. This emphasis on qualifications was driven home with the institution of a variety of examinations. From mid-1860 judicial posts of more than Rs. 30 a month in salary were reserved for those who had passed an annual examination in law. The engineering department began competitive examinations--for 'any class or caste'--in 1864, and pleaders' examinations were held for the first time in the following year. A new regulation for magistrates in 1872 laid down certain minimum qualifications.[32] Not surprisingly, after only a year of operation, the government vernacular schools were said to be 'so eagerly thronged...that they cannot but be multiplied...'[33]

In establishing the vernacular school system, Madhava Rao laid down three requirements which he felt were vital if vernacular education was to be successful: the linking of sirkar employment, even in the lower grades, to academic qualifications; the eventual introduction of a grant-in-aid code, which would allow the sirkar 'to provide for the education of the whole of the youth of Travancore at very moderate additional expenditure' and--though this was not stated--to absorb and partially control indigenous and mission schools; and the establishment of a book committee to translate and write textbooks of all kinds. Madhava Rao proposed to begin by creating a normal school for teachers in

Trivandrum, establishing thirty taluk schools supervised by two inspectors, and admitting 2,000 boys. The curriculum was to consist of reading, writing, arithmetic, geography, history, morality, health, political economy and Sanskrit, 'so far as a knowledge of it may assist the vernacular'.[34]

Kerala Varma, poet, sybarite and husband of the senior Rani, presided over the book committee, which, he later confessed with typical modesty, 'owes everything to me'. From 1867-72 the committee brought out large Malayalam editions of twelve books, including Euclid, Duncan's *Geography of India*, treatises on truthful evidence and health, and a history of India.[35] It also co-operated with the sirkar Book Depot, set up in 1866 as the first book-selling venture in Travancore when no private merchant could be induced to stock books. The Book Depot, which published lists of titles in the *Gazette*, allowed its clients to pay their local tahsildar and submit his receipt to Trivandrum. The books were sent post free. By 1870 the Book Depot was offering four dozen Malayalam titles, as well as books in English and Tamil.[36]

The first government vernacular school under Madhava Rao's plan was opened in Trivandrum in August 1866. By the end of 1867, thirteen were in operation, and the Normal School in Trivandrum had produced thirty-six masters.[37] By 1869 there were forty-nine schools, all using the same books and teaching the same syllabus. Pupils numbered 3,500, about forty-eight per cent Nairs and twenty-five per cent non-Malayali Brahmins, with a sprinkling of Tamil Sudras, 'other Hindus' and only a few Christians and Muslims. The fears of guardians that the schools would weaken religion, and the reluctance of young men to attend the Normal School, had both been overcome. Indeed, all seventy graduates of the Normal School (thirty-six of whom were non-Malayali Brahmins) had been provided with jobs.[38] In 1870 the Normal School turned out sixty-four graduates (forty-seven of them non-Malayali Brahmins), all of whom were given jobs,[39] and by 1871 vernacular schools were established in most of the state's 245 pravrattis. Each pravratti school was to begin with one master on Rs. 7 a month; inspectors on Rs. 30 a month were each to have the supervision of fourteen schools.[40] By 1875 the enrolment of government and aided vernacular schools was 11,500; by 1880, nearly 30,000; by 1905, nearly 100,000.[41] The following table indicates the growth of vernacular schools over forty years.[42]

*TABLE 3.1*

| *Year* | *Vernacular Schools (Sirkar and aided)* | *Pupils* |
|---|---|---|
| 1865-66 | 12 | 855 |
| 1866-67 | 20 | 1,383 |
| 1867-68 | 49 | 3,455 |
| 1868-69 | 48 | 3,639 |
| 1869-70 | 53 | 3,075 |
| 1870-71 | 188 | 8,064 |
| 1871-72 | 216 | 8,452 |
| ... | ... | ... |
| 1874-75 | 233 | 11,466 |
| 1879-80 | 598 | 29,363 |
| 1884-85 | 857 | 43,513 |
| 1889-90 | 979 | 47,044 |
| 1894-95 | 1,606 | 82,820 |
| 1899-1900 | 1,283 | 83,058 |
| 1904-05 | 1,483 | 99,757 |

By 1871 expenditure on education had risen from a few hundred rupees when Madhava Rao became Dewan to Rs. 1.23 lakhs,[43] two per cent of the annual budget.

Sirkar schools were open only to high castes. Madhava Rao seems to have recognised the danger of driving low castes into the arms of the missionaries, for in September 1865 he asked the LMS educational agents for their opinion of a scheme to establish separate sirkar Anglo-vernacular schools for low-caste boys. Three of the four missionaries rejected the proposals as 'a retrograde policy' and doubted whether enough Shanar boys would attend schools on such degrading conditions.[44] But one missionary concluded–perhaps with greater candour, for Shanars were hitherto dependent on mission schools, and missionaries, in many ways, on Shanar converts–that sirkar schools for low-castes 'would be decidely taken advantage of'.[45] Satisfied perhaps that the missionaries saw low-caste schools as potentially harmful to themselves, Madhava Rao suggested the establishment of such schools in his administration report. At that stage, however, the Resident and the Madras government stepped in to veto the scheme 'as tending to sanction the continuance of distintions which are most injurious to the people of Travancore'.[46]

Sirkar schools remained for the next forty years virtually the exclusive property of high castes and those Syrians and discreet Christian converts who chose to attend them. Madhava Rao's reforms, in effect, brought western-style education to high-castes as the missionaries had brought it to Syrians and the low.

Was he trying to put a brake on missionary influence? Certainly his proposals for low-caste schools indicate an awareness of the dangers of complete missionary control of low-caste education. The CMS missionaries, moreover, were sceptical of the grant-in-aid code when it came, for they saw it as a way of limiting their freedom to use their schools to proselytise. The poorer LMS pressed for grants-in-aid.[47] Earlier, Joseph Peet had characterised Madhava Rao as 'a Young Bengal'--that is, 'one who glories in the creed which practically believes in nothing,' when the Dewan refused to buy a CMS-produced Malayalam spelling book with a heavy Christian bias. Similarly, the Bible was removed from the curriculum of the High School in Trivandrum, and the book committee, a CMS agent noted with displeasure, 'in selecting books eliminate anything relating to Christianity'.[48]

The sirkar's enthusiastic support of education broke the missionary monopoly and destroyed any chance of high castes being forced to attend mission schools in large numbers. The sirkar both stimulated and satisfied their educational needs. This is not to say, however, that mission involvement in education flagged. Indeed, the Christian interest in education in terms of investment and enrolment continued for years to be at least as great as the sirkar's. In the 1860s the well-organised schools of the LMS and CMS had an enrolment of about 10,000 while the disorganised schools of the Jacobites, Romo-Syrians and Latin Catholics were said to have 40,000 pupils.[49] To exercise some control over Christian schools became a recurring aim of the sirkar; but the government system created in the 1860s had at least given high castes easy opportunity to get a good education yet avoid Christian schools.

The sirkar education system also created a small network of jobs, patronage and prestige which was reserved for the high castes. In small towns and even villages, schools ceased to be haphazard gatherings held in the compound of a wealthy taravad by a hereditary teacher paid in rice and vegetables. Qualified masters who viewed teaching as the first rung on the ladder of government service received salaries and were subject to inspection. V. Nagam Aiya, A. Govinda Pillai, P. Thanu Pillai and P. Ayyappan Pillai (see Biographical Notes), to name only four who rose to high positions, all began their careers as sirkar school masters on a few rupees a month.

Although most sirkar schools were closed to low castes, the continuing emphasis on educational qualifications awakened expectations. The question was to be increasingly asked: if graduates are preferred for government service, why not Ezhava graduates? Why not many more Syrian Christians? However, for the 1860s and 1870s the supremacy of Nairs and Brahmins in the administration was adequately reinforced by their hold on the new sirkar schools system.

## *CYNICISM AND CIVIL RIGHTS*

Francis Maltby, the Resident, had been sent to Travancore in 1860 with instructions to work for the abolition of the civil disabilities, especially in matters of dress, of low castes. To both the royal family and the Dewan, it was clear that unless Travancore made concessions to the liberal sentiments of British governments, the state would win no praise and its rulers no honours. Moreover, there was a danger, undoubtedly evident to men like Madhava Rao, of driving low castes into the nets of those fishers of men, the missionaries. Yet dress distinctions and distance pollution were part of the foundation of Malayali society and helped to maintain the position of the high castes. To tamper with such traditions was to tamper with a system of relationships highly beneficial to the high castes.

Under Madhava Rao the sirkar began to walk a fine line. It issued 'enlightened' proclamations lessening the disabilities of low castes; it conciliated the missionaries to lessen their militancy; yet it strove to give a minimum of offence to conservative high-caste Hindus, not the least of whom was the Maharaja, Ayilyam Tirunal, himself. The policy was successful, if cynical.

Many of the proclamations had no reality beyond the statute books, but British governments were satisfied. On the ground in Travancore, Nairs were able to maintain many of the old distinctions, and sirkar servants either actively supported them or turned a blind eye.

The spiritual aspects of Christianity exercised no great appeal to low castes, and by administering the sirkar's laws with reasonable fairness, making a few concessions and promising a few more, the Travancore government was able to minimise the low castes' need for missionary aid. After the old regime, such improvements were noticeable and appreciated. A CMS agent writing in 1867 indicated the success of the sirkar's policy:

> How miserably the lower castes were held under and ground down by the higher 20 years ago. They were without protection and could obtain no redress. Was it not a very natural thing, under such circumstances, that these poor oppressed classes should fly from their oppressors to the Missionary whom they knew to be independent of the government and yet believed to be all powerful in asserting their claims, in order to effect with sahib's influence what in those days they could hardly hope to effect without...
>
> ...[But now] an enlightened and beneficient government is first levelling all ranks and imparting to all that protection and favour which it is the part of an upright government to bestow upon its subjects. All classes may assert and maintain their own rights. The courts are open and justice is administered to the rich and the poor, the high and the low. A letter from 'Sahib' is not now a *sine qua non* to secure attention when a man has to appear before the Magistrate, as it once was. Now all this has had a good effect on the 'appreciable results' of our [missionaries'] work. There is little or no inducement now for a heathen to join our church unless he is really convinced of the truth and joins solely in consequence of his convictions.[50]

This missionary had succeeeded Joseph Peet and was dealing chiefly with Anglican Syrians and established converts, which helps to explain his fulsome praise. The account of a Resident was rather different:

> Roads are public to all good castemen ... but certain lower classes are prohibited altogether from using them. ... lower caste men generally cannot enter--sometimes cannot approach–the courts, cutcherries, registry offices, etc. If the evidence of a low caste man has to be taken by a judge or magistrate, as the witness cannnot come to the court, the court must go to the witness. But it must not go too near him, and the frequent result is that the witness's evidence is taken by the court, or a Goomastah deputed for the purpose, calling the questions to an intermediate peon, and the peon shouting them to the witness and repeating his replies to the presiding officer... however desirous the higher officers may be to keep justice and show mercy, it is simply impossible for them, in such circumstances, to prevent oppression and corruption on the part of their underlings.[51]

Faced with apparently conflicting evidence, one must ask: what were the sirkar's measures which had so disarmed at least some of the missionaries? First, the sirkar cultivated the missionaries, invited them to special functions and saw to it that their converts were not harassed, Second, Madhava Rao introduced a fairer, less corruupt administration of the old laws, which went some way towards satisfying the grievances of low castes. And where low-caste aspirations and British pressure were irresistible, the sirkar conceded gracefully and did its best to allay the indignation of high castes.

The right to an upper covering, which was granted to Hindu and Christian Shanar women in 1859, was extended to all classes and castes in 1865, although the style used by Nairs was still forbidden to the low castes. The original intention was to bring only Ezhavas within the terms of the earlier proclamation, but when the Resident suggested that all castes might be included, Madhava Rao added a hasty pencilled note: 'If there are other classes, the Notification will apply to them also, and nothing but good will result from such a measure'.[52] Ezhavas, however, reaped most of the benefit, for they had already been affecting the upper covering. The ex-slave castes, on the other hand, were too poor and despised to attempt such pretensions. In Paravur in Quilon district, where Ezhava women first flaunted the upper covering, they were attacked by Nairs, 'but the police immediately interfered and set matters aright'.[53] Ezhavas did not seek missionary aid in this case, because they did not need it.

In 1865 the sirkar also granted the right to all castes to use wheeled vehicles (ten years earlier there were not enough roads to make it an issue), and repeated an earlier proclamation allowing low-caste women to wear certain types of jewellery without having to obtain special sirkar permission. By 1865, *uriyam*, was no longer demanded.[54]

But the question of low castes' rights to use roads and public buildings remained. More than any other, it shocked British governments and pushed low castes towards the missionaries. In 1870, however, Madhava Rao made a calculated gesture. Only a few weeks after the Resident had submitted a long report on caste disabilities to Madras and before it could be examined by the Madras government,[55] the sirkar issued a circular throwing open all roads in the state which it chose to designate as 'public'.

Madhava Rao's district officers–three Nairs and his first cousin–were unenthusiastic about such a measure and unsure of its results. All held the view that the low castes were a minority of the population and that to let them use the high roads would be to give 'a *small* advantage, to a *small* portion of the community', while bringing 'a large amount of pain to the *greatest* bulk ...' This of course was nonsense as the 1875 census was to show, but they further argued that enforcement would prove a problem: 'the majority of the gorvernment officials are bigoted Hindus'.[56] Nevertheless the proclamation was issued, and on specified roads low castes were to have the right to move freely.

At the same time, judges were instructed to take steps to hear the cases of low castes barred from certain kutcherries and public buildings near temples. Such offices were eventually to be shifted, Madhava Rao wrote, to more suitable locations. To all other kutcherries, low castes were to have free access.[57] The Madras government received news of this 'liberal instruction' with 'very great satisfaction'.[58]

Yet the measure was basically prudent, and its liberality continued for many years to exist mainly on paper. Low castes were still kept out of kutcherries and off roads, either as a result of the approval or indifferences of sirkar officials. The fact that the circular was reissued with a similar updated notification in 1884 indicates that it was never much more than an administrative pronouncement.[59] But the sirkar could claim to have shown its good intentions, and the onus of maintaining caste disabilities was transferred to private citizens.

There could, however, be little doubt where the highest members of Travancore society really stood. When a pravrattikkaran near Trivandrum announced by beat of drum that, regardless of the sirkar's notification, Pulayas were not to use certain roads, Madhava Rao dismissed him from the service. Within three weeks he was reinstated with a fine of a month's salary, 'the matter having come under His Highness the Maharaja's notice'; His Highness deemed this 'sufficient punishment'.[60] Having one eye on the all-India stage, Madhava Rao was prepared to treat the cherished notions of high-caste Travancoreans lightly at times. Ayilyam Tirunal, however, had only one state, and he had to live there.

Generally, the sirkar's policy regarding the disabilities of low castes met with considerable success in the 1860s and 1870s. Missionaries were wooed and won; existing laws were fairly administered; some concessions were made and British governments impressed; yet high castes, especially Nairs, were left to enforce their social privileges much as before. It was twenty years before the rebuffs handed out to educated low-caste men like P. Palpu revealed the cynicism of the circulars and the sirkar's pronouncements.

## *TOWARDS A CASH ECONOMY*

The sirkar's policies regarding education, government employment and civil rights were of obvious importance. 'Respectable' castes were urged to educate their dependents, and the carrot of government jobs was held out as encouragement. Proclamations removing caste disabilities disarmed British governments, while a general increase in administrative probity–though it left untouched many of the old discriminatory caste practices–lessened the militancy of missionaries and the grievances of low castes. By such means, the theory at the time seemed to run, Travancore could be 'improved' without altering the basic relationships between various groups. Everyone would rise a little; but the people on top would remain there.

However, from the point of view of Travancore society, the vital aspect of Madhava Rao's activities lay in the strides made towards the establishment and extension of a cash economy. In the course of his administration, Rs. 1.5 crores of land value was created when 200,000 acres of land were made alienable, the export trade and the price of labour doubled, a plantation industry was firmly established; monopolies were struck down, and communications vastly improved. Some groups more than others had institutions and traditional occupations which were able to capitalise on these wide economic changes.

## *Land*

As we have seen, nearly half the rice-growing land in the state–about 200,000 acres–was held under the sirkar pattam tenure which gave the sirkar the rights of a janmi. If it chose it could evict tenants almost at will, while they could neither mortgage the land nor expect recompense for improvements. Much of the sirkar pattam land–probably more than half–was held by Nairs and in some areas such holdings were 'looked upon as a positive infliction' [*sic*].[61] Because the sirkar could not sell the land for non-payment of rent and because tenants were reluuctant to take on such land anyway, the government experienced great difficulty in collecting its dues. Tenants, on the other hand, saw such land as having no value beyond the rice it produced.

Madhava Rao's solution to this stagnant situation was to issue in 1865 a proclamation granting full ownership rights to the holders of the 200,000 acres of sirkar pattam land. He estimated that Rs. 1.5 crores of land value were thus created.[62] The measure probably affected most Nair taravads, many Syrian Christians and lesser numbers of other groups. Holders of sirkar pattam suddenly acquired a windfall of saleable, mortgageable land.

The proclamation had more important consequences for Nairs than for others, not merely because Nairs were the largest group affected. Sirkar pattam land was now capable of providing cash for education or the performance of costly ceremonies *like talikettukalyanam*, lavish celebrations of which enhanced a taravad's prestige. Moreover, when dissension threatened a taravad and younger members demanded partition, the excuse that the family's sirkar pattam land was inalienable could no longer be used against them. Indeed, the obvious profit to be had from the taravad's newly gained land may well have appealed to the avarice or independence of frustrated younger members. At the same time, the proclamation gave Syrian Christians, who had interests in trade, held land and wanted more, increased opportunities to extend their holdings. The relationship between land and cash became much closer, and Nair institutions and traditions were to prove less able to cope with the change.

In 1867 the sirkar issued a second proclamation effectively curtailing the powers of the state's few thousand janmis, who had become more demanding of their tenants as a result of the increasing population and value of land. A decision of the Sadr Court in 1856 recognised the janmi's right to extract better terms or evict his tenants on the expiry of the customary twelve-year lease. The court's decision was not surprising, for the chief justice, Krishna Parameswaran Nambudiri–'a lamentable specimen of complete inefficiency'[63]–'was himself a janmi and had largely purchased *Janmam rights* from other janmis'.[64] Applying rigid court decisions to the old, lax tenure system led to a rise in the number of evictions and the dissatisfaction of tenants. The proclamation of 1867 gave tenants security of tenure and virtually automatic renewal of leases, without enhancements, at the end of the twelve-year agreements. Provided the tenant paid his dues, the janmi had no right of eviction, and, indeed, the proclamation made it difficult for the janmi to recover arrears through the courts. Madhava Rao planned a third proclamation to ensure the janmis' rights, but this was not realised until twenty years later when the janmis, experiencing more and more difficulty with their tenants, began to petition the sirkar.[65] As a result of Martanda Varma's annexations, janmis in Travancore were fewer in number than in British Malabar; the proclamation of 1867 served to reduce their collective influence further. They lost their economic leverage against their tenants, who–whether Nairs, Syrians or even Ezhavas--gained independence and room for manoeuvre which was unique in Kerala.[66]

The land reforms not only won the approval of British governments but made Travancore an area of many thousand small proprietors and secure tenants. With cash values now imparted to all land, family arrangements which permitted efficient management became important, as did familiarity with cash transactions and business techniques. On neither count were Nairs at an advantage.

### *The Implications of a Public Works Department*

To the Secretary of State for India, Travancore had become by 1867 'something like a model Native State'.[67] Part of the favourable impression which the state now made on visitors, readers of official reports and even those who lived there, resulted from the activities of the public works department, created entirely after Madhava Rao's assumption of office. To use the popular phrase of the day, the PWD 'opened up the country'; that was obvious. But it had more subtle, yet more important effects. By involving thousands of low castes in salaried employment as labourers, it introduced them to a cash economy, just as the land reform of 1865 had started to bring similar implications to many landholders. As well as encouraging trade, exchange of ideas, and entrepreneurship, the PWD widened the scope for labourers and forced up their wages.

After an abortive start in 1860, the organisation of the public works department began in earnest in 1863 with the arrival of William Barton as chief engineer. The establishment he found was 'unfit even to carry out the works already sanctioned and utterly inadequate to take up those in contemplation'. His first step was to get from the sirkar an annual guaranteed sum of two lakhs of rupees to be spent on public works. Another Rs. 20,000--an immense amount at the time, for it was more than half of the total expenditure on public works in some years under Krishna Rao--was set aside annually to pay a permanent establishment of clerks, overseers and supervisors.[68]

But since *uriyam* had fallen into disuse, labour was hard to find. Barton wrote that '...coolies refused to work and bandies to ply for hire, in the belief that they are prohibited by sirkar orders, or, oftentimes, simply to demonstrate the power of their new position...'[69] Convicts were used as coolies, but they were unsatisfactory and sometimes removed by sirkar officials to perform other work.[70]

The labour problem was solved by raising wages and ensuring their regular payment. In 1865-66 nearly 10,000 Ezhavas and slave-caste coolies were on daily wages from the public works department. The scale was not extravagant, but the four annas a day which was paid to men, represented an increase of three or four times the rate before the establishment of the PWD.[71] Earlier, 'the ordinary cooly in the village used to get only an anna and a half, and one meal for a day's work... [In 1875] a labourer cannot be hired for less than four annas and one meal, though his hours of work have also been diminished since formerly'.[72] By 1876 it was advisable that all missionaries be able to ride a horse: 'A few years ago men were carried in chairs or went in boats, but the cooly [hire] is so high that a man cannot do it now'.[73]

The benefits of these changes fell to those who were prepared to work as labourers. Given an alternative form of employment, the slave castes gained a little leverage against their old masters. Hundreds of Ezhava women became PWD coolies. Indeed, the sirkar sought to demonstrate its enlightenment by ordering 'the clothing of the upper part of the person a condition of the employment of women'.[74] The 1875 census returned eighteen per cent of the population as 'labourers',[75] and most of these were affected by the spread of, and the rise in, wages.

Travancore landholders, most of whom had been accustomed to farming their land with slaves or cowed subtenants, were also affected; payment for labour had been in kind where there had been payment at all. Now, however, landholders were to be increasingly forced to handle cash and to compete, at least to a small extent, for labour.

The PWD, moreover, encouraged contractors and entrepreneurs. When Barton began work, none existed.

> The entire absence of contractors, not only for the construction of any portions of the works but even for the supply of the most ordinary materials required by the department, make the labour extremely hard.
>
> We have had to make our own bricks, quarry the stone, dive for the shells and burn lime, and even to fell the timber required for our works...
>
> The most trifling aid is not forthcoming; every nut

> and screw, bolt or nail has to be constructed in our own workshop; and when work was first started, we had to burn the charcoal and manufacture the gunpowder before blasting operations could be commenced... [76]

But within a few years the situation had improved; contractors–non-Malayali Brahmins, Syrians, other Christians and Tamil Sudras–came forward; and Syrians had sufficiently appreciated the potential of the PWD that one of their number was on the way to becoming Travancore's first Bachelor of Civil Engineering.[77]

In spite of the initial difficulties in finding labour and contractors, the public works department continued to expand. By 1865 its permanent staff, mostly non-Travancoreans, numbered thirty-five, drawing nearly 4,000 rupees a month in wages, and by 1872 it required a complete reorganisation, because 'the operations of the Department are now of such a magnitude...'[78] From the miserly Rs. 38,550 spent on public works by Krishna Rao in 1855-56, the expenditure rose to Rs. 5.61 lakhs in 1865-66. In 1871-72, Madhava Rao's last year in office, the sirkar put Rs. 12.21 lakhs (twenty-four per cent of the total budget) into public works.[79] For labourers, contractors and landholders, the consequences were to be considerable.

The activities of the public works department, however, had more obvious and easily measurable results. Its road-building programme was remarkable. The absence of roads in pre-British Kerala has been described as 'striking',[80] and although roads were built to facilitate the movement of British troops after Velu Thampi's rebellion in 1809, by 1845 these had fallen into disuse and disrepair. Cullen complained that '... the communications in Travancore are greatly neglected, in many places are almost impassable at particular seasons...and little or nothing is done...to provide for the wants of an increasing population and Commerce'. The north-south road from Trivandrum to Quilon was used only by the troops, and the east-west line through the Ghats to the Tamil country was totally unreliable. All traffic from the east came through the Aruvamozhi Pass to Nagercoil and then proceeded north by water, and what roads there were, to Trivandrum, Quilon and even Alleppey.[81] The sirkar showed no enthusiasm for road-building, and shortly before Cullen became Resident, had successfully side-stepped a proposal for a north-south road by agreeing to it and then forgetting about it.[82] Rev. John Cox thundered in 1857 that 'there is not a single road to be called passable for the entire length of the province, and not one from the sea to the interior'.[83] In the interior, those who could afford it, and whose caste was high enough to warrant the dignity, travelled by palanquin along paths through paddy fields, cocoanut gardens and jungles; the rest walked.

There were major hindrances to communications. The country was rugged and rolling; roads had to wind around hills and through valleys. Travancore was crosscut by fourteen major rivers, which, coupled with the extensive backwaters, not only required technical skill to bridge, but offered an easier alternative means of communication. Such water routes, however, did not lead to every part of the state, and they could be disrupted by lack of rain, weed growth or accumulation of silt.[84]

Madhava Rao realised the importance of a good road system for the commerce of the state and its prestige with British governments. Roads were monuments of good government, measurable indices of progress. Within a few months of the new Resident's arrival in the state in 1860, the Dewan presented a memorandum outlining 'the works required for the improvement of this state'. Maltby concurred in all Madhava Rao's recommendations, and first importance was given to the Trivandrum-Nagercoil road which was 'much out of repair'. A road from Kottayam due east to Mundakayam, with a view to eventually linking with Madura, was also sanctioned. Within eighteen months the southern road had been repaired–albeit not very well–and the twenty-mile trace from Kottayam to Mundakayam was completed and work had begun to open it to cart width.[85]

The master plan was to build a good north-south road from Nagercoil to Alleppey and Kottayam and two east-west roads into the hills, which would eventually link Kottayam with Madura, and Quilon with Shenkotta. Feeder roads were to be constructed to connect with the trunk lines. In 1866 the public works department had opened 195 miles of road suitable for 'rapid wheeled traffic of any sort'. By 1869 the figures had risen to 266 miles, and in 1872 Barton estimated that 1,000 miles of road would be open for cart traffic 'in the course of another eighteen months or two years'.[86] The Quilon-Shenkotta road was completed by 1872 and was taking an average of twenty carts and forty-five pedestrians a day across the Ghats; previously Quilon district had not possessed 'a wheeled conveyance out of the town of Quilon'. The road from Kottayam to Pirmed was completed in the same year, and the final link with Madura in 1876. In one year alone the public works department constructed fifty bridges and culverts with spans greater than five feet.[87]

Cart traffic between Madura and Kottayam increased steadily. 'The Madura carts bring grain from the Cumbum Valley for the use of the estate coolies', the Resident wrote in 1877, 'cart the coffee crop to Kottayam, and return to the Madura District with betel-nut, pepper and other west-coast produce'.[88] Along the same road, waste land was taken up; as early as January 1861 ryots had applied for 380 plots on the first dozen miles of the road. It is worth emphasising that Kottayam was the district in which Syrian Christians were traditionally most numerous and powerful. The new network of roads, wrote another Resident, was changing 'the whole character of the country'. He continued:

> In not a few taluqs where but a few years ago there were literally no communications, save the river courses, a few rude tracks traversable by pack-bullocks or coolies only, and wild elephant paths, a spring-carriage may now be driven along a well-traced, drained and bridged high road.
>
> In some sections these roads traverse forests which along the immediate line are rapidly giving way to a succession of clearings.
>
> ... At other sections the country traversed is comparatively open, jungly only in patches, boldly undulating with valleys and slopes of considerable productiveness. But the people seem to have rested curiously remote from intercommunication; wheeled traffic of any sort has never been known. It is indeed strange that some of the districts should have remained as isolated as they still are for so long when comparative progress was going on around.[89]

### *Commerce and Planting*

At the same time that the public works department was bringing the beginnings of a cash economy to thousands of labourers and landlords, Madhava Rao was carrying out reforms and promoting schemes which were expressly intended to advance commerce. To put the state's finances in order was his first duty if Travancore was to lose its reputation for delinquency with the Madras government. Moreover, Maltby's instructions when he came as Resident in 1860 were to achieve the abolition of the sirkar monopolies which brought annoyance to the Madras government and offence to the free-trade principles of the age.

The pepper monopoly, which was bringing the sirkar only a lakh of rupees annually, was abolished in November 1860 and an export duty substituted which was equal to the duty charged at British Cochin.[90] A guarantee was given that pepper vines would not be taxed. Local traders were now free to buy pepper from inland ryots and sell it in the best market. Smuggling to Cochin became unprofitable and Alleppey assumed new importance as Travancore's chief port and trading centre. However, the trade had become highly disorganised, and it was not until 1871-72 that pepper exports began to show any stability. In that year, they were Rs. 2.42 lakhs and averaged Rs. 2.84 lakhs for the next nine years until the pepper boom began about 1880.[91]

The tobacco monopoly was more difficult, for with the tighter administration of Madhava Rao it had brought the state seventeen lakhs of rupees in revenue in 1859-60. However, it was also the most vexatious monopoly for foreign traders and thus was constantly brought to the attention of the Madras government. In 1863 it was abolished, and import duties, varying with the place of origin of the tobacco, were established. Previously, the sirkar had been the sole supplier of inferior tobacco at inflated rates. Now petty traders could acquire their tobacco cheaply for themselves. With the sirkar middleman removed, the trade became more profitable for the retailer. As we have seen, these petty traders tended to be non-Malayali Brahmins, Muslims and Syrian Christians.

Commercial adjustments were completed in 1864 by treaties with the Cochin sirkar and the British government. Prior to the treaty British governments had regarded Travancore as a foreign country in matters of trade: export to, and imports from, Travancore were subject to duty. The effect of these duties was to encourage smuggling, discourage legitimate trade and divert most Travancore transactions to British Cochin, to which Travancoreans had access either by stealth, or by paying a small transit tax to the

Cochin sirkar. The new treaty placed Travancore ports on the same footing as those of British India; most goods coming from, or going to, other parts of India paid no duty. Exports from Travancore, especially from Alleppey, rose dramatically. In the seven years from 1861-62 to 1868-69 they more then doubled–from Rs. 35.45 lakhs in 1861-62 to Rs. 72.76 lakhs in 1868-69.[92] Most of the exports were agricultural–cocoanut products, cardamoms, spices–and the impact was felt to some degree at all levels, even down to the Ezhava climbing the palm tree.

Madhava Rao's administration also introduced an efficiency and a striving for budgetary surpluses which impressed the Madras government and perhaps had some influence on those who did business with the sirkar. Madhava Rao's first year of government, 1857-58, produced a surplus of Rs. 1.67 lakhs, and an increase of a lakh of rupees in the revenue from the tobacco monopoly as a result of 'greater vigilance'.[93] The year 1859-60 brought a surplus of five lakhs, the highest revenue collection in the state's history (Rs. 51.5 lakhs, Rs. 11.5 lakhs more than the average for the previous fifteen years), and the conclusion of the Madras government that all this was 'most creditable to the administration of the Dewan Madhava Rao'.[94] In his fourteen years in power, Madhava Rao produced only three small deficits which were more than covered by large surpluses in other years.

In setting the finances in order the new Dewan also exposed the errors of his predecessor which he dutifully reported to the Resident who passed them on to Madras. A difference of Rs. 4.5 lakhs was found between the actual cash in the treasury and the book accounts. The loan of five lakhs of rupees which a desperate Krishna Rao had obtained from the Padmanabhaswami Temple in 1856, far from being interest free, was discovered to require interest payments of Rs. 2.5 lakhs. A conspiracy of government officials to corner the tobacco market and sell to the sirkar at more than one and a half times the normal rate was broken up.[95] From such penetrating investigations, the Dewan derived considerable credit, while the emphasis on businesslike procedures resounded throughout the sirkar service and the state.

But these reforms of the state's finances and revenue techniques could have touched most Travancoreans only indirectly. Much more important for many was the stimulus the sirkar gave to the plantation industry. Although the exotic crops of the Kerala coast had been one of India's major attractions for Europeans from the fifteenth century onwards, Travancore had no tradition of large gardens devoted solely to export crops.[96] Ryots grew a little pepper and sold it to the sirkar, hill tribes collected wild cardamoms. In the late 1830s when the price of coffee was rising rapidly in the United States, an Englishman, William Huxham, began planting coffee on the hills east of Quilon. The quality being reputed 'equal, if not superior, to any in the world', the sirkar toyed with the idea of starting a coffee monopoly, similar to its pepper monopoly, by distributing seeds to landholders. It greatly feared a shortage of agricultural labour if high-paying European planters were allowed to establish themselves in the state.[97] The plan, however, was dropped, and the state's notoriety under Krishna Rao did not encourage planters.

However, under Ayilyam Tirunal, Madhava Rao and Maltby, the sirkar's policy quickly changed to one of active encouragement for planters. Work on the road from Kottayam towards the Ghats resulted in two coffee estates being opened by early 1862. By August of the same year planters had obtained the rights to 15,118 acres, and six European planters were soon working in the state. The value of coffee exports rose from Rs. 0.80 lakhs in 1864-65, the first year in which statistics were kept, to Rs. 5.97 lakhs in 1871-72, Madhava Rao's last year in the state. In 1876-77 they reached a peak of Rs. 9.89 lakhs.[98] The two chief planting areas were at Pirmed on the hills east of Kottayam, and in the Ashambu Hills north of Nagercoil. Kottayam and Nagercoil towns were the Christian centres of the state, and the impact of planting on Christians and missionaries, as we shall see in the next chapter, was to prove important.

The sirkar gave a good deal of help to planters. It realised Rs. 5.78 lakhs from sale of land (at a rupee an acre in most cases), tax and export duty, but it spent Rs. 2.21 lakhs on roads, road-building subsidies to planters and surveys. A cart road was opened from Nagercoil to the foot of the Ashambu Hills; tracks for bullocks were cut to connect with the Kottayam road at Pirmed. The sirkar also ran its own experimental gardens for a time at Pirmed.[99]

The sirkar's interest stemmed partly from the direct involvement of Madhava Rao and the First Prince, Vishakham Tirunal, who was a keen botanist, credited with popularising tapioca in Travancore.

They jointly owned a 150-acre coffee estate in the Ashambu Hills, which was managed for them at first by John Cox, missionary turned planter, and then by P.D. Devasagaim, the most successful planter among the London Missionary Society's adherents. Madhava Rao and Vishakham Tirunal were said to have gone into planting only to demonstrate the dignity of commercial pursuits, but when Madhava Rao finally disposed of the estate in the 1880s it brought him a lakh of rupees.[100] In the 1870s when coffee was proving profitable, Ayilyam Tirunal, the reigning Maharaja, who was noted for his thrift and acquisitiveness, had to be told by the Madras government that the sirkar could not open coffee estates to enhance its own revenues.[101]

The expansion of planting did not create the shortage of labour which the sirkar had feared, for the population was increasing rapidly. Moreover, low-caste Malayalis were reluctant to abandon their traditional occupations to go to the hills. Much of the labour came from the Tamil districts of British India, and on some estates all the labourers were Tamilians.[102] Yet the estates, coupled with the public works department, helped to increase the cost of labour, while educated Malayalis, especially Christians, took up most of the clerical and managerial posts.

## *THE SYMBOL OF TRIVANDRUM*

To appreciate the dramatic changes of Madhava Rao's administration, it is helpful to look at the capital city of Trivandrum. There, between 1865 and 1873, the public works department completed three ambitious public buildings–the General Hospital (1865), the Public Offices (1867) and the Maharaja's College (1873)–which changed Trivandrum from an anonymous temple town to something closer to the Victorian idea of a capital.

Built in a depression on the flat ground a mile or two from the sea, old Trivandrum huddled round the Padmanabhaswami Temple. Within the walls of 'The Fort', at the centre of which was the temple, were the Maharaja's palaces, the kutcherries, and a Brahmin agraharam similar to those found in the Tamil country. Entrance to the Fort was restricted to the high castes. Outside the walls, on the level palm-covered ground stretching west to the sea and east to the Karamanai River, were taravad houses of Nair families, the homes of some Brahmin officials and the palaces of the wives of the Maharaja and princes. At the village of Karamanai was another agraharam. To the north-west, thickly covered in cocoanut, lay the village or suburb, of Pettah, inhabited by Eurasians, Ezhavas, Shanars and Latin Catholics. Two miles to the north of the Fort, up a long gradual slope, were the cantonment and the Church of England church.

For the Public Offices and College, the sirkar selected plots within about eight hundred yards of each other on the high ground between the Fort and Christ's Church; the hospital was built half a mile to the west of the Public Offices. Thereby given a new, northern focal point, the town began to expand to the salubrious hills to the north-east, where Europeans and wealthy Indian officials, like Madhava Rao, Rama Rao and Nanu Pillai, acquired property and built houses on the western model with names like 'Cotton Hill House' and 'Hill View'.[103]

One of the aims in constructing the new public buildings on a grand style was to give 'an architectural ornament to the capital..., dignity to the State and respect to the Courts and Cutcherries...'[104] Success was indicated by the report of a sycophantic north Indian that 'all the institutions in Calcutta...can be seen in Trivandrum, the capital of Travancore, in miniature'.[105]

Calcutta in miniature was an exaggeration, but certainly by 1872 the public works department had changed the physical appearance of Trivandrum, and, indirectly, some of its cultural and social characteristics. Apart from the three major public buildings, the department constructed the bandstand in the public gardens where the band of the Nair Brigade now played on alternate Fridays; it did the maintenance on the old bungalow housing the museum, which sometimes drew three thousand visitors a month; it was involved in planning a grand and grotesquely memorable new museum; it brought the first steam engine to Travancore, gave demonstrations to the Raja of Cochin and 'astonished...natives...in thousands'; its improvement and extension of the capital's roads consigned 'Palankeens to desuetude' and brought 'spring carriages into use instead'.[106] Moreover, as Madhava Rao proudly pointed out, the extension of the country roads was bringing all parts of the state into easy communication with Trivandrum and its novelties and facilities.[107]

The 'modernisation' of Trivandrum made it the grandest city in Kerala. By backwater and canal, and over the expanding system of roads, men were increasingly drawn to the capital, whether to take up a case with government, get an education, cure a disease or merely gawk at the new steam engine. The ideas they took away with them are immeasurable, but indisputably important.

The change in the face of Trivandrum was concrete and visible. It symbolised the other less obvious, but more important, changes which the Madhava Rao administration had wrought in Travancore. The Maharaja's College, for example, was the apex of a sirkar system of education which linked government employment with academic qualifications. It was, moreover, the preserve of high castes; an Ezhava did not gain admission until a few years after Madhava Rao left the state. Even in Trivandrum, under the noses of the highest and, in theory, most 'enlightened' officials, the sirkar's proclamations removing caste disabilities remained largely a dead letter.

Over the short-term, the sirkar's policies in education, employment and civil rights strengthened the high castes. But the long-term consequences of other innovations were different. The growth of a cash economy, which was encouraged by land reform, extensive public works (the Public Offices alone cost Rs. 1.5 lakhs), increased trade and large scale planting, helped to undermine the 'communality' of the Nair matrilineal joint-family. Nor did the style of life which Trivandrum made fashionable among the western-educated do anything to bolster the taravad. Over the next twenty years, numbers of those groups–Syrian and other Christians, non-Malayali Brahmins and Ezhavas–who had less burdensome family institutions, who were prepared to attempt new occupations, and who had some experience in dealing regularly with money, were to improve their economic position in relation to Nairs. How this came about, we shall see in the following chapter. Travancore even by 1891 was far from being a society in which money was the only resource worth having; it did not necessarily bring status or political power. However, the steps made in that direction did not favour most Nairs.

# 4

# Cash, Caste and Customs: The Effect of New Resources, 1872-91

Madhava Rao left Travancore under a cloud in 1872. The timid Maharaja, Ayilyam Tirunal, angered at Madhava Rao's involvement with his brother's faction and at the Dewan's lack of respect, finally succeeded in getting his minister's resignation, but only after much intrigue.[1] Madhava Rao was replaced by his close friend and classmate, A. Sashiah Sastri, a Smartha Brahmin, a product of E.B. Powell's Madras High School and head sheristadar of the Madras Board of Revenue. Over the next twenty years–with the exception of the period from 1877 to 1880 when a Travancore Nair was Dewan–Madhava Rao's schoolfellows and kinsmen held the Dewanship and generally maintained Travancore's reputation as a 'model state'.

During the same period members of various groups in Travancore were attempting to adapt to the changes which the reforms of the 1860s helped to impel.

Between 1875 and 1891 the population increased by ten per cent, and by the latter year the density on arable land was calculated at 609 people to the square mile.[2] Travancore, which in the 1840s was said to have been a rice exporter, was by the 1880s importing rice to the value of fourteen and a half lakhs of rupees annually.[3] The increase in population had much to do with this, but there was also 'the general improvement of the circumstances of the lower castes, who can now afford to eat more rice...'[4] That improvement had come about largely through the increased demand for labour and the dramatic increase in, and spread of, wages. As we have seen, in the 1850s coolie labour was worth an anna a day if it was worth a cash wage at all. By the 1870s it was worth four annas a day, and skilled workmen like carpenters could earn up to a rupee a day by the 1880s.[5]

To be sure, the cost of living also rose. A survey taken in Cochin in 1891--conditions in north Travancore at least would have been similar--concluded that the cost of living had increased by 103 per cent between 1850 and 1890. But the wages of non-agricultural labourers--for example, those employed by planters, the public works department or in the coir industry--had risen by 167 per cent and those of artisans by 140 per cent.[6] The survey calculated the cost of living for a man at Rs. 42 a year, and the average cost of living, including women and children, Rs. 29½ a year.[7] Little wonder that jobs in government service paying six or seven rupees a month looked so attractive. The survey concluded that large land-holders--who were not numerous in Travancore--had 'no doubt enormously benefitted during the last forty years by... the marked increase in the price of food grains'. At the same time, the standard of living of many of the low castes had improved. It was the small landholding family which may have found itself in difficulty,[8] especially if it had clear notions about what constituted 'respectable' employment.

In Travancore, probably the majority of Nair matrilineal joint-families were small landholders. They were clear about their respected position in society and how it must be maintained. Already in the late 1830s and 1840s, for example, one family burdened with carrying out in accordance with the family's position the *talikettukalyanam* and *terundakuli* ceremonies for eleven daughters, was impoverished. It subdivided by consent, and each branch appears to have been left with only a few paras of land.[9] This family's experience was probably typical of many others.[10]

By 1891 Travancore had passed through a period of boom-and-bust in the coffee-estate industry, and was on the verge of a new and enduring enterprise in tea. There were said to be forty European planters and about a hundred estates covering

37,500 acres.[11] The value of exports of copra doubled and those of coir nearly tripled between 1871 and 1891.[12] In 1881 the public works department was maintaining 975 miles of road; by the mid-1890s the figure had risen to 2,000 miles.[13] Such expansion of government responsibilities brought an increase of government servants from 14,700 in 1875 to 20,200 in 1891.[14] Yet education more than kept pace with the demand for literate men. As we have seen, the numbers of students rose from about 8,500 in 1872 to 50,000 in 1890. By 1891 the Maharaja's College in Trivandrum had produced 264 graduates of the Madras University.[15]

These changing conditions led to a questioning of ritual privileges and sanctity. Increased mobility became possible for all castes. Indeed, it was encouraged, as boys were sent to distant high schools and colleges and as planters and the public works department recruited labour. That 'territorial segmentation' which supported 'the hierarchical order of castes by permitting greater mobility ... for those at the top' began to break down.[16] Moreover, the new values and administrative standards encouraged by Madhava Rao stipulated that a B.A. degree was better than mere matriculation. Was, therefore, an Ezhava or Syrian Christian graduate to be given a post in the sirkar service in preference to a less educated Brahmin or Nair? By the same token, were the Smartha Brahmins gorging themselves in the free feedinghouses such admirable and holy men after all? They had no degrees or educational qualifications. Were they not in fact leeches and parasites? And what of Nairs? Did they not claim to be Hindus of good caste? Yet they lived in a state of 'universal concubinage', as even *The Hindu* of Madras–and there were many less charitable critics–was prepared to remind them.[17] Nairs became increasingly aware that seen in relation to the standards of Hinduism in the rest of India, their marriage customs appeared scandalous and comic.

Some groups responded to these challenges more successfully than others. For non-Malayali Brahmins, the alternatives were fewest. They already occupied a formidable position in the sirkar service in 1875, and their numbers in Travancore remained constant over the next twenty years. They retained their large share of government patronage. Since the Dewans, with one exception, were non-Malayali Brahmins, this was not surprising.

Smartha Brahmins maintained their interest in trade, and the level of education among non-Malayali Brahmins continued to be the highest of any group in Travancore. Yet other castes and religions were expanding as traders, improving their educational qualifications and demanding places in the government service. In relative terms the influence of non-Malayali Brahmins could only decline.

Through the 1870s and 1880s Syrian Christians were preoccupied with sectarian struggles. Romo-Syrians, who represented more than forty per cent of all Syrians, made little progress in western-style education until the late 1880s, in spite of the landed wealth of some of their members. Syrians, however, had the advantages of a wider network of connections than most Hindus. Their organisation into bishoprics had always permitted substantial mobility beyond the *desam* for a few of their members, and the coming of the CMS opened up opportunities in Madras and even Britain. It was not coincidence that the first joint-stock company in Travancore was started in 1889 by Syrian Christians.[18]

Ezhavas, too, were able to take advantage of the missionaries. By 1891 there were thirty English-speaking men among Travancore Ezhavas, and probably most of them owed part of their education to the missionaries. As a result of the increasing value of the abkari or liquor trade and the growing demand for cocoanut products in the world market, many Ezhavas were experiencing a new, if modest, prosperity. Like low-caste Christian converts whose financial resources had also grown, some Ezhavas were unwilling to accept quietly the traditional disabilities which were still enforced against them.

On the surface, Nairs also appeared to benefit from the changing circumstances of the 1870s and 1880s. They flocked to the government schools, and their male literacy rate rose from twenty-one per cent in 1875 to thirty-seven per cent in 1891. No other group approached this sixteen per cent increase. At the same time, Nairs captured more than a quarter of the choicest posts in the sirkar service--those on salaries of more than Rs. 50 a month. Yet Nairs' share of such jobs was slightly less than that of non-Malayali Brahmins, though their population was seventeen times greater. Here lay the makings of a grievance.

Nairs, however, had another, greater problem. The impartible matrilineal joint-family, the taravad, increasingly proved an embarrassment and a handicap. Educated Nairs winced at the taunts that 'no Nair knows his father', while taravads were torn by feuds over money and land. The idyllic 'communality' of interest which should have characterised the taravad began to crumble. Finding it difficult to raise capital, and having fixed ideas about what constituted respectable employment, Nairs took little part in the commercial activities which allowed some Syrians, Ezhavas and Christian converts to improve themselves materially.

In 1891 educated Nairs, worried by the state of the taravad and the declining prosperity of Nairs, gathered as many allies as possible from other castes and religions and led an assault on the heavy non-Malayali Brahmin representation in the sirkar service. If Nairs could re-establish their political supremacy of pre-British days, the argument seemed to run, all could be made right with the taravad. But that supremacy could never be recaptured, and by 1905 Nairs were to find themselves divided within, resisted by non-Malayali Brahmins, and under pressure from Syrians and even Ezhavas.

It was the spread of a cash economy and the increased value of land which were perhaps most important, though least noticeable, to men living in the 1870s and 1880s. What was readily apparent was the burgeoning government school system and the advantages of sending one's dependents to school. Yet this education helped to undermine many of the old Malayali values and led to intense competition for the best jobs in the government service. For the matrilineal joint-family of Nairs the sum of these changes added up to tension, dispute and decay.

## *NON-MALAYALI BRAHMINS*

When Madhava Rao left Travancore in 1872, non-Malayali Brahmins were at the height of their power in the state. Still enjoying the traditional veneration which Travancoreans accorded to Brahmins, they had captured the best jobs in the sirkar service through their educational attainments and the patronage of the Dewans.[19] Malayalis had hardly begun to object to their disproportionate influence in the government. As early as 1873, it is true, there were polite notices in a Syrian-owned Malayalam newspaper about the injustice 'of bringing foreigners (who have little or

*TABLE 4.1*

*Numbers, Literacy Statistics and Sirkar Jobs of Four Social Categories in 1875 and 1891*

| | *Number* | | *% age of men literate* | | *No. of men literate in English* | | *Sirkar jobs Rs.10-50* | | *Sirkar jobs Rs. 50 plus* | |
|---|---|---|---|---|---|---|---|---|---|---|
| | *1875* | *1891* | *1875* | *1891* | *1875* | *1891* | *1875* | *1891* | *1875* | *1891* |
| Non-Malayali Brahmins | 27,700 | 28,100 | 50 | 56 | — | 645 | 220 (25%) | 1,035 (31%) | 57 (27%) | 101 (27%) |
| Nairs | 441,000 | 483,770 | 21 | 37 | — | 572 | 410 (47%) | 1,620 (48%) | 35 (60%) | 99 (27%) |
| All Christians | 468,550* | 526,900* | 12 | 21 | — | 534 | 10 (1%) | 95 (3%) | 4 (2%) | 21 (6%) |
| Ezhavas | 383,000 | 414,200 | 3 | 12 | — | 30 | 0 | 0 | 0 | 0 |

* About 60% Syrian, 25% Latin Catholics and 15% Protestant converts. Europeans, Eurasians, Tamil Sudras and other *savarna* Malayali Hindus provided the remainder of the job holders. See *Census*, 1881, pp. 242-43, for a breakdown.

Percentages in parentheses are of the category's share of that classification. Thus, non-Malayali Brahmins in 1875 had 25% of all jobs on Rs. 10-50 a month.

*Source: Census*, 1875 and 1891 and *List of Public Servants of the Tranvacore Government* for 1872-73 and 1893-94.

no sympathy with [the Maharaja's] subjects) to hold high positions in the State...', but these were sporadic and easily ignored.[20] The newspaper habit had not yet taken hold. Nor were there organised protests about the state's forty-two *uttupuras*, where Brahmins could receive two free meals a day, and which cost the state four lakhs of rupees a year by 1891.

In the twenty years after Madhava Rao's departure, non-Malayali Brahmins maintained their position in the sirkar service and their numbers in government schools. They readily responded to--indeed, anticipated--the sirkar's demand for qualifications. By 1868-69 the sirkar had nine graduates in its employ; seven were non-Malayali Brahmins.[21] It was their speed in acquiring qualifications from the Madras colleges which allowed them to justify their numbers in the government service. 'It is to be sincerely regretted', wrote Madhava Rao in 1869,

> ...that there is a great paucity of Nairs on the benches of the higher courts. The Sudr Court has not one Nair judge... The Government is fully alive to the desirableness of employing largely this purely native element. But qualified persons have, unhappily, been not available. It is, however, gratifying to note that there is a fair prospect of this cardinal want being speedily supplied.[22]

Even when the Maharaja's College, Trivandrum, which was affiliated to the Madras University, began turning out graduates in the 1870s, they were mainly non-Malayali Brahmins. The first such graduate was V. Nagam Aiya in 1870. He was immediately taken into the service--he had already been a schoolmaster--and over the next thirty-seven years became one of its leading officials. Between 1870 and 1879, the College turned out sixty graduates; thirty-one were non-Malayali Brahmins. From 1880 to 1889 it produced 157 graduates; seventy-seven were non-Malayali Brahmins.[23]

These educational attainments were translated into power in the sirkar service. In 1890 the Dewan was T. Rama Rao, Madhava Rao's cousin, and three of the four dewan peshkars were non-Malayali Brahmin graduates. A non-Malayali Brahmin headed the revenue survey and settlement; ten of its twenty supervisors were non-Malayali Brahmins. They held ten of eighteen Zilla and High Court judgeships, and comprised one hundred and forty-five of two hundred and thirty-one licensed vakils and pleaders. Fifteen of twenty-nine tahsildars and seventeen of thirty headmasters of government English schools were non-Malayali Brahmins.[24]

From such statistics, the hold of non-Malayali Brahmins on the sirkar service is obvious. Yet by 1890 there was a vital difference from the situation in 1872. Many Malayalis, especially Nairs, were also graduates, and they were no longer ready to accord veneration to Brahmins or accept such extensive Brahmin influence. Indeed, from the early 1880s anti-Brahmin feeling began to make itself evident in the expanding Travancore press. A newspaper correspondent in 1882 typified this view of 'the deceitful and treacherous character' of non-Malayali Brahmins,

> ...many of whom, as mere destitute immigrants from Tinnevelly and other places, first settle here with the object of partaking of the charitable distribution of food in the Brahmin feeding houses here, and then, taking advantage of the credulity of the natives, borrow money from them, and begin petty trades, and when they have, by a course of swindling, made large sums of money, which they take care to invest in lands in their own countries and in the name of their relatives, they pretend insolvency to defeat the just claims of their creditors...[25]

The commercial activities of non-Malayali Brahmins, primarily Smarthas, were an obvious target, for no one loved a moneylender, and many moneylenders were Brahmin merchants. In the 1880s Travancore had about eight hundred non-Malayali Brahmin traders.[26] A third of the Trivandrum merchants listed in the *Travancore Almanack* for 1881 were non-Malayali Brahmins who dealt primarily in rice, cloth and tobacco.[27] Such traders were to be found 'in all parts of the country, especially in north Travancore. [They]...live here single', Nagam Aiya continued, 'returning to their families in their villages on the eastern coast once a year or so'.[28] One case may serve as illustration. Picchu Aiyar came to Alleppey as a cook about 1880. He began to deal in rice, as non-Malayali Brahmins long had, and then to lend money. Later he bought land and built an imposing house. The nearby junction still bears his name.[29]

Such traders maintained their connections on the other side of the Ghats through marriage, and by offering opportunities to young relatives or by sending their own children to kinsmen in the Tamil country. They confined their business to the family circle, and could always find a casteman, if not a relative, highly placed in the sirkar service in their locality. Their caste had long given them freedom of movement and the right to government appointments.

But from the 1880s the old privileges could no longer be taken for granted. Educated Malayalis, especially Nairs, increasingly objected to the sirkar's soft spot for non-Malayali Brahmins who were subject neither to capital punishment nor rigorous imprisonment. When Brahmin prisoners objected to changes in the management of the Central Jail, the Superintendent was told to overcome their protests 'by tact and gentle suasion' and to make the men see 'that no interference with cherished sentiment or long existing usage is contemplated'.[30]

It was the *uttupuras*, the free feeding houses for Brahmins, which rankled most with Malayalis. Non-Malayali Brahmins, the argument ran, owed all their material advantages to the *uttupuras* which enabled them to live free while they were getting an education or conducting a petty trade. Not having to worry about subsistence, they were able to devote all their energies to surpassing and exploiting Malayalis, especially Nairs, to whose women they already had access in some instances. 'It is for pocketing some money', wrote a disgruntled Quilon correspondent of the *Travancore Times*, 'that they (the back-tufted intruders) come from Pandy [the Tamil country], [and they do so] by taking their meals in the ootupuras'. A writer from Trivandrum noted that 'the price of paddy has grown in the streets. Why? Because the Brahmins are consuming much. Who will oppose this statement and condemn it as a scurrility?' Later the *Madras Standard* joined the fray: '...the government of Travancore encourage a class of indolent and unscrupulous Brahmins... to fall back upon it for support and existence'.[31]

The picture of the parasitical, trouble-making Pattar grew in popularity and became a useful stick with which to beat Brahmins. How true was it in the 1880s? Probably most Smartha Brahmin government officials, traders and landowners had relatives who took advantage of the *uttupuras*. Indeed, in 1907 Nagam Aiya had occasionally to feed 'forty or fifty kinsmen' at his

Trivandrum house.[32] Doubtless some of them were regular visitors to the *uttupuras*. A Brahmin could travel throughout the state with the certainty of finding free food and probably accommodation. Poor students took their meals in the *uttupuras*. Yet there was a stigma to frequenting the feeding houses, and Desastha Brahmins rarely did so: nor, it seems likely, did successful Smarthas. Access to the *uttupuras*, however, was a real advantage to poor Smarthas who could, as Malayalis complained, prosecute their trades or studies with little expense. At least 1,500 Brahmins were fed in the forty-two *uttupuras* each day.[33] It was a useful privilege which Nairs, beginning to feel the want of such things as student hostels, increasingly resented.[34]

Non-Malayali Brahmins experienced additional hostility after 1885 when it became apparent that the new Maharaja, Mulam Tirunal, was under the influence of a Brahmin favourite, Saravanai Ananda Narayana Aiyar. Saravanai– 'the ICB (illiterate cook boy)', as he came to be known to everyone from the Resident down[35]–had been the Maharaja's servant from the ruler's childhood and was appointed to the revived office of Fauzdar Commissioner on Rs. 500 a month. His sole duty was to sign death warrants. The Resident wrote that:

> ...the favourite is a most mischievous man...he is credited with even more influence than he possesses and his favour is sought and paid for by persons desiring appointments or advancement in the State service... The Maharaja is completely under his influence–the impression of the natives is that he has bewitched the Maharaja.[36]

Saravanai's rise to prominence provided a focus for the growing feeling against non-Malayali Brahmins. *Kerala Patrika* made the connection when it complained of 'the undue influence in State matters of the Maharaja's favourite, the Fauzdar Commissioner' and the disregard of 'the claims of the natives of the country for a share in the appointments in the public service'.[37] But although Saravanai helped to intensify the resentment of educated Malayalis against non-Malayali Brahmins, he was by no means a disadvantage to his Smartha castemen and other Brahmins. He was, it is true, said to be as interested in money as caste affinity; but Nairs later argued that only when a Nair favourite was established in the palace beside Saravanai were they able to compete with Brahmins for the ear of the Maharaja.[38]

In the 1880s when proposals to bring the railway into Travancore were being discussed, the *Madras Standard* averred that the mass of ignorant Brahmins opposed the extension of the railway, especially to Trivandrum. 'By Brahmins we simply mean those classes which are sucking the life blood of the country', the *Standard* continued blithely. It concluded that 'the country [was] literally seething with intrigue' as Brahmins sought to use their influence on 'the young Maharaja'.[39] The railway did not come to Travancore until 1903 and then it entered through the Shenkotta Pass to Quilon, the Maharaja having refused to allow it to desecrate Trivandrum.[40] Perhaps there was something to the *Standard's* charges.

Non-Malayali Brahmins of course were far from being a homogeneous group. The Marathi-speaking Desasthas and Tamil-speaking Vaishnavites in Travancore looked down on the Tamil-speaking Smarthas who were the chief beneficiaries of the *uttupuras*. Yet for Malayalis such subtle distinctions were unnecessary: non-Malayali Brahmins were *foreign* Brahmins, and that was designation enough. Desastha, Smartha and Vaishnavite officials lent substance to the Malayali view by banding together socially. The Shanmadi Vilasa Sabha, founded in 1882 in Trivandrum as a cultural association, was exclusively Brahmin, Its first president was V. Ramiengar, the Dewan, who was succeeded about 1885 by K. Krishnaswami Rao, the Chief Justice. Its membership included numbers of Smartha, Desastha and Vaishnavite officials.[41] The Fort Reading Club, founded in 1885, was patronised by Vishakham Tirunal and one or two Kshatriyas and aristocratic Nairs, but the large majority of its members were non-Malayali Brahmin officials.[42]

Madhava Rao wrote proudly of 'Brahmins' as a *varna*: 'You have safely survived all ... domination, not by your personal prowess or proficiency in arms, or even the strength of your numbers, but by your intellectual and moral superiority'.[43]

There was another division among non-Malayali Brahmins, yet one which was perhaps more apparent than real. This was the supposed clash of ideas between the western-educated elite and their conservative castemen. Among Nairs a similar conflict was to have important implications, as we shall see. But among non-Malayali Brahmins the contrast was surprisingly less spectacular, in spite of the obvious difference between the English-educated official in his office and his illiterate casteman in the *uttupura*. A large part of the reason was that many educated Brahmins remained intensely conservative in social matters and saw no reason to preach social reform among their uneducated kinsmen.

If an educated non-Malayali Brahmin in Travancore attempted innovations, he could expect little support. The most dramatic incident occurred in 1872 when a Vaishnavite Brahmin of Nagercoil, a vakil of the Sadr Court, proposed the re-marriage of his widowed pre-pubescent daughter.[44] He appealed for a second Vaishnavite groom, and the offer of a large dowry brought several responses, the London Missionaries being invited to 'express an opinion on the merits of the various candidates'. The opposition of orthodox Brahmins was so great, however, that there was a riot near the vakil's house the night before the wedding. The marriage took place, but the vakil and his family were excommunicated, and their local temple was then purified at the sirkar's expense.[45]

The vakil petitioned Madhava Rao and the Resident for a proclamation legalising Brahmin re-marriage in Travancore, for without such an act, children of the second marriage would be considered illegitimate. The Resident consulted the Maharaja who was 'very cautious in expression and merely said he would consider the matter'. Madhava Rao told the Resident that the Maharaja was 'strongly averse' to such a proclamation and pointed out–'his [Madhava Rao's] countenance belied him if it was not with considerable inward satisfaction'[46]–that a British Indian Act of 1856 had been unpopular and inoperative. The Resident argued that the Madras government should press for a proclamation, but the Madras Council allowed the matter to drop. Two years later the vakil was still petitioning.[47]

The view of educated men like Madhava Rao was that no social reform among Brahmins should be instituted 'till there is a generally expressed desire on the part of the [Brahmin]] public'. The Resident concluded that 'the period of inactivity' was intended to be 'of very long duration'.[48] Sashiah Sastri, Madhava Rao's schoolmate and successor, refused an invitation to testify before the Select Committee on Indian Finance in London in 1873 because of 'my health and the necessities of my social position as a Brahmin...I should willingly travel many thousands of miles if on land, and to a more genial climate'.[49] He survived until 1903. Nor did he and Madhava Rao take a radical line on marriage questions:

> '*Widows* do you call them?' said Sashiah, 'they are god-ordained saviours of the Hindu household–ministering angels of home, finding their joy in the joy of those around; how round them are twined the hearts of all the family!

Madhava Rao's most radical suggestion on the subject was to prohibit the marriage of girls 'before nine years of age'.[50] And when V. Ramiengar, Dewan from 1880 to 1887, toyed with the idea of abolishing the *uttupuras*, the arguments and protests of large numbers of non-Malayali Brahmins were said to have quickly dissuaded him.[51]

Educated non-Malayali Brahmins tended to be sympathetic towards the prejudices and customs of their unschooled kinsmen. Their position was fundamentally different from that of educated Nairs. The traditional style of life of south Indian Brahmins was, in theory, a model of Hindu virtue as understood throughout India; a man might acquire English education yet see no need to renounce his identification with such high standards of ritual purity. Educated Nairs, on the other hand, were made increasingly aware that, though they claimed to be Hindus of good caste, their customs did not conform to the all-India model. Their social problems, moreover, were much more acute than anything Bramins were to experience, and their educated men were to be bitterly divided over remedies. There were, to be sure, obvious divisions among non-Malayali Brahmins,[52] but they had enough in common to make them appear to Malayalis as a fairly solid group.

In the 1870s and 1880s, non-Malayali Brahmins in Travancore maintained their share of higher posts in the sirkar service, their numbers in government schools, their interests in trade and their traditional privileges. But Nairs also maintained their large numbers in the sirkar service and produced graduates and matriculates in ever-increasing numbers. Syrian Christians,

Christian converts and even Ezhavas extended their commercial interests in an expanding economy and also sent their children to school. The spread of education helped to undermine 'the high veneration' which non-Malayali Brahmins had traditionally enjoyed in Travancore. In short, Brahmins continued to walk, but other groups began to run; the relative position of Brahmins could only be undermined. By 1891 their role in the sirkar service was under heavy attack. Yet because of their high level of education, their established strength, their traditional privileges, their mobility, their diverse interests and their considerable solidarity, they were to prove well able to defend themselves over the next twenty-five years. But having to defend themselves at all was something new.

## *SYRIAN CHRISTIANS*

Throughout the 1870s and 1880s, Syrian Christian leaders, as a European missionary wrote, were preoccupied with litigation and sectarian disputes, and 'all their clergy generally speaking are employed in litigation'.[53] During the same period, numbers of Syrians extended their landholdings by taking up waste land, acquired educational qualifications, expanded their interests in trade, and through European planters, got a cursory introduction to cash crops and the plantation system. Moreover, the sectarian skirmishes, which had divided Syrians into four major churches by 1890, provoked an educational competition which brought church schools within easy reach of virtually every Syrian in the state. By 1890 even the most numerous, wealthy and educationally backward section, the Romo-Syrians, were beginning to establish western-style schools. Education was to lead to demands for more equitable representation in the government service.

### *Sectarian Disputes*

After the split with the CMS in 1836, some reforming Syrians who had no wish to remain with the Anglicans, arranged to send the future Mar Athanasius from the CMS school in Madras where he had been studying, to the Patriarch of Antioch in Mardin in Armenia. The Patriarch consecrated him bishop in 1843, and Mar Athanasius returned to Travancore. After overcoming the opposition of other candidates, he was recognised by the sirkar as head of the Jacobite Church in Travancore in 1852. Opposition, however, remained, especially to Athanasius's low-Anglican views about images and relics and his occasional injunctions to proselytise among the low castes.[54]

In 1862 an orthodox section of Jacobites, following the example of Athanasius, sent the future Mar Dionysius to Mardin where he was made a bishop by the Patriarch in 1864. Having returned to Travancore, he claimed that the Patriarch had excommunicated Athanasius in 1852 and that he, Dionysius, was the rightful head of the Travancore Jacobites. Athanasius held the upper hand until 1869 when he attempted to have funds amounting to half a lakh of rupees, which had been held in the Resident's treasury since the split with the CMS, made over to him and his party. The CMS was agreeable, and the Resident, G.A. Ballard, a staunch Anglican, had 'no hesitation in affirming that a very large and powerful majority [of Jacobites] acknowledge Mar Athanasius as Metropolitan...' Ballard asked the Madras government for permission to release the money.[55]

The government's refusal encouraged Dionysius and his followers, whose strength lay in Cochin and north Travancore, to press their claims more strongly. They won the support of Patriarch Ignatius who put their case to the Archbishop of Canterbury when he visited London in 1874. The Archbishop, apparently well briefed by the CMS, suggested leaving the Syrians in Kerala to Athanasius.[56] Undeterred, the Patriarch, who was short of money, came to India in 1875, had an interview with the Governor of Madras at Ootacamund, and with the instructions of the Madras government to render him all assistance, proceeded to Cochin and Travancore.[57] There he employed as his agent H. M. Walker, an Englishman married to a Eurasian Roman Catholic. In the following year, Walker--'a man of the worst possible character', thought the Resident--became editor of the *Western Star*, the first English newspaper in Travancore, founded in 1865 by C. Curien, a supporter of Dionysius.[58] Walker's work for the Patriarch was brief but effective. Writing on the best monogrammed stationery, he asked the Travancore sirkar to provide a bungalow, a carriage and a guard of honour, and was successful in extracting accommodation and an official welcome.[59]

Parishes immediately began to switch their allegiance to Dionysius, and within a few months, Sashiah Sastri, the Dewan, was pressing the Resident to be allowed to recognise Dionysius.[60] Athanasius still claimed to have the allegiance of 137 out of 162 parish churches and 350,000 out of 400,000 Jacobites, including those in Cochin. His estimates, however, were undoubtedly exaggerated, and the struggle to win over parishes, many of them 'richly endowed', began in earnest. In 1876, on the instructions of the Madras government, the sirkar withdrew its recognition of Athanasius and instructed both sides to go to the courts.[61]

The death of Athanasius in 1877 delayed the legal battle, and it was not until 1879 that Dionysius filed suit in the Alleppey Zilla Court against Thomas Athanasius, the cousin and successor of the late metropolitan. The case dragged on for ten years, commanding the attention of leading Syrians and devouring large sums of money. Dionysius, for example, raised Rs. 3,000 from a few of his churches in 1880; this gave 'some idea of the great wealth of the Syrian Church' to at least one European missionary.[62] Dionysius won in the Zilla Court in 1884, then defeated appeals to the High Court in 1886 and finally to a special royal court in 1889. All Jacobite property and assets were awarded to him and his party, but Thomas Athanasius and his followers, refusing to acknowledge Dionysius's spiritual authority, founded the reformist Mar Thomite church.

It was not only the Jacobites, however, who knew litigation and schism. The Romo-Syrians, too, had been warring among themselves. Moreover, the disputes of one sect often involved another. It was not uncommon for Syrians to move from the Jacobites to the Romanist party or from the Anglicans to the Jacobites. Families might have relatives in different sects, and there was some inter-marriage. The vital fact was that all were Syrian Christians.[63]

The Romo-Syrians, as we have seen, were those who remained loyal to Rome after the oath of the Coonen Cross in 1653. Although many of them were devoted to the Pope, they had no liking for the foreign hierarchy of Portuguese, Italian or Spanish bishops appointed by Rome. Nor were such bishops, who often spoke neither English nor Malayalam, of much help to their adherents. For two hundred years they had largely contented themselves with fighting schism through interpreters.

When the Church Missionary Society began to proselytise from the 1840s, the useful connections of its agents in education, planting, commerce and government loomed as an attraction to Romo-Syrian congregations. The foreign hierarchy banned Romo-Syrians from attending CMS College, Kottayam, to which all other Syrians freely resorted, and from reading publications of the CMS press.[64] Prohibited from attending the leading educational institute of the area, and with their own bishops uninterested in English education, Romo-Syrians saw others gain posts in government service, in commercial offices in Cochin and on coffee estates.

Resentment against the foreign hierarchy showed itself in the Rokos schism of 1861-62,[65] and more importantly in the Mellus schism which began with the arrival in Travancore of Mellus, Archbishop of Acre, in 1874. Mellus claimed to represent the Pope through the Patriarch of Babylon, and soon became the master of the Romo-Syrian churches in Cochin and north Travancore. In the south he won the support of the wealthy Fr. Mathew Palakkunnel of Kuthirapalli near Changanacherry, and might have succeeded in seducing all the Romo-Syrian parishes if Fr. Emmanuel Nidhiry, another wealthy priest of the large parish of Kuravilangad, had been willing to join him. Although a militant nationalist in church matters, Nidhiry remained loyal to Rome, the Papal party counter-attacked in the civil courts, and Mellus, excommunicated by the Pope, left Kerala in 1882.[66] He left behind, however, a few schismatic parishes and the conviction among Nidhiry and other leaders that the only solution to the dissensions and backwardness of Romo-Syrians was for them to have their own Malayali bishops.[67]

## *Education, Sirkar Service and Commerce*

Those Syrians who remained with the CMS after the break of 1836-40 numbered only three to four thousand, but they became the Syrian vanguard in education, and were the first Syrians to express discontent at being rejected for the sirkar service. When Madhava Rao left Travancore in 1872, Indian Christians of all kinds held only ten of eight hundred eighty government jobs on Rs. 10-50 a month and four of two hundred fifteen jobs on more than Rs. 50 (see Table 4.1). There were no Syrian magistrates or sub-magistrates, and the only Syrian important enough to find his way into the *Trivandrum Almanack's* list of top public servants was the headmaster of a district school.[68]

In the same year, the first Malayali to study in Britain returned to Travancore. He was T.C. Poonen, a CMS Syrian, who had been a student in CMS College, Kottayam, the Government Provincial School, Calicut, and Presidency College, Madras, where he took a BA in 1869. From 1869 to 1872 he lived in London and was called to the bar from the Inner Temple in 1872.[69] When Poonen applied to the Travancore sirkar for a post, he was refused. He practised briefly as a vakil in Tellicherry in Malabar district before accepting a judgeship in Cochin state. 'Suppose he had been a Nair or a Pattar', *Paschima Taraka* commented testily, 'how easily and how long ago he would have received a proper office'.[70]

Poonen's case illustrated two points: the usefulness of CMS connections and the reluctance of the sirkar to employ any except caste Hindus. From the mid-1850s the products of CMS College were 'much sought after' by British merchants in Cochin.[71] Similarly, Poonen's travels to Calicut, Madras, London and Tellicherry had been facilitated by CMS contacts. Yet such travelled, educated men were not welcomed by the sirkar. *Jnana Nikshepam*, a CMS newspaper published in Kottayam, ascribed 'the Syrians' want of success...to there being none to represent their case to the Maharaja who is noted for his generosity'.[72] But there were more cogent reasons. Except for their brief period of favour during John Munro's Residency, Syrians had no tradition of sirkar service. The non-Malayali Brahmins and Nairs who conducted the administration had no wish to divide still further the choicest appointments, and in a Hindu state, reasons could usually be found to explain the exclusion of non-Hindus. Because revenue and executive officers all had duties connected with the temples, one explanation ran, only caste Hindus could be employed.

This argument, however, came from a government which had repeatedly emphasised its search for qualified men. As the number of educated Syrians rose, the justifications for keeping them out of the government service sounded increasingly hollow. Syrians claimed to have as many matriculates and graduates as

Nairs, yet in 1880 they held only twenty-five of 1,424 posts in the sirkar worth more than Rs. 10 a month.[73]

Whether Syrians had in fact turned out as many academically qualified men as Nairs in the 1870s and 1880s is doubtful. Many Syrians, it is true, went to Madras to do their B.A. (CMS College taught only to First Arts standard), but by 1890 fewer than twenty-four had graduated from the Maharaja's College, Trivandrum.[74] Indeed, even CMS College had produced only eighty-six Christian matriculates between 1879 and 1889, and only eight of these had gone on to graduate.[75]

Part of the reason for the lack of graduates was that Syrians readily found jobs outside the government-service network. A glance at the occupations of the 86 CMS College matriculates illustrates this:[76]

| | |
|---|---|
| Graduates (job unspecified) | 8 |
| Still studying in Arts | 23 |
| Still studying in Medicine or Engineering | 3 |
| Travancore Medical Service | 5 |
| Teachers and writers | 18 |
| Employed by CMS | 23 |
| Unemployed | 2 |
| Dead | 4 |
| TOTAL | 86 |

Only five were dependent on sirkar service, and they were all in the medical department. The CMS itself had absorbed twenty-three of its old boys, and another eighteen had found work as teachers and writers. Being excluded from much of the government service forced Syrians to be independent and reinforced their traditional interests in commerce. Indeed, some of the tamer Syrian spirits in 1891 attributed the paucity of Syrians in the government service to the fact that 'until lately [they were] devoted to the pursuits of religion, agriculture and commerce'.[77]

It is true that well-organised, large-scale education conducted by Jacobites and Romo-Syrians did not begin until the late 1880s. Sectarian disputes gave it a surprising impetus. In 1879 when the litigation between the two Jacobite factions began,

Thomas Athanasius's party controlled eighty-two grant-in-aid schools with an enrolment of 3,4000; Dionysius's adherents had fifty-two schools with 2,100 pupils. The following table shows the expansion.[78]

*TABLE 4.2*

*Christian Schools Receiving Grants-in-Aid, 1879-95*

| | 1879 | 1885 | 1890 | 1895 |
|---|---|---|---|---|
| Mar Thomas Athanasius | 82 | 87 | 96 | 103 |
| Mar Dionysius | 52 | 88 | 93 | 92 |
| All Roman Catholic | 0 | 5 | 23 | 49 |
| Protestant | 207 | 231 | 331 | 468 |

By 1885, as Dionysius's fortunes waxed in the courts, the number of his schools rose to eighty-eight; Thomas Athansius had eighty-seven. The rival metropolitans were competing for the control of parishes and people, and one way of gaining and demonstrating that control was to conduct schools. If one of the rivals were able to open a parish school, he stood to gain a sirkar grant-in-aid, the gratitude of the congregation and the loyalty of the parish leaders.

Even more striking than the increase in educational interest among the competing Jacobite parties was the attitude of Romo-Syrians in the late 1880s. In 1885, in the wake of the Mellus schism, a number of Romo-Syrians led by Fr. Nidhiry petitioned the Vatican for their own Malayali bishop.

> The want of a Bishop in our own nation and rite is the cause of our deterioration in the ecclesiastical and social affairs...[O]ur Jacobite Brethren who having Bishops of their own nation and rite and having been encouraged by them to pass the University Examinations...hold high and responsible offices in the Government.[79]

While questions of bishops and hierarchies were decided, slowly, in Rome, Nidhiry and others concluded that education was the only way to head off the schismatics and Protestants who 'are daily advancing on us with alluring offers'. Romo-Syrians could 'count no member of theirs as graduates of the university, nor a single one who holds a responsible or respectable office in the government...'[80] In 1885, only five grant-in-aid schools were under Roman Catholic management, and they may have been under the control of Eurasian Latin Catholics with whom Romo-Syrians did not normally associate. The *Bombay Catholic Examiner* concluded that 'the cause of education...would appear, unfortunately, to have been sadly neglected, and hence, no doubt, the fatal facility with which Jacobitism...had hitherto been spreading...'[81]

The first effort to lead Romo-Syrians into western-style education had come in 1883. With the Jacobites deep in litigation, some Romo-Syrians formed the Syrian National Union Association in co-operation with Mar Dionysius. The aim of the association was the 'national and social well-being' of the Syrians, an end which was to be achieved through education and commerce.[82] The chief figure in the organisation appears to have been Fr. Nidhiry, who hoped to bring Dionysius and the Jacobites into communion with Rome. During the next few years, Nidhiry wheedled Rs. 20,000 and a bargain price for the twenty-two acre Woodland Estate out of James Darragh, an American Roman Catholic who was in the coir business in Alleppey. The money was to be used to found a joint Romo-Syrian/Jacobite college at Kottayam. Trying to win over the Jacobites, Nidhiry had the money paid to Dionysius who used part of it in his litigation.[83]

The college scheme was finally crushed by the opposition of the Romo-Syrians' European bishops. Suspicious of any fraternization with heretics, and distrusting Nidhiry's claim that he had 'the secret consent of Mar Dionysius to abjure Jacobitism and become Catholic after the establishment of ... a college',[84] they forced Romo-Syrians to drop the college proposal and the Woodland Estate in 1888.[85] Yet at the same time the European hierarchy was made aware of the necessity of providing western-style schools for Romo-Syrians. By 1890 there were twenty-three schools under Roman Catholic management; by 1895, forty-nine. In 1888 a seminary was founded in Changanacherry, the Romo-Syrian heartland, which grew into St. Berchman's High School, an English teaching institution, in 1891.[86]

Those Syrians who associated with–though they did not necessarily have to belong to–the Anglican church in Travancore were the first to get an extensive western education and to aim at employment in the sirkar service. K.K. Kuruvila, who became a Bachelor of Civil Engineering in 1877, was a Jacobite, but he had been partly educated at CMS College and his parents had been briefly connected with the CMS. Kuruvila entered the Travancore public works department and became the highest ranking Syrian public servant of his generation. A few years his junior was E. Poonen, a CMS Syrian, who received his early education in Kottayam and studied medicine at Aberdeen University in the early 1880s. He rose to be the highest-ranking Indian in the Travancore medical department.[87]

The CMS connection had uses beyond education. As planting increased on the hills east of Kottayam, young Syrians found employment as clerks in export merchants' offices in Alleppey or Cochin. Planters such as George and William Baker, sons of Rev. Henry Baker, Sr., and F.G. Richardson, a ward of the Baker family, patronised the families of Syrian Christians. Richardson wrote of his employment of 'Kottayam Syrian Christians' and of his friendship with one of the early CMS clergymen, Rev. George Matthan.[88] When the Rev. Henry Baker, Jr. had an interest in a coffee estate, his manager was a Nair convert who was trying to assimilate as a Syrian.[89] Planting was at its lowest ebb in 1885, but there were still said to be three hundred Christians, excluding labourers, on the hills all year round and more at crop time.[90]

Having been introduced to the skills and opportunities of planting, a few Syrians took up coffee land around Pirmed on their own account. One who did so was Thomas Matthai, a CMS Syrian, a matriculate of CMS College, and the father of John Matthai, the first Indian finance minister in the government of India. The holdings of these few early planters appear to have been large. In at least two cases, they extended to five hundred and eight hundred acres, although it is doubtful whether they were able to find the finances to plant much of this in coffee.[91] The auctions of waste land in 1874 brought Rs. 2.25 lakhs to the sirkar and disposed of 8,000 acres, mostly to Indians.[92] When coffee failed disastrously after 1879, Matthai lost his investment and left planting (his CMS connections helped him to move to

Calicut as a schoolmaster and inspector). A few Syrians, however, persevered on the hills and were in a position to take advantage of tea when it began to prosper in the 1890s and later to popularise rubber among their fellow Syrians who held land on the rising ground between Kottayam and the hills.[93]

The expansion of planting and public works in the 1860s had brought other benefits to Syrian traders. The road-building programme connected the Syrian centre of Kottayam with Madura in the Madras Presidency, and the coffee estates which flourished around Pirmed in the 1870s relied for their provisioning on Kottayam as well as Madura. By 1879, just before leaf disease ruined coffee throughout most of south India, the prosperity of Kottayam traders was obvious and owed 'so much to the Coffee Interest... which gives...markets for their produce [and]...employment for their bandies and bullocks...'.[94]

The Kottayam-Madura road, completed in 1876, opened up large tracts of sloping garden land in the area of Travancore where Syrians were most numerous. Of the change that overtook the land east of Kottayam, F.G. Richardson wrote about 1905:

> There was time when, starting from Kottayam on his pony ride to Peermaad there were only six places on the long and weary track of 45 miles where a planter could obtain fire to light his cheroot! Now, however, along the whole length of the road there are houses and gardens and a thriving population...[95]

One estimate places the increase in land under cultivation in Travancore in the fifty years before 1911 at nearly two per cent a year, or a virtual doubling of cultivated land.[96] In the area around Kottayam much of this land was taken up by Syrians. The profitability of cash crops was becoming obvious, and in addition to their commercial interests, Syrians had a strong farming tradition. Unlike Nairs, they were not encumbered by an impartible matrilineal joint-family. In youth, Syrians had the advantage of a recognised paternal obligation to provide education and a start in life, but individuals were nonetheless expected to make their own way later. Nairs, on the other hand, were legally guaranteed a living from the income of the joint-family.

By the late 1880s all the Syrian sects were turning their attention to education, while individual Syrians were finding greater scope for trade and farming. Syrians, too, established a commanding position in journalism. The sectarian skirmishes made it desirable for each of the factions to own a press.[97] Jacobites owned the *Western Star,* founded in Cochin in 1865 and moved to Trivandrum in 1893. The same family held the abkari contract for most of Kottayam division.[98] Another Syrian started the first Malayam newspaper, *Paschima Taraka* in 1864.[99] The CMS had published a number of journals in Malayalam and English from the 1840s, and a unknown Syrian Christian, in collaboration with a CMS missionary and his wife, was responsible for publication of what was arguably the first novel in Malayalam.[100] *Kerala Mitram* was started by a Gujarati in Cochin in 1881, but its editor was K.I. Varghese Mappillai, a Jacobite, and perhaps the leading Malayalam journalist of his time. In 1887, under the auspices of the Syrian National Union Association, Fr. Nidhiry established *Nasrani Deepika*, the oldest Malayalam newspaper still publishing today. Two years later Varghese Mappillai formed the first joint-stock company in Travancore to found *Malayala Manorama*, the most famous Malayalam newspaper, whose present offices stand on the land Nidhiry acquired for the unsuccessful college scheme.[101] In mid-1893, after some Hindu ventures had fallen by the wayside, all ten newspapers publishing in Travancore were Christian owned.[102]

By about 1890 Syrians had set their own house–or more correctly, houses–in order, and four major sects, Romo-Syrians, Jacobites, Mar Thomites and Anglicans had emerged. The sectarian disputes of the 1890s gave an impetus to education. Schools were a way of rallying a sect's adherents and of demonstrating its control of a parish. Western-style education, which had been largely confined to those Syrians willing to associate with the CMS, was becoming widely available to members of all sects by 1890. With the increase in the numbers of educated Syrians came growing indignation at their virtual exclusion from the government service. As *Paschima Taraka* observed in 1877, 'many are studying English not with a view to acquire knowledge, but for the purpose of making a profit',[103] and perhaps the most desirable way to profit and power was through the sirkar service. In 1891, Anglicans, Mar Thomites, Romo-Syrians and some

Jacobites were prepared to align themselves with educated Nairs to protest to the Maharaja about the dominance of non-Malayali Brahmins of the best jobs in the sirkar service.

But as the numbers of western-educated Syrians grew and their commercial enterprises prospered, they found that their path to sirkar preferment was blocked not so much by Brahmins as by apprehensive Nairs. If recruitment to the sirkar service was to be based on academic qualifications–and that was largely what the government had been saying since Madhava Rao's day–Syrians in the 1890s had the resources to produce as many educated men as any group in the state. By 1896 roughly ten per cent of the total population of Anglican, Jacobite and Mar Thomite Syrians were students.[104]

## *CONVERTS AND EZHAVAS*

The reforms of Madhava Rao offered little advantage in education and sirkar patronage to Ezhavas and low-caste Protestant converts who were regarded by both caste-Hindus and Syrian Christians as being beyond the limits of 'respectable' Travancore society. Most government schools were closed to them, and by 1890 no Ezhavas, and only three or four Protestant converts, had posts in the sirkar service worth more than Rs. 10 a month. Yet thousands of converts acquired basic literacy, a few became graduates, and even among Ezhavas by 1890 there was a medical doctor and a Bachelor of Arts. Such men were bound to question the caste rules of Travancore government and society which so manifestly worked against them. At the same time, the growth of a cash economy opened up areas where Ezhavas and converts could profitably employ themselves without annoying, or coming into contact with, high castes. Such pursuits would eventually give them an economic advantage over the high castes.

Converts of the London Missionary Society in south Travancore were able to use the education which they acquired from the missionaries to advance in planting and in commerce. North of Quilon, however, the converts of the Church Missionary Society found themselves in a church already dominated by Syrian Christians who appropriated for themselves most of the good things which the missionaries had to offer. For Ezhavas, on the other hand, the activities of both missionary societies were helpful and important. Although relatively few Ezhavas embraced Christianity, many attended Christian schools and had contacts with European missionaries. From the 1890s, the threat of conversion to Christianity was a useful weapon for Ezhavas trying to extract recognition of enhanced status from caste Hindus, particularly Nairs. Moreover, the increased demand from the 1880s for the products of the cocoanut palm enabled some Ezhavas to improve their economic position considerably and brought to thousands of Ezhavas the benefit of cash payment for their labour. By 1890 some Ezhavas, having acquired educational or economic resources at least equal to those of the so-called high castes, were beginning to object to their enforced social inferiority.

### *Converts of the LMS*

In 1875 there were 35,000 baptised Christians and another 25,000 adherents of the LMS in the six southernmost taluks of Travancore. This represented more than ten per cent of area's population. It was not a coincidence that the southern division had a literacy rate of 7.42 per cent, the highest of the state's four administrative divisions.[105] Nor was it surprising that in the years after Madhava Rao assumed office conflicts between the missionaries and the sirkar almost ceased. Although Madhava Rao was not a special admirer of missionaries–in 1868 he wrote that some of them seemed to think they could enforce the civil rights of their converts 'even to the extent of shooting down those that would resist such action'[106]–he usually took pains to conciliate them. Under his administration, many of the causes of missionary grievances were removed. Moreover, by the late 1860s, the pace of proselytising had slackened; the sizable, second-generation Christian community had first call on the missionaries' attention.

Unlike the Church Missionary Society, which was generally better financed in England and had the support of a few well-to-do Syrians in Travancore, the LMS was constantly searching for ways to support its chapels, schools and clinics. The vast majority of its adherents were Shanars and Parayas who made their livings as field labourers or as climbers and tappers of the palmyra palm. A few owned a little land, but the readiness with which they joined the mission was probably indicative of their poverty.

From the 1840s, educated converts had been going to Ceylon to work on coffee estates. In 1866 the mission received donations totalling Rs. 150 from three of its members who were acting as managers of estates in Ceylon. There were fifteen other donations of less than Rs. 10 from clerks and writers on Ceylon estates.[107] In 1859, P.D. Devasagaim, a Shanar convert born in 1822, who had been educated in the Nagercoil boarding schools of the LMS, returned to Travancore after nearly twenty years' experience of planting in Ceylon. He opened an estate called 'Victoria' in the Ashambu Hills, twenty-five miles north of Nagercoil, and began to plant coffee. He regularly gave a tenth of his income to the mission, and until coffee failed about 1880, gave Rs. 200 to every Christian widow who remarried. His was the first two-storey Christian house in Nagercoil and brought loud objections from caste Hindus. In 1874 he helped his wife's nephew, P.C. Joseph, to start the *Travancore Times* which represented Christian opinion in south Travancore for the next eighty years.[108]

Devasagaim's enterprise attracted the attention of the missionaries. When the Rev. John Cox, who had led the attacks against the sirkar before the breastcloth disturbances, married a Shanar convert and left the mission in 1861, he retreated into the Ashambu Hills and began planting coffee. At one stage his holdings extended to 1,800 acres.[109] The family of Cox's wife joined them on the hills, and other Christians were employed as clerks and conductors, not only on Cox's estate but on those which he, and later Devasagaim, managed for Madhava Rao and Vishakham Tirunal.[110] Missionaries began planting: first, a modest eight acres to support their hot-weather bungalow in the hills; then a hundred and fifty acres to finance an additional European teacher for the Nagercoil Seminary; and ultimately, their own company, formed with some of their converts. The Glenallyn Coffee Company initially held fifty-two acres of land and was divided into ten shares, six of them held by converts and the rest by the missionaries, James Duthie, William Lee, Samuel Mateer and James Emlyn.[111] There were other missionary ventures, a few briefly successful,[112] but leaf disease destroyed coffee and the missionaries' enthusiasm about 1880.

Only a few Christian converts became estate owners–probably not more than a dozen families[113]–but as coffee prospered in the early 1870s, the missionaries found difficulty in keeping boys in the Nagercoil Seminary. 'Many of our acquaintances and friends [the boys said] who have less learning than we have are earning respectable wages as overseers of Coffee Estates...'[114] It was recognised that the prosperity of the mission owed a great deal to 'a few [converts] whose incomes as conductors of Coffee Estates are good, and who are not unwilling to subscribe liberally to the cause of God'.[115] As Graph 1 indicates, contributions to the mission roughly coincided with the fortunes of the coffee industry. The missionaries, who viewed coffee only as a potentially profitable sideline, sold or abandoned their interests after the collapse, but their converts moved farther afield or experimented with other crops. A.V. Thomas (1891-1968), for example, left south Travancore to find work in Alleppey as a youth and became one of the wealthiest planters on the west coast of India.[116] In 1881, with coffee at its worst, forty-three out of seventy contributors to the 'Mission to Coolies' fund were converts who gave estates as their addresses; their occupations ranged from conductors to cooks and stable hands.[117] By 1891 coffee exports had fallen lower than ever before, but mission contributions reached a new high, as new crops like tea began to prosper in south India.

The opportunity provided by coffee allowed LMS converts and adherents to make material advances which would have been imposible in the pre-plantation social and economic system of south Travancore. As a newly-shaped community with little stake in tradition or the status quo, the converts were readier to attempt a new enterprise. Their mission education made them valuable employees, and the involvement of sympathisers like John Cox, and of the missionaries themselves, brought the converts' skills to the attention of virtually every planter in Travancore. Such an effective introduction helped to compensate initially for the converts' lack of capital. For all who cared to look, Devasagaim's two-storey house was a symbol of a changing order in which caste alone would not determine a man's rank or status.

Coming from the poor and low castes, the converts badly needed a new route to economic prosperity and power, for the

## Graph 1

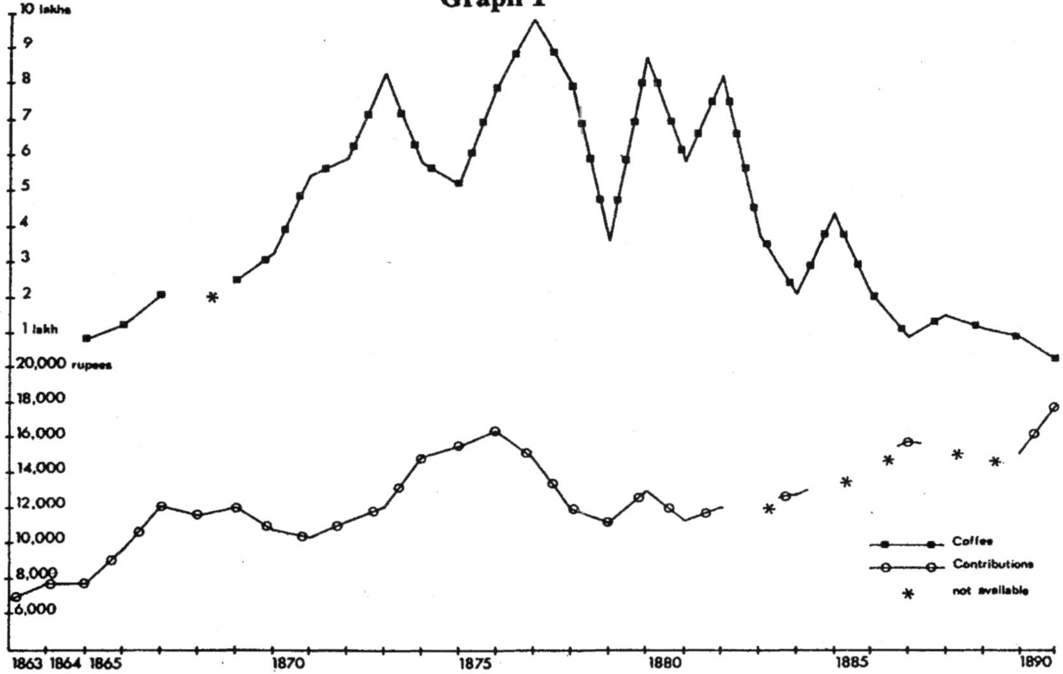


Value of coffee exports from Travancore and contributions to the London Missionary Society's Travancore mission, 1863-91. Sources: <u>Travancore Administration Reports</u>; London Missionary Society, Travancore District Committee, <u>Annual Reports</u>.

government service was virtually closed to them. Yet in spite of the sirkar's blatant discrimination against the converts, a strange warmth generally came to characterise relations between LMS adherents and the sirkar in the 1870s and 1880s. The reasons were partly personal. Two Dewans, Nanu Pillai (Dewan, 1877-80) and Rama Rao (Dewan, 1887-92), were educated in the Nagercoil Seminary and often acknowledged their debt to the missionaries; Rama Rao donated property at Quilon, the income from which was used for the education of poor childern; Nanu Pillai was reputed to read the Psalms daily, attended missionary magic-lantern shows on such subjects as the 'Life of Christ' and left the Nagercoil Seminary Rs. 1,000 when he died.[118]

The status of converts also rose through their association with powerful Europeans. In 1851, Rev. Charles Mead, nearly sixty, married a nineteen year-old Paraya convert and was banished from the mission. He moved to Trivandrum to manage the sirkar press and supervise sirkar schools; he took with him his wife and her family. Such behaviour, however scandalous to Europeans, seems likely to have made converts appear more influential to caste Hindus. There were other infiltrations of Trivandrum Society. C.M. Agur, a graduate, and the great-grandson of the first Shanar convert, became manager of the Resident's office where he worked for more than twenty years until his death in 1904. P.D. Devasagaim's career was frequently held up by Vishakham Tirunal as an example of hard work and self-help.[119]

Cordial relations between educated converts and educated Hindus were aided by the fact that neither side saw itself in competition with the other. Christians, becoming modestly prosperous in commerce and planting, accepted their exclusion from the sirkar service with apparent understanding. When the sirkar made concessions, LMS agents and converts were suitably grateful. In 1890, for example, Rama Rao's administration appointed two converts as sub-magistrates in Padmanabhapuram division, and the missionaries rejoiced at 'the enlightened rule of the present Maha Rajah'.[120] There was no resentment that Rama Rao's Christian contemporaries at the Nagercoil Seminary had not been able to enter government service. Similarly, the *Travancore Times* was usually prepared to defend the government, and even when Rama Rao was under attack in Travancore and

Madras newspapers, the *Times* would write of 'our highly popular Dewan'.[121]

A naive ideal of personal friendship, however, was not alone responsible for the missionaries' and converts' cordial relations with the sirkar. In Padmanabhapuram division in the 1880s, Hindus outnumbered Protestants by at least six to one.[122] Because of the presence of famous holy places like the Suchindram Temple and Kanyakumari, the division was a centre of Hindu orthodoxy, and most uneducated high-caste Hindus bitterly resented the missionaries. Moreover, great areas of rice-growing land were owned by Nairs and Nanjanad Vellalas; the latter, though Tamil speakers had adopted Malayali customs and had a long tradition of ostentatious loyalty to the Travancore royal house.[123] Many of the LMS adherents depended for their livelihood on agricultural labour. There was a consequent feeling that Malayalis ruled and Tamils were ruled. Surrounded by a resentful Hindu community which was economically and politically dominant in local affairs, the LMS and its adherents cultivated Hindu and European friends in the sirkar service. The administration might not be inclined, or able, to give much support to mission causes, but a sympathetic, passive government was better than an actively hostile one. Occasionally, too, there were pleasant surprises, as in the case of Rama Rao's Protestant magistrates. In the years after Madhava Rao's departure, good relations with the government became highly desirable for the missions as a counterpoise to its powerful and antagonistic high-caste Hindu neighbours.

By 1890, the organisation of the LMS encompassed 45,000 baptised Christians and perhaps another 20,000 adherents in south Travancore.[124] Some, having taken up planting and commercial activities related to it, had achieved a modest prosperity. In 1891, adherents contributed Rs. 18,000 to the support of the mission; thirty years before, their contribution had been Rs. 5,000. At the same time the missionaries and their pastors and catechists introduced a sense of community among converts. Church services, school inspections and religious programmes went on constantly, and when a Christian was in trouble, he immediately turned to the church. 'They seem to imagine', lamented Alfred Thompson, 'that the function of the missionary is to settle all their disputes, to send pleaders to the law courts, to help them in their pecuniary difficulties, and to obtain for them good and remunerative employment'.[125] Low-caste Hindus, observing the advantages which converts derived from having an institution like the church to fall back on, were later to adopt some of the techniques of the mission.

## *Converts of the CMS*

From association with the London Missionary Society in south Travancore, converts could obtain protection, education, economic advantage and membership in a community which claimed for itself 'respectable' status in society. Caste Hindus might scoff at such a claim, but European missionaries were willing to accord devout low-caste converts considerable respect.

In the area north of Quilon, however, where the Church Missionary Society was established, the situation was different. The CMS did not begin to proselytise among Hindus until about 1840 after its final break with the Jacobites. The CMS retained a few thousand Syrian followers, and they appropriated for themselves many of the advantages of the mission, while denying equal status to low-caste converts. In the 1860s and 1870s, against the advice of missionaries like Joseph Peet (d. 1865) and Henry Baker, Sr. (d. 1867), the CMS accepted thousands of Pulaya converts. 'These', Baker forecast with great accuracy, 'will continue a separate class for generations to come'. Baker argued that the CMS should cultivate its Syrian congregations, for the respected position of Syrians in Hindu society 'removes an objection commonly made to X'nty [Christianity] among the higher classes'.[126] Through Syrians, Nairs and Brahmins might be won. But the emancipated slaves were easy converts for younger, less calculating missionaries. By 1880, the CMS had 16,000 adherents, more than half of whom were Pulayas. About a quarter were Syrians. The rest were Ezhavas and other low castes; a very few were Nairs and Tamil Brahmins.[127]

Pulaya converts were excluded from the churches of CMS Syrians in almost every area. When a European bishop tried to bring them into a Syrian church in 1893, 'the Syrians all bolted out of the church through the windows'.[128] Prior to 1887, Syrians provided all the clergymen and most of the teachers in CMS pastorates and schools. Few other CMS adherents managed to find a place in CMS College, Kottayam. Pulayas constituted virtually a separate church.[129]

Ezhava converts fared only a little better. They were generally permitted to sit in the same church with the Syrians and to use the same schools, but Syrians would not inter-dine or inter-marry. For their part, Ezhava converts would have nothing to do with Pulaya Christians and towards them bore themselves 'as men of the superior caste'.[130] After the influx of Pulayas in the late 1860s, few Ezhavas were converted.[131] It was 1887, moreover, before an Ezhava convert was ordained as a CMS cleric, and he was a third-generation Christian whose background was kept as secret as possible. He had, in effect, become a Syrian, but it had taken three generations.[132]

Because most of the advantages and assets of membership in the Anglican Church were reserved for Syrians, and because Syrians were unwilling to accept converts as equals, the material attractions of conversion were drastically reduced. At the same time, the fact that more than half the church membership was composed of Pulaya converts was a serious deterrent to the conversion of higher castes, who might otherwise have sought the benefits of mission protection. For Ezhavas in the 1870s and 1880s, conversion did not hold the promise of elevation to the status of Syrian Christians, and may, on the contrary, have carried the threat of debasement to the level of Pulayas. The possibility of conversion, however, was to remain a useful lever against the high castes. Meanwhile, missionary activities--in 1887 for instance the CMS started the Travancore Christian Family Provident Fund for its members[133]--offered helpful examples of what organisation could achieve.

### *Ezhavas*

Compared to Shanars, few Ezhavas converted to Christianity,[134] and to discuss Ezhavas in conjunction with missionaries implies a debt to European evangelism which perhaps few Ezhavas today would be prepared to acknowledge. However, in the 1870s and 1880s, as their economic position improved with the increased demand for cocoanut produce and the increased profitability of their traditional occupations, Ezhavas associated with Christian evangelists, used their schools and observed their techniques. Ezhavas stopped short of conversion to Christianity, but they were to use the threat of conversion for forty years, until the Temple Entry Proclamation of 1936, to try to extract recognition of enhanced status from high-caste

Hindus. 'Government', petitioned the Ezhava doctor, P. Palpu, in 1895, '...is showing the converts the encouragement they deserve. But to the Tiyas [Ezhavas] that remain within the pale of Hinduism, a Hindu Government [will] not extend the same consideration'.[135]

Let us look first at the economic improvement which many Ezhavas experienced in the 1870s and 1880s, and then at the disabilities which they sought to overcome and which in turn led them to a flirtation with the missionaries.

The traditional occupation of Ezhavas was the tapping and tending of the cocoanut palm. Between 1870 and 1890, the value of exports of cocoanut products from Travancore more than doubled.[136] Exports of coir, the rot-resistant fibre of the cocoanut husk, used for making ropes and mats, rose from Rs. 9.27 lakhs in 1871 to Rs. 26.22 lakhs in 1891. Exports of copra, the dried kernel of the cocoanut, increased from Rs. 21.06 lakhs to Rs. 42.37 lakhs in the same period.[137] (See Graph 2).

It would be foolish to suggest that all the proceeds of this trade, which by 1891 amounted to about 60 lakhs of rupees, were finding their way to the Ezhava labourers who collected the raw materials. Merchants from Europe, America and other parts of India, handled the exporting in Alleppey and Cochin, while Nair, Syrian or Nambudiri landholders generally owned the trees. Yet the trade could not be conducted without Ezhavas. Their expertise was essential; in caring for the cocoanut palm, they enjoyed what might be called a closed shop. The production of coir was an unpleasant, semi-skilled, labour-intensive task. The cocoanut husk had to be soaked in the backwaters, then the fibre separated from the rotted pulp and finally spun into yarn. Between 1881 and 1890, the value of coir exports went from Rs. 12.55 lakhs to Rs. 24.55 lakhs as a result of 'the increasing demand for this article in America'.[138] In an expanding market for coir, Ezhavas would at least have found full employment for men as well as women, while the traditional aim of poor Ezhavas–to own or rent a few palm trees–had the advantage not only of status but of increasing profit. By the turn of the century a few Ezhavas owned coir factories, while Ezhava women who collected and sold cocoanut shells for fuel were said to earn more than enough to feed their families.[139] Ezhavas' classic occupation was, in short, an economic asset. This was different from the cases of other low castes, such as potters or blacksmiths, to whom the greater availability of manufactured goods in the late nineteenth century was injurious.

# Graph 2

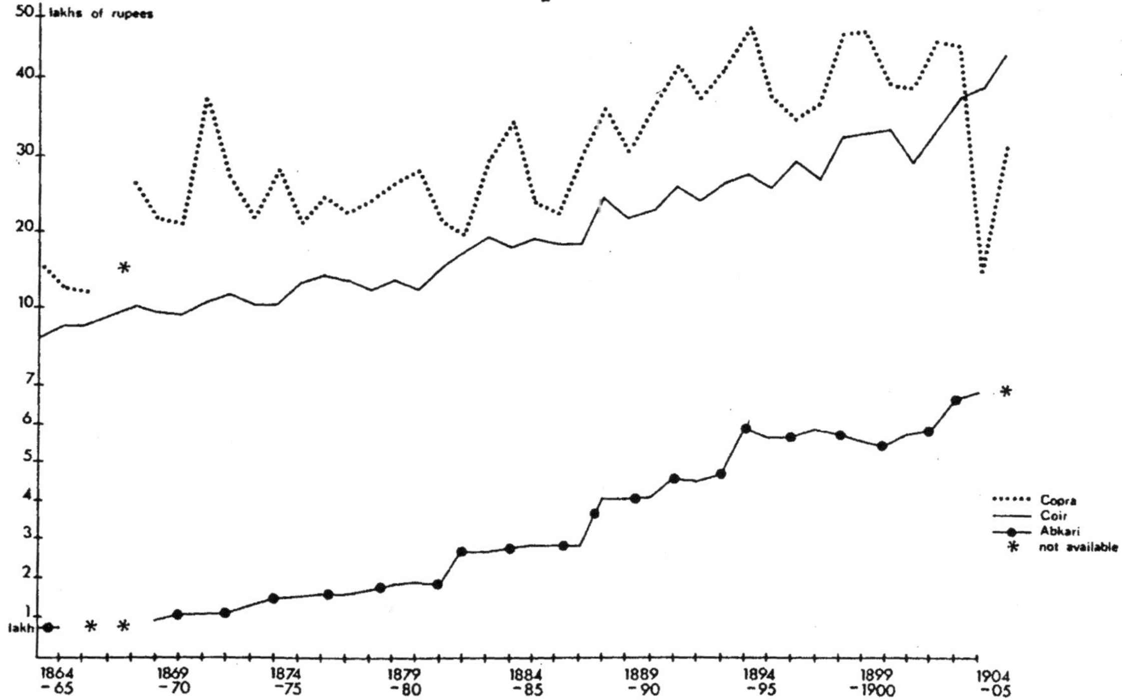


Value of Travancore copra and coir exports and abkari revenue, 1865-1905, in lakhs of rupees.

Source: Travancore Administration Reports.

Another aspect of Ezhavas' traditional vocation was embarrassing yet profitable. This was the toddy and arrack trade which more than doubled between 1860 and 1880.[140] The sirkar regularly auctioned licences to sell intoxicants, and these were usually bought by rich Tinnevelly Shanars, Syrians, Eurasians and occasionally Europeans.[141] But the actual vendors were mainly Ezhavas,[142] and the men who tapped the palm and made the intoxicants in areas from Trivandrum north were exclusively Ezhavas. When the LMS made an Ezhava convert in 1874, the missionary praised the man's devotion, for he had given up 'the profitable employment which specially belongs to his caste, viz. the distillation and sale of ardent spirits...'[143] To the despair of the legal abkari contractors, Ezhavas were able to run illicit and remunerative businesses. In 1889, a Trivandrum contractor complained, probably extravagantly, to have lost Rs. 1.5 lakhs in two years because

> ...the large Elava population that live solely upon liquor trade contrives various means of carrying on the trade without the contractor's knowledge. They distil at night and deposit underground or transmit to their customers... Even though great efforts are put forth, only one fourth of the liquor that is now consumed belongs to the contractors.[144]

Occasionally illegal toddy vendors were apprehended, but generally Ezhavas seem to have been able to pursue the profitable if shady business with only minor interruptions.[145]

Ezhavas also worked as carpenters, masons, coolies and farm labourers. They had a tradition as weavers, and some Ezhavas opened small handloom factories towards the end of the century.[146] As ayurvedic doctors, they enjoyed a high reputation throughout Travancore, and at the founding meeting of the Sri Narayana Dharma Paripalana Yogam in 1902, sixteen of the sixty people present were ayurvedists.[147] Such occupations as these put money into Ezhava hands, and money brought social ambitions.

As early as 1884, British governments were receiving petitions from Travancore Ezhavas which complained at the disabilities enforced against them:

> The Chogans [Ezhavas] and other low caste people are not allowed to come near any public office whether it be of the 1st Class District Magistrate or [the lowest]

> of the tax collectors. They are put to the greatest inconvenience whenever they use any of the public roads, inasmuch as they have to move a considerable distance away from high caste men whom they meet on the roads. They have, in speaking to people of higher castes, to use certain technical expressions, which if they do not, they are taken to task for it. There are many Chogans [Ezhavas] in the state but not a single one of them has ever had a situation under government.[148]

In 1870, the Resident wrote:

> There can be no doubt that the spirit which prevented Elavars from keeping milch cows; from using oil mills, metal vessels and umbrellas; from wearing shoes and any but coarse cloths and ornaments, is still alive and active in many parts of the country... [149]

Ezhavas were increasingly resentful of such discrimination and increasingly able to challenge it.

In 1865, P.T. Palpu, an Ezhava of the Trivandrum suburb of Pettah, encouraged by the sirkar's emphasis on academic attainments, applied to write for the first Travancore pleaders' examination. His application fee was accepted, but when it was noted that he was an Ezhava he was refused permission to appear for the examination. His fee was never refunded.[150] Palpu, whose family had been carpenters, had acquired a general knowledge of English from Christian converts and European missionaries who had visited his house, and indeed one branch of the family was converted to Christianity.[151] The difficulties which two of Palpu's sons, P. Velayudhan and P. Palpu, encountered in trying to get an English education illustrate the conflict between Ezhava ambition and sirkar conservatism in Travancore after Madhava Rao.

Although the government was conducting an expanding education programme, its schools in 1870 remained firmly closed to the state's 383,000 Ezhavas. Ballard, the Resident, wrote that 'a boy professing Christianity would probably be admitted' to the High School in Trivandrum, that a Shanar from the Madras Presidency 'would pass if at all discreet as a "Pandy"', but that 'an Elavan or Chogan would hardly effect an entrance, and if he did so would probably find the position too uncomfortable to maintain for long'. In the outlying towns an Ezhava could not 'even theoretically' be admitted to government schools, but if converted to Christianity, 'with ordinary discretion on the part of the converts the point would not generally be raised against them'.[152]

P. Velayudhan, the eldest of P.T. Palpu's sons, became the first Ezhava admitted to the Maharaja's College and High School about 1874. His enrolment was an act of some daring, both on the part of Velayudhan and of John Ross, the Scottish principal. The younger Palpu, having studied under the local *asan,* began at the age of twelve to take English tuition from a Eurasian. Eventually he was able to attend the Maharaja's High School; he matriculated in 1883.[153] In the previous year, Velayudhan had graduated from the College and applied for government employment. His application was rejected, and he entered the British service in the Madras Presidency where he rose to be a deputy collector and was granted the title 'Rao Bahadur'.[154]

P. Palpu wrote the entrance examination for the Travancore medical class, passed second and was refused admission because he was an Ezhava. In 1885 he went to Madras and 'having managed partly by borrowing and partly by subscription to make up a sum of Rs. 140', enrolled in the Madras Medical College. He was awarded an honour certificate for the first year's work, but in 1885, deep in debt, he petitioned Madhava Rao for help:

> Your Honour need not be told that the 'Ilavers' of Travancore are considered so low a caste of people that they are not allowed at all to hold any post in that Government and the incentive to education being thus denied them, they are a very backward class. The Petr., however, without remaining in the state in which his caste-men are, made up his mind to study the English language... [155]

Madhava Rao, living in comfortable and adulated retirement in Mylapore, Madras, sent a cheque for Rs. 50 and arranged for Palpu's petition to be sent to Ramiengar, the Travancore Dewan and Madhava Rao's old friend. The sirkar, however, had to be careful: a scholarship would have led Palpu to expect a government post after completing his course, and the sirkar had no intention of making such an offer. Instead, the Maharaja sent a donation of Rs. 50 which was repeated after Palpu twice petitioned for it the following year.[156] He was awarded the Licentiate in Medicine and Surgery (LM&S) degree in 1889, applied and was rejected for a post in the Travancore Medical Department, worked for a time in Madras and in 1891 entered the service of another princely state, Mysore. From Bangalore, for the next thirty years he was to promote Ezhava causes.

As we have seen, Palpu's father learned English from the missionaries and one branch of the family converted to Christianity. This association with the missionaries seems to have been fairly typical among aspiring Ezhavas. In 1872 Rev. Samuel Mateer opened a school near Anjengo for fifty 'highly respectable' Ezhava boys who 'were refused admission to the Sircar School at Sherankil...'[157] Mateer received more requests for mission schools than he was able to meet, and noted with regret that 'the very interesting Ilavar people' north of Trivandrum 'who were willing to receive instruction' have not been sufficiently impressed to join us outright...'[158] The story in the CMS area of north Travancore was similar. Ezhavas met the missionaries or their evangelists, accepted Bibles and asked for schoolmasters.[159] Where government schools were closed to them, Ezhavas sought admission to CMS institutions. But there was one major difference from the situation around Trivandrum. Syrian Christians kept the low castes at a distance and were reluctant to associate with Ezhavas. Ezhavas, on the other hand, would not attend the CMS schools maintained for Pulayas. This led Ezhavas to ask the missionaries to provide masters for separate Ezhava schools. Although such requests held out the prospect of conversions, the missionaries were generally short of teachers and were growingly aware of Ezhavas' reluctance to become Christians.

Yet why were Ezhavas reluctant when Shanars, whose position in south Travancore appeared comparable, were converted in large numbers? Throughout the 1870s and 1880s Ezhava pretensions, assertiveness and frustrations were growing; missionaries offered education and in some cases protection. Converts 'have their Missionary to press their claims on government and get them some consideration', a letter writer to the *Madras Mail* pointed out; Ezhavas had no one.[160] By 1890, however, Mateer could write that 'Iravas do not largely join us now...', and that the Ezhavas near Anjengo, for whom he had opened the school in 1872, 'hate Christian teaching'.[161]

The matrilineal system partially followed by Ezhavas had much to do with the paucity of converts. As we have seen, in northern Travancore Ezhavas were pure marumakkattayis; in the south, half a man's property went to his children and half to his sister's sons. If an Ezhava converted to Christianity, he took with him only what he could prove were his self-acquired property and possessions; all else belonged to his family. Even if the senior male of an Ezhava family in north Travancore was converted, the position was the same; although he was the administrator of the family property, he did not own it. At the same time, the matrilineal system provided a loose, flexible marriage tie, or, as the missionaries thought, no marriage at all. 'Hence we require', wrote Mateer, 'Iravas who embrace Christianity to marry in due form the women with whom they are living...'[162] This was an irksome condition, but one on which the missionaries would not compromise.

On the question of inheritance, they pressed the sirkar for an act entitling marumakkattayam converts to a share of their family property. A court decision of 1885, which we shall return to later, had ruled that converts had no inheritance rights at all, and various appeals by the missionaries brought no change in the law.[163] While this difficulty of property and inheritance deterred prosperous Ezhavas from conversion, the rigorous missionary view of marriage discouraged the poor and self-seeking. Moreover, as Ezhavas increased in prosperity, they were able to imitate cautiously the manners of Nairs. A respected place in Hindu society was a far more desirable goal than a doubtful Christian role between contemptuous Syrians and polluting Pulaya converts. As the Rev. Jacob Chandy, Sr. lamented in the 1850s, Ezhavas 'could not see any spiritual motive for embracing Christianity; rising in caste and freedom from the opposition of the high castes were all that [they] cared for'. What did Ezhavas ask of Christianity? Chandy answered: to 'be raised to the position of Syrians in the country'.[164]

Ezhava aspirations within Hindu society, and the help derived from the missionaries, were neatly illustrated in an incident recorded by a missionary near Kottayam in 1882. He

> ...met a fine looking man. Even those with me mistook him for a Nair at first. He turned out to be a wealthy Chogan [Ezhava] who had learnt as a boy in our mission school, hence his superior ways. He...has no real love for Christ or desire to serve Him.[165]

The growing Ezhava aim, unstated, but perceptible from the 1880s, was to achieve the status of Nairs, many of whose customs also came to be Ezhava customs. Nairs, for example, generally cremated their dead. Ezhavas, largely because of the cost, cremated only the eldest member of a family and buried others.[166] After government-enforced caste restrictions were removed in the 1860s, Ezhava women began to discard their own distinctive jewellery and wear that of Nairs. Wealthy Ezhavas started to build their houses in the same style as Nairs.[167] Ezhavas and Nairs had common rights over a few temples.[168] '...The Iruvers', wrote Samuel Mateer, 'seem to have adopted Nair customs'.[169] There were persistent claims that before the nineteenth century Ezhavas had been as much a military class as Nairs.[170]

At the same time, Ezhavas were discarding their old caste government in favour of a system in which wealth was more important than birth. In 1885 a hereditary Ezhava village priest, angered at not being called on to preside at the marriage of the daughters of a moderately wealthy casteman, sued for his fee of five rupees and for Rs. 500 in damage 'for loss of dignity'. The case reached the High Court which ruled that a proclamation of 1851 had removed legal recognition from hereditary caste officers who now existed only on sufferance. 'The office has under the altered state of the country become obsolete...'[171]

Between the censuses of 1875 and 1891, literacy among Ezhava men increased from 3.15 per cent to 12.1 per cent, although the number of Ezhavas in government schools remained small.[172] Their association with the missionaries and their improving economic position allowed increasing numbers of Ezhava children to get a basic education. The outcome was predictable. In 1891, Palpu and Velayudhan, Travancore's only Ezhava graduates, associated themselves with the Malayali Memorial, as we shall see in the next chapter. Into it was written a demand for the admission of Ezhavas to the sirkar service. The demand was rejected, but it marked the beginning of a campaign conducted by Palpu in the 1890s to win Ezhavas admission to sirkar schools and the government service. It was 1908 before an Ezhava graduate was granted a minor judicial post. By that time their successful economic activities were causing alarm among Nairs.

*NAIRS*

When Madhava Rao left Travancore in 1872, Nairs held a place of dominance which appeared both comfortable and secure. Amounting to 20 per cent of the population, they held much of the land and 60 per cent of the 14,700 jobs in the government service.[173] More than 20 per cent of the men were literate, and they were responding enthusiastically to the sirkar's educational programme. Yet Madhava Rao noted two areas of inadequacy and potential dissatisfaction. He pointed, as we have already seen, to the 'great paucity of Nairs on the benches of the higher Courts', and on another occasion, though warning of the dangers of over-legislation, concluded that

> ...it has to be declared lawful for any member of a Malayali (native) family to insist upon a division of common property so far as he or she is individually concerned, if he or she wishes to separate. Not that such a law would be generally acted upon at once. The feeling in favour of relatives living together in an undivided state of property is too strong to yield to reason in the present generation. But it is obviously the province of government to see that a general feeling of the kind does not operate as an instrument of tyranny over individuals.[174]

Questions of the taravad and of patronage in the higher echelons of the government service were to preoccupy Nairs for the next sixty years.

In the costly sphere of college education, Nairs led all other Malayalis, but could not compete with non-Malayali Brahmins. By 1891, the Maharaja's College had turned out 232 Bachelors of Arts; sixty-seven were Nairs, but one hundred twelve were non-Malayali Brahmins.[175] These proportions were reflected in the sirkar service, where, out of one hundred twenty-nine graduates, sixty-two were non-Malayali Brahmins and thirty-six Nairs.[176]

Nairs were to argue that the dominance of non-Malayali Brahmins in the government kept Nairs from their just share of patronage and discouraged them from taking degrees. Among themselves, they dewelt on the cost of higher education and the question of who was to pay: the father of the child or the child's taravad.

Madhava Rao, as we have seen, intended to give a spur to his education system by making academic qualifications necessary for sirkar employment, even in the lower grades. Nairs quickly read his message and sent their dependents to school. There were nearly 50,000 Nair children in government or grant-in-aid schools by the 1890s.[177] If there were 30,000 Nair taravads in Travancore, nearly all had at least one member studying in a government-inspected school.[178] The question of education concerned virtually every taravad, and usually meant increased costs and changed attitudes.

What did students learn in these government-supervised vernacular schools? At the lowest level was the unaided vernacular primary school, the traditional village school, but now occasionally visited by the local school inspector. From such institutions, though they accounted for a third of the total enrolment, 'the regeneration of the masses' was not to be expected.[179] This was realistic if we are to judge by the first school to which Mannath Padmanabha Pillai (Mannam) was appointed as a teacher in the 1890s. The school had two classes, two broken-down benches, a blackboard, a wornout cane chair and a wobbly table. Though there were twenty boys on the register, only five or eight ever attended; the first teacher, a Syrian Christian named Thomas, had no hesitation in marking all twenty present each day. Thomas himself would spend Wednesday and Thursday sleeping, and Friday at noon would sign a leave form and proceed to his village whence he would return about noon the following Tuesday. If an inspector came in the meantime, Mannam had instructions to report that the first teacher was on leave.[180]

In aided schools, however, a certain set of books was prescribed and in theory at least, a rough syllabus was followed. By 1869 textbooks in vernacular schools included *Moral and Social Duties*, *Moral Maxims*, *Treatise on Health* (by Vishakham Tirunal), *Truthful Evidence*, the first book of Euclid, Duncan's *Geography of India* and *Easy Lessons on Money Matters*. Later, histories of Travancore, England and India, and Blackie's *Self-Culture* were added.[181] At the level of the district English schools and the Maharaja's High School and College, leading figures like Vishakham Tirunal urged students to read Ruskin, Kinglake, Carlyle and Samuel Smiles.[182] It is reasonable to suggest that such studies helped to propagate an individualism which was incompatible with the 'communality' of the old taravad. One may speculate, for example, on the effect *Easy Lessons on Money Matters*, which was in Malayalam from the 1860s, may have had on youths from a taravad in which money was only handled by a thrifty, self-seeking karanavan. Similarly, *Self Help* was probably the wrong reading for a man whose self-acquired property could descend only to his nephews and remoter relatives in the matrilineal joint-family.

The new education system also promoted mobility and independence. If a boy was to obtain the required qualifications for a job in the sirkar service, he often had to leave his village school and travel to the nearest town. If he wished to matriculate–and about three hundred Travancore Nairs had done so by 1890[183]–he had to enrol in CMS College, Kottayam, the Nagercoil Seminary or the Maharaja's High School, Trivandrum. In travelling to and from school, in living in a town and in eating meals away from the taravad house, Nair youths experienced new influences. In the upper schools there were team sports, debating clubs and dramatic societies, sometimes with officers elected from among the boys. Students were exposed to teachers of different castes, to European missionaries, and even to a 'a clever Cambridge atheist', H.N. Read, the Scottish science professor and later principal of the Maharaja's College.[184]

Students could not avoid hearing open attacks on Nair marriage and morals. Augusta M. Blandford, who spent forty years evangelising among Nairs around Trivandrum and whose Fort Girls' School produced the first Nair woman matriculate, described 'the customs of their caste with regard to marriage' as 'very revolting'. Rev. A.F. Painter, who moved freely among Nairs in north Travancore for more than twenty years, wrote of 'a system so horrible that even its defenders are ashamed of it as it stands'.[185] What was worse for Nairs, however, were the jibes of other Hindus. Nagam Aiya in his 1875 census report felt obliged to make a brief apology for 'the looseness of the prevailing morals and the unbinding nature of the marriage tie which possesses such fascinations for the majority of our population'.[186]

Growing numbers of Nairs were coming to agree with the Tamil Brahmin. In pre-British days, as we have seen, polyandry was practised among Nairs, and either the man or woman could end a liaison virtually at will. Nambudiris, Pottis, Kshatriyas and non-Malayali Brahmins were also permitted to enjoy Nair women.[187] Yet, by 1875 the Rev. Henry Baker, Jr. suggested that 'in many respectable families' there was not 'that state of profligacy the want of a *legal* marriage tie would imply'. Baker knew of Nair couples who had been faithful to each other for seventeen years.[188] Perhaps in imitation of Smartha Brahmins, sambandham between first cousins was said to be the ideal among many Nair families.[189] However, even if such examples of lasting marriages were the rule, there were enough examples of the old laxity to embarrass educated Nairs.[190] Newspapers inveighed against the repudiation of wives by their husbands and husbands by their wives, which was 'so reprehensibly practised among Sudras'.[191] Missionaries like Samuel Mateer were ready to give a twist to the knife or a stir to the pot. Mateer gave wide circulation to the charge that within the taravad incest was common. By 1891 he was proclaiming that 'educated Nairs', were 'ashamed of the absence of real marriage' and that 'the publicity...and the ridicule' being given to their customs 'naturally mortify them'.[192]

Education affected Nair attitudes, but it also affected the taravad economically. Few taravads were so wealthy that they could afford school fees for half a dozen or more boys. The question of which boys were to be educated created dissension in the taravad and forced fathers to make alternative arrangements for their sons. It is a well-known fact, a leading Nair wrote, 'that most Malayalis, whose karanavans are distant kinsmen, owe their education to their fathers'.[193] But such fathers obviously had taravads and nephews of their own who should have had first call on their affections and resources. '...The old, ignorant, self-willed karanavans educate only their direct nephews and bring up their distant Anandaravers as agriculturalists or as servant boys in the tarawad house', wrote O. Chandu Menon in his preface to *Indulekha* in 1889. In the novel itself, the hero laments the parsimony of his karanavan towards a young cousin: '...he has no idea about that small boy Shinnan, except to bring him up like a bull calf, but I will never consent to this. I will take him away myself and have him educated'.[194] The speech indicated the dissatisfaction of a generation of Nairs with the taravad system. Although Nairs, even as youths, wanted education,[195] the taravad was often unable or unwilling to provide the cost. And if it did pay, it was generally after arguments and intrigues over which boys were to benefit.

The taravad was increasingly unable to bear financial strains. The largest of the joint-families might profit from the rise in the value of their surplus rice, but this could also mean more spoils to fight over, more dissension within. For the smaller landholding taravads--and Travancore was an area of moderate-sized holdings, as we have seen--the abolition of slavery, and the rising cost of labour and rice, were calculated to strain resources. Moreover, members of the taravad showed a growing concern for their own, rather than the joint-family's, interests.

Madhava Rao's Pattam Proclamation of 1865, which gave ownership rights to tenants on 200,000 acres of sirkar pattam land, helped to accelerate the decay of the taravad. In the year after the Pattam Proclamation, litigation in munsiff's courts rose from 9,804 cases to 18,441, as people attempted to realise the new value of land.[196] Still more striking, and directly concerning Nairs, were the suits for the partition of taravad property. In the five years after the proclamation, these totalled 284.[197] For dissatisfied members of taravads, the proclamation made partition more desirable. The joint-family could now sell its holdings of sirkar pattam land, and the share of each member would be enhanced thereby. However, after repeated court decisions refusing to grant partition–in accordance with the 'well established rule that division cannot take place unless all those who would be entitled to a share agree to it'[198]–suits in the second quinquennium following the proclamation fell to only twenty-eight.[199] However, in the 1880s, as the stresses within the joint-family grew and were accompained by economic pressures, suits for partition again increased. Between 1881 and 1891, they numbered 660.[200] The cases which reached the courts–especially since the courts were widely known to be unreceptive to the partition plea–represented only a tiny fraction of the discontent within the taravad.

This tension and economic pressure, however, were mitigated in the 1880s by Nairs' continued numerical dominance of the sirkar service. By 1881 their share of jobs in the expanding government service had increased to more than 65 per cent,[201] and a large proportion of taravads had at least one member working for the sirkar. To be sure, most Nairs were in jobs worth less than Rs. 10 a month, but with the average cost of living at about Rs. 30 a year, such positions were a vital asset to taravads increasingly unable to live solely from their land. Moreover, control of the lower levels of the government service allowed Nairs to enforce their caste privileges. In 1890 the Resident wrote that, contrary to orders, 'in the inferior courts low caste people are frequently kept at a considerable distance from the Judge--questions and answers being passed down a line of constables or peons'.[202] Similarly, Ezhavas were kept out of most government schools, and advertisements for sirkar jobs carried the warning that 'the social position of candidates should be such as not to interfere with their general usefulness...'[203] Nairs came to regard control of the sirkar service as an economic and social necessity and to object increasingly to the preponderance of non-Malayali Brahmins at its higher levels.

By the mid-1880s two problems troubled educated Nairs in Travancore. The first was the decay of the taravad: the dissension within it, the ridicule it provoked, the mismanagement to which it was prone. The second problem was the hold of non-Malayali Brahmins on the most powerful positions in the sirkar service. Having eschewed trade and the plantation business, Nairs more than ever needed to find extensive employment in the government. Yet they saw their way to the top being blocked.[204] College-educated Nairs came to view reform of the matrilineal system as something which could be effected only after Nairs had regained supremacy in the highest positions under government. In the 1880s they formed the Malayali Sabha. Its original purpose was to promote education and work for modest social reform. But it soon became involved in the agitation over preferment in the government service which is the subject of the next chapter.

In June 1889 a committee of officials recommended the virtual abolition of *viruthi* tenure. This dated from the eighteenth century and provided for land to be held on favourable terms in exchange for the supply to the sirkar at fixed prices of various foods, handicrafts and services. Why was *viruthi* now obsolete? The committee wrote:

> In bygone days, owing to the undeveloped state of inland trade and the absence of roads and other facilities for communication, the government had to devise means for drawing supplies... But the times have completely changed. Provisions of all sorts and qualities could [sic] be commanded now, to any extent and at a given notice from the markets or centres of trade... [205]

The demise of the *viruthi* tenure summed up the changes of the 1870s and 1880s. Where communication had been difficult, it was now relatively easy. Where trade had been rare, it now flourished. Where Travancore had once been a rice exporter, it now imported rice in large quantities, both as a result of growing population and of the increased ability of low-caste people to afford rice. They could afford rice because wages had increased faster than the cost of living. Yet it was more than that: wages had become available to thousands of men and women whose ancestors had been debased sub-tenants and labourers, who were paid in kind and lived at a level of bare subsistence. This is not to say that all of them suddenly blossomed into dazzzling prosperity. Indeed, the large majority remained poor. But it was a poverty with alternatives. A low-caste man could become rich; poverty no longer had to be the concommitant of low ritual status. To eat rice was in one sense an affirmation of an improved standing.[206] So too was the desire for education. The western-style education which was increasingly propagated, and demanded, in Travancore tended to devalue ritual sanctity, to substitute achieved for inherited status: the new 'Brahmin', the argument could run, ought to be the Master of Arts graduate, regardless of the caste or religion of his birth. And where ought such a man to be? In the higher reaches of the government service, where, as government increasingly interfered in the lives of the people, real power was seen to lie.

Different groups had characteristics which helped or hobbled them in the new race. Non-Malayali Brahmins, with their influence in the government service and the palace and their interest in trade, were well able to look after themselves. Syrian Christians--landholders, traders for generations, respected by caste Hindus, befriended by European missionaries and planters--found positive advantages in the new conditions. So too did low-caste

Christian converts and Ezhavas though they had still to contend against formidable prejudices and poverty. Yet Nairs, who held by far the largest share of government jobs and were the best educated of Malayalis, were to lead the first agitation about preferment in the government service. This was understandable, for the issue was basically the predominance of non-Malayali Brahmins in the higher grades; Nair officials saw their way blocked. Yet the Malayali Memorial, which is the subject of the next chapter, showed symptoms of other problems common to many Nairs: the growing economic difficulties of the taravad, and distress and embarrassment over traditional marriage customs. The taravad, too, offered no incentive or capital for Nair youths to attempt trade or planting. 'A Nair has at present hardly any motive to exert himself', William Logan wrote of Malabar in 1881, 'because the fruits of his labours ... pass to persons with whom he has little sympathy'. Such a situation 'is fatal to individual industry and thrift, ... the consequences to the ruling caste will be disastrous'.[207] Among college-educated Nairs in Travancore the feeling grew that they must first recapture the control of the government which they believed they had enjoyed in pre-British times. That done, the problems of the taravad could be remedied. The Malayali Sabha, founded in 1885 to work for social reform, was soon near the centre of a campaign to curtail the influence of non-Malayali Brahmins in the sirkar service.

# 5

# *The Malayali Sabha and the Malayali Memorial: Out of Change, Conflict, 1886-89*

Between non-Malayali Brahmins and Nairs there was an incipient rancour. In fields such as education, where they had traditionally led, Brahmins were confident that they could not be overtaken. One declared, it was said, that he would cut off his moustache if a Nair ever passed the Master of Arts examination of the Madras University.[1] For a Desastha Brahmin, the removal of his moustache would have been an emotional and humiliating gesture. The enthusiasm of Nairs for education, however, could not long be denied. In 1880, the 26-year-old P. Thanu Pillai, who was teacher in the Maharaja's College in the 1870s, and in 1879 was promoted to be manager of the Dewan's office by the Nair Dewan, N. Nanu Pillai,[2] became the first Malayali to take an M.A. Over the next twenty years, until his death in 1902, Thanu Pillai was the leading Nair official and 'an enlightened, safe and trusted leader of the Nair community of Travancore...'[3]

Although he seldom appeared at the head of delegations or in the chair at public meetings, his influence on more active Nair public figures was considerable. It stemmed from his time as a teacher in the college. He was said to have been the idol of his students, many of whom were only a few years younger than he, and around him in the 1870s grew up a cultural association called the Malayali Social Union, which was encouraged by the two Scottish professors, John Ross and Robert Harvey.[4] The Malayali Social Union often met at Thanu Pillai's house--where the *Fortnightly* and *Contemporary Reviews* and the London *Times* were available--and among its members were a number of young Nairs who graduated between 1879 and 1881. They included P. Ayyappan Pillai, V.I. Keshava Pillai, M. Kunchukrishna Panikkar, C.V. Raman Pillai and the Nanjanad Vellala, C.M. Madhavan Pillai; all went directly into the sirkar service.[5] Members read papers on subjects like female education, marriage customs, literature and social reform.[6] At the same time, they were exposed to Thanu Pillai's suspicion, if not hostility, towards non-Malayalis in the sirkar service.[7]

However, in 1883 Thanu Pillai was transferred from Trivandrum to Quilon, and interest in the Malayali Social Union quickly flagged. It was revived by C. Krishna Pillai, who graduated in 1875 and by the 1880s was a government school inspector. As a result of Krishna Pillai's prodding, the Social Union was reincarnated about 1884 as the Malayali Sabha, 'with the object of promoting the welfare of the Malayali community, by aiding the diffusion of Western knowledge, by encouraging female education and by reforming the marriage system'.[8] Early in 1886 the Sabha began to publish a Malayalam newspaper, the *Malayali*, edited by C.V. Raman Pillai, who was to become the first, and perhaps the greatest, historical novelist in Malayalam.

Although the Sabha had a few non-Nair members and at least one of its early meetings was attended by a non-Malayali Brahmin,[9] its social aims were peculiarly Nair. The emphasis on female education and marriage reform stemmed directly from the embarrassment which educated Nairs felt at the jibes of both Christians and Brahmins. A Christian newspaper, for example, used the following letter, said to be from a Nair girl:

> ['Keralam maid'] informs the Editor that a Brahmin has tied on her 'Tali' [sic] (marriage badge) and taken his departure, and she now requires someone to look after her. What is she to do? Is she to remain single with the badge of marriage round her neck. Or is she to be the lady of all who make her a present? If she happens to have children on whom are they to be fathered? Her elder sister has ten children, and 'the maid' herself has

> twice that number of brothers and cousins, but she has never yet heard of their having a male parent.
>
> 'The maid' is indignant that women should be compelled to play the harlot, and go about with bosoms bare to catch a lover as a fish is caught with bait.[10]

Leading members of the Sabha saw it as a mediator between the small educated Nair elite and the large majority of conservative landholders. There was no reason, Krishna Pillai wrote in 1885, for the Sabha to be careless of the reasonable interests of the janmis. The Sabha should not offend the conservative rural folk, but should rather coax and lead them to accept new ideas and change disreputable customs.[11]

At first, the Sabha enjoyed official approval and some success. 'It had succeeded', wrote the *Travancore Times* in 1885, 'in rousing the Malayalees from the state of torpor and lethargy in which they have hitherto been sunk, and they have woken to a sense of their own wants and weaknesses as compared with other castes of Hindus'. Among its achievements, it had helped students at the Maharaja's College and the Civil Engineering College, Madras, patronised a few vernacular schools, and founded an industrial school. Most of the credit belonged to Krishna Pillai. 'Let him withdraw from the Sabha now', wrote the *Travancore Times*, 'and it will come to a standstill at once'.[12] The Maharaja was persuaded to allow his name to be used as the Sabha's patron, and other members of the ruling family became vice-patrons.[13] Initially, it took great care not to offend the government. The *Malayali*, wrote the *Travancore Times*, 'seems intent upon criticising no official injustice inasmuch as the organ would secure a loss in the number of subscribers, especially the officials...'[14] So influential was the Sabha among Nair officials that it was able--to the Resident's dismay--to hold a meeting in Alwaye in the unoccupied Residency.[15] By early 1887 the Sabha was said to have nine hundred members, twenty-five schools, fourteen branches, and a trading company which was earning Rs. 5,000 a year.[16]

However, the Sabha's apparently happy relationship with the sirkar and the royal family was not to last. In 1887 the Maharaja, his Brahmin favourite and the Brahmin element in the sirkar service began to come under bitter attack in a Madras newspaper, the *Standard*, and as a result, members of the Sabha came under suspicion. The instigator of these attacks was G. Parameswaran Pillai, a Trivandrum Nair, who had been expelled from the Maharaja's College and forced to flee Travancore in 1882 for publishing anonymous articles, critical of Brahmin influence, in the *Cochin Argus*. Parameswaran Pillai graduated from Presidency College in 1888 at the age of twenty-four. Throughout his college career, he was said to have contributed to Madras newspapers, and even after he became a translator in the Madras High Court, he wrote anonymously in the *Standard*, often under the pseudonym, 'A Lover of His Country'.[17]

In August 1887 Nair government servants who were members of the Malayali Sabha began to complain of harassment by their Brahmin superiors, and the *Standard* opened its scathing, and occasionally scurrilous, campaign against the Maharaja, the Dewan and non-Malayali Brahmin officials. Who fired the first shot is now impossible to say, but the armies were already drawn up in battle order.[18] On 15 August the *Standard* attacked the Maharaja and Rama Rao, both of whom, it claimed, were completely under the influence of Saravanai, the palace favourite, 'an illiterate menial of notorious character'.[19]

Parameswaran Pillai's attacks were well-informed, and he did not hesitate to refer to the Malayali Sabha in his arguments. Many of its members had of course been his school fellows. The announcement that Lord Connemara, the governor of Madras, would visit Travancore intensified the controversy. The *Standrard* wrote that many leading Malayalis wanted to petition the governor, but were afraid to do so.

> Among the educated portion of the Sudra population, there is also some discontent; and the Malayalee Sabha, an organisation...for the advancement of Sudra interests, are desirous of having an interview with the Governor... Their main grievances are that the Sudra landed gentry are in great measure the mainstay of the wealth of the country, yet they are excluded from their legitimate share in the Government.[20]

The real question, wrote 'A Lover of His Country' was jobs:

> ...to serve the royal man as his menial ..., Malayalis alone are wanted and Malayalis alone could be found. But to enjoy the comforts of the country, to fill all the higher appointments in the State, to obtain the highest honours of the land, to deserve all gifts, donations and rewards, foreign Brahmins alone are wanted and Brahmins alone are sought.[21]

In late September, or early October, Parameswaran Pillai published a pamphlet, 'An Open Letter to Lord Connemara', under the pseudonym of 'Pro Patria'. In it he attacked the Maharaja, the Resident and the Travancore chief secretary, a Eurasian, as well as Brahmin influence and the harassment of members of the Malayali Sabha.[22] At about the same time, the *Standard* charged Saravanai with arranging women for the Maharaja's pleasure; one was said to have been the young wife of an official who was also a member of the Malayali Sabha. When he learned of it, the husband immediately 'put his wife away'.[23]

The gesture of the cuckolded husband was intended to indicate that educated Nairs were as strictly and conventionally moral as other educated high-caste Victorian Hindus. It vividly illustrated, too, the anxiety, despair and resentment which were the ingredients of the agitation at this stage. Educated Nairs saw themselves as traditional rulers of the country, yet events had forced them into a position subordinate to a few thousand non-Malayali Brahmins. The latter not only dominated the best jobs under government, but took advantage of the old, lax system of Nair marriage to enjoy Nair women. The father of Parameswaran Pillai himself had been a non-Malayali Brahmin.[24]

It is likely that members of the Malayali Sabha were providing Parameswaran Pillai and the *Standard* with much of their information. However, when the campaign began to take such a scurrilous tone, Sabha members in Travancore came under increasing suspicion, and the *Standard* attempted to absolve them of responsibility. When Krishna Pillai and another Sabha member were transferred to less pleasant stations. 'A Lover of His Country' objected strongly.

> The *Sabha* itself is suspected to be a political association, started with the object of bringing about the downfall of the sovereign... The *Sabha* is a purely social organisation, started for the amelioration of the condition of the people. Its object is to effect a change, if possible, in the system of marriage prevalent among Malayalis, to make it more economical, to encourage female education and technical instruction, to support poor and helpless students, and to root out old superstitions and old and useless customs prevalent in the country.[25]

The Sabha, too, played an innocuous role when Connemara came to Travancore. It presented an address which merely confessed to Malayalis' inability to 'keep pace with the march of progress, owing chiefly to a spirit of conservatism and contentment carried to a fault'.[26] Connemara, well-prepared, ironically praised it for its 'most loyal feelings towards His Highness', and later wrote that as a result of the attacks, 'I have...gone out of my way to support [the Maharaja]'. The Maharaja got the K.C.S.I. soon after.[27]

Attacks on the 'Rao-ridden' Travancore sirkar continued in the *Standard*. In some articles all non-Malayali Brahmins were indicted; in others, only 'Raos'; and in a few, only 'this particular clique of Raos'.[28] However, the examples of unjust patronage tended to include all Brahmins. The appointment of A. Sitarama Aiyar, a non-resident Brahmin, to the High Court was objected to, and cases of discrimination against Nairs and preferment of non-Malayali Brahmins were produced in abundance.[29] When Thanu Pillai was passed over for a dewan peshkarship in December, the *Standard's* outrage was boundless: '...he lacked those special qualifications which enable one to surrender his wife to the embrace of another without the least scruple. Many others have been disqualified for promotion on similar grounds...'[30]

The same issue of the *Standard*, however, carried a letter from the Sabha's secretary, C.V. Raman Pillai, which disclaimed all responsibility for the *Standard's* attacks and affirmed the staunch loyalty of Sabha members to their official superiors and the Maharaja. '...Nothing can be farther from [the Sabha's] real object and aim', wrote Raman Pillai, 'or more opposed to the deep and genuine feelings of loyalty which notably characterise the community which the Sabha represents than to sympathise with, or render any aid to, anything which would cast the least slur on the name of His Highness, its Patron and Sovereign.' Unrepentant, the *Standard*, declared that the letter had been dictated to the unfortunate Raman Pillai by Raghunatha Rao, the dewan peshkar, whose daughter was married to the Dewan's son.[31]

In Travancore itself the Sabha was experiencing difficulties, even among Nairs. Thanu Pillai, who kept very much in the background, had written earlier that in Quilon and Alleppey many important men misunderstood the Sabha's ideals, which were thought to be atheistic or political. It was these conservative, landholding Nairs whom the Malayali Sabha saw itself reforming and whom it claimed to represent. Thanu Pillai insisted that these misconceptions must be dispelled through articles in the *Malayali* which would set out the Sabha's true aims.[32] But while members of the Malayali Sabha protested their political innocence in Travancore, the *Standard* in Madras continued to attack the Dewan, the favourite and the Maharaja. The cry was taken up by Malayalam newspapers outside Travancore.[33]

The justice of some of the *Standard's* complaints was undeniable. As we have already seen, the Resident too was appalled at the influence and corruption of the royal favourite, Saravanai. Moreover, in the field of patronage, Dewans of Travancore traditionally had wide scope and large soft spots for their relatives and castemen. In 1843 the Madras government reprimanded Reddy Rao for employing two of his sons in the huzur cutcherry. Madhava Rao himself drew a similar reprimand in 1863 when it was discovered that six of his relatives, including his son-in-law and Rama Rao, were in posts worth a total of Rs. 550 a month.[34] This trend was said to have continued and Brahmin favouritism to have reached a new peak under Ramiengar.[35] Such a contention is debatable,[36] but there is no doubt that the large non-Malayali Brahmin element was at least maintained, while the number of educated, unemployed Nairs was increasing. Parameswaran Pillai, himself driven out by Ramiengar, was quick to seize on the Rama Rao administration, in which the Dewan's son was his private secretary, his brother found a post in the palace and his daugheter-in-law's uncle became a Zilla Court judge. '...When any vacancy occurs, one need only refer to the long list of Rows to choose the right person, and it is only a question between one particular Row and another'.[37]

Yet the objection, one feels, was not the principle of such oligarchic patronage but to the fact that Nairs were not the chief dispensers and beneficiaries. When Parameswaran Pillai asked rhetorically whether the golden virtues of four early Travancore heroes would ever again guide the state, all four of his examples were Nairs.[38] Moreover, the *Standard* objected not only to Rama Rao's partiality for Brahmins, but also to his friendly relations with Christians. One of his principles, complained a letter writer, was that 'Syrian Christians, as a class, are more intelligent than the natives (Malayalis and Brahmins)'. Here again was the implication that the only real Malayalis were Nairs. The town of Kottayam was referred to as 'the centre of his [Rama Rao's] beloved Syrian Christian sect', and the *Standard* objected to the fact that some mission schools were receiving larger grants-in-aid than the schools of the Malayali Sabha.[39]

Throughout 1888 and 1889 the *Standard* fulminated intermittently. 'A Lover of His Country' denounced the Maharaja as 'a weak and imbecile prince, given up to momentary pleasures, with no thought of his country's good'. The favourite, Saravanai, was said to have twice assaulted the ruler. The charges of anti-Nair bias continued. 'Padmanabha Pillai', wrote 'A Lover of His Country', when a Nair was passed over for the headship of the Salt Department, 'has committed the atrocious crime of being a Malayali, and as it is impossible for him to be born anew, he must rot in the place where he is'. In mid-1889 the *Standard* announced that Rama Rao had epilepsy, and about 1890, Parameswaran Pillai published another anonymous pamphlet, 'Travancore for the Travancoreans'. In it, he repeated the charges which had been retailed in the *Standard* and returned to the theme of past glories:

> ...held in in subjection by a class of foreigners who have not conquered them by the sword, ...who are not intellectually their superiors nor physically their betters, ...can Travancoreans never expect to rise to that personal distinction and that political influence which were the glory, the pride, the richest heritage and the brightest possession of their ancestors?[40]

Parameswaran Pillai was not alone in his view of the glories of the Nair past. P. Ayyappan Pillai, a member of the Malayali Sabha and close friend of C.V. Raman Pillai and Thanu Pillai, lectured to the Maharaja's College on 'Raja Kesava Das and His Times'. The lecture, which was published as a pamphlet in 1889, lauded the late eighteenth-century Nair Dewan as one of Travancore's greatest heroes. It also allowed the *Standard* to point out that soon after Kesava Das's death the state was brought to ruin by a young ruler who 'like the present Maharaja, was a weak and depraved Prince who was under the influence of a scheming Brahmin'.[41] C.V. Raman Pillai himself was engaged in a larger and more important piece of work, the writing of his great historical novel, *Martanda Varma*, which was published in 1891. The character of the title was Maharaja Martanda Varma, the builder of Travancore in the eighteenth century, but the real hero was Ananda Padmanabhan, a brave and faithful young Nair.[42] Nairs, the *Standard* concluded, were experiencing a 'regeneration'. It was becoming obvious that they were

> no longer contemptible enemies, and that among them were many self-denying and courageous men who were prepared to face every danger and every difficulty in order to ameliorate the condition of their downtrodden countrymen...
> No future administration will be able to ignore the Nair factor in Travancore politics...the Nairs will once more occupy an honourable position, and...their Native-land which they love so ardently, will soon regain its lost title of 'Model State'.[43]

This was heady stuff to mix with the strong and simple brew of jobs-for-the-boys.

Meanwhile, in Travancore the Malayali Sabha continued its programmes, in spite of the fact that Krishna Pillai, its chief organiser, had been transferred–as a punishment, it was said[44]–from Trivandrum to Mavelikara. C.V. Raman Pillai became secretary in Trivandrum, while Krishna Pillai was able to use his position as a travelling school inspector to propagate the ideas of the Sabha in the central and northern taluks.[45] The Maharaja could not have been completely alienated–or he hoped to lessen the

Sabha's spleen—for early in 1889 the palace sanctioned a grant of Rs. 200 to the Quilon branch of the Sabha after it had presented an address.[46]

Sabha members, however, were no happier, and in October 1889 C.V. Raman Pillai, finding, according to the *Standard*, that his job in the High Court 'obstructs his independence and usefulness to his countrymen', went to Madras to take the British pleadership examination.[47] In Madras he stayed with Parameswaran Pillai and N. Raman Pillai who was the son of N. Nanu Pillai, the former Dewan, and who had been expelled from the College with Parameswaran Pillai in 1882. He also spent time with K.P. Sankara Menon, a Madras vakil and son of the former dewan peshkar P. Shankunni Menon. Madras at that time abounded with young Nairs from Travancore, Cochin and Malabar, all studying for various examinations. On Sundays they gathered for discussions and entertainment.[48] Parameswaran Pillai himself had already met Eardley Norton, the Rugby and Merton barrister and radical who was then the darling of educated Indian opinion in Madras.[49] Out of such meetings grew the plans for the Malayali Memorial.

Authorship of the Memorial is now disputed,[50] but it seems likely that Raman Pillai took a draft with him when he returned to Travancore early in 1890. Circulation began in February, and it was claimed that by June 10,000 people had signed it. As a result of printing difficulties, however, it was not submitted to the Maharaja until January 1891.[51] In circulating the petition, members of the Malayali Sabha played the leading role. C. Krishna Pillai used his itinerating duties in northern Travancore to meet people and acquire signatures; C.V. Raman Pillai is said to have led the campaign in Trivandrum. When Parameswaran Pillai and Sankara Menon came to Trivandrum to stir up enthusiasm in December 1890, the job of collecting signatures appears to have been largely done. Raman Pillai, however, is said to have sold his wife's jewels to pay the expenses for the visit of the two Madras men.[52]

The Memorial itself was typical of the genteel petitions of the time. Parameswaran Pillai and the members of the Malayali Sabha were steeped in English political history. They found both logic and excitement in using the methods of the early parliamentarians and the Chartists. Such methods, moreover, because of their revered antecedents, were proof against British disapproval, as members of the Indian National Congress were also aware. At the same time, palace politics–the old intriguing around the Maharaja, Dewan and Resident– were effectively closed to members of the Malayali Sabha. Eighty years of non-Malayali Brahmin Dewans, a superstitious Maharaja with a Brahmin favourite and the 'proper channels' of the modern bureaucratic system (which existed on paper, at any rate) saw to this. Later, C.V. Raman Pillai and other Nairs were to capture influence within the palace, but in 1890 they were still on the outside, and this fact dictated the scope and nature of the memorial.

Given the need for numbers, for signatures, for leading articles and eventually for public meetings, it became imperative to have allies and present the appearance of a 'national' movement. A memorial presented by the Malayali Sabha, a group of official Nairs, complaining about the exclusion of Nairs from the public service, would have been unconvincing and easily brushed aside. Indeed, even if the Sabha's claim to speak for all Nairs had been acknowledged, these would have represented only 19 per cent of the population. The Sabha, therefore, went out to capture allies. In Madras P. Palpu, the young Ezhava medical graduate, was recruited; his brother, P. Velayudhan, Travancore's first Ezhava graduate and a head clerk in the British service, was induced to sign; and a paragraph on the disabilities of Ezhavas was written into the Memorial. In the same way, Raman Pillai assiduously courted Fr. Emmanuel Nidhiry, the Romo-Syrian priest, and was disappointed when Nidhiry, who had to be careful of his European superiors, was unable to sign. However, Nidhiry spoke in support of the Memorial, and his brother signed it and was in the delegation which later met the Dewan.[53] The Memorial claimed to express the grievances of all 'Malayalis'–Nambudiris, Nairs, Syrians, other Christians and Ezhavas.

Only the names and occupations of its first 250 signatories were printed and have thereby survived. They indicate Nair predominance in the Memorial and the attempt of the Malayali Sabha to act as spokesman for, and educator of, the large number of conservative Nair landlords. The following table shows Nair influence:

*250 signatories of whom:*

| | |
|---|---|
| Landlords | 132 (about 90 Nairs) |
| Employed by government or retired | 63 (about 55 Nairs) |
| Vakils and pleaders | 27 (about 23 Nairs) |
| | 222 (about 168 Nairs) |

Distributed among the 250 signatories were such stalwarts of the Malayali Sabha as C.V. Raman Pillai, C. Krishna Pillai, P. Ayyappan Pillai, K. Neelakanta Pillai and others. Forty-four Christians were among the 250, while the remainder of the signatories was made up of Nambudiris, Ambalavasis, Ezhavas, Eurasians and Hindus whose caste is not apparent.[54]

Before the agitation ended there had amassed a wide assortment of memoranda, propositions, replies, and replies to replies. However, in its first and most revealing form the Malayali Memorial stressed, with suitable obsequiousness, 'the grievance which affects the most important classes of your Highness's subjects...[:] the denial to them of a fair share in the government of their country and their systematic exclusion from the higher grades of its services'.[55] The trick, however, was to define 'the most important classes' in such a way as to make the signatories appear representative of a large and aggrieved Travancore majority, yet to exclude non-Malayali Brahmins like Rama Rao, the Dewan, who had been born in Travancore and lived most of their lives there.

The Memorial began by excluding from consideration Europeans, Jews and Muslims, the latter being dismissed with the remark that among them 'education is at a very low ebb'. The remainder of the population was divided into three classes: (i) Malayali Hindus, 'meaning thereby all Hindus who follow the Marumakkatayam system of inheritance or a mixed system of Makkatayam and Marumakkatayam and whose *kudumi* or tuft of hair is in the front'. These were said to comprise 59.8 per cent of the population; (ii) 'Foreign Hindus', who included 'the foreigners who have settled and domiciled in Travancore' (13.14 per cent) (iii) Christians (20.76 per cent). Statistics were introduced to show the advantageous position of 'foreign Hindus' in the government service, especially in the grades drawing more than Rs. 10 a month. In this class, Ezhavas held 'not a single appointment' and '76 alone are held by that ancient community of Syrians'.

However, the Memorial's early concern for Ezhavas and Christians and its references to 'foreign Hindus' gave way to an open statement of the wrongs done by non-Malayali Brahmins to Nairs. In spite of Nair progress in education, a long line of Brahmin Dewans 'regularly and systematically ... without exception not only introduced their relations, castemen and friends into the State, but tried their best to oust the Nairs and prevent them from filling any of the higher appointments'. The plight of Nairs was 'all the more deplorable when it is remembered by Your Highness that they were from time immemorial till within the last few years the chief administrators of the State. History records a distinguished line of Dewans who had sprung from the Nair class...' Now, too, the 'Malayali Hindus' were handicapped in the competition for education by 'their peculiar system of inheritance', while 'the foreign Brahmins' were 'as comfortable as ever; a vast number of them have no taxes to pay, they are fed gratuitously at the choultries, and the increase of school fees means simply a little more exertion on their part to obtain more gifts and donations from the State and the people at large'. Further, 'Travancore certainly cannot with any amount of truth to [sic] be said to have been conquered for the foreign Brahmins; and they are in no way entitled to play the Englishmen in this state'. Towards the end of the Memorial, Syrian Christians and Ezhavas disappeared altogether:

> As the Malayali Sudras are the most loyal portion of Your Highness's subjects, as they are in point of intelligence, general culture and attainments not behind any other class in the country, as they were from the earliest times till within the last few years the ruling race in the land, and as it is that they mainly contribute to the resources of the State..., their claims on Your Highness's Government are far stronger than those of any other class in the country.

The Memorial made only one concrete request. It asked for

the introduction of a regulation to define 'a native of Travancore' on the lines of the British government's definition of 'a native of India'. Such a person was born and domiciled within the dominion of Her Majesty in India of parents habitually resident in India and not established there for temporary purposes only'. It seems doubtful whether even strict application of a similar regulation in Travancore could have excluded leading Brahmins like Rama Rao and the dewan peshkar Sankara Subbaiyer, all of whom had been born in Trivandrum. Indeed, the members of the Malayali Sabha probably did not expect any sort of regulation to result from the Memorial. Rather, the Memorial was a way of serving notice on the Maharaja, the Dewan, whose term was drawing to a close, and other high-ranking Brahmin officials: 'Come to terms with us, official Nairs, or we will make your lives unquiet indeed'.

K.P. Sankara Menon, who became the titular leader of the Memorial campaign, sent it to the Maharaja on 10 January 1891. For three months there was silence while the doddering Rama Rao, the Maharaja and the Resident considered the matter.[56] In April Rama Rao sent an endorsement to Sankara Menon in which he defended the government's employment policies, set out his own statistics to disprove those of the Memorialists and pointed out that the definition of 'foreigners' which the Memorialists suggested would not embrace the majority of government officials to whom they were objecting. However, at the command of the Maharaja, he agreed 'to meet a small deputation from the Petitioners, not exceeding six in number and hear and discuss with them any plans they may have to lay before government...'[57] This was the signal for non-Malayali Brahmins to begin looking for allies for a 'counter-Memorial'

The leaders of the Counter-Memorial were E. Ramier, a vakil of the Travancore High Court from the Tamil taluk of Shenkotta, and R. Ramanatha Rao, also a High Court vakil and the son-in-law of Sir T. Madhava Rao. In their petition, the Counter-Memorialists ridiculed the claims made in the Memorial, deployed their own statistics and argued that 'intellectual and moral worth and professional attainments alone must be qualifications for Government employment'.[58] They met the accusation that they were being encouraged by the Dewan and other government servants with the counter-charge that the organisers of the Memorial had been 'zealously helped by the Malayali officials'.[59]

The Counter-Memorialists enlisted the support of Muslim merchants, who had taken umbrage at their curt dismissal in the Memorial, and of the London Missionary Society's Tamil converts in South Travancore, who relied on cordial relations with government officers as a counterpoise to their dependence on Nair and Nanjanad Vellala landlords. One such convert explained his position in a letter to the *Madras Mail*. '...The Malayali Sudras are bitterly opposed to the political and social advance of our class, and ... whatever encouragement and support have been held out to us have been by Brahmin administrators'.[60] The Counter-Memorialists were also able to recruit Syrians, Nambudiris, Vellalas and a few Nairs. June, the rainiest of the monsoon months, was a time of public meetings, and by its end, the Counter-Memorialists were claiming 27,000 signatures; 1,000, however, seems a more likely figure.[61] Rama Rao agreed to meet delegations from both sides on 2 July.

Throughout June both sides held public meetings in the major towns of Travancore's four districts. The proceedings illustrated the anxieties and aims of the two sets of organisers. Members of the Malayali Sabha were careful to stay in the background, and both sides took pains to find chairmen from other groups or religions. However, the principal concerns of educated Nairs sometimes emerged. In Kottayam, K. Narayanan Thampi, the Nair district munsiff, emphasised to his listeners the peculiar social problems of Nairs. No karanavan was inclined, or able, he said, to educate all the boys in the taravad, and only the inducement of government service would spur karanavans to greater efforts.[62] In Quilon, where G. Parameswaran Pillai was the leading attraction and key speaker, another Nair, K.C. Keshava Pillai, attacked 'the foreign clique' in the government and said that liberal English education was now making it possible for Malayalis to demand their rights. The Maharaja, he was confident, loved the people 'in spite of the advice of foreign Brahmins'. At the same meeting, Kavalam Neelakantha Pillai, landowner, member of the Malayali Sabha and retired vakil, also attacked non-Malayali Brahmins, especially traders, 'who being fed gratis in the numerous feeding houses in the country, are able to undersell their Malayali brethren... The amount they derive from us each year may be reckoned as a tax paid to them annually'. Parameswaran Pillai turned to the theme of former glories and contrasted the past and present conditions of the natives of Travancore in the service of their country'. He spoke also of the disabilities of Ezhavas.[63]

The meetings of the Memorialists were chaired by Mar Thomas Athanasius, the leader of the Mar Thoma Syrian church, in Kottyam, by Kavalam Neelakantha Pillai in Quilon, by T.F. Lloyd, a retired Eurasian judge, in Trivandurm, and by P. Sivan Pillai, a Nanjanad Vellala landlord, in Nagercoil.[64] Since the Memorialists held their meetings first, the Counter-Memorialists were able to collect overlooked and offended notables for their meetings. Existing local disputes provided ready recruits for both sides. The Counter-Memorialists' session in the northern district was held in the Muslim and mercantile centre of Alleppey, with Mar Gregorious, a Jacobite bishop, in the chair. He assured the government on behalf of 'all Christians present, nay, of the Christian population in Travancore', that Christians 'have no complaints to make...'[65] Mar Thomites having lined up with the Memorialists, it was not surprising that some Jacobites, victorious adversaries of the Mar Thomites in the ten-year litigation, should have sided with the Counter-Memorialists. A similar pattern was followed in other Counter-Memorial meetings. In Quilon, a Nair was voted to the chair, in Trivandrum, a Nambudiripad, and only in Nagercoil was the chairmanship bestowed on a non-Malayali Brahmin.[66]

E. Ramier branded the Memorial as 'the Nair Memorial', and charged that 'the Nair Memorialists held their meetings under the direct patronage of Government officers'.[67] One Counter-Memorialist warned Nairs that in attempting to compete with Brahmins they were 'running their head against the rock of hereditary aptitude and wisdom...' Another argued that Kerala was made for the Brahmins and 'that the Malayalis came in as slaves'.[68] In the Madras press opponents of the Memorial had already been poking Nairs in their tenderest spot:

> ...The Malayalees as a class are the most idle and homesick of the whole Hindu community, owing to the enervating influence exercised on their character by their peculiar system of inheritance and their obnoxious system of promiscuous marriage, or rather no marriage.[69]

In Trivandrum, the Nambudiripad chairman of the Counter-Memorial meeting attacked from the conservative flank. He deeply regretted 'that some of your young men educated in English should dare to make such a misrepresentation (as the Memorial) about our government'.[70]

Such unprecedented political activity—'not a day passes', wrote the *Madras Mail* in June, 'without one or other of the two parties communicating its proceedings to us...'[71]—undoubtedly caused the Travancore sirkar some concern. Mulam Tirunal, unlike his uncle and predecessor, tended to avoid public discussions, while Rama Rao was a sick man. On 30 June the sirkar issued a notification forbidding any government servant to attend a political meeting where his presence was 'likely to be misconstrued or to impair his usefulness as an official'.[72]

The outward manifestations of the agitation ended with a whimper two days later when the two delegations met the Dewan at his office in Trivandrum. Sankara Menon led the carefully balanced Memorialist delegation with Parameswaran Pillai hovering in the background as 'secretary'. It included two landholding members of the Malayali Sabha--Kavalam Neelakantha Pillai and P. Sivan Pillai--Syriac Nidhiry and P.K. Palpanabha Pillai, the first Travancore graduate and a retired district judge. E. Ramier headed the Counter-Memorialists, who included a Muslim merchant, a Syrian, a non-Malayali Brahmin, a Vellala vakil, and P.C. Joseph, the LMS Christian who edited the *Travancore Times* of Nagercoil.[73] The meeting with the Dewan lasted only half an hour. Rama Rao accepted statements and memoranda from both sides, but the Memorialists, wrote *Malayala Manorama* approvingly, 'refused anything to do' with the other delegation.[74] Rama Rao assured everyone of his consideration and fairness; Sankara Menon assured Rama Rao of their confidence in him. At this stage, Parameswaran Pillai perhaps felt obliged to turn away. The meeting ended, and with it, the agitational aspect of the Malayali Memorial.

In its immediate aftermath, members of the Malayali Sabha found themselves out of favour. There were no promotions for Nair officials under Rama Rao's administration,[75] and supporters of the Memorial were hard put to find small victories.[76] Interest in the Malayali Sabha understandably waned. The agitation, however, commanded wide coverage in the Indian press, and the Memorialists won the support of the *Mail* and to a certain extent of *The Hindu* in Madras,[77] as well as the *Standard*. In achieving such notoriety, they gave warning of their potential to roughen the waters on which the Travancore ship of state sailed. Mulam Tirunal, and many highly placed non-Malayali Brahmin officials, had a horror of political seasickness.

Such fears, as we shall see in the next chapter, prompted the new Brahmin Dewan, appointed in 1892, to reach a tacit understanding with official Nairs in an effort to ensure a smooth administrative passage. For elite Nairs like C.V. Raman Pillai, an accommodation which brought them quick promotion was the next best thing to the Nair rule of former times. In this sense, within two or three years the Memorial largely achieved the purpose of its key organisers.

However, the Memorial also pointed to the serious divisions of attitude among Nairs. The tiny band of elite Nairs–perhaps amounting to three or four dozen–who were the chief workers in the Malayali Sabha, claimed to speak on behalf of thousands of landlords. Yet the Counter-Memorialists were able to draw some support--notably the chairman of their Quilon meeting--from conservative Nair landlords who were appalled at the *lèse majesté* of challenging the authority of the Maharaja and the sanctity of Brahmins. Moreover, while western-educated Nairs of C.V. Raman Pillai's generation might be able to fulfil their ambitions in the government service, a younger generation was to find that there were not enough sirkar jobs to go round. Similarly, when the older generation talked of 'social reform', it usually meant a marriage law to remove the slur against Nair morals. However, the economic difficulties of the taravad, which the Memorial hinted at, were increasingly to make younger Nairs talk of radical reform of the joint-family; such reform, in the eyes of men like C.V. Raman Pillai, would strike at an institution which was responsible for many of the glories of the Nair past.

Moreover, in having brought western-educated members of other groups into association with the Memorial, the Nair elite had helped to awaken aspirations which were not satisfied. Syrians and Ezhavas began to harbour a growing suspicion of the motives of official Nairs and of the glorification of Nair rule in former times. By 1896, a correspondent in the *Madras Mail*, who was probably P. Palpu, was writing of the Malayali

Memorial as a Petition of 'over 10,000 Nairs'. And by the early years of the twentieth century, *Malayala Manorama* was indignantly describing the grievances of Syrians as 'far greater...than the Nairs had some ten years back', while the *Malabar Herald*, a Romo-Syrian newspaper, could refer to the organizers of the Memorial as 'those shrewd men' who 'reaped the fruits of this memorial, and thus had their selfish ends gratified'.[78]

The fruits which the Malayali Memorial brought to its organisers suggested to other groups that similar campaigns might be equally rewarding. But the fruits of the Memorial did nothing to solve the problem of the matrilineal joint-family, and this was the concern of growing numbers of Nairs.

# 6

# The Brahmin-Nair Official Elite and its Competitors, 1891-1904

In the years immediately following the Malayali Memorial, the Malayali Sabha withered and died as official Nairs of C.V. Raman Pillai's generation found an accommodation with the new Tamil Brahmin Dewan, S. Sankara Subbaiyer. The Dewan's policies, however, antagonised Christians, and led Syrians into an attempt to organise politically. At the same time, ordinary Nairs were becoming increasingly aware of the improvement of the economic condition of Syrians as well as Ezhavas. Nairs, on the other hand, were experiencing a growing crisis in the matrilineal joint-family which led them into feuds, litigation and alienation of land. The problem of the taravad demanded attention, but there were differences about the proper solutions. By 1904 a younger generation of educated Nairs was finding the notions of caste-Hindu respectability and past Nair glories, which were important to C.V. Raman Pillai and his Trivandrum-based friends, less and less relevant to the practical difficulties faced by Nairs throughout Travancore. This chapter tells how the official Nair elite came briefly to terms with Brahmin officials, yet failed to alleviate the problems of Nairs. These problems were aggravated and dramatised by the growing prosperity and assertiveness of many Syrians and Ezhavas.

## *THE OFFICIAL ELITE*

Although the Memorial appeared to end anticlimactically, and K.P. Sankara Menon was writing in June 1892 to ask the sirkar whether any new employment policies had in fact been implemented,[1] official Nairs in Travancore soon gained much of what they had sought. By August 1892 Rama Rao had retired and been replaced by 'a native', albeit a Tamil Brahmin, but, Nairs consoled themselves, one who had been born in Trivandrum. They chose conveniently to ignore the fact that Rama Rao himself was Trivandrum-born.

C.V. Raman Pillai later claimed that under Sankara Subbaiyer, Nair officials received suitable recognition and promotion. In *Videshiya Medhavitvam* ('foreign rule'), written in 1920, he concluded that Sankara Subbaiyer had ruled 'faultlessly' and had distributed jobs with the wisdom of Yudhisthira, the eldest of the five Pandava brothers of the *Mahabharata*.[2] This was high praise indeed for an administration which the leading Syrian newspaper described as having 'gone from bad to worse' and having reached a level similar to that of 'the days previous to the advent of Sir T. Madhava Rao'. The Dewan was 'rightly held by the people as responsible for all the evils that now exist...'[3]

Sankara Subbaiyer arrived at an understanding with the leading Nair officials who had been the mainstay of the Malayali Sabha and the chief workers for the Malayali Memorial. A later Dewan wrote that Sankara Subbaiyar's administration 'made a systematic attempt to conciliate the Nair community by employing educated men of that community more largely in the public service of Travancore'.[4] Nair officials advanced rapidly. P. Thanu Pillai, the cautious intellectual leader of the old Malayali Social Union, was promoted to the powerful post of Chief Secretary about 1895, and other stalwarts of the Malayali Sabha shot up the official ladder.[5] In 1898 K.P. Sankara Menon himself accepted a district judgeship from Sankara Subbaiyer and when G. Parameswaran Pillai returned to Travancore to die in 1903, he too was offered a place on the bench.[6] *Malayala Manorama* had no doubt what Sankara Subbaiyer had done:

> He could well see that the one element which harrowed his predecessor and held up his administration to the

> ridicule of the whole world was the enmity of the Malayali Sudras... [To avoid this enmity] he would seem to have thrown overboard his own party and entered into a secret compact with his former enemies promising to hand over to them the sole monopoly of all offices of State if they would not lacerate him by newspaper articles, indignation meetings, deputations and counter-deputations, anonymous letters and numerously-signed petitions. Such an understanding places the dewan's claim to be a very shrewd man of business beyond any doubt. The result has been to put the handle that turns the wheel of the State into the hands of one or two disreputable cliques.[7]

*Manorama's* case had more to it than pique at the continued exclusion of all but a few Syrians from government service. After Sankara Subbaiyer's assumption of office the Malayali Sabha and the *Malayali* newspaper ceased to function. Part of the reason may have been the sirkar's notification forbidding officials to conduct newspapers or be members of political organisations. This forced C.V. Raman Pillai's withdrawal from the overt supervision of the *Malayali*. Yet even Parameswaran Pillai's *Madras Standard* seems to have remained untypically quiet on the subject of Sankara Subbaiyer, and when it criticised the appointment of too many European department heads in Travancore in 1896, it named Sankara Subbaiyer as Dewan of the hypothetical non-European Travancore administration which it constructed. It would not have made the same genuflexion to Rama Rao.[8] As well as a suspension of most open hostilities between Nairs of the defunct Malayali Sabha and non-Malayali Brahmins, missionaries detected a keen new anti-Christian bias in the government.[9]

One of the *Madras Standard's* manifold criticisms of Rama Rao had been his supposed belief 'that Syrian Christians and Christians as a class are more intelligent than the natives...'[10] As a product of the LMS Seminary, Nagercoil, Rama Rao enjoyed good relations with the missionaries. One described him as 'such a kind friend' whom 'I believe...to be near to the Kingdom of God'.[11] Sankara Subbaiyer's exposure to Christianity, however, however, had been less happy: a relative had converted and brought shame to the family. His education, moreover, had been completed before John Ross reformed the Trivandrum High School and raised it to the standards of the Madras University, and he had gone directly into the sirkar service as a protege of Madhava Rao. His early contacts with Europeans–and, indeed, with any society except that of Travancore--had therefore been limited. he was described as 'a Brahmin of the Brahmins; a conservative of the conservatives; according to Hindu views a throughly religious man'. He carried out the marriage of his granddaughter when she was only eight or nine; even his mentor, Madhava Rao, no radical in such things, thought nine to be the bare minimum.[12] To such a man, a policy of arresting Christian pretensions, maintaining Hindu orthodoxy against low-caste requests and coming to a tacit understanding with the Nair officials who had so plagued his predecessor had much to recommend it. It offered the possibility of a quiet life, which as a local man on the point of retirement he undoubtedly valued, while it did not run against the grain of conviction. For their part, Nairs of the Malayali Sabha did not come suddenly to cherish non-Malayali Brahmins, even those born in Trivandrum. But it ill-behoved a dewan peshkar or High Court manager to criticise the sirkar's personnel. The truce was never perfect, and hot-tempered organisers like C. Krishna Pillai, who remained a school inspector all his life, were probably never party to it. Nairs did not join the Brahmins' Union Club in Trivandrum, nor were Brahmins invited to enrol in the National Club of Nair officials. Yet with the obvious increase in the organisational and economic power of Christians, and even Ezhavas, official Nairs may have concluded that there was much to be gained from quietly cooperating with the Dewan and his castemen. Agitations about the paucity of Nairs in the services would do nothing to lessen the pressure from Chirstians and Ezhavas. The latter were becoming more of a threat to Nairs' view of their traditional place in society than Brahmins were a hindrance.

Moreover, as well as the pressure from without, the decay of Nair social institutions became increasingly clear during the 1890s. This decay affected the vast majority of Nairs, not merely the educated elite who felt embarrassment at the absence of a marriage law. Leading officials like Thanu Pillai saw that Nairs' position in society was threatened by the basic inadequacy of their social institutions; but their attempts at remedy were mild and unsuccessful. In spite of the grievances of the Malayali Memorial, the old system had generally been good to such men, and the glories of the Nair past exercised a powerful hold on their emotions.[13] It was difficult—indeed almost impossible–for most of them to advocate radical social reforms and thereby disavow those customs which had contributed to the traditional greatness of Nairs.

The major problem for Nair society was its impartible matrilineal joint-family. It is necessary now to discuss in some detail the complexities of the taravad, and particularly the role of the eldest male member, the karanavan or manager. In the ideal taravad of pre-British times, the karanavan was selfless. A seasoned old soldier, devoted to the interests of his house and locality, he was charged with the supervision of the women, land and slaves, thus leaving the young men free to follow their raja and to fight. In the ideal taravad, there was a perfect 'communality' of spirit. Although the number of relatives in a single house might exceed a hundred, they were seldom at home together, for each taravad had responsibilities in war and government.

This was the ideal type, and whether it had actually existed was not so important by the 1890s as the fact that some Nairs believed that it had. It was part of a golden age when Nairs moved through the country as prosperous soldiers and gentry, respected and feared. With such a picture, the situation in the 1890s compared unfavourably. 'Incessant disputes, heart burnings and litigation spring up; many families are sinking into ruin', wrote one well-informed, though not disinterested, observer, 'and the Nairs are, on the whole, diminishing in wealth and position'.[14] The karanavan had become a greedy villain, and the taravad the scene of endless dissension among aggressive mothers, layabout youths and scheming elders.

The large ideal taravad had probably begun to dissolve in Travancore before other parts of Kerala as a result of Maharaja Martanda Varma's subordination of the Nairs in the eighteenth century. Certainly by the 1870s, as we have seen, monogamous marriages–though they were not enforced by the courts–were becoming common. At the same time, taravads were increasingly agreeing to divide themselves into a number of branches, each with its own house and lands; but these divisions were similarly without the force of law and could be overturned in the courts.

It is difficult not to burlesque the potential legal troubles of a taravad, but let us examine a hypothetical case for illustration. The following diagram may help to make the situation clearer:

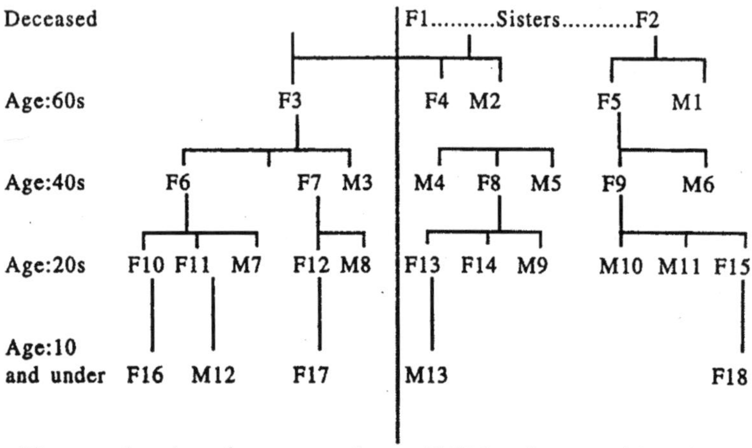


*Figure showing descent and possibilities for partition in a hypothetical taravad*

F1 and F2 are sisters, both dead. They have twenty-nine descendants, and the taravad has extensive, scattered holdings of land. The karanavan is M1, the eldest male descendant of the two sisters. M3, dissatisfied with M1's management, persuades his mother, F3, and his sisters, F6 and F7, and their families, to establish themselves on family lands a few miles distant from the old taravad house; there, M3 acts as the manager. Legally, however, M1 is solely responsible for the administration of the whole taravad. He can claim the revenue from the lands on which M3 is living, and, indeed, can alienate them if he can convince the purchaser or mortgagee (and by extension, a court) that the alienation is for taravad necessities. M3, on the other hand, can challenge such alienations on the grounds that the karanavan did not have the consent of all the adult members of the taravad.

The permutations of even such a simplified example, and the scope for mismanagement and litigation, are extensive. For example, the karanavan, M1, may have been supporting his wife and childern with taravad resources and neglecting even his own nephew, much less the nephews of his cousin, M2. M6, unlikely ever to be karanavan though he holds a well-paying government job, leaves the taravad to set up his own household with his wife in Trivandrum; his resources are lost to the taravad, and his nephews, M10 and M11, are neglected and unproductive. On his death, however, his nephews and taravad are his legal heirs and can claim all his self-acquired property, thus leaving his wife destitute, or at best with only her own taravad to fall back on. F13 is permitted to have sambandham with a penniless non-Malayali Brahmin who is unable to pay her confinement expenses and eventually disappears.[15] The possibilities demand a Malayali Gilbert and Sullivan.

Litigation–'that constant flood...which is the ruin of the country'[16]–increased steadily. In the decade 1879-80/1888-89, there was an average of sixty suits a year for taravad partition, in spite of the known policy of the courts to grant such decrees only when all the adult members of a taravad agreed. From 1889-90, the average increased to eighty suits annually; from 1899-1900 to 1903-04, when figures stopped being published, the average was ninety-six a year.[17] Thus in twenty-five years, nearly 1,800 taravads of the perhaps 30,000 in Travancore had taken the extreme step of going to law; as an indication of the malaise affecting the taravad, these cases were only the tip of the iceberg.

By 1890 appalling stories were circulating about the state of poverty to which some families had been reduced by foolish litigation and haphazard management. It was said that some taravads were forcing their young girls into sambandhams with old Brahmins who could afford to pay a price.[18] Nairs had always permitted sambandhams with non-Malayali Brahmins, but the latter were less attractive husbands than Nambudiris, Kshatriyas or even some sub-castes of Nairs. As educated Nairs came to know more of Hinduism in the rest of India, their embarrassment at a custom which other Hindus regarded as both comical and disgraceful grew. G. Parameswaran Pillai's father, for example, was a Pattar, and Parameswaran Pillai's son has suggested that this was important in making him 'an uncompromising opponent of social injustice'.[19] Certainly it made him independent, for as a polluting Nair he had little to do with his father and received no financial support from him.

The remedies suggested for the decaying taravad were various. Some men, embarrassed by jibes at the laxity of Nair morals, advocated a more binding marriage tie, recognised by law. Others asked how a mere marriage law could ameliorate the condition of the taravad, while a few radicals called for partition on demand: the right of any member to ask for and receive his share of the taravad's assets. The prevailing system, one writer argued, rendered Nair women 'coarse' and men 'avaricious'. Without their disproportionate share of posts under government, 'most of the Nair families would soon be ruined. As it is many are'.[20]

One of the aims of the Malayali Sabha had of course been reform of Nair marriage customs; but by 1890 the Sabha's leading figures were deeply involved in the Memorial and the sirkar-service issue. In that year, however, C. Sankaran Nair, a member of the Madras Legislative Council and the leading Nair in the Madras Presidency, introduced a bill to permit Nairs in British India to register their sambandhams. This would make the sambandham legally binding and enable Nairs to dispose part of their self-acquired property on their wives and children. The proposed bill met with immediate opposition–from Nairs who defended the old system in its entirety, from Nairs who urged cautious slow changes, and from Nambudiris, Kshatriyas and non-Malayali Brahmins who saw their traditional domestic arrangements threatened.[21]

The Madras government created the Malabar Marriage Commission, headed by Sir T. Muthuswami Aiyar, the most distinguished Brahmin in the Presidency, to examine the whole subject. Originally, Kerala Varma, a Kshatriya, the poet and husband of the senior Rani of Travancore, was to have been one of the six members, but he withdrew and was replaced by the Raja of Parapanad, a Kshatriya, born in Travancore but living in Malabar. His family traditionally supplied husbands for the Ranis of Travancore.[22] The commission examined witnesses in Malabar in mid-1891, and requested written opinions from Travancoreans, including Rama Rao, the Dewan, and judges A. Govinda Pillai and T. Kunhi Raman Nair, a Malabar man who had entered Travancore service. All three favoured legislation to recognise or clarify Nair marriage, but there was uncertainty about what form the law should take and what it could be expected to do. Rama Rao told the commission that 'the educated portion of Malayalees... would hail any measure which will have the effect of making the marital tie more real and binding...', while Govinda Pillai stated flatly that educated Malayalis (as so often, Malayali here meant Nair) 'demanded' a change of the marriage system and 'all classes' would 'welcome' a change; he did not go into detail. Kunhi Raman Nair opposed major changes in the system of inheritance, which, he felt, would destroy the taravad.[23]

The Commission's report was published towards the end of 1891 and suggested a modest, voluntary bill. But the report was forwarded to the Government of India, where it rotated with other files for two years, and it was not until 1896 that the Malabar Marriage Bill became law. Under its provisions people of any caste in Malabar following the marumakkattayam system could register their sambandham with the government. This made the sambandham a legal marriage, entitled a man to make over his self-acquired property to his wife and children, and conferred on marumakkattayis such benefits of English law as bigamy, adultery and divorce. Yet the act was purely permissive: to those who did not register, it did not apply. During its first ten years on the statute books, fewer than a hundred people registered their marriages; by 1906 it was pronounced 'a dead letter'.[24]

The terms and passage of the act were watched closely in Travancore, especially after the Memorial and the virtual dissolution of the Malayali Sabha. Thanu Pillai pointed out that the error of Sankaran Nair's bill was in not recognising a public sambandham ceremony as a legal marriage, and this was the burden of Kunhi Raman Nair's evidence to the Malabar Marriage Commission.[25] Only by granting such recognition could the large majority of marumakkattayis be brought within the scope of the law and minimal rights given to wives and children.

As early as 1882, the Special Commission on Malabar Land Tenures, headed by William Logan, drew attention to the need to give Nairs the right to make a will and to leave their self-acquired property to their wives and children. The situation as it stood was 'fatal to individual industry and thrift, and if the law is not soon changed the consequences to the ruling caste will be disastrous'.[26] In 1887 the Malayali Sabha circulated a draft of a marriage bill among its members, but the Travancore sirkar showed no inclination to accept legislative proposals from an organisation which it regarded as suspect.

It was a measure of the good relations existing between leading Nair officials and the new Dewan when early in 1896 Sankara Subbaiyer 'advised, encouraged and prompted' Thanu Pillai to introduce a bill in the Travancore Legislative Council.[27] The bill, which C.V. Raman Pillai helped to draft,[28] provided legal recognition for all marriages solemnised by 'the presentation of a cloth or some other recognised ceremony'. It did not undertake to change the system of inheritance; on a man's death, his taravad and his nephews remained his rightful heirs. But it removed any doubt about a man's right to provide for his wife and children from his self-acquired property during his lifetime, and it aimed to end the ridicule directed at the laxity of Nair morals.

In his speech introducing the Bill, Thanu Pillai emphasised the latter aspect which seemed more important to his educated circle than the economic difficulties in which the taravad found itself:

> Whether from ignorance or prejudice our critics seem to have no qualms of conscience in levelling against us the reproach: 'Your wives are concubines and your sons are bastards'.
>
> ...[But in fact the sambandham] union is intended to be permanent and is, in the vast majority of cases, practically so. Though there is no civil right in theory, every father feels it is his duty to make some provision, according to his means for his wife and children.
>
> ...In Travancore–at all events in most parts–the sons have to perform sradha and observe deeksha for the father [on his death]. The wife and children also observe pollution. In some parts of Travancore the father's name and not the karanavan's is used as the second name in describing the *full* name of the individual. The wife is invariably taken to the husband's house, lives and messes with him and is not at liberty to leave his house even to visit her own relations without her husband's permission... If one would cast off all prejudices and preconceived

> notions and impartially and dispassionately investigate the subject, he will find that the conjugal union... is not a casual or fugitive connection formed for the purpose of sexual gratification, but a serious and solemn alliance, and that the intention of the parties is to make the union a life-long one.

He read opinions favouring the measure from Kerala Varma, from the Kshatriya husband of the late junior Rani, and from Kunhi Raman Nair who agreed that some measure had to be taken 'against the present state of things which allows anyone to commit adultery with another's wife with impunity...' The bill was referred to a select committee of Thanu Pillai, K. Krishnaswami Rao, the chief justice, the Raja of Parapanad, and K. Kuruvila, a Syrian Christian.[29]

In the course of the next six months the bill became 'the chief subject of discussion' in the state; opinions were 'greatly divided'.[30] The select committee presented a majority report, signed by Krishnaswami Rao, Thanu Pillai and Kuruvila, in January 1897. It recommended only one change in the proposed bill: the provision of optional registration for those who wished to make recognition of their sambandham unquestionable. There was, however, a dissenting memorandum from the Raja of Parapanad, who displayed a curious concern for the feelings of low-caste marumakkattayis such as Ezhavas. '...Only the Nair community do feel the want of marriage legislation', he asserted. 'I doubt the wisdom of thrusting on a class a social legislation of which they never felt the want'. He concluded with one of the wounding asides which educated Nairs found so hard to bear. It was not a desire 'to make their marriage more binding or to make divorces more difficult'–not, therefore, a desire for morality–which prompted Nairs to press for this change. Rather, it was purest self-interest: to keep one's self-acquired property out of the hands of one's taravad and rightful heirs and to use it 'to make ample provision...for the wife and childern'. The Raja's argument cleverly blended Victorian morality, for which all other marumakkattayis and most Nairs were not ready, with an implicit glorification of the 'ideal' taravad which some Nairs were seeking to betray.[31]

The Raja's disinterested innocence was less than childlike. The bill promised to affect the domestic and sexual arrangements of Kshatriyas, including the Maharaja, of Nambudiris and of non-Malayali Brahmins. One of the legends of the origin of Kerala held that Nair women were created for the enjoyment of the high castes. Many of these had sambandham with Nair women, and while some were faithful husbands, others flitted from flower to flower. The *Madras Standard* had gone unchallenged when it accused Mulam Tirunal's Brahmin favourite of arranging three Nair women– one of them the wife of a sirkar official and member of the Malayali Sabha–for the Maharaja's pleasure, and later described the ruler as 'grossly sensual, sparing...no woman in his lust'.[32] Nair women in the countryside were still expected to bare their breasts as a mark of respect to high-caste men, and even in towns 'it is in this semi-nude fashion they are required to accompany state processions...'[33]

In the long term, Thanu Pillai's bill could be seen as a step towards ending the hypergamy of Nair women and their deference to the high castes. Its immediate effect would be to make high-caste men, who had performed sambandham with a pretty Nair girl and later changed their affections, liable to a criminal prosecution for adultery and bigamy. Educated Kshatriyas like Kerala Varma did not oppose–indeed they supported–the bill, but as a whole, Kshatriyas, the acting Resident wrote, 'have not taken advantage of the educational facilities offered by the state and stand too much on their dignity...'[34] Nambudiris, if anything, were worse, and non-Malayali Brahmins who had sambandham with Nairs were generally among the least educated. Yet all three groups had considerable influence in the palace: the Maharaja was related to most Kshatriyas; his favourite, Saravanai Ananda Narayana Aiyar, the 'illiterate cook boy', was an uneducated Brahmin; and Nambudiris and Pottis were great landholders, the most important priests and the beneficiaries of the sexennial *murajapam* ceremony.

The marriage bill continued to excite interest throughout 1897,[35] but it was virtually pushed off the Legislative Council agenda and never appeared likely to become law. During the next five years, though never formally killed, it languished and died, the victim of Brahmin-Kshartiya intrigue, according to C.V. Raman Pillai's biographer. *Malayala Manorama* wrote of 'a howl of opposition' which caused it 'to be shelved for an indefinite period'.[36] The sudden death of Thanu Pillai at the age of forty-eight in May 1902 removed the most influential

Nair in the sirkar service and the bill's sponsor.

Educated Nairs, however, had achieved a small reform in 1899 with the passage of the Travancore Wills Act. Again their apparently satisfactory -relations with Sankara Subbaiyer and, initially, with his successor, Krishnaswami Rao, who had been in Travancore service from 1884, first as chief justice and then as Dewan, facilitated action in the Legislative Council. The bill conferred on marumakkattayis the right to bequeath up to one-half of their self-acquired property to their wives and children. In the absence of a will, their taravads and nephews remained their sole legal heirs. Because the bill made no alteration to the law affecting marriage, it aroused less enthusiasm among educated Nairs; the stigma, the taunts and the exploitation of their women remained. Yet opposition was also lessened, and the bill passed without difficulty. Govinda Pillai, five years Thanu Pillai's senior but probably more radical in his social views, called the bill 'the first instalment of reform'.[37]

## *THE COMPETITORS*

### *Syrians and Other Christians*

At the turn of the century, however, Nairs had little cause for jubilation. The uncomfortable accommodation which some Nair officials had arrived at with Sankara Subbaiyer proved increasingly impractical with his successor. Growing numbers of educated unemployed Nairs had little contact or sympathy with the middle-aged members of the old Malayali Sabha who were now in positions of power and comfort. Only C. Krishna Pillai retained the reformist zeal of the 1880s, and as we have already seen, promotion eluded him. Moreover, Christians of all kinds, growing in economic power and assertiveness, were no longer prepared to accept exclusion from the sirkar service, especially when members of that service could use their position to discriminate against Christian activities. There was no doubt among Syrians and European missionaries that an anti-Christian era began with Sankara Subbaiyer's dewanship, and that 'those who have got power into their hands move Heaven and earth to prevent others from sharing in its privileges'.[38]

Three major developments, accompanied, it was claimed, by petty harassments, proved to the satisfaction of most Christians that the Sankara Subbaiyer administration was 'decidedly hostile to Native Christians and Christian Missions...'[39] These were (i) the introduction of a new grant-in-aid code for education, (ii) strict application of a court decision that Christian converts from marumakkattayam castes lost their inheritance and maintenance rights, and (iii) a provision in the criminal code setting out penalties for building places of worship without consent.

In the last case Syrian Christians had largely themselves to blame. Following the victory of Mar Dionysius and his party in the Syrian court case in 1889, the defeated Mar Thomites surrendered the churches they held and prepared to establish new ones. But the Jacobites (i.e. the Mar Dionysius party) resolved to make matters for the defeated faction as difficult as possible. In some cases, they approached the sirkar with the warning that there would be a breach of the peace if the Mar Thomites were allowed to build their church close to a Jacobite Church. In response, the sirkar reissued a notification of 1829–the same notification which granted an upper covering to Shanar converts–which forbade the building of places of worship without express consent. In 1889 missionaries protested at the reissue of the proclamation and asked the Resident for a clarification. The matter appeared to die.[40]

But in 1894, when Krishnaswami Rao introduced amendments to the Penal Code Bill in the Legislative Council, they were found to include provisions for fines and imprisonment up to two years for those who built places of worship without consent or who failed to demolish places of worship built illegally. The outcry from Christians was immediate. *Malayala Manorama*, which was generally cautious in its criticisms of the administration, attacked the provision as being aimed specifically at Christians and illustrating 'what opinion Krishnaswami Rao holds on matters connected with religious liberty'. The occasion gave *Manorama* an opportunity to air another grievance: the fact that no Indian Christian had yet been appointed to the Legislative Council to defend the interests of the community from such assaults as these.[41] The *Madras Mail* took up the issue, and the long debate which followed in its correspondence columns elicited further charges of anti-Christian bias.

The second issue which aroused Christians was the application of a High Court ruling of 1885. A full bench, with Krishnaswami Rao as chief justice, and including two Nairs, a European and a Tamil Christian, ruled against a Nair woman and her son who had been converted to Christianity and who sought to retain the lands which their taravad had earlier assigned for their support. The court held that converts from a marumakkattayam caste had no right to maintenance from their taravads or to a share of the property; to find otherwise, wrote the lower court judge, 'would completely destroy the present law of inheritance'. Only Arianayagam Pillai, the Tamil Christian, found in favour of the converts.[42] The missionaries claimed that previously Nair converts, who were never numerous, had been able to negotiate a financial arrangement with their families. Now, however, that would be impossible: Nair converts were 'civilly dead'. As a result of a missionary petition, the sirkar set up a committee of officials to investigate the question in 1888; its members included Krishnaswami Rao, Sankara Subbaiyer, Kunhi Raman Nair, a Eurasian Roman Catholic and a European. The committee reported that it would be 'highly inexpedient' to grant Nair converts any rights to family property.[43] The missionaries were preparing to petition again when the Malabar Marriage Commission was established; they decided to await its report.[44]

Their interest in the Malabar Marriage Commission was understandable, for they were aware of the difficulties the taravad system was experiencing. Men like Samuel Mateer of the LMS and A.F. Painter of the CMS had regular dealings with many Nairs, and although such relations were usually friendly, the missionaries were never reluctant to point out the ridiculous and immoral aspects of the taravad. Among missionaries there was a feeling that the Nair social system was crumbling and that if the missionaries were ready to pick up the pieces, the great breakthrough–conversion of large numbers of high-caste people, which men like Peet had worked for–could be achieved. The immediate aim was to win for Nair converts the right to a share of the taravad property and guardianship of children. If such an innovation were introduced, if Nair converts were granted a right to taravad partition which Hindus were denied, would not many Nairs be led to convert to Christianity in order to enjoy a civil advantage which increasing numbers badly wanted? Missionaries also frequently assured themselves that many Nairs were sympathetic to Christian teaching but were not prepared to sacrifice the material comfort which they derived from their family property.

In 1894 the Malabar Marriage Commission's report was still being considered at various levels of government, and Brahmins, claimed Painter, were fighting a vigorous delaying action.[45] Painter's letter to the *Madras Mail*, which denounced the disabilities imposed on Nair converts, led the missionaries to revive their campaign.[46] In 1895, at the same time that Sankaran Nair was presenting his revised Malabar Marriage Bill to the Madras Legislative Council, the missionaries petitioned Lord Wenlock, the governor of Madras. They claimed that a Nair convert to Christianity lost not only his property, but frequently had his children taken away by their legal guardians, their uncles. In short, such converts were treated 'worse than a leper or an adulterer or a thief'.[47]

There was little likelihood, however, of the administration of Sankara Subbaiyer, involved as it was in a tacit alliance with leading Nair officials, ever conceding the missionaries' requests. Their petition had little success. The Madras government instructed the Resident to urge the introduction of a law similar to Act XXI of 1850 in British India, which would give Nair converts a right to maintenance from their taravads. Even this, however, the sirkar opposed. In a letter to the Resident, Sankara Subbaiyer argued that the change in the law was sought solely by the European missionaries, 'while the converts themselves do not appear to have felt any prompting in this direction'. Moreover, the Roman Catholic missionaries did not seek any change, and there were few Nair converts anyway; legislation was unnecessary. He concluded by pinpointing and ridiculing 'the chief remedy' which the missionaries sought–'the doing away with the Marumakkattayam custom'. It was indeed too ridiculous to think about.[48] Checked in Travancore and Madras, the missionaries switched their attention to the government of India, but by 1900 it was obvious that they could expect no help.[49]

Although Syrian Christians had shown little interest in the question of Nair converts, *Malayala Manorama* later wrote that the issue had well illustrated Sankara Subbaiyer's 'hatred of Christians'.[50] Syrians, however, were more concerned with the sirkar's new grant-in-aid code and reorganisation of education instituted in 1894. In the last year prior to the introduction of the code, Christians controlled half of the aided schools in the state with 53 per cent of the enrolment.[51] Moreover, as we have seen, Romo-Syrians and Latin Catholics were just beginning to turn their resources to education.[52] In the first year after government began to recognise and accredit teachers in 1897, 42 per cent of the newly-licensed teachers were Christians.[53] The Christian interest in education was obvious, and to some, ominous. As early as 1888, *Kerala Patrika*, a Nair paper published in Calicut in Malabar, was warning Kerala Hindus 'not to send their children to mission schools as education in these schools will bring many evils'.[54]

The new grant-in-aid code was introduced in 1894 with little warning. Basically, it was a move towards some centralised control of the aided schools which were expanding rapidly and haphazardly. The code aimed to improve standards by demanding better facilities and more highly-qualified staff, and by setting out the curricula and, in some cases, the text-books to be used in aided schools. But more important for Christians and missionaries was the provision that pupils could receive religious instruction only with the consent of their parents. Coupled with the controversies over permission to build churches and converts' rights to family property, the new education code convinced many Christians that 'under the present Administration the general drift of all effort is to repress and restrain progress of liberty of religious thought and life'; the education code embodied 'the intolerant spirit now being manifested by the men in high positions in this State'.[55] The sudden introduction of the code, which led to administrative delays, helped to confirm their opinion, and the payment of grants-in-aid–especially, it appeared, to Christian schools–fell into arrears. Was this a way, one writer asked, 'to chastise the naughty missionaries'?[56]

The sirkar, however, had a number of defenders who bitterly attacked the scheming, self-interested missionaries. The *Mail's* Travancore correspondent led the assault,[57] and others joined in. The missionaries were accused of offering inferior education, resisting improvements which would cost money, and using education only 'as a means towards their own particular ends'–conversion. Grants to mission schools represented money awarded by a Hindu sirkar to a 'proselytising agency'.[58]

In the course of the next three years, missionaries claimed that the sirkar's attitude on the three issues–convert inheritance, permission to build churches and grants-in-aid–was encouraging government servants, who were overwhelmingly Brahmins and Nairs, to seize any pretext on which to harass and oppress Christians. Under the terms of the 1829 proclamation, officials challenged Christians who had built one-room schoolhouses without permission.[59] Difficulties were made for Christian converts who tried to register waste land; missionaries were no longer used as agents for the distribution of famine relief; government school inspectors intimidated Christian schoolmasters; grants-in-aid were often late.[60] Government officials harassed mission schools and catechists, and bullied and assulted mission adherents.[61] One of the missionaries was prompted to write to the Maharaja: 'Rightly or wrongly, the vast body of Christians feel that the present government is hostile to them. Your Highness has no more loyal subjects than they, and yet they are often regarded with distrust and suspicion'.[62]

Yet was 'the vast body of Christians' really involved? As we have seen, to talk about 'Christians' in Travancore, as if they were a body with some unity, was as useful as to talk of 'Hindus'. At first, only the question of permission to build churches affected the Syrians. The Mar Thomites and Jacobites, whose sectarian conflict had raised the issue, were intent on retaining their members, and this could only be done by erecting new buildings in areas where they lost control of the exsting churches.[63] Moreover, the administration had its Christian defenders in Trivandrum. Both the Latin Catholic vicar and the Anglican chaplain, who was not a CMS man, wrote of the government's concern for their interests and their complete satisfaction with the government.[64]

*Malayala Manorama* gave its fellow Christians only cautious support at first. Pointing out that the missionaries were naturally shocked by the government's attempts to make them observe religious neutrality, *Manorama* criticised the grant-in-aid code as a foolish step towards a strangling centralisation. The government, it felt, should immediately withdraw its insistence on Christians' obtaining permission to build churches and schools.[65]

Another element, however, began to creep into the controversy.

Before the end of the century it had devoured the three original grievances and grown immensely. The new element was the question of Christian representation in the sirkar services. Expressing the relief felt in the south at the transfer of an anti-Christian dewan peshkar, a letter writer drew the obvious conclusion: '...how small a proportion of [Christians] are admitted to responsible offices under government'.[66] This was increasingly to be the theme: a government service virtually without Christians was bound to oppress them: only a large representation within the public service, which was involved in more and more areas of Travancore life, could guarantee the rights of Christians.

Under the present regime, even where Christians did gain entry to the government services, claimed the Rev. John Caley, they were held back and discriminated against. He submitted a table showing the rank and salary of the eighteen new magistrates appointed since 1887.[67] Five were Christians, but none had risen to a salary of more than Rs. 70 a month; none of the remaining thirteen Brahmin and Nair magistrates drew less than Rs. 125. The government service lists for 1893-94 named the occupants of 5,850 jobs; one hundred and seventy-four had Christian names, and fifty-five of these were in the Forest and Cardamom Department. Ninety-one jobs carried salaries of more than Rs. 200 a month; five were held by Christians.[68] Moreover, in Kottayam taluk, where Christians, most of them Syrians, were a third of the population, the tahsildar was a Nair and his two immediate subordinates, Brahmins. There were only two Christians in the taluk office, and of the taluk's thirty-five pravrattikars, who presided over the smallest administrative units, only one was a Christian.[69]

The reason for their exclusion from posts of dewan peshkar and tahsildar, Christians had long been told, was that these officers had also to supervise the *uttupuras* and state temples, and none but a high-caste Hindu could approach the temple precincts. These executive posts were the offices where real power lay: control of the land assessment and registration, the revenue and the police. Representation in the Forest and Cardamom Department, working amongst the tribal people and the malaria of the Western Ghats, lacked the charm of the peshkar's kutcherry. Supervising gangs of coolies was a poor substitute for presiding over school prize days or interviewing petitioners. Even in the

Medical Department, the other sirkar agency in which Christians were well-represented, there was a tendency to try to keep their numbers down. In 1898 when the European head of the department employed two Syrians, one a graduate of Edinburgh and Glasgow on Rs. 70 a month, he received a sharp note from Sankara Subbaiyer which insisted that he must make no more hirings.[70]

Towards the end of Sankara Subbaiyer's administration, Syrians began to advance arguments which sounded more and more like the testimony of the Malayali Memorialists six or seven years earlier. They ridiculed as fraud the fastidiousness about temple pollution which kept the jobs of tahsildar and peshkar in the hands of Brahmins, Nairs and the occasional Tamil Sudra. *Manorama* wrote:

> Now this objection, if at all, is equally applicable to Sudra officials. Neither Christians nor Sudras will be admitted into the places where Brahmins are feasted; arrangements for this, which have in either case to be made from without and through subordinates, can be as efficiently carried out by a Christian official as by a Sudra. For in point of social status, the Syrian Christians who constitute the most important portion of the Christian community in Travancore, are in no way inferior to the Nairs. To their unsurpassed and unsurpassable loyalty and industry, the greatest of the Sovereigns of Travancore [Vishakham Tirunal] has borne eloquent testimony.

The newspaper pointed out that Syrians had degrees, held posts in Mysore and Madras and had sent the first Travancoreans to study in Britain. 'Moreover all Christian officials, unlike many of their more fortunate Hindu brethren, have attained their position only through the possession of more than the required qualifications'.[71]

The implication that Syrians were socially inferior to Nairs was a slight which Syrians would not bear. Although the conflict might be over jobs and power, the question of status gave it edge. For their part, Nairs could impishly choose to lump all Christians together: Syrians could not hold certain posts under the sirkar because Pulaya converts were so offensive. It was a charge which Syrians rejected, yet it led them to keep as remote as possible from the converts.

> ...The Syrian Christians in their every-day habits [*Manorama* wrote] and their intercourse with other people differ very little from the Nairs among whom they live. Their recognised social status is also high–higher certainly...than that of several of the so-called Nair castes ... [Yet] the accidental peculiarities of certain sections of Christians are now used as a dead weight to drag down all Christians alike even from that stage of tolerable pre-eminence so long enjoyed by them.[72]

In April 1898 the growing dissatisfaction with the Sankara Subbaiyer administration led Syrians to form an association 'to watch the interests of the Travancore and Cochin Christian community'.[73] Although it was called the Travancore and Cochin Christian Association, it was intended only for Syrians, and at first it had remarkable success in bringing together the various sects. The organisational meeting, held on 21 April, was called by T.C. Poonen, a CMS Syrian and the first Malayali to study in Britain; he was elected president. K. Kuruvila, the retired engineer and the first Syrian member of the Travancore Legislative Council, proposed the first resolution. It dealt with the discrimination Syrians were experiencing from Sankara Subbaiyer's government whose 'settled policy' towards Christians had been 'to reduce them to a position of distinct inferiority'. Yet the association resolved to be strictly loyal and launch no 'unfair agaitation'. *Manorama* observed that without 'the widespread discontent that now prevails among the Christian Community such antagonistic sects as the Protestants, the Roman Catholics, Jacobites and Reformed Syrians [Mar Thomites], could not have met on a common platform as they did at this meeting'.[74] Even Father Emmanuel Nidhiry, the leading Romo-Syrian, whose influence C.V. Raman Pillai had been so eager to win for the Memorial, was ready to participate, in spite of the disapproval of his European superiors.[75]

Yet why did Syrian protest come at this time? Except for a brief period under John Munro, Syrians had always been excluded from the sirkar service. The three major issues which disenchanted the protestant missionaries with the Sankara Subbaiyer administration had less importance for Syrians. The latter, moreover, were still recovering from the Jacobite-Mar Thomite litigation, the Romanists were ruled by a European hierarchy suspicious of all contacts with other sects, and Anglican Syrians were felt to be harming the whole community by their membership in a church which included low-caste converts.

In part, formation of an association was a reaction against litigation and sectarian strife. The intra-Syrian feuds had awakened 'the cultured men in all the different parties...to the conviction that their strength lies in their union...'[76] Strength, they thought, was necessary. The rise of an educated, ambitious Nair party in the sirkar service in league with Sankara Subbaiyer came to disturb Syrians as much as missionaries; nor did the assumption that the administration was anti-Christian depart with Sankara Subbaiyer. In 1899, K.P. Sankara Menon, the Malayali Memorialist and now a district judge, sentenced a Syrian sub-magistrate to two and a half years' rigorous imprisonment and a fine of Rs. 1,500 for wrongfully detaining and charging a Brahmin engineer of the Public Works Department. The outcry reached Madras where the *Mail* called the sentence 'monstrous'.[77] The High Court quickly reduced the sentence to a fine of Rs. 500, but the incident was the first in a series which was to win Sankara Menon the reputation of a staunch, partisan caste Hindu.[78] Similarly, when the European High Court judge went on leave in 1899 and was replaced by a Brahmin, for the first time in years the High Court was without a Christian judge. Syrians again smelled a plot.[79]

By the end of the century, leading Syrians were chastened and troubled. Yet, at the same time, many of them enjoyed an increasing economic power. Indeed, this added to the sense of grievance; the community with the only 'England-returned men' was excluded from the most powerful offices under government, and in those branches where its members did find entry, their progress was often hindered and retarded. A correspondent of the *Madras Mail* wrote that 'Syrian Christian merchants are getting the trade of the country into their hands. In the villages the hard-working Syrian is ousting the Sudra and the Nambudiri'.[80] T.C. Poonen had started the first wholly Travancore bank in Kottayam in the early 1890s, and although it had not prospered, in 1900 M. Pouloose, a Jacobite, founded the Tiruvalla Bank which operated successfully for a number of years.[81] By 1900

Travancore had twenty-four registered joint-stock companies. Nine of these were various kinds of provident funds operating from Shenkotta taluk, the Travancore enclave in the Madras 'Presidency; three were European. Of the remaining twelve, six were obviously Syrian, and the ownership of the other six is now uncertain. The first of these companies was *Malayala Manorama*, registered in March 1889.[82] In 1904 when the first session of the Popular Assembly was called, three trading organisations were each granted a representative. Two were companies based at Alleppey, one owned by Americans, the other by Bombay Muslims. The third was the Kottayam Traders' Association, led by M.M. Varghese and representing–in theory, at least–the interests of scores of Syrian merchants.[83]

Among themselves Syrians recognised no concept of ritual purity, although they were ostentatiously careful to regulate their relations with the low castes so that they would not be accused of carrying pollution to Nairs and Brahmins. But Syrians never allowed this concern for high-caste sensibilities to interefere with their commercial activities. They were ready to turn their hand to most enterprises, and by the turn of the century they had an impressively broad range of interests. The abkari contract for most of the taluks in Kottayam division had been held for twenty years by the Jacobite family which also owned the *Western Star*, the oldest English newspaper on the west coast.[84] Syrians dominated the newspaper business. By 1903 Travancore had fourteen Malayalam periodicals, ranging from the bi-weekly *Malayala Manorama* to the quarterly *Syrian Evangelist*; total circulation was estimated at 11,000. Syrians ran nine of these publications with a circulation of 6,700.[85] Moreover, the boom in tea at Pirmed and in the High Range from the 1890s had brought renewed prosperity to Kottayam and jobs for young Syrians. F.G. Richardson, the longest resident on the hills, had always enjoyed good relations with Syrians and employed them often. Although the labour was mostly Tamil, the clerical and artisan staff of most estates was Syrian. In this way, many Syrians learned the planting business and spread the idea of cash crops among their kinsmen in the lowlands, who were already profiting from pepper and who were later to grow rubber.[86] Lamenting the unadventurousness of other communities, a correspondent of the *Madras Mail* wrote in 1903 that 'a forest of fruit trees has grown up on the high lands' occupied by Syrians east of Kottayam.[87]

For Nairs, however, the most concrete and alarming manifestation of Syrian prosperity was their acquisition of land. We have already seen how Syrians were quick to take up waste land along the Kottayam-Madura road in the 1870s. Between 1877 and 1890 Rama Rao's administration introduced measures to encourage ryots to reclaim backwaters and low-lying land.[88] By 1903, 'a large extension of cultivation' was said to have taken place in Kottayam division.[89] Not all of it belonged to Syrians. Indeed, Kavalam Neelakantha Pillai, who had helped to finance the Memorial, was said to have been responsible for the reclamation of 2,000 acres in this area.[90] But much of the land reclaimed belonged to Christians; had it been otherwise, the anxiety of leading Nairs would not have been so great. That anxiety was well-founded, as we shall see in the next chapter, and was expressed in a much quoted speech by Thanu Pillai to a Nair meeting in Trivandrum in 1901, less than a year before his death:

> While a Brahmin friend of mine was travelling on government duty in the Kottayam Division with a smart local officer, the latter said in reply to repeated questions about the country and people–'whenever you see a person that is strong in physique, smart and of good bearing, you many infer that he is either a Syrian Christian or an Ilavan; and if you see one that is weak in physique, pale and listless in bearing, your inference that he is a Nair will not often be mistaken. Similarly, if you see a garden land with a good hedge and first-rate cocoanut palms in it, you can infer that the owner is a Syrian or Ilavan–if hedgeless and unattended, you can be sure that the land belongs to a Nair'. My friend, the Brahmin official, found out subsequently that all the local officer had said was true... The same condition of things I have found to be true more or less in the South of Travancore also...[91]

Thanu Pillai was attempting to rouse his audience. Some Syrians, however, used the speech as an occasion for jubilation:

> The Nairs have had special favours shown to them, and such favours are likely to be continued, perhaps in

> increasing measure. The Christians have had no adequate encouragement and are not likely to have for some time to come. But the tide of prosperity decidedly has set in favour of the latter. Will that tide be stemmed? The answer is not difficult. It is natural and moral forces that have been bringing about the prosperity of the Syrian Christians.

The writer concluded with the usual jibe at the Nair marriage system. As long as Syrians retained 'the qualities of thrift, self-reliance and purity' and their 'spirit of enterprise', they could 'afford to desire that their Nair friends and neighbours should leave off those pernicious customs that have been eating into the vitals of the community'.[92]

Yet Syrians had by no means supplanted Nairs as the economic power in the state. Both Thanu Pillai's pessimism and the anonymous Syrian's exultation were overdone. Nairs and Brahmins still controlled the public service, and the Travancore and Cochin Christian Association could do nothing to change matters. In 1899 it presented a memorial to the new Dewan, Krishnaswami Rao, calling for the removal of temple duties from executive officers, competitive examinations for the higher posts in the service and a more representative character to the composition of the administration.[93] *Manorama* warned darkly that when representation failed, 'people are justified in resorting to other and less mild forms of political agitation',[94] and pointed out that of eighty-six Syrian graduates, only thirty had found jobs under the sirkar.[95] The wandering Syrian graduate, forced to leave his native land, became a favourite theme; it was very like the one Nairs had played in 1891.[96] Getting no satisfaction from the sirkar, the association eventually petitioned the viceroy, but Curzon declined to interfere.[97]

Syrian unity was a precarious thing. By 1903 the Jacobites were suing the CMS, and Father Emmanuel Nidhiry, whom *Manorama* hoped would take the presidency of the 'sleepy' association, was ordered to withdraw from it--along with all Romo-Syrians--by his European superiors.[98] When the first session of the Sri Mulam Popular Assembly was called in the second half of 1904, it was found that even in Kottayam division wealthy Nair landlords were predominant. Of 361 landlords paying more than Rs. 100 a year in land tax, 154 were Nairs.[99]

| | |
|---|---|
| Nairs | 154 |
| Christians | 98 |
| Malayali Brahmins | 34 |
| Tamil Brahmins | 18 |
| Muslims | 14 |
| Kshatriyas | 10 |
| Ezhavas | 8 |
| Europians | 5 |
| Ambalavasis | 3 |
| Others | 17 |
| TOTAL | 361 |

Nairs were not about to be swept away. They were, however, beginning to feel a pressure which was to make them cling all the more tenaciously to their hold on the sirkar service. And with twenty-four newspapers[100] ready to attack each other, and numbers of public speakers ready to warn of the need for harmony and the dangers of communal discord,[101] conflict became self-sustaining.

*Ezhavas*

The main conflict at the turn of the century was between educated Syrians and the Nair elite which controlled much of the sirkar service. Elite Nairs had varying relations with the non-Malayali Brahmin element in the sirkar service. Nair-Brahmin harmony and Nair influence were at their height under Sankara Subbaiyer; later, Brahmin Dewans from outside Travancore were less responsive to Nair pressure. Yet between Nairs and Brahmins there was only one source of contention: government preferment, an issue which affected only a small percentage of Nairs. Syrians, on the other hand, could be seen not only as challengers for posts under the sirkar, but as aggressive landholders, enterprising businessmen and ambitious educationists. They were unquestionably Travancorean; they were counted in lakhs, not thousands, and they lived in close touch with ordinary Nairs who could see the aggrandisement of Syrians as a much more serious threat to their own status and influence than the employment of a few thousand Brahmins in government service. What is said here of Syrians could increasingly be applied to Ezhavas.

Thanu Pillai included Ezhavas in his admonitory speech of 1901, and from the mid-1890s there were growing indications of 'an awakening among the Elavars... They are beginning to assert themselves and to claim attention from the government. The movement has in it a very strong religious element also...'[102] Rama Rao claimed with little tact but some justification that Ezhavas had been 'imported into the Memorial' in 1891, and it seems true that Parameswaran Pillai and his associates were happy to use an acquaintance with Palpu to add four lakhs of people to their statistics.

Palpu, however, proved a doughty fighter. The failure of the Memorial--from the Ezhavas' point of view at least--and his own appointment in the Mysore service did not lessen his concern for his castemen in Travancore. In 1895 he submitted a long English petition to Sankara Subbaiyer which outlined the disabilities suffered by Ezhavas. He reiterated that under existing government policies, Ezhavas had only one course open to them if they wished to educate their children or enter sirkar service: conversion. 'This induced conversion is prejudicial to the interests of all the religions concerned...'[103] After eight months and a number of reminders, Palpu had no reply. He went to Trivandrum in February 1896 and received an assurance from Sankara Subbaiyer that qualified Ezhavas would receive consideration on their merits for all departments except Revenue; as many government schools as possible would be opened to them. But when a few Ezhava graduates immediately applied for jobs, they were told that there were no vacancies.[104]

Again taking leave from his job in Mysore, Palpu returned to Travancore and began to organise an unsuccessful Ezhava Sabha and a mass memorial similar to that of 1891; this, however, was to be signed only by Ezhavas. Within a few months, more than 13,000 Ezhavas, nearly half of them payers of land tax, had signed the petition, which was submitted to the Maharaja and released to the Madras newspapers in September 1896.[105] Claiming that Ezhavas paid more taxes that any other community, the petition lamented the fact that government schools were virtually closed to them and that they were denied the incentive to education which employment in the sirkar service provided. The 1891 census showed at least 25,000 'educated' Ezhavas, all of whom were working loyally in such pursuits as ayurvedic medicine, weaving, shopkeeping, the abkari trade and astrology. Those few with English education had left the country in search of employment. It was a source of regret that although Tiyyas in Malabar and Christian converts in Travancore were entertained in the goverment service, Ezhavas in Travancore were excluded. The memorial asked for entry to government schools and employment under the sirkar.[106]

Sankara Subbaiyer's reply offered little comfort. In his vague, discursive style, never using a concrete noun when two or three abstract ones would do, he wrote that Ezhavas themselves were great sticklers for caste customs and that in a state like Travancore, government had 'to feel their way'–a favourite phrase–'lest any violence should be done to social order and harmony'. Most of the higher schools in the state were open to Ezhavas, but to open lower schools would be to drive out the high castes. Special Ezhava schools would be started instead; some were already operating. 'Thus for all practical purposes the Memorialists are at no real disadvantage'. In the public service, the sirkar had now agreed that Ezhavas would be eligible for some departments, and this, government hoped, would 'meet the aspirations of the community having regard to their present educational condition'.[107] Ezhavas might have been forgiven for not dancing in the streets.

Within two weeks a letter from 'A Travancorean', almost certainly Palpu, appeared in the *Madras Mail.* It pointed out that only a few months before, Ezhavas had been rejected for posts in the very departments to which the Dewan now recommended that they should apply. (Not surprisingly, the Forest and Cardamom Department was one.) The superintendent of police, the letter claimed, was willing to employ Ezhavas but the Dewan would not consent; there were no Ezhavas in the police except for a few Christian converts.[108]

'A Travancorean' returned to the attack six weeks later when he reported that an Ezhava graduate whom the Dewan had told to apply to the Public Works Department had been rejected; a Brahmin undergraduate had been hired. Moreover there were only five special Ezhava schools in the state for a population of nearly five lakhs. And an Ezhava run school attended by four Nair pupils had been told by the school inspector, P. Ayyappan Pillai, to drop them from the rolls; thus caste distinctions, concluded the writer, were intentionally fostered.[109] Throughout his petitioning, Palpu had the support of Parameswaran Pillai who was editing the *Madras Standard.* Parameswaran Pillai raised the issue of the rights of Ezhavas in a speech at the National Social Conference in Poona in 1895, editorialised on their behalf in the *Standard* in 1896, and engineered a question in the House of Commons about their condition when he was in England in 1897. By 1898, however, Parameswaran Pillai was occupied with less glamorous affairs,[110] while Palpu seems to have concluded that attempting 'to claim the attention of government' was effort ill-spent. The direction of Ezhava activity changed, and moved towards the 'religious element'.

Shortly after Palpu took up service in Mysore, Vivekananda visited the state. Palpu appears to have got to know him well,[111] and many of Vivekananda's teachings were to find their way into the Ezhava movement as it developed at the turn of the century. Palpu became receptive to the idea of Hindu revivalism and reformation, but a western-educated, western-dressed doctor in government service in a distant state could exert little appeal to the emotional cravings of his castemen. In Sri Narayana Guru, one of the most famous Indian ascetics of the last hundred years, he found an ideal complement.

Born about 1855 near Trivandrum, Narayana was the son of an Ezhava *asan* (traditional schoolmaster) and cultivator. The chronology of his early life is difficult to piece together, but he was certainly educated in Malayalam, Tamil and Sanskrit. It appears that as a youth he helped his father in the fields and was remarkably devout. The latter may explain why he was allowed about 1877 to join a Sanskrit school run by a wealthy Ezhava family in Karunagapalli taluk in Quilon division. He remained there four years. When he returned to his home, he began small vernacular schools and acquired the title, Nanu Asan. He was married against his will to his cousin about 1882; it is uncertain whether the marriage was consummated. His parents died soon after, and he left home to wander as a sanyasi. In 1887 he founded a small Siva temple at Aruvipuram, near

Neyyattinkara, about fifteen miles south of Trivandrum. He used this as his base while he continued his wanderings in central and south Travancore, Tinnevelly and Madura district, where he was acquiring a reputation as a distinguished holy man. By about 1890 his remote hermitage and temple were attracting so many pilgrims that he had to establish a kitchen to feed them. In 1893 a sanyasi from Suchindram offered to make over his encumbered property if Narayana would pay off the debt. Two of Narayana's followers collected subscriptions, the debt was paid, the property registered, and P. Parameswaran, Palpu's elder brother, became manager of the temple properties. It was undoubtedly through Parameswaran that Palpu and Narayana met.[112] By 1896 Narayana's fame was widespread, and the annual Sivaratri festival drew 10,000 people, mostly Ezhavas to Aruvipuram. An LMS evangelist wrote:

> At the close of January we went to a festival, known as Sivarathri, held at Aruvipuram. It is a place 14 miles to the south of Trivandrum, famous for its shrine. It is situated near a waterfall, and dedicated to Siva by one Sanyasi (an Ascetic) named Nanen Asan, an Elaven by birth, greatly respected for his good behaviour and profound study of Hindu Vedas. He is called Swami and is very attractive in personal appearance.[113]

In the course of his travels Narayana met an Ezhava trader 'of moderate means' who had a studious, intelligent son. The son was N. Kumaran Asan who was to become the first secretary of the Ezhava caste association and perhaps the greatest modern Malayalam poet. Asan learned Sanskrit and Malayalam as a child, worked briefly as a merchant's accountant and left an advanced Sanskrit school after an argument with the master over the meaning of a sloka. At fourteen he met Narayana, and four or five years later, about 1892, he joined Narayana at Aruvipuram and studied yoga under him for two years. In 1894, Narayana visited Palpu in Bangalore, and arrangements were made for Asan to join the Sanskrit college there. With financial help from Palpu he studied Sanskrit and picked up English in Bangalore, Madras and Calcutta between 1895 and 1899 when he finally returned to Aruvipuram.[114]

Having acquired more funds and property, the Aruvipuram ashram was reorganised in 1899 as the Aruvipuram Temple Yogam; Asan was elected secretary-teasurer. He and Narayana toured as far as Malabar district to raise money, and another temple was started in north Travancore.[115] Finally in December 1902, ten shareholders, paying Rs. 100 each for a life membership, met at Aruvipuram to found the Sri Narayana Dharma Paripalana Yogam (SNDP Yogam), literally, the society for the propagation of the moral teachings of Sri Narayana. It was registered as a limited company in March 1903.

Palpu did not attend this inaugural meeting, nor was he one of the ten original shareholders. However, his absence underlined the fact that the Yogam had more resources than his to rely upon and that it was Narayana's spiritual message, rather than Palpu's more overtly political one, to which Ezhavas responded. Of the ten shareholders, four were from Neyyattinkara, and two each from Trivandrum, Kottarakara, and Mavelikara, the latter two places in Quilon district. But although the Yogam was organized around an ashram, its bye-laws were business-like and detailed. Its 'main object' was 'to promote and to encourage religious and secular education and industrious habits among the Elava Community...'[116] This included strict monogamy and the abolition of the tali ceremony and other expensive but unbrahminical customs.

By January 1904 when the Yogam met again in Trivandrum –this time Palpu attended--Asan had put out most of the society's capital on loan to Ezhavas and Eurasians; the interest was paying the salary of a Sanskrit master employed to teach Ezhava boys. About sixty people attended this meeting, including sixteen Ezhava ayurvedists, who were said to be quite wealthy. The wealthiest Ezhava landlord in Travancore sent a telegram of support.[117] The Yogam began to attract attention in Madras in 1904,[118] and under Palpu's inspiration it set about organising an industrial exhibition to coincide with its annual meeting in Quilon in January 1905. The exhibition, as we shall see, was so surprising a success, and Ezhavas so assertively optimistic as a result, that it was later said to have contributed to the Nair-Ezhava riots which followed within a few weeks.[119]

Palpu, Narayana and Asan were the right combination to tap the great reservoir of Ezhava yearning and discontent. But they did not create it. The economic condition of Ezhavas had improved with the spread of a cash economy.[120] (It must be remembered that payment of tax in kind continued in Travancore on some tenures until 1904.) The growth in the demand for coir products in America and Europe had brought prosperity to a few, and regular, cash-paid work to many. The abkari trade, which was dependent on Ezhavas in its tree-tapping stages, grew increasingly profitable, and some Ezhavas managed to become abkari farmers. Others were weavers. In his autobiography, C. Kesavan, the Ezhava leader, describes how his mother in the 1890s employed three or four weavers and used to weave herself. The weaving, plus a little farming, allowed her to raise a family of eight without great hardship.[121]

Although they shared some of the matrilineal customs of Nairs, Ezhavas, being poorer, were not handicapped by the large impartible taravad. Kesavan's mother had a polyandrous relationship with his sickly father and uncle, and this made available the resources of two adult males to the small family of about twelve members.[122] Being closer to the nuclear, patrilineal model, Ezhava families offered greater incentive for the individual; traditional occupations imparted useful skills. Asan's father was a trader, Palpu's had learned English in the 1860s and Narayana's had had his son educated in three languages, including Sanskrit. These were aspiring people. Moreover, some Ezhavas did own land. As we have seen, eight paid more than Rs. 100 in land tax in Kottayam division in 1904, and Alamuttu Channar, 'one of the richest landlords in Travancore', who had telegraphed his support to the inaugural meeting of the SNDP Yogam, paid 12,000 paras of rice and Rs. 15,000 in tax annually.[123]

There was, therefore, an Ezhava elite, albeit a tiny one. In many senses it was at least a generation behind the Nair elite typified by Thanu Pillai and his circle. But this was not necessarily a bad thing. While Nairs acquired BAs and BLs, scrambled for the sirkar service, formed genteel associations (usually, one feels, with Cobden and Bright strongly in mind) and preached about the dignity of labour and the need for social reform without doing much about either, necessity forced Ezhavas into more practical organisations. In spite of their crumbling institutions, Nairs could still afford to play at social reform; Ezhavas could not.

As early as 1887, the *Travancore Times* reported the formation of an Ezhava association at Vaikam in north Travancore. It levied a tiny monthly subscription from every Ezhava family in the neighbourhood and 'a few schools are being conducted ...for the education of their children who have no access to a sirkar school'.[124] In 1892 an LMS agent wrote that an Ezhava organisation at Paravur in Quilon district was holding regular monthly meetings to promote local education and was pressing him to start an English school.[125] By 1896 there were 16,000 Ezhavas in schools inspected by the sirkar (about 10 per cent of the total enrolment),[126] and in 1900 a correspondent of the *Madras Mail* superciliously reported 'a rather remarkable mania' among Ezhavas. The Ezhava youth 'aspires to be a religious teacher, gets off by rote tags of Sanskrit verse and takes to discipleship and begging...' The writer blamed the phenomenon on the throwing open the doors of the educational institutions of the province to the backward classes...'[127] Such cases were fairly common. In 1900 the LMS station at Attingal, between Trivandrum and Quilon, had not received a single Ezhava convert for a number of years, although most of its adherents were Ezhava converts of twenty years' standing. The missionary in charge attributed this recent absence of interest in Christianity to 'an increased activity on the part of the Eluvar caste everywhere to secure social and political recognition... To this end they have established associations of their own, have promoted education amongst themselves and have increasingly fitted themselves to take a part in the larger life and growth of the state'.[128] The CMS experience was similar: '...it is as easy to make a convert from the Brahmins as from the Chogans'.[129] And where the CMS had Ezhava converts these became increasingly demanding and unwilling to accept Syrian dominance of the Anglican Church.[130] Although conversion was to remain a useful threat for Ezhavas to use against caste Hindus, a junior partnership among Christians ceased to be an attractive alternative when respectability among Hindus became a possibility.

Sankara Subbaiyer, the first Dewan appointed after the Malayali Memorial, was a Tamil Brahmin, but his home was in Trivandrum, and he had been thirty years in the sirkar service. Having seen the trouble which western-educated Nair officials had made for his predecessor–or perhaps having a genuine liking for men whom he had known since their youth–he reached an accommodation with them. Nairs advanced in the sirkar service and pronounced his rule beneficial and beneficent. At the same time, policies which hindered and angered Christian missionaries were prosecuted, and Ezhava petitions calling for basic civil rights were dismissed. Eventually, the sirkar's actions towards Christians began to bring opposition from prosperous Syrians who sought a role in government equivalent to their educational and economic position. Yet for Syrians to point to their prosperity merely alarmed western-educated Nairs and made them cling more tenaciously to their remaining privileges under the sirkar. Where Nairs were losing land, Syrians were acquiring it; where Nairs were plagued by litigation, indolence and the taravad, Syrians were experimenting with banks, joint-stock companies and cash crops. Indeed, by 1904 even Ezhavas whose initial advantages were far fewer than Syrians, were seen by some Nairs as a potential threat to Nair pre-eminence.

Meanwhile, Sankara Subbaiyer's retirement eventually brought an end to the accommodation between official Nairs of C.V. Raman Pillai's generation and their non-Malayali Brahmin colleagues and superiors. Both Syrians and Ezhavas demanded a share in the administration, Brahmins showed no signs of abdicating, and British governments began to press gently for greater opportunities for non-Nairs and non-Brahmins. At the same time, a younger generation of educated Nairs began to feel increasing impatience at the palace politics and elite intrigues which so appealed to C.V. Raman Pillai and some of his friends. Although there might be agreement in Nair-controlled newspapers about the evils of Brahmin dominance of the government service, there were growing divisions among educated Nairs over the need for, and nature of, taravad reform.

On the other hand, the large majority of less educated, conservative Nairs was becoming conscious of the assertiveness of Ezhavas and, to a lesser extent, apprehensive of the expanding economic influence of Syrian Christians. In October 1904 the first Travancore representative assembly was called in an effort to bring the leading men of the various groups together harmoniously. In January 1905 Ezhavas held an impressive industrial exhibition at Quilon. Within a month, Nair-Ezhavas riots had broken out.

# 7

# 'Social Civil War': Nairs at Bay 1902-08

After twenty years in the Travancore service, fifteen as Chief Justice and five as Dewan, K. Krishnaswami Rao retired to 'Beaconsfield Gardens', Egmore, Madras, in February 1904. 'Old Krishnaswami Rao should be well content', wrote a former Resident. 'He has had a quiet life for many years in Travancore and has never been given to expense. As a Dewan I could not rate him highly; that he was complaisant to his Chief [the Maharaja] was no doubt his best commendation to him, but it certainly was not so to the State'.[1] Krishnaswami Rao had overstayed his time. Well before he retired, signs of inefficiency and corruption were apparent in the administration and the palace. Moreover, wider changes were in progress which ensured that no Travancore Dewan would have a quiet life again. Violent political activity among Maratha Brahmins in the rest of India even led some to question the old Dewan's loyalty to the British.[2] Curzon, moreover, was a viceroy who disapproved of quiet lives and was prepared to interfere in princely states.

In Travancore the Dewans since 1887 had been men from the Maharaja's service. Administrators had grown fat and the administration rusty. The land survey and settlement, begun in 1883, was still seven years from completion in 1904. Within the administration, the first generation of college educated Nairs–the stalwarts of the Malayali Sabha–'had risen to important positions and were intent on recapturing the power which they felt traditionally belonged to Nairs. By 1900 a Nair favourite was firmly established in the palace, and through him Nair officials like C.V. Raman Pillai were attempting to advance their interests. For the large majority of Nairs outside the administration, however, such ploys had little meaning. Nair taravads were in decay, and power in the palace could do little to save them. Nairs were alienating land at an alarming rate to Syrian Christians and, to a lesser extent, Ezhavas. Both Syrians and Ezhavas were increasingly resentful of the hold of *savarna* Hindus, especially Nairs, on the government service, and of the civil disabilities which applied in varying degrees to all who were not *savarna* Hindus. The aroma of power emanating from the new Popular Assembly, created in 1904 and modelled on the one which had met happily for twenty years in tranquil Mysore, whetted appetites rather than dulled them. A high rate of literacy and a flourishing vernacular press brought conflict increasingly into the open. By 1908 conservative Nairs were holding desperately to their old privileges against challenges from Syrian Christians and *avarna* Hindus; some Nairs carried on the battle against Brahmin dominance and exploitation. But the real problem for Nairs, and the one which concerned virtually every Nair in the state, was the decay of the matrilineal joint-family.

## *PALACE POLITICS*

The wife of Mulam Tirunal, the Maharaja, had died in child birth in 1882. For many years the Maharaja did not remarry. In the 1890s, however, he developed an affection for a Nair woman. She divorced her husband–here was the loose marriage tie which so embarrassed educated Nairs–and married the Maharaja, who gave her ex-husband a place in the palace and the title of 'Thampi'. T. Sankaran Thampi, who was to outlive Mulam, married his ex-wife's sister. All lived within the palace precincts,[3] and Sankaran Thampi's influence came to rival that of the early favourite, Saravanai Ananda Narayana Aiyar, 'the illiterate cook boy'. Sankaran Thampi, born in 1860, was a contemporary of the official Nairs of the Malayali Sabha, and two of his brothers were tahsildars.[4] The connections and the opportunities were obvious.

C.V. Raman Pillai's biographer later claimed that his subject cultivated Sankaran Thampi merely to try to lessen the influence of non-Malayali Brahmins and to advance the interests of P. Thanu Pillai, who was the Nair hope for the Dewanship until his death in 1902.[5] Palace politics, however, were vicious and corrupt, and, what was more, they became less and less relevant to the pressing social problems of the majority of Nairs.

As early as 1890 a Resident had seen the growing defects of the Maharaja's government as 'the tendency to develop a palace bureau–outside the ordinary administration...'[6] The Maharaja had important powers. He could veto the proposals and appointments of the Dewan and press his own. The annual palace budget which ran into lakhs of rupees could be spent largely at his whim. The palace could also occasionally bypass the 'proper channels' of the Dewan's kutcherry and instruct officials to carry out its will without reference to the Dewan in the towns and taluks of Travancore. With a compliant Dewan like Krishnaswami Rao, such irregularities were unimportant. In exercising his powers, the Maharaja heavily relied on his favourites. 'He is,' wrote the governor of Madras,

> in a singularly isolated position as he has no relations whatever, and nobody with whom he can make friends. This and his dependent character oblige him to have somebody with whom he can be on intimate terms and if the present 'favourites' were dismissed there is no doubt that he would find others and perhaps worse ones.[7]

The favourites sold appointments and grew rich.[8] 'The state of the Court here is very bad', wrote the Anglican bishop. 'Unworthy favourites rule and we hear of great scandals'.[9]

The question of the favourites and the maladministration of Travancore pressed itself on British governments after the body of a young Nair girl was found in the palace gardens in May 1902. The scandal reached the Madras newspapers and ultimately Curzon, who instructed the Madras government to seek an inquiry.[10] Ampthill, the governor of Madras, concluded that 'there is nothing in the evidence to justify the suspicion of murder' and asserted that the Maharaja was innocent of any complicity.

Curzon, however, was less sure,[11] and when an attack on the Travancore administration came to him in July 1903, he seized it eagerly.

This indictment, which ran into eighteen printed pages, came from R.S. Lepper who had been appointed as professor of history in the Maharaja's College, Trivandrum, in 1900.[12] Lepper's style was pompous and melodramatic, but Curzon was impressed and chose to believe most of Lepper's charges. 'The really dangerous influence at present', Lepper wrote, 'is the corrupt bribe-taking influence of the favourite', by whom he meant Sankaran Thampi, who was over-shadowing his rival, Saravanai. Lepper continued:

> ...Brahminical interest is latterly much on the decline, the Nairs having organised themselves in what are really anti-Brahmin clubs all over Travancore to resist the Brahmins everywhere, believing themselves to have been victimised by the Brahmins for centuries. The all-powerful favourite, Sankaran Thumpi, is a Nair, and not a Brahmin, and uses his influence against Brahmins.

Lepper concluded that there were three weak men in power—'the Maharaja, Krishnaswami Rao and G.T. Mackenzie, the bumbling Resident--and consequently the favourites had wide scope for profitable mischief. He also alleged that the Nair girl in the palace had been murdered and that C.M. Madhavan Pillai, the Travancore tour agent for the Delhi durbar, had siphoned off thousands of rupees for himself. Madhavan Pillai had been the investigating magistrate in the murder case.[13] Lepper recommended a new Dewan, 'preferably a Brahmin not belonging to Travancore', and a slipper-beating and banishment for Sankaran Thampi.

Ampthill was furious at Curzon's unquestioning acceptance of Lepper's charges. This was, he felt, the beginning of an attempt by the viceory to remove Travancore from the jurisdiction of the Madras government and bring it into direct relations with the government of India.[14] Yet he had to admit that the Resident was incompetent, that Krishnaswami Rao was 'not a strong man' and that bribery and corruption existed 'to a serious extent'. There was, he wrote, no evidence to suggest that civil and criminal justice was corrupt, though 'the highest appointments in Travancore are probably bought and sold'. The Resident unfortunately had fourteen months to serve before he was due to retire, and the successor to Krishnaswami Rao was 'a matter of some difficulty'.[15]

From August 1903 the search was on for a new Dewan who would be able to curtail the influence of the favourites and lessen the intensity of the rivalries in which the favourites were always ready to become involved. 'But here is the difficulty', Ampthill wrote. 'There is nobody in the whole of our service who is marked out for the post...'[16] As Ampthill expected, the Maharaja wished to appoint a pliable Travancorean to the Dewanship and pressed for V. Nagam Aiya–'that windbag', as one Resident snorted.[17] The Madras government refused to approve the appointment, and the Maharaja, well prompted in the palace, objected to all the Madras government's suggestions. There the matter remained until February 1904 when the name of V.P. Madhava Rao, suggested by 'a mere Press Reporter',[18] was mentioned to Ampthill.

V.P. Madhava Rao was not related to Sir T. Madhava Rao, although both were Desastha Brahmins from Tanjore. Indeed, V.P. Madhava Rao's career was comparable in a number of ways to that of his older namesake. Born in 1850, he studied at Kumbakonam College under W.A. Porter, as legendary an educationist as Sir T. Madhava Rao's mentor, E.B. Powell. V.P. Madhava Rao graduated in 1869 and immediately entered the Mysore service where he served under Dewans V.C. Ranga Charlu and K. Seshadri Aiyar. He was headmaster of the royal school, a district officer and inspector general of police before becoming revenue commissioner and first member of council in 1901. Ampthill concluded that 'there was no man in Southern India better fitted for the post'[19] and after much negotiation and 'about a score of personal letters',[20] he persuaded the Maharaja of Travancore to accept Madhava Rao. Madhava Rao was induced to take the post 'to help the Madras government out of a difficulty and thereby render imperial service'.[21]

Madhava Rao's appointment was largely directed against the favourites, particularly Sankaran Thampi. It was not surprising that the latter sought to frustrate the new Dewan. C.V. Raman Pillai's biographer wrote that Madhava Rao's appointment spoiled the vision of the future of men like Raman Pillai and that 'the people' saw Brahmin dominance poised to reassert itself.[22] Raman Pillai attacked the Dewan anonymously in the local press, and a case concerning the proper dress for the Dewan to wear in the Padmanabhaswami Temple was trumped up to embarass him.[23] Brahmins in Trivandrum conducted a newspaper called the *Malabar Mail; Subhashini*, a Nair paper for which Raman Pillai often wrote, dubbed Madhava Rao 'the *Malabar Mail's* Mysore bull'.[24] Within a year of Madhava Rao's appointment, it was apparent that against him 'local intrigue is gaining ground, so that there is an unpleasant prospect of a political crisis...'[25]

Yet Sankaran Thampi and his friends did not make all the running, and for a time Madhava Rao was confident of success. In July 1904 he reported that 'the so-called favourite has...retired into private life and has left His Highness to transact State business solely in consultation with his responsible advisers'.[26] Ampthill's appreciation was more accurate: 'they [the favourites] are most probably lying low, cunning fellows as they are, and waiting for their opportunity'.[27] The Maharaja's position was given suitably ambivalent expression in a letter he wrote to the acting governor of Madras: 'As for the very rapid progress that is being made, Your Excellency will forgive me for saying that I am not responsible, although I give my utmost support to [the dewan]'.[28]

Madhava Rao's greatest victory over the favourites came when it was too late to matter–in February 1906, just before he resigned the Dewanship to return to quieter Mysore as Dewan. The High Court, presided over by the new chief justice, T. Sadasiva Aiyer, a well-educated liberal imported from Madras, brought down a judgement in a bribery case which implicated Sankaran Thampi and exposed the dealings of C.M. Madhavan Pillai who had died in 1904. Sadasiva Aiyer wrote:

> It seems to have been the impression of plaintiff and several others–it is not necessary to say whether it was a right or wrong impression–that Mr. Sankaran Tampi could be influenced by bribes to have palace orders issued in favour of any party he wished to favour, that the Fouzhadar, Mr. Anantha Rama Iyer (called usually Sarvanaswami) could also be induced to favour parties, and that if one party tried to influence Mr. Sankaran Tampi, the opposite party ought to go to Mr. Anantha Rama Iyer if he wished to counter-balance the weight

of Mr. Sankaran Tampi.[29]

The decision discomfited Sankaran Thampi, but did not defeat him. Madhava Rao issued a notice in the *Gazette* that all petitions were to be directed to the Dewan's kutcherry, not the palace, and sent a confidential circular to district officers telling them to take orders only from the Dewan. 'These salutary changes', the new Resident wrote, 'seriously affected the favourite's influence and income and he swore vengenance on the Chief Justice'.[30] But Sankaran Thampi's influence with the Maharaja remained 'as strong as ever'. In the period of uncertainty after Madhava Rao's resignation, 'Nair officers under the control of the Palace were actually put into many minor appointments'. Only the Resident's veto prevented the appointment of V.I. Keshava Pillai–'a corrupt and useless official,' wrote the Resident, as head of the survey and settlement.[31] Keshava Pillai, like the late Madhavan Pillai, was a close friend of C.V. Raman Pillai, a member of the old Malayali Sabha and a signatory of the Malayali Memorial. Raman Pillai himself is said to have received gifts from Sankaran Thampi and the Maharaja.[32]

For those Nairs of Raman Pillai's background and generation, there was profit and exhilaration in these palace intrigues. But British governments and Residents strongly disapproved, and educated Syrian Christians and Ezhavas were virtually excluded from any part in the administration. One of Madhava Rao's aims when he came to Travancore seems to have been to bring politics into the open and to encourage those groups which still suffered traditional disabilities. To this end in the latter part of 1904 he established the Sri Mulam Popular Assembly, a large consultative body of local notables which would meet for a few festive days each year in Trivandrum to keep the government informed of the needs of the country. It was an attempt to provide a dignified and constructive arena–all else that was available was the scurrilous vernacular press, the small Legislative Council and the palace–for increasing numbers of educated Travancoreans. The importance of palace intrigues could thereby be diminished, while the Dewan would no longer be alone in trying to combat the favourites. Educated Syrian Christians, for example, showed no hesitation in exposing 'the vagaries of an illiterate menial' or 'the accession of Sankaran Thampi'.[33]

## *THE SRI MULAM POPULAR ASSEMBLY*

Soon after Madhava Rao arrived in Travancore, he filled two vacant places in the eleven-man Legislative Council with non-Malayali Brahmins. Almost immediately a delegation of 'non-Brahmins', said to represent Nairs, Syrian Christians and Ezhavas,[34] asked to meet the Dewan to protest at the composition of the Legislative Council, which now had six Brahmins, none of whom was a landholder. The delegation was led by Mallur K. Govinda Pillai, a twenty-six-year-old lawyer patronised by C.V. Raman Pillai.[35] Madhava Rao met the deputation, accepted its petition and took the opportunity to deliver a lengthy lecture. He was, he said, surprised to find that in Travancore people having similar interests did not form associations to give continuous expression of their opinions to government instead of engaging in 'spasmodic' petitioning. There was a 'want...of any public spirit', and therefore he was happy to see even this delegation, for it indicated 'signs of political life in you, however nascent they may be'. He defended his appointees as the ablest men available and advised the delegation to turn its attention to much needed activities like the education of the backward classes. He hoped that the delegates would not again 'forget the larger interests of the country' as they had in their petition, a document confined 'to class and sectional considerations'.[36]

Such a dressing down–especially one so rapidly communicated to the Madras press--was not calculated to place Madhava Rao first in the hearts of educated Nairs. However, his remarks about the desirability of organisations and political activity appear to have had more sincerity than unctuousness about them. Less than a month later he began preparations to call a new body, the Sri Mulam Popular Assembly, to allow landholders and merchants to inform the sirkar of 'their requirements, wishes or grievances...' District officers were to choose the representatives, who must be non-officials over eighteen and either pay more than a hundred rupees in land tax or have an income in excess of Rs. 6,000 annually. The town improvement committees of Trivandrum, Nagercoil, Quilon, Kottayam and Alleppey were each to nominate a member, and other associations, especially of planters, would be given representation. District officers were told to emphasise that the Popular Assembly was being created solely to give the people an opportunity of raising subjects for the sirkar's attention; it would have no legislative powers.[37]

Madhava Rao looked on the Assembly as a means of diverting the communal antagonisms which troubled the state. In a speech in September 1904 he condemned 'such suicidal distinctions as Brahmin and non-Brahmin and Hindu and non-Hindu' and claimed that the Assembly 'will be a powerful factor in promoting good understanding between different sections of the community, removing class and caste prejudices and advancing the general good of the country'.[38] A letter writer to the *Madras Mail* agreed that the Assembly would help to create 'a spirit of union among the now separated classes of the people'. Another more pessimistic writer, however, felt that the Assembly would 'only serve as another instrument in the hands of party leaders in their conflicts arising every day from the clas[h ]of their questionable interests'.[39]

The first session of the Assembly, however, was a model of amity. Perhaps it could not have been otherwise, for the time and date of the inaugural meeting were altered to 11 o'clock on the morning of 22 October on the advice of Travancore's leading astrologer.[40]

In the composition of the Assembly, Nairs predominated. The thirty-one taluks sent sixty-five representatives; twelve were identifiable as Nairs and another eight were probably Nairs, although their caste is not given. A total of eighty-eight members attended the session, but seven of these were powerful townsmen, like E. Ramier of the Counter-Memorial, who had somehow been overlooked and were appointed to represent an area or an organisation, more than a quarter were Nairs. Syrian Christians and non-Malayali Brahmins made up an eighth each. There were seven Malayali Brahmins--two of whom spoke, one to recite a Sanskrit verse and the other to complain about temple maintenance--and six Kshatriyas. Ezhavas, Shanars, Protestant converts and Latin Catholics totalled about six. The landed interest was overwhelmingly dominant. Of the forty-three taluk representatives from the districts of Padmanabhapuram, Trivandrum and Kottayam (Quilon statistics have not survived), thirty-one were landed proprietors.

This emphasis on the landed interest was what educated Nairs had been understandably demanding since the Malayali

Memorial. At least half of the landed proprietors represented in Table 7.2 were Nairs, and another seven (including janmis) were educationally backward Nambudiris and Kshatriyas, many of whose interests as landed *savarna* Hindus corresponded with those of Nairs. The reasons for Nairs' concern for the representation of landed proprietors becomes clearer when one looks at the caste or religion of non-landed or multi-interest delegates to the Assembly. Of the nine shown in Table 7.2 (excluding janmis), only one was a Nair, while of the nine representatives of towns and associations (excluding seven Europeans) in Table 7.1 only two were Nairs. As long as the qualification for representation was based on landholding, Nairs held an advantage over both non-Malayali Brahmins and Syrian Christians. In any legislative arrangement involving a limited franchise based on a landholding qualification, Nairs could expect to dominate. Yet–and here was the rub for many educated Nairs—the breakdown of the taravad was not only hindering Nairs' use of their greatest asset, the land, but was indeed forcing them to alienate land at an alarming rate.

*TABLE 7.1*

*Showing Castes of Representatives from Taluks, and from Towns, Associations and Businesses, to Assembly in 1904*

| Caste | Taluk reps. | Merchant, planter, town and association reps. | Total |
|---|---|---|---|
| Nairs | 12 | 2 | 14 |
| Probable Nairs | 9 | - | 9 |
| Non-Malayali Brahmins | 9 | 2 | 11 |
| Syrian Christians | 8 | 2 | 10 |
| Malayali Brahmins | 7 | - | 7 |
| Kshatriyas | 6 | - | 6 |
| Muslims | 3 | 2 | 5 |
| Ezhavas | 1 | - | 1 |
| Probable Ezhavas | 1 | - | 1 |
| Latin Catholics | 1 | - | 1 |
| Shanars | 1 | - | 1 |
| Probable Protestant Converts | 1 | 1 | 2 |
| Europeans | - | 7 | 7 |
| Uncertain | 6 | - | 6 |
| TOTAL | 65 | 16 | 81 |

*Source:* TGER, TPD, File 113A of 1904.

The distinguished observers who were given seats on the dais for the opening session were a disconcerting feature of the Assembly for Nairs--and even more so for Christians and Ezhavas. Among them were twenty-seven Europeans and Eurasians, twenty-two non-Malayali Brahmins, twenty Kshatriyas, Nairs and Tamil Sudras and two Christians.[41] That dominance of the highest spheres of Malayali life, which Nairs of C.V. Raman Pillai's generation saw as their birthright was still far from reattainment. Nor were Christians and Ezhavas likely to ignore their virtual exclusion from the ranks of the invited guests.

The two-day session of the Assembly, however, passed off happily in a festive atmosphere. Representatives were given the same travelling allowances as tahsildars, and careful arrangements were made for their stay in Trivandrum.[42] The proceedings opened with a speech by Madhava Rao which outlined the aims in calling the Assembly and the activities of the government during the past year. Madhava Rao was followed by E. Ramier, who made a long and obsequious speech praising the Maharaja's generosity. This set the tone, and loyalty and gratitude became the theme of most speakers, even those who questioned the Dewan or raised local problems. The most striking feature of the session, according to the correspondent of the *Madras Times*, was 'that the Nambudires [sic], the highest class of Brahmins, and Elavas, the lowest [caste] were brought together under the same roof'.[43] The reference would not have pleased Ezhavas, but the writer's point was well taken. Had the suggestion of such an assembly been made in the youth of some of the delegates, it would have provoked laughter and incomprehension.

With the Assembly pronounced a success by all, it seemed certain that it would be summoned again in 1905. The first session had recognised the claim of special groups or associations: three merchant concerns and the South Travancore Native Christian Association had been permitted to send delegates. A well-known organisation obviously had a good chance of being asked to send a representative. Palpu and Kumaran Asan undoubtedly were aware of this when they planned a programme to enhance the reputation of the SNDP Yogam in 1905. The consequences of that programme were to be more widespread than its planners expected.

*TABLE 7.2*

*Occupation by Caste or Religion, of the Taluk Representatives from Padmanabhapuram, Trivandrum and Kottayam Divisions to the Assembly of 1904*

| | *Nairs* | *Probable Nairs* | *Syrians* | *Non-Malayali Brahmins* | *Malayali Brahmins* | *Kshatriyas* | *Muslims* | *Others* | *Uncertain* | *Total* |
|---|---|---|---|---|---|---|---|---|---|---|
| Landed proprietors | 10 | 4 | 4 | 1 | 0 | 4 | 0 | 4 | 4 | 31 |
| Vakil and landed proprietor | 1 | 0 | 0 | 1 | 0 | 0 | 0 | 0 | 1 | 3 |
| Trader and landed proprietor | 0 | 0 | 0 | 0 | 0 | 0 | 2 | 0 | 0 | 2 |
| Priest and landed proprietor | 0 | 0 | 1 | 0 | 0 | 0 | 0 | 0 | 0 | 1 |
| Janmis | 0 | 0 | 0 | 0 | 3 | 0 | 0 | 0 | 0 | 3 |
| Vakils | 0 | 0 | 0 | 2 | 0 | 0 | 0 | 0 | 0 | 2 |
| Traders | 0 | 0 | 0 | 1 | 0 | 0 | 0 | 0 | 0 | 1 |
| | 11 | 4 | 5 | 5 | 3 | 4 | 2 | 4 | 5 | 43 |

## *THE SNDP YOGAM'S INDUSTRIAL EXHIBITION AND THE NAIR-EZHAVA RIOTS*

By mid-1904 the SNDP Yogam was receiving notice in the Madras press, operating a few schools and temples and publishing a monthly magazine, *Vivekodayam,* edited by Kumaran Asan and showing in its content its debt to Vivekananda. Across its masthead was the English slogan, 'God helps those who help themselves'.[44] A month after the 1904 session of the Assembly, the Yogam announced that it would hold an industrial exhibition in Quilon to coincide with its second annual general meeting in January 1905. Only Ezhavas were permitted to enter. The exhibits were to be of crafts or produce, and there was to be a special competition for knowledge of Sanskrit.[45]

The exhibition had a wide impact. C. Kesavan, then a boy of thirteen wrote a vivid four-page account in his autobiography nearly fifty years later.[46] He recalled the dress of the leading men: their dark suits, long coats and turbans. It was rare then, he wrote, for an Ezhava even to wear trousers; the honourable dress was a single cloth around the waist and another draped around the shoulders.[47] He remembered also the typewriter which he saw for the first time, the skilful exhibits of Ezhava craftsmen and agriculturalists and the resentment of *savarna* Hindus at such Ezhava pretensions. As a result of the meeting and exhibition, he wrote, Ezhavas began to awaken.[48]

The success of the exhibition probably surprised even its organisers. Dozens of exhibits of cocoanut and other agricultural products were submitted, and 3,000 Ezhavas, a few from as far north as Cannanore in British Malabar,[49] attended. Palpu, moreover, was able to attract support from many quarters. The Maharaja sent a contribution of Rs. 300, and the Dewan, who had promised to open the exhibition but later withdrew, sent Rs. 50. A total of Rs. 3,000 was raised to defray costs. The twenty-six Sanskrit entrants were judged by Kerala Varma, a Kshatriya and self-confessedly Travancore's leading man of letters, and A. Govinda Pillai, by this time a judge of the High Court.

When the Dewan, whom Palpu had known in Mysore, was unable to come, Palpu got T.F. Bourdillon, Travancore's Conservator of Forests and brother of Sir James Bourdillon, a former Resident in Mysore, to perform the opening ceremonies. Bourdillon, an old Travancore hand, was probably more perceptive in his encouragement than the Dewan would have been. '... You [Ezhavas]', he told the gathering, 'have a great advantage in being accustomed to manual labour and trained in special industries. ... You have ...the entire control of the cocoanut-fibre industry in your hands, at all events in its early preparation'. Before the ceremonies began, Sri Narayana Guru was met at the Quilon landing jetty and taken in procession through the streets to the meeting place, which was decorated with pictures of himself, the King and Queen, the Maharaja and the Dewan. Palpu proudly told the meeting that the Yogam had six hundred paid-up members.[50] *Malayala Manorama* wrote of the 'interest and admiration' which 'the very successful exhibition' excited.[51]

As C. Kesavan's recollections emphasise, the exhibition gave many Ezhavas a sense of pride and wider community which had hitherto been lacking. It was proof that Ezhavas could organise and create–and that they could wear long black coats and trousers, like other educated Indians and Englishmen, in the eighty-degree heat of a Kerala January. Moreover, the respect accorded to Sri Narayana as a genuine holy man, even by men of higher castes, was proof of Ezhavas' place within Hindu society and perhaps of the possibility of improving that place. For conservatives among higher castes, however, the exhibition and the new self-confidence of Ezhavas were signs of an assertiveness which cried out to be resisted and destroyed.

On 22 January 1905, about ten days after the end of the exhibition in Quilon town, fighting broke out between Nairs and Ezhavas at a temple festival at a village in the northern part of Quilon division. Following the successful exhibition, Ezhavas were said to have put on airs, and when the temple procession took place, they dressed their women in imitation of Nairs and pressed closer to the idol than custom allowed. Nairs retaliated by beating the disrespectful Ezhavas and sometimes stripping their women to the waist. At about the same time in Haripad, the nearest small town, Nairs beat Ezhava schoolboys who had refused to move off the public road to allow Nairs to pass unpolluted.[52] At Haripad the real sore point was the government school to which Ezhavas had been admitted over Nair opposition in 1903. Some Nairs had withdrawn their children while others had continued to grumble at the innovation.[53]

Ezhavas, who had a local organisation affiliated to the SNDP Yogam, were quick to respond to these incidents with telegrams and petitions, and also, even at this early stage, with despatches to the Madras newspapers.[54] The European superintendent of police travelled north to investigate and posted a Christian inspector, an LMS convert, to replace the Nair officer who had been in charge. All the officials in the area were Nairs. Although there were reports of scattered clashes and of intimidation of Ezhavas on their way to the district headquarters in Quilon, the trouble seemed to subside. The Maharaja and the Dewan went on tour to Madras as scheduled, and Nagam Aiya was left in charge of the huzur kutcherry. He viewed the situation more seriously--or perhaps he enjoyed the self-importance of sending orders. On 9 February he wrote to the dewan peshkar of Quilon, V.I. Keshava Pillai, to warn him of 'serious breaches of the public peace' similar to those between Shanars and Maravars in Tinnevelly in 1899. He instructed Keshava Pillai 'to take *immediate* steps to prevent the quarrels developing into serious faction fights in which the whole population may take sides'.[55]

Whatever measures Keshava Pillai took, they were ineffective, and, Ezhavas later charged, provocative. On 20 February there were further disturbances ending in bloodshed in Karunagapalli, Kartigapalli and Chengannur taluks of Quilon division, and Keshava Pillai telegraphed to Trivandrum for extra police and troops. He got little sympathy from Madhava Rao who by now had returned from Madras. Scribbling a marginal note about peshkars 'keeping too much at hdquarters [sic] and ... to desk work', Madhava Rao replied that 'the whole thing will subside if you visited [sic] the scene of the so-called riots and brought your personal influence to bear... The calling out of troops will invest the whole affair with greater importance than it deserves'. None of 'the extraordinary measures' which Keshava Pillai called for was to be implemented.[56]

If Ezhavas were getting the worst of these clashes in Quilon division, they were getting the best of them in the Madras press. On 21 February the *Mail* reported the persecution of Ezhavas in Quilon taluk and a week later the *Times* wrote that worried Ezhava leaders had telegraphed for Palpu to come from Mysore.[57] Some newspapers in Kerala presented the Nair case,[58] but on the propaganda front Ezhavas were generally better organised. When the disturbances intensified in March, Ezhavas in Quilon division wired a petition to the sirkar in Trivandrum–and to the *Madras Times*.[59] The SNDP Yogam held an emergency meeting on 4 March, and Kumaran Asan forwarded to the government its resolution appealing for support. He pointed out that he had received letters and petitions from Yogam members in Quilon division and that intimidation had prevented some from attending the emergency meeting at Aruvipuram.[60]

Ezhavas maintained a solidarity which gave them an advantage in putting their case. Educated men like Asan and his associates in the Yogam advised those who collided with Nairs, and organised the petitions and telegrams. Educated Nairs, however, were on the defensive. They may have had some sympathy with their conservative castemen, and Nair officials probably did show partiality, as Ezhavas charged. However, the causes of the disturbances–enforcement of distance pollution and exclusive schools–were not ones with which educated Nairs would have wanted to be publicly associated, regardless of their private feelings. For Ezhavas, the problem was fairly simple. Very much the challengers for a respected place in Malayali society, they had far fewer influential men. Consequently, there was a feeling that all must hang together to avoid hanging separately.

The disturbances continued into March. Ezhava homes were entered, men beaten and women 'compelled to remove their upper cloth'.[61] *Sujanandhini*, an Ezhava newspaper published at Paravur south of Quilon, called on the Resident to intervene and wrote that Ezhavas planned to ask the British government and the rulers of Cochin and Mysore for grants of land where Ezhavas might settle. 'Many', it continued, 'are contemplating a change of religion. It is under discussion whether Christianity or Mohammedanism will afford the neccessary relief'.[62] Shortly after the publication of this editorial, the office of *Sujanandhini* was burned down–by Nairs, the editor claimed.[63] No one was ever prosecuted for the fire. The incident resulted in Madhava Rao himself going on tour in Quilon division. He met the editor of *Sujanandhini* and a number of Ezhava delegations, and guaranteed them protection if they went to Quilon to file formal complaints.[64]

Madhava Rao also appears to have encouraged a public meeting of reconciliation which was held on 19 March in the Malayali Hall, built by the old Malayali Sabha, in Quilon. It was chaired by Kavalam Neelakantha Pillai. It heard fifteen speakers and passed five resolutions; about 1,000 people were said to have attended. At least six of the speakers were Ezhavas, and two of the resolutions represented clear advances for them. One urged members of both sides to seek education by taking advantage of the sirkar's order of 1904 which opened most government schools to Ezhavas. The other thanked the sirkar for it's attempts to select government employees from all communities.[65] With the meeting, the disturbances ended; only the recriminations remained. These included an unsuccessful Nair attempt to trump up a bribery charge against the Christian police inspector[66] and allegations that Nairs were setting fire to the houses of non-Malayali Brahmins as part of a plot directed against all their competitors.[67]

A few Ezhavas emerged bruised from the disturbances, but no one was killed on either side. The crisis helped to enhance the reputation and confidence of the SNDP Yogam which had brought Palpu from Mysore at the height of the trouble to lend moral support.[68] At the end of April the Yogam was back on the offensive when it petitioned the sirkar either to allow Ezhava children into a school at Changanacherry or to help Ezhavas build a school of their own. The petition, neatly written in English, bore the marks of twenty-eight iliterate residents and not a single signature in Malayalam or English. This, concluded the *Malabar Herald*, was the work of Kumaran Asan and Palpu.[69] At about the same time, Ezhavas boycotted a temple festival at Cranganore in Cochin in which they had traditionally taken part—from a deferential distance. Their 'spiritual head', it was reported, was arranging to build another temple in the area.[70] Finally in June a Yogam meeting in north Travancore passed a resolution requesting the sirkar to permit the Yogam to nominate a representative to the Popular Assembly. The request was granted in 1907.[71]

The success of Ezhava leaders in publishing their version of the disturbances and in communicating with large numbers of their illiterate castemen was clearly apparent to Nairs. It is not a coincidence that Nair efforts to carry on a united, vigorous caste association were renewed in 1905. But Nairs, unlike *avarna* Hindus, lacked the binding tie of common grievances. Conservative Nairs still set much store by the old subcaste distinctions, while among the educated there were factions and disagreements.

## *ATTEMPTS TO ORGANISE NAIRS*

After the Malayali Memorial, the Malayali Sabha had virtually died. The accommodation with Sankara Subbaiyer meant that its leading spirits found comfortable billets in the sirkar service, while the rise of Sankaran Thampi gave them a channel into the palace as well. By 1895, the number of schools under the Malayali Sabha's control had fallen to two and the Malayali Hall in Quilon was supervised by a few local Nairs.[72] Other genteel associations grew up, but the reforming zeal was absent. The Vidhya Abhivardana Sabha (society for the growth of knowledge) was established in Trivandrum in 1897 and held annual meetings addressed by Thanu Pillai himself and others of his circle. It was at such a meeting that Thanu Pillai made his speech about the decay of the Nairs. But the activities of the society did not go beyond speech-making about the need for taravad reform and the virtues of thrift, enterprise and legal marriage.[73] C. Krishna Pillai, still working in northern Travancore, became estranged from his friends in the Thanu Pillai circle in Trivandrum,[74] and conservative rural Nairs were preoccupied with quarrels, disputes and ceremonies.[75] As one Nair wrote to another in January 1904, while Ezhavas were advancing in the newspaper business, English study, female education, ayurvedic medicine and the coir, copra and rice trades, Nairs passed their time in envy, jealousy and wasteful ceremonies.[76]

The palace politics which were now open to Nairs of the old Malayali Sabha offered gains and opportunities. But the palace network appeared remote to growing numbers of educated young Nairs. The manipulators of the palace political system had little to offer them and in spite of a certain amount of lip service, seemed basically unconcerned with the very real problems of the matrilineal joint-family. Indeed, for many younger Nairs, who did not share Raman Pillai's inflated ideas about the Nair past and who knew the poverty and dissension of the decaying taravad, palace politics appeared ridiculous, pernicious and often irrelevant. Such men tended to gravitate towards C. Krishna Pillai whose view of Nair society--and perhaps his own irascible temper--never allowed him to co-operate for long with the educated, palace-politicking Nairs of his generation.

Three young Nairs who had an association with Krishna Pillai help to illustrate and explain the new attitudes. K. Ramakrishna Pillai was born in 1877, the son of a Potti Brahmin, near Neyyattinkara; Mannath Padmanabha Pillai, in 1878, the son of a Nambudiri Brahmin, near Changanacherry; and Changanacherry K. Parameswaran Pillai, in 1877, the son of a Nair, at Changanacherry.

K. Ramakrishna Pillai became a journalist in 1899 and for a brief period edited the revived and anti-Brahmin *Malayali* in 1903-04. He resigned after a disagreement with the board over the propriety of attacking the palace. In January 1906, however, he was given a free hand to edit *Swadeshabhimani*, and for more than four and a half years, until his deportation from Travancore in September 1910,[77] he laid about him with gusto, savaging the Maharaja, Dewans, favourites, Brahmins and palace-oriented Nairs. His attacks tended to be scurrilous and exaggerated, but his targets were often well-chosen: Saravanai and Sankaran Thampi; C.V. Raman Pillai, P. Ayyappan Pillai and V.I. Keshava Pillai; every Dewan since 1885 with the important exception of V.P. Madhava Rao; the cringing weakness of the Maharaja; the libidinous nature of the Dewan P. Rajagopalachari[78]. In the latter's opinion, however, 'the most serious thing against the *Swadeshabhimani* has always been the remarkable persistency with which it preached the gospel of government by the people, and the exhortation which it held out to the people of Travancore to unite and demand self-government'.[79] Yet Ramakrishna Pillai was no leveller, and *Swadeshabhimani* was suspicious of Christians and opposed to the sirkar's order allowing Pulaya and Paraya children to attend government schools.[80]

Ramakrishna Pillai had the encouragement of C. Krishna Pillai in many of his activities, and, fiercely criticised the writings of C.V. Raman Pillai.[81] He acted as publisher in 1906 for a cuttingly satirical novel, *Parapuram* (on the rock), by

K. Narayana Kurukkal, an Ambalavasi. The book ridiculed the concept of princely rule and especially the court politics of Trivandrum.[82] When Kurukkal was dissmissed from his job as an assistant school inspector, *Swadeshabhimani* took up his cause.[83]

Ramakrishna Pillai represented a curious mixture. He was part of a Nair faction–the Dewan thought him a poor man who obtained his funds from others[84]–but many of the views he offered were iconoclastic. He damned the palace and the whole system of princely rule which had traditionally provided the focus for warring factions. He emphasised that 'the important factor in government is the will of the people',[85] but opposed the admission of Pulayas and Parayas to government schools because 'hereditary differences in intellect...cannot be ignored'.[86] The same man wrote the first Malayalam biography of Karl Marx. Ramakrishna Pillai was prone to schoolboyish extravagance and melodrama; he aimed to apply the fashionable lessons of the wider world–whether the murder of the King of Portugal or deportation of Lajpat Rai–to Travancore; his charges were often hilariously fantastic.[87] Yet he represented an important break with the past. His wife was the first Travancore Nair woman to graduate,[88] and he himself found no honour in having been fathered by a Brahmin. Though one feels that, had he not died of tuberculosis in 1916, the Justice Party might have been his eventual refuge, some of his egalitarian ideas–'the rights of the people are...the same everywhere'[89]–took firm hold among many members of succeeding generations in Travancore. He was the most striking early product of the breakdown of traditional Malayali society.

Mannath Padmanabha Pillai's father was also a Brahmin, a Nambudiri. Mannam–to use the name by which Padmanabha Pillai has become best known–was the first male child for a generation in a poor taravad. Both his mother and grandmother were illiterate, and the decline of the family had been hastened by lack of proper management. His Nambudiri father ended the marriage relationship with Mannam's mother soon after Mannam was born. Poverty forced him into a number of jobs, including that of an actor, and prevented him from studying beyond the fourth class. About 1894, however, C. Krishna

Pillai appointed him as a teacher in a local vernacular school in north Travancore on five rupees a month, and he taught in the school for ten years.[90] After a career as a pleader, he and a few friends founded the Nair Service Society in Perunna near Changanacherry in 1914. In the clashes within the Keraliya Nair Samaj at the time of the First World War, Mannam was firmly attached to C.Krishna Pillai's party.[91] He later led the Nair Service Society in the campaign for individual partition and abolition of the marumakkattayam system. Unlike Ramakrishna Pillai, Mannam never abandoned Malayali dress; nor was he tempted by biographies of Marx. He was brought up on classical Hindu stories, performed them during his acting career as a youth, and remained a staunch Hindu all his life. Perhaps this accounts for his success in reaching ordinary Nairs. Yet Mannam's eagerness to abolish the marumakkattayam system marked as much a break with the past as Ramakrishna Pillai's flights of democratic fancy.

The same may be said of Changanacherry K. Parameswaran Pillai. Unlike Mannam and Ramakrishna Pillai, Changanacherry's father was a Nair and a government servant. When the father was transferred to Trivandrum about 1887, the family accompanied him. Changanacherry's parents died within ten months of each other about 1891, and he seems to have been able to complete his studies through help from C. Krishna Pillai and others. He matriculated at fifteen and later graduated. He taught in a school in Trivandrum and took the Bachelor of Law degree.[92] By 1905 he was prominent enough in public affairs to take part in the reconciliation meeting of Nairs and Ezhavas in Quilon, and in January 1907 he was a delegate to the third session of the Sri Mulam Popular Assembly where he attempted to speak on the marumakkattayam question.[93] In the same year he published a sweeping criticism of marumakkattayam which concluded: 'All that we want is out and out partition and that at the instance of any member who desires it'.[94] He too was in C. Krishna Pillai's party when the Keraliya Nair Samaj split. He later became president of the Nair Service Society and was responsible for piloting the legislation which provided for individual partition of the matrilineal joint family in 1925.

All three men were products of the poverty and disarray which confronted Nairs in the late nineteenth century. For all three, the old society was manifestly deficient. 'The political, social and economic conditions', wrote Changnacherry K. Parameswaran Pillai, 'which gave rise to the particular system...have disappeared and other conditions based upon totally different aspects of life have been forced upon us so that it has become positively disadvantageous to continue the old order of things'.[95]

C. Krishna Pillai, their patron, agreed. In 1903, estranged from many of his contemporaries in Trivandrum and still stationed in northern Travancore, he formed the Travancore Nair Samajam. This was a modest organisation of thirty-one members which aimed to reform Nair customs and avoid palace politics by working in the countryside. Unlike the old Malayali Sabha, membership was restricted to Nairs. Criticism came quickly from non-Nairs who saw the branch organisations as 'secret societies', dedicated to the arousal of communal animosities and providing indications of 'impending disturbances'.[96] These charges were rebutted by the editor of *The Nayar*, a short-lived monthly published from Changanacherry, who wrote that non-Nairs were welcome to attend meetings as observers and that the sole aim of the organisations was to strive for 'all desirable reforms in the customs and the social institution of the Nayars'.[97] By the end of 1904, Krishna Pillai, backed by the wealthy Kavalam Neelakantha Pillai, who was the president, had enrolled three hundred eighty members and established twelve branches.[98] Mannam later wrote that in a small way such activities even reached Changanacherry.[99]

The Nair-Ezhava riots provided a shock for the disunited elite of educated Nairs. In late January or early February 1905, while the disturbances were still going on, Krishna Pillai came to a reconciliation with his old Trivandrum associates, notably C.V. Raman Pillai, and P. Ayyappan Pillai. They agreed to form a joint organisation called the Keraliya Nair Samaj, which would unite Krishna Pillai's country branches with Raman Pillai's influence in the capital.[100] It was a union of different viewpoints and interests: of an official elite, immersed in palace politics and able to gain certain benefits thereby, and a larger section of generally younger Nairs whose immediate concern was the economic deterioration of the majority of Nair taravads. The disquiet at Ezhava competition, and the potential power for reform which a united Nair association might wield in the

Popular Assembly and elsewhere, were instrumental in bringing the two sides together.

Early in October 1905, shortly before the Assembly session, the eighth annual meeting of the Vidhya Abhivardana Sabha was held in Trivandrum in combination with a session of the Keraliya Nair Samaj. C. Krishna Pillai, 'the leader of the Nair community', presided. Partly agreeing with those who said that Nairs must imitate the Japanese--speech-makers throve on the rise of Japan–he attacked subcaste distinctions and government corruption, which, he said, were among the important issues facing Nairs. He concluded with 'some rabid remarks on the Brahmins', which wounded the innermost feelings of a few high officers...'[101] Such a speech emphasised the element of compromise in the union of Nair factions and organisations. Krishna Pillai's criticism of the sirkar could not have pleased C.V. Raman Pillai and his highly placed friends, but all were probably prepared to listen to an attack on Brahmin influence. An external threat, real or imagined, was useful for fostering unity.

With the Assembly session approaching there was flurry of activity among Nairs. The Quilon Malayali Sabha was revived,[102] and a 'monster meeting' of the Keraliya Nair Samaj was held in Trivandrum to coincide with the Assembly itself. Over that gathering P. Ayyappan Pillai presided, and some Nambudiris, Kshatriyas and a lone Tamil Brahmin attended. It was said that Rs. 15,000 was pledged for the organisation's projects, but little was ever collected. Typically, the speakers 'all strove...to picture the low position the Travancoreans occupy in the industrial world and spoke emphatically upon the necessity of taking immediate steps for the industrial, social and moral regeneration of the people...'[103]

The Assembly itself, some of whose members were now returned by an electorate of 3,200 voters, was another exercise in speechifying and self-congratulation,[104] a criticism similar to that frequently levelled against Nair caste associations. 'We mean no offence', wrote the *Malabar Herald* in May 1906,

> when we venture to say that ... some of the leading members of the Nayar community have been talking a

> lot, but practically they have been doing very little for the good of those whom they represent.[105]

The Assembly, though as yet it had no power, had an obvious attraction for men who wished to be recognised as leaders. It offered the trappings of power and a captive audience under sirkar patronage. Implicit in the Assembly, moreover, was the idea that real power would eventually be devolved on it. When that day came, those who had already been members would be in the best position to benefit.

V.P. Madhava Rao resigned early in 1906 to become Dewan of Mysore. After some difficulty, he was replaced in Travancore by S. Gopalachari, the Brahmin district judge of Tinnevelly in the Madras Presidency. The choice was immediately unpopular and became more so when it appeared that Gopalachari, in consultation with the Maharaja who in turn was prevailed on by the favourites, was not going to call the Assembly in October. The resulting series of protest meetings, at which the majority of speakers were Nairs, recalled the Malayali Memorial,[106] and the sirkar soon weakened and announced that the Assembly would be called for January 1907. Among Nairs there was a growing awareness that they would dominate an Assembly elected on a narrow franchise based on landholding. If such an Assembly were to have a certain amount of power, it could be used to rectify the problems of the matrilineal joint-family and thus preserve Nairs' hold on the land. Indeed, if Nairs could present a unified front such an Assembly would provide them with much of the old dominance which men like C.V. Raman Pillai felt was their birthright.

Various organisations of Nairs began petitioning the government for representation at the session of January 1907. Most were successful. The Quilon branch of the Keraliya Nair Samaj and the Quilon Malayali Sabha, whch had virtually the same membership, were each granted a delegate.[107] In Trivandrum, where the voters at a meeting in the town hall returned three Nairs, there were complaints that the meeting had been manipulated. In the southern division, the Brahmin dewan peshkar was said to have disqualified a Nair whose criticism he feared. The Nair, who was one of Thanu Pillai's heirs, came to Trivandrum and got a seat anyway.[108] For the first time, there was real bite to the contest for admission, partly because of the attempt to let the Assembly lapse and because of the issues some of the delegates felt prompted to raise. Two questions preoccupied Nair representatives: their continuing antagonism with non-Malayali Brahmins and the problems of the crumbling taravad.

Even between well-placed Nair and Brahmin government servants there was cool distance, as Krishna Pillai's speech in 1905 had shown. In Trivandrum each group had its own clubs: the Sri Mulam Union Club, almost exclusively for Brahmins, and the National Club for Nairs. The latter club dated from 1899; the former, from about 1902, although a Brahmin reading club at Karamanai village went back to 1888. There was also a Trivandrum Syrian Club.[109]

With such exclusiveness among the well-educated and prosperous, the strident animosity between less elevated Brahmins and Nairs was not surprising. *Sudharma*, a short lived Trivandrum monthly, delivered fairly typical attacks against 'aliens and Pandy Pattars..., a race of wicked people that ought to be banished at once and forever...'[110] Travancore by this time had more than twenty newspapers and journals, excluding those like the vitriolic new incarnation of the *Malayali* published from British India or Cochin. Few of these newspapers survived long, and most were conducted on the smallest of budgets. 'In Travancore', one observer wrote, 'we have the Brahmin interest, the Nair interest, the Syrian interest, the Ezhava interest, etc., and ...there are journals to support each one's cause...'[111]

The causes were so well supported that 'a Brahmin stinks in the nostrils [of] a Nair nowadays...' There were complaints about the 'mean malignancy and partisan perversity' which governed the discussion of 'Brahmin officials in Sudra organs', and assertions of the 'unsleeping racial jealousy' between Brahmins and Nairs.[112] The situation, one correspondent concluded, was one of 'social civil war', with Nairs and Brahmins at each other's throats, and Nairs trying at the same time to keep an eye on Syrians and Ezhavas.[113] The position was as awkward for Nairs as the metaphor suggests.

The second issue which some Nairs were prepared to raise at the Assembly in January 1907 was the reformation of the taravad. This was related to the competition with other castes and religions: if Nair families were failing economically, they could not hope to compete. But the Assembly of 1907 proved an uncongenial forum. Gopalachari, the new Dewan, had spent his career in the judicial service and was 'absurdly sensitive' to criticism. '...He is', the Resident continued, 'quite unable to withstand the influence of the Palace and is not endowed with any great natural ability as an administrator'.[114] In short, he was out of his depth in the rips and undertows of Travancore politics. Having been forced to call the Assembly, Gopalachari did his best to get it over with quickly. His performance, however, did more to arose opposition than avoid it. Printed copies of his speech were not delivered to the members beforehand, and when a Nair rose at the conclusion of the speech to thank the Dewan, as had been the custom, Gopalachari waved him down. No question received a direct answer, and only placemen were permitted to speak. T. Sankaran Thampi watched all the proceedings intently and was said to be reporting to the Maharaja. 'Ugly incidents' of the Dewan silencing speakers likely to criticise officials or palace favourites rendered the Assembly, in the opinion of the *Malabar Herald*, 'a meaningless institution'.[115] The Dewan accepted a memorial from Quilon Nairs asking for an investigation of the taravad, but when Changanacherry K. Parameswaran Pillai began to speak in support, Gopalachari stopped him.[116] The session ended on the same note as it had begun:

> ...the dewan took up the last subject and was giving the reply when all of a sudden, he sprang up from the chair to the great surprise of all, saying the words, '*With this, out bustness closes*', and disappeared from his seat.[117]

This was the Assembly's only experience of Gopalachari. The Dewan resigned in July. His attempt to lessen the importance of the Assembly had in fact enhanced its reputation. The fact that he had been forced to call it, apparently against his will and the will of the favourites, added to the Assembly's popularity and established it as an annual institution. His attempts to confine the proceedings to controlled formalities so annoyed representatives that for the first time, it became respectable in the Assembly to try to attack the Dewan and the administration. The Assembly had lost its school-outing innocence. With the realisation that the Assembly did not have to be merely a speech-making society, that it could bring real pressure to bear on the administration, those Nairs who wanted taravad reform began to see demands in the Assembly as a way of pressing their case. Their preparations for the session at the end of 1907 were made accordingly.

## *THE MARUMMAKUTTAYAM COMMITTEE OF 1908*

The Keraliya Nair Samaj's second annual conference held in Trivandrum in October 1907, shortly before the Assembly session, attracted the largest gathering of Nairs hitherto seen in Kerala. One of British Malabar's leading Nairs, M. Krishnan Nair, a lawyer and member of the Madras Legislative Council, accepted the chairmanship, and delegates attended from British Malabar and Cochin. For the first time a Nair meeting passed resolutions making specific recommendations for the reform of Nair customs. In his opening speech Krishnan Nair stressed the urgent need for such reform, the key to which was a change in the law governing taravad partition. He described the position of Nairs as not only 'very deplorable', but as one which was 'fast deteriorating'. Although the 'enormous litigation' going on among Nairs was the direct cause of their economic decline, this was, he claimed, only 'the outer fringe of the evil'. The whole body of the community was 'diseased'--with the impartible, matrilineal joint-family system. Only legalising partition could solve the problem, and only governments could change the law. He realized, he said, that his outspoken advocacy of radical reforms would cause 'violent disturbances' but the time for such reform was ripe.[118]

The resolutions were not as radical as his speech called for, but this was probably because C.V. Raman Pillai and his followers seem to have controlled the meeting.[119] The first and most important resolution, moved by P.G. Govinda Pillai, a Travancore High Court vakil, prescribed cautious moves towards a patrilineal family in view of 'the declining condition of the Nairs'. Stopping short of individual partition, it advocated:

(i) giving children a legal claim for maintenance from their fathers; (ii) making a man's self-acquired property heritable only by descendants of that branch of his taravad originating from his mother; (iii) allotting half of a man's self-acquired property to his wife and children on his death. Put into practice, such measures would not have ended the taravad, but they would have encouraged remotely related branches to sever all connections and partition family property voluntarily. The prospect of the whole taravad–and thus distant relatives–benefiting from the death of an enterprising member would have ended, and with it one of the reasons why there were always a few taravad members ready to resist a unanimous and voluntary partition. Now, too, a man would no longer have to resort to complicated and sometimes illegal methods to provide for his wife and children after his death.

The second resolution was mild enough: it called for recognition of the ceremony of sambandham as a legal marriage. Other resolutions advocating dissemination of education among Nairs and the organisation of village branches or *karayogams*, recalled Nair meetings of earlier years. The two resolutions requiring changes in the law were forwarded to the governments of Travancore, Cochin and Madras.[120]

Within a month, the Assembly met in Trivandrum under the presidency of the new Dewan, P. Rajagopalachari, a Brahmin who jokingly claimed to behead his enemies with a pen. The story impressed Nairs.[121] A member of the Statutory Civil Service, Rajagopalachari had been Dewan of Cochin from 1896 to 1901 and was registrar of cooperative societies in the Madras Presidency when he was persuaded to come to Travancore.

On the third day of the session, after the completion of the customary speeches and formalities, he announced the creation of a committee of four Nairs and a matrilineal Samanta–three non-officials to be elected by Nair members of the Assembly and two officials to be appointed by the sirkar. The committee was directed to investigate ten proposed reforms of the joint-family, marriage and inheritance customs of Nairs. Chief among these suggested reforms were: the recognition of sambandham as a legal marriage; statutory controls over the power of karanavans;

and, the rights to bequeath all one's self-acquired property, to arrange partition of distantly related branches of taravads and to claim a share, for wives and children, of the self-acquired property of a man dying intestate.[122]

The three members chosen by the Assembly were M. Krishna Pillai, a retired district judge, K.P. Padmanabha Menon and K. Krishna Pandalai (a Samanta), both High Court vakils. The sirkar appointed A. Govinda Pillai, a High Court judge and the highest ranking Nair in the government service, as president, and N. Raman Pillai, excise commissioner, as secretary. The committee was obviously elitist, and closely enough connected with the old Thanu Pillai circle to make one expect from it great caution. M. Krishna Pillai, N. Raman Pillai and Padmanabha Menon were all in their late forties, old school fellows and signatories of the Malayali Memorial. Govinda Pillai at fifty-six was the oldest member and the only one to have done a full course of study outside Travancore; he graduated from Presidency College, Madras, in 1869. Krishna Pandalai at thirty-four was the youngest member. N. Raman Pillai was the son of the Dewan, N. Nanu Pillai, and fled Travancore with G. Parameswaran Pillai in 1882. Padmanabha Menon was the son of peshkar P. Shankunni Menon and brother of K.P. Sankara Menon. The committee, however, produced a virtually unanimous report which was decidedly radical, and a body of evidence which depicted the economic plight of Nairs as starkly as any reformist pamphleteer.

The committee toured the state throughout 1908, heard 1,021 witnesses and published its report at the end of the year. It recommended the recognition of the ceremony of sambandham as a legal marriage; the outlawing of polyandry and polygamy; divorce by mutual consent certified by registered document; compelling karanavans to keep careful accounts of their use of taravad assets; the grant to wives and children of a half share of the self-acquired property of a man dying intestate; and the right of any branch of a taravad descended from the same woman to demand partition.[123] The last recommendation fell short of the right of individual partition which men like Changanacherry K. Parameswaran Pillai were advocating, but it would have been enough to destroy the big taravad. In a taravad of twenty members, for example, a mother, her brother, her three children and their two children, would have been empowered to demand 7/20ths of the taravad assets and separate themselves completely.

It would be wrong, however, to suggest that because the committee's recommendations were unanimous on most points, no critics came forward to give evidence. Chief among the opponents of any kind of partition was C.V. Raman Pillai who circulated a Malayalam pamphlet on the subject and appeared before the committee. Arguing in favour of some kind of registration of marriage, he opposed any attempt at 'breaking up what belongs to the commonalty'. One of his fears was the creation of small proprietors and the fragmentation of holdings. Yet he claimed that among Nairs, 'what is notoriously wanting is the spirit of enterprise'. The question of partition, he argued, needed much more consideration.[124]

C.V. Raman Pillai's opposition to partition and exhortation to individual initiative were not necessarily illogical. His view of Nairs as the military gentry of Kerala, living on large ancestral estates, following an idyllic way of life and preserving the tranquillity of society,[125] may not have been accurate, but it was firmly held. To tamper with the taravad was to destory the great families and put at risk one of Nairs' greatest assets: their hold on the land. His concern about fragmentation of holdings was shared by others. P.K. Keshava Pillai told the committee:

> The partitionists' proposal in the wide way in which it is put forward by some, is like a proposal to pull down the fortification which protects an ill-disciplined force and break up its existing organisation just when the siege has become close.[126]

A letter to the editor of the *Madras Mail* stated the fears specifically:

> [Partition will] reduce a good portion of the Nair gentry to the condition of peasant proprietors and the remainder to that of landless men. The keen competition that is

> going on for land in Travancore and the relative strength and strategic skill of the competitors make me fear that the Nair landholders will succumb if the protection which the law affords to *Tarwads* is now taken away.[127]

The committee met such opposition with statements of the virtues of competition. 'The creation of small proprietors... is in fact the very thing that promotes enterprize [sic]', it concluded. Moreover, partition would 'strengthen the community ... by bringing into operation the universal law of the survival of the fittest'.[128] But the conclusive argument in favour of some form of partition was the chaotic state of the taravad, which was proved to the satisfaction of the committee by an impressive array of statistics. Partition might not be the complete solution, but clearly matters could not continue as they were.

Like the opponents of partition, the committee's first concern was the land. It collected figures on all sales and mortgages in the state for eighteen months prior to the begining of the Malayalam month Makaram (January-February) 1908. Table 7.3 shows the findings. Under a system which in theory made property inalienable without proof of necessity or the consent of all adult members of the taravad, Nairs had alienated by sale or mortgage property worth Rs. 18.77 lakhs more than they had acquired. Samantas, a matrilineal caste numbering no more than a thousand or so in north Travancore, had a similar net loss of Rs. 35,651. Among patrilineal groups, on the other hand, Christians of all kinds had net gain of Rs. 11,71,007 worth of property; Ezhavas, Rs. 2,94,386; and Shanars Rs. 83,009.

Christians and Ezhavas were acquiring land. Where was it coming from? The answer was obvious: from Nairs. And what was happening to the money which Nairs gained from alienating their land? That question led the Marumakkattayam Committee to its second concern: litigation.

## *TABLE 7.3*

***Alienations and Acquisitions of Property by Nairs, Christians, Ezhavas, Shanars and Samantas in Travancore for 18 months prior to 1 Makaram 1083 (about 15 January 1908)***

| *Category* | *Sales in rupees* | *Mortgages in rupees* | *Total in rupees* | *+ or — in rupees* |
|---|---|---|---|---|
| **NAIRS** | | | | |
| **---Buyers or mortgagees** | 12,20,264 | 76,40,804 | 88,61,068 | |
| **--Sellers or mortgagees** | 17,39,607 | 89,98,463 | 1,07,38,070 | — 18,77,002 |
| **CHRISTIANS** | | | | |
| **--Buyers or mortagagees** | 22,44,641 | 80,07,137 | 98,51,778* | |
| **--Sellers or mortgagees** | 19,82,647 | 66,98,124 | 86,80,771 | + 11,71,007 |
| **EZHAVAS** | | | | |
| **--Buyers or mortagagees** | 11,71,197 | 42,31,665 | 53,92,862 | |
| **--Sellers or mortgagees** | 10,53,763 | 40,44,083 | 50,98,476* | + 2,94,386 |
| **SHANARS** | | | | |
| **--Buyers or mortagagees** | 3,08,643 | 12,49,291 | 15,57,934 | |
| **--Sellers or mortgagees** | 3,03,261 | 11,71,664 | 14,74,925 | + 83,009 |
| **SAMANTAS*** | | | | |
| **--Buyers or mortagagees** | 11,829 | 63,423 | 75,252 | |
| **--Sellers or mortgagees** | 17,298 | 94,605 | 1,11,903 | — 36,651 |

*Source: Maru. Report,* Appendix IV, p. 74

* Samantas were a matrilineal caste ranking between Nairs and Kshatriyas and found in limited numbers in north Travancore. They were more numerous in Cochin and British Malabar. See Ananthakrishna Iyer, *Cochin Tribes*, Vol. II, p. 146. K. Krishna Pandalai was a Samanta.

* Apparent errors in addition are in the original report. They do not affect the general conclusions.

*TABLE 7.4*

*Suits Involving Karanavans, Brought by Taravad Members, 1073-1082 M.E. (1897-8/1906-7)*

| *Type of Suit* | *Number* |
|---|---|
| 1. Suits to cancel a karanavan's alienation | 4,365 |
| 2. Suits to remove a karanavan | 295 |
| 3. Suits to set aside decrees made against a karanavan's alienations | 142 |
| 4. Suits to set aside attachment of taravad property for a karanavan's debts | 67 |
| | 4,869 |

*Source*: *Maru. Report,* Appendix I, p.73

As Table 7.4 shows, disputes over the karanavan's management provoked an average of 487 suits a year over the preceding ten years. Changancherry K. Parameswaran Pillai estimated the annual expenses incurred by Nairs in legal disputes arising from the marumakkattayam system at Rs. 2 lakhs.[129] If a Nair won such a suit, another Nair lost, and the fruits of victory were eaten up in litigation. The only Nairs to gain were vakils.

Finally, the committee produced statistics to show a growing movement against the taravad way of life. (See Table 7.5) Agreed partitions had risen from 301 in 1896-07 to 516 in 1906-07.

*TABLE 7.5*

*Partitions, Allotments for Maintenance and Gifts to Children Executed in the Courts in Three Selected Years*

| *Type of Agreement* | *1896-7* | *1901-2* | *1906-7* |
|---|---|---|---|
| Partition | 301 | 342 | 516 |
| Allotment for maintenance | 205 | 281 | 385 |
| Gifts to children | 293 | 473 | 601 |

*Source: Maru. Report,* Appendix I, p. 73

From such figures it would appear that over the ten-year period more than 3,000 taravads had unanimously agreed to partitions of one kind or another, and had executed the partition in the courts. At the same time, more members wishing to live apart from their taravad negotiated agreements for maintenance. In 1896-97, 205 such agreements were executed; in 1906-07, 385. In the same period, gifts to children, legally carried out, doubled. These figures, moreover, were undoubtedly only a tiny fraction of the *de facto* gifts, partitions and maintenance grants which were arranged without reference to the courts.

To these statistics the committee added its opinion that 'residence [of the mother and children] with the father should be encouraged by the law on the ground of public policy'.[130] It also endorsed the view of one witness that in 'the great majority' of taravads,

> instead of unanimity and mutual co-operation what one really finds is disunion and ill-will. ...The credit of the average existing Tarwads will likewise be found to be very low, and it cannot be otherwise, for the credit of a country where civil war is being waged with determination on both sides, cannot ordinarily be high. And lastly, if prestige has any place, it is surely not in a Tarwad, one of the common pastimes of whose members is the institution of criminal proceedings against each other for assault, theft, forgery and even attempts to commit murder.[131]

Having endorsed such views, the committee not surprisingly advocated a modified form of partition. Yet in doing so it was acknowledging that the condition of Nairs was so serious that the very basis of their traditional organisation had to be abolished if they were to retain the power which had been theirs in the past.

The committee's report was a recogniton by Nairs of the precariousness of their position. It marked the first step towards the withdrawal of legal recognition from the matrilineal joint-family. There would be die-hards to fight the movement towards individual partition, but they would be continually confronted by the committee's findings on land transfers and litigation. The data produced by the committee confirmed what had been increasingly apparent:

Syrians and Ezhavas prospering in trade, services and education, were also acquiring land from dissent-ridden taravads and were no longer prepared to be quietly excluded from the sources of administrative power. It was all very well for educated Nairs to rail at non-Malayali Brahmin officials or for less educated Nairs to try to intimidate Ezhavas into traditional submission, but these attacks were symptomatic of the decline in which Nairs felt themselves to be. Such attacks offered no practical solutions.

For some Nairs, the Assembly suggested remedies. To begin with, it was a counter-balance to the favourite, Sankaran Thampi, who was a mainstay of the palace-politicking faction of official Nairs. In the Assembly the latter could be attacked, their misdeeds exposed and their conservatism about taravad reform overcome. An Assembly, moreover, might eventually acquire some useful powers. If the qualifications for membership in such an Assembly were based on fairly high landholding or educational requirements, Nairs could be expected to dominate. They still, after all, provided more large landholders than any other group,[132] and there were now more English literates among them than among non-Malayali Brahmins.[133] In an Assembly with real powers, controlled by Nairs, might not all be made right with the matrilineal joint-family and might not the traditional Nair role of leadership and dominance be reasserted?

Such a hypothesis presupposed that Nairs could behave as a political community, a united group. The evidence in 1908 was not encouraging. The subcaste distinctions of traditional society had still to be overcome,[134] while the factions among educated Nairs were only brought together with difficulty and were to fly apart again in 1915.[135] Moreover, the fact that the largest Nair landholding families had been able to cope with the changes of the past sixty years while lesser families had not, pointed to incipient class divisions which were to become increasingly pronounced. Where the old subcastes withered and died, class distinctions took root.

By 1908 the unquestioned dominance which Nairs had enjoyed sixty years earlier had vanished. It had been replaced by a situation in which Nairs, to be sure, still held many advantages. But these were no longer unchallenged, and the economic power of the majority of Nair families was manifestly on the decline.

# Epilogue

## *End of Matriliny: Beginning of Disillusion*

It was November 1912 before the report of the Marumakkattayam Committee resulted in legislation, and the regulation which was then passed did not grant taravad partition on demand, even to branches of taravads. The draft bill which was initially presented to the Nair members of the Legislative Council contained the committee's provision to allow branches descended from the same woman to demand partition. However, the three Nairs in the Legislative Council were conservatives, fearful of partition, and they fought successfully to have the partition clause dropped from the Bill.[1]

Regulation 1 of 1088 of the Malabar Era recognised a public sambandham as a legal marriage, and gave wives and children of Nairs dying intestate the right to half of the husband's self-acquired property. A man could dispose of all his self-acquired property by making a will. A husband, moreover, was made the legal guardian of his wife and children if they lived with him; wives and children were given a right to maintenance against the husband, without prejudice to their right to be maintained by the wife's taravad. The powers of the karanavan were limited, simple procedures for divorce were laid down, and subcaste distinctions among Nairs were intentionally ignored.[2]

In the 1890s such a measure would have satisfied most shades of educated opinion. The recognition of public sambandham as a legal marriage was the major aim of Thanu Pillai's bill in 1896. Moreover, the bestowal of half the self-acquired property of an intestate Nair on his wife and children would have helped to satisfy the critics who claimed that to awaken their initiative, Nairs needed the incentive of being able to provide for their families.

By 1908, however, the dissension in the taravad and the self-interested attitude of most karanavans made the matrilineal joint-family appear irreparable to many Nairs. While conservatives like C.V. Raman Pillai might see the maintenance of the taravad as the only way to preserve Nair landed interests and position in society, younger men advocated partition for the same reason. One wrote:

> ...the evils... [of partition] are more than counterbalanced by the freedom which every shareholder obtains to improve his share: and as against the reckless conduct of a shareholder we have to take into account the equally reckless conduct of quarrelsome joint owners, which ultimately brings ruin on their Tarwad property and tends to scatter it among fortune-seeking moneylenders. That the property of many a Nair Tarwad has thus passed into others' hands is plain... Most of the *Karanavans* of these days mind more their own private interests than the interests of members committed to their charge... Free partition of Tarwad property has become a matter of necessity.[3]

The fact that Nair members of the Legislative Council could ignore the pressing demands for partition merely emphasised the divisions among educated Nairs and the unrepresentative character of the Council.

The problems of the taravad affected thousands of Nairs and appeared soluble only through legislative action. Nairs, therefore, were drawn towards both the Legislative Council and the Popular Assembly. From 1913, Changanacherry K. Parameswaran Pillai led Nair demands in the Assembly for an expansion of the Legislative Council and an increase of its powers.[4] This was not surprising, for Nairs had won every seat but one in the

Assembly elections for seats on the Council.[5] A Council with real power, chosen on such a basis, would be dominated by Nairs.

The trick, however, was to overcome the divisions among Nairs–the factions among the educated, the subcastes among the rural and conservative--and thus enable them to act as a political community at the state level. Nairs lacked those common grievances so useful for uniting Ezhavas. C. Krishna Pillai brought the question of subcastes to a head in 1909. At a feast commemorating the death of Vishakham Tirunal's wife, he and his followers insisted that the Thampis–Nairs descended from Kshatriyas–eat with them. The Thampis refused, and Krishna Pillai and his followers left the gathering.[6] About a year later, Mannath Padmanabha Pillai was elected secretary of a local Nair association at Perunna, his native village, near Changanacherry. This *karayogam* included members of all Nair subcastes in the area; its aims were subcaste fusion, interdining and abolition of *talikettukalyanam* and other wasteful, embarrassing ceremonies. By 1912, the *karayogam* had built its own offices,[7] and in October 1914 Mannam and a few friends founded the Nair Service Society and vowed to devote their lives to social service. By 1922, a Malabar Nair could write enviously that in Travancore the process of subcaste fusion was almost complete.[8]

But while there was progress towards the elimination of the old divisions among Nairs, there were factional battles among the educated elite, and indications that class would one day divide Nairs as effectively as subcaste ever had. In November 1915, the Keraliya Nair Samaj split acrimoniously. C.V. Raman Pillai and his followers tried to pack the annual general meeting in Trivandrum with their supporters, and C. Krishna Pillai, Changanacherry K. Parameswaran Pillai and their followers left in protest.[9] Personal rivalries played a part in the split. C.V. Raman Pillai's influence in the administration, for example, had grown with the appointment of M. Krishnan Nair, a Malabar lawyer, as Dewan. However, C. Krishna Pillai's party tended to come from less affluent Nair areas of central and north Travancore and to favour individual taravad partition. The followers of C.V. Raman Pillai were from the more aristocratic Trivandrum and south Travancore taravads; individual partition threatened their large holdings.

Following the break, Krishna Pillai's followers formed the

All-Kerala Nair Samaj, and Changanacherry K. Parameswaran Pillai used its meetings to call for reform of the Legislative Council.[10] In September 1916, T.K. Velu Pillai, another member of the Krishna Pillai party, got permission to introduce a bill in the Council for branch partition of the taravad.[11] The progress of the Bill dragged on slowly; the Dewan, Krishnan Nair, was cool towards it, and only with the expansion of the Legislative Council in 1919 and again in 1921 did legislation for taravad partition become possible.[12] The turning point came in November 1920, when supporters of individual partition attended a meeting of C.V. Raman Pillai's Keraliya Nair Samaj in Trivandrum. The meeting was intended to pass a resolution in favour of branch partition, but after three hours of wrangling, a resolution in favour of individual partition was carried overwhelmingly.[13] It was another four years, however, before a bill providing for individual partition became law.[14]

Regulation II of 1100 of the Malabar Era (October 1924) virtually legislated away the matrilineal joint-family. 'Every adult member of a Tarwad' became 'entitled to claim his or her share of the properties of the Tarwad'. A wife was made the legal heir of all her husband's self-acquired property. There were a number of qualifications and conditions, but the effect of the new regulation was to allow thousands of Nairs to take their share of the taravad's assets and leave the joint-family.[15]

The results in some ways justified the worst fears of the anti-partitionists. In the five years following the act, Nairs recorded an average annual net loss of property worth Rs. 48.7 lakhs. In the same period, Christians showed an annual net gain of property worth Rs. 33.5 lakhs.[16] By 1931, more Nairs probably owned land than any other group, but numbers alone did not constitute economic strength. Nair holdings of wet land appear to have been fragmented and subdivided,[17] and much of the land Nairs did own was heavily mortgaged.[18] Nevertheless, paper ownership of the land allowed Nairs to control the reformed bicameral legislature, established in 1932, which continued to base the franchise on payment of Rs. 5 in land tax.[19]

The problem of the matrilineal joint-family had preoccupied educated Nairs for more than thirty years. The propaganda it had provoked was also in effect propaganda for a wider community. Nairs were continually told that they were Nairs, that they shared many traditions, that they had once ruled and that they would rule again when the problems of matriliny were solved. If, as Mannath Padmanabha Pillai later wrote, Nairs in the nineteenth century had little consciousness of belonging to a Travancore-wide community,[20] the organisational attempts to reform the matrilineal system did much to propagate such awareness. Nair organisations, moreover, reinforced in the minds of other groups--Ezhavas, Christians, non-Malayali Brahmins--the exclusiveness of Nairs. In 1916, it was impossible to allow the students in the Maharaja's College, Trivandrum, to vote among themselves for the outstanding boy, because 'caste prejudice played a great part in the elections and ... merit was ignored'. Kumaran Asan was 'astonished' to discover, when two Nairs canvassed him for votes in the Assembly elections to the Legislative Council, that they 'wanted no Ezhava member in the Legislative Council. [One] went so far to [sic] say that Ezhava educational status would not come to such a level for ten or fifteen years to come'.[21]

Appeals to caste and community became fashionable and oft repeated in the period between 1910 and 1920. Ezhavas relied for patronage on Kumaran Asan's friendly relationship with P. Rajagopalachari, who was Dewan until 1914.[22] There were public meetings of Kuravas, Pulayas, Latin Catholics and Nambudiris to press for sirkar help for their 'communities', but the associations which grew out of such meetings never attained the coherence of the SNDP Yogam.[23] Educated Syrian Christians, however, grew impatient at their continued exclusion from the executive branches of government, and in 1918 formed the Civic Rights League at a meeting in Kottayam. The League claimed to represent twenty-six lakhs of Christians, low-caste Hindus and Muslims, and demanded equal rights in the public service and in public institutions for all Travancoreans.[24] It was quickly pointed out that Syrian Christians overwhelmingly dominated the League.[25] The League waged a campaign of public meetings and speeches similar to that of the Malayali Memorial. It won a small victory in 1922 when the devasam or temple department was separated from the revenue department, and non-caste Hindus were thereby permitted into the executive service.[26] By 1925 there was a Syrian Christian district officer.[27]

The militancy of the Indian National Congress, which had become so pronounced in British India from 1919, left Travancore relatively untouched. Because Travancore was a princely state, Congress leaders regarded it as beyond the scope of their activities. There were, however, occasional forays of the Malabar-based Kerala Provincial Congress Committee into Travancore,[28] and the students' strike in Trivandrum over fee increases in September 1921 owed some of its inspiration to the non-cooperation movement in British India.[29] The aftermath of the strike produced the first calls for responsible government in Travancore.[30]

The failure of non-cooperation in British India turned the nationalist leadership towards council entry and 'constructive' programmes. At the Kakinada session of the Congress in 1923, a resolution was passed which committed the Congress to work for the eradication of untouchability. One of the instigators of the resolution was T.K. Madhavan, a Travancore Ezhava who had sought an interview with Gandhi at Tinnevelly in 1921 to inform him of the disabilities of Ezhavas.[31] The way for Ezhavas had not been easy. Although by 1921 there were 4,500 literate in English and their male literacy rate in Malayalam was thirty-six per cent, educated Ezhavas were largely kept out of the government service and legislature. The rural poor were excluded from most temples, certain roads and a few public buildings.[32] Madhavan became president of the SNDP Yogam and gave it a more militant stance. When Congress activities elsewhere were in hiatus early in 1924, he succeeded in getting Congress support and national attention for a satyagraha at Vaikam in north Travancore. At Vaikam, *avarna* Hindus, as well as being banned from the main temple, were not permitted to use the roads which ran near it. The satyagraha, according to *The Hindu* correspondent writing at its outset, was to be 'a truly glorious fight, one to establish the dignity of man and his right of free movement in public places'.[33] The satyagrahis did not ask for temple entry but only the right to use nearby roads. There was, however, some irony in the way Madhavan was able to use the Congress' need for suitable agitations. During non-cooperation Ezhavas had generally supported the British government,[34] and Kumaran Asan had accepted a medal from the Prince of Wales. The gentlemanly Vaikam satyagraha dragged on for more than a year and was eventually settled with a compromise which admitted *avarna* Hindus to most of the roads around the temple. The satyagraha, however, publicised the disabilities of Ezhavas and lent impetus to a movement for temple entry for *avarna* Hindus.

Such issues were to dominate Travancore politics until the Temple Entry Proclamation of 1936. Early in 1933, Ezhavas, Muslims, Syrians and other Christians formed the Joint Political Congress to oppose the new legislative reforms. These had increased the size of the Council and Assembly, but by retention of the Rs. 5 land-tax qualification and a careful gerrymander, left the control largely in the hands of Nairs.[35] The Joint Political Congress was fairly successful in inducing Christians, Muslims and Ezhavas to boycott the elections of 1933.[36] Tension with Nairs ran high, and the vernacular press bristled with attacks by members of one community against others. At the same time, Ezhava leaders were using the Joint Political Congress and the SNDP Yogam in attempts to force the government to throw open its temples to *avarna* Hindus. Prominent Ezhavas threatened that they would lead their castemen into Christianity, Islam, Buddhism and even Sikhism if the temples were not opened to them. Others recommended atheism and Karl Marx.[37]

In 1936 Sir C.P. Ramaswami Aiyar, an old friend of the ruling family who as 'constitutional adviser' had been the *eminence grise* in Travancore since 1931, became Dewan. In a flurry of activity in 1935 and 1936, the franchise qualification was reduced to payment of Re. 1 in land tax, a Public Services Commission was established to supervise government appointments, and in November 1936 all temples under government management were thrown open to Hindus of all castes.[38] Ramaswami Aiyar's aim was to isolate the extremists in the Joint Political Congress, most of whom he saw as being Syrian Christians. He was largely successful. By 1940 the SNDP Yogam, and most other caste or religious associations, were carefully supporting the government.[39] A new political organisation, the Travancore State Congress, led by Pattam Thanu Pillai, a south Travancore Nair, and supported by members of the old Joint Political Congress, was formed in 1938 to campaign for responsible government. However, after a concerted effort in 1938, it rarely threatened the sirkar again until Indian independence was imminent in 1947.

The nature of Travancore as a princely state, in which the Maharaja was sacrosanct and even unhappy subjects began their petitions with expressions of loyalty, led aspiring leaders into a particular style of political activity. Since the Malayali Memorial of 1891 their quest had been for issues which could be presented as panaceas. The Maharaja's loyal subjects had grievances which required solution; once solved all would be well. Such grievances, however, especially those with a state-wide significance, were invariably related to the customs or disabilities of particular castes or religious groups. The campaigns for removal of a grievance reinforced a state-wide community consciousness. For many Nairs, the right to individual partition of the matrilineal joint-family was regarded as the ultimate solution to their problems:

> Emancipated from the thraldom of the family the junior member learns to look upon himself not as a zero as he formerly was but as a unit...he becomes industrious and prudent... The net result is to supply an incentive to produce industry. Partition supplies not only the incentive to industry but also the means to start it.[40]

Syrian Christians pressed for separation of the revenue and devasam departments so that they might acquire influence in the executive branches of government commensurate with their economic power. Ezhavas demanded concessions in the government service and the civil rights of *savarna* Hindus. As a princely state, Travancore lay outside the main sweep of the nationalist movement; nationalist ideology and leadership were not available to sublimate the passions generated by local issues.

The goals of most of these local campaigns were eventually achieved. The Travancore public service became the preserve of Travancoreans. The matrilineal joint-family became individually partible. The revenue and devasam departments were separated, and a Public Services Commission established. Temple entry was granted to all *avarna* Hindus. Indeed, by 1948 even responsible government had been gained under a three-man ministry of Pattam Thanu Pillai (a Nair), T.M. Varghese, (a Mar Thomite Syrian) and C. Kesavan (an Ezhava). Yet none of these solutions satisfied the hopes they had raised. They were, to begin with, essentially the goals of the wealthier, western-educated sections of each 'community'. Such men set out to present themselves as leaders of their 'community'. First, however, they had to overcome the old geographical and subcaste differences which traditionally divided Nairs; among Syrians there were competing sects. And as these old crevices were bridged, new fissures of class began to appear.

Between 1901 and 1941 the population of Travancore more than doubled from 2,950,000 to 6,070,000. The density by 1941 was eight hundred people for every square mile in the state. That figure too disguises the real density, for much of the state was backwater or mountain, or turned over to the cultivaton of plantation crops. The literacy rate was 47 per cent, including women, and among Christian and Nair men it was 73 per cent.[41]

It was not surprising that a high density of population, high rate of literacy, high unemployment and a shattered social system among sections of the population led to a strong Communist Party. As early as 1926, the Travancore Unemployment Enquiry Commission was pointing to 'the growing fascination which socialistic and communistic ideas... exercise upon the minds of the young men educated in our colleges'.[42] In 1934 Congress Socialists won control of the Kerala Provincial Congress Committee in Malabar, and in 1939 they formed a Communist Party.[43] One of the leading members was P. Krishna Pillai, a north Travancore Nair from a liquidated taravad.[44] Members of the Communist Pary worked both within and without the Travancore State Congress, and during the Second World War built a firm base among the coir workers around Alleppey. The war brought acute rice shortages and an increased cost of living. In October 1946 the hungry, frustrated labourers of villages near Alleppey attacked police stations and killed a few policemen. This was the 'Punnapra-Vayalar rebellion'. Martial law was proclaimed on 25 October, and the fighting lasted only three days. The government later claimed that only 190 people were killed,[45] though there were reports of as many as 7,000 deaths.[46] Punnapra-Vayalar, however, provided the Communist Party with an incident which was elevated to evocative mythology.

Sir C.P. Ramaswami Aiyar announced in June 1947 that Travancore would become an independent state after the British left India. Opposition to the independence plan united most groups in the state. In July Ramaswami Aiyar was attacked and wounded on the face in Trivandrum. Soon after, Travancore signed the act of accession, and he resigned the Dewanship.

Responsible government in 1948 made real power available to Travancore leaders and intensified their struggles with each other and with the economic conditions of the state. In the period from 1948 to 1956 Travancoreans had seven governments and an interval of President's rule from New Delhi. In 1949 Travancore and Cochin were integrated into a single state of Travancore-Cochin. In 1956 Malabar district was added and Kerala state formed; the Tamil-speaking taluks of south Travancore were ceded to Madras. The elections of 1957 returned a communist government under E.M.S. Namboodiripad; but by July 1959 a 'liberation struggle', led by the Roman Catholic churches and the Nair Service Society under Mannath Padmanabha Pillai, had induced the Government of India to dismiss the administration and impose President's rule. In the twenty-five years after Indian independence in 1947, Travancore experienced thirteen governments, eight chief ministers and four periods of President's rule. By 1971 the population of Kerala had increased from roughly 11.5 million in 1941 to nearly twenty million; the literacy rate was 60 per cent.[47]

So much of the promise which had accompanied the breakdown of traditional society remained unfulfilled. Malayali domination of the sirkar service provided no solution to the growing problem of supplying a satisfactory standard of living to an increasing and literate population. Nor was the abandonment of the marumakkattayam system or the granting of equal civil rights to all castes and religions; nor was responsible government, a united Kerala or even a communist administration. An elderly Travancore Nair writing on the first anniversary of the death of Pattam Thanu Pillai made the disillusionment clear. After the fall of the first Pattam ministry in October 1948, Travancore's fate was determined by

> the whims and fancies of fifth-rate politicians who were jealous of Trivandrum and the people who built up a prosperous Travancore. The result was Travancore Cochin Integration, ... and the transfer of the High Court from

> Trivandrum to one of the dirtiest towns in the world [i.e. Cochin], followed by the appointments of briefless lawyers–whose only qualification was jail life for a few months when Sir C.P. was Dewan–to high judicial and executive offices. Corruption and nepotism ran high and allegations against ministers were frequent and too many... On the 1st of November 1956 a trunkated [sic] Kerala State was born..., after giving away a well developed and fertile South Travancore, the real original Travancore, to the State of Madras (which was another political blunder) in exchange for an undeveloped Malabar District.[48]

This was a far cry from the self-confidence of seventy years before, when another Nair could write that 'we have every right to expect that, in course of time, the Malayali community will come by the recognition due to it as the most progressive community in south India'.[49]

# Conclusion

In the last half of the ninteenth century a society which had survived fundamentally unchanged for seven hundred years came unhinged.[1] A movement from inherited to achieved status began, a movement from the interdependence of castes to the competition of individuals, from traditional authority to modern bureaucracy. The missionaries, with their emphasis on the equality of men before God, their involvement with the low castes and their willingness to challenge the Travancore sirkar, lent impetus to this process. Without them, the impact of British suzerainty would have taken much longer to be felt in a princely state like Travancore. As the Maharaja lamented to the governor of Madras in 1856:

> The great increase of their number in late years, and their dispersion all over the country, have unavoidably led to disputes respecting Caste and local customs, and ... have tended in some degree to impair the control heretofore exercised by the Government over its Hindoo subjects.[2]

The bad name which the missionaries helped to give Travancore with the Madras government forced the sirkar to 'modernising' efforts in the 1860s, and these were enthusiastically pursued by the brilliant young Dewan, T. Madhava Rao. The land reforms, the abolition of commercial monopolies, the encouragement of European planters and the vigorous programme of public works stimulated the growth of a cash economy. The system of courts spread throughout the country and the secular law, particularly in relation to social institutions, was increasingly appealed to and formalised. The employment policy of government stressed the need for educational qualifications, which *savarna* Hindus could now obtain in the new government school system. Wages rose dramatically, and their use spread through a wide section of the population. The price of rice also rose, and it had to be imported in large quantities. This was partly a result of an increase in population, but also of an improved standard of living among *avarna* Hindus, many of whom were now able to afford rice occasionally.

In the 1870s and 1880s different groups responded differently to these economic, legal and educational changes. Those who had traditions in trade and were without prejudices about what constituted respectable employment were better able to cope than the proud, small-landholding, matrilineal joint-families of Nairs. Ezhavas, indeed, found their traditional occupations put them much in demand as the abkari revenue and exports of coconut products rose. At the same time, the connection between educational qualifications and employment in the government service sent Nairs enthusiastically into schools and led them to challenge the control and nepotism of non-Malayali Brahmin officials. Ritual status was no longer sufficient reason for the latter's preferment; a Nair graduate should be chosen over a Brahmin matriculate. This, however, was potentially dangerous doctrine for Nairs. By 1890 there were two Ezhava graduates, and Syrian Christians claimed to have as many college-educated men as Nairs. Both Syrians and Ezhavas came to use the same arguments that Nairs deployed against non-Malayali Brahmins.

Such emphasis on achievement, however, was farther than members of the first generation of college-educated Nairs were prepared to go. In their view, the new emphasis on merit and qualification was to be used only to ensure equality among *savarna* Hindus; others must remain slightly inferior, outside the ruling circle. Nairs would thus regain their ancient position of authority. The accommodation which these educated Nair officials reached with their Brahmin counterparts in the government service in the 1890s came close to fulfilling such aims. Christians and *avarna* Hindus were resisted, while the glamour and patronage of the palace were shared more equally among *savarna* Hindus. As C.V. Raman Pillai and his friends saw it, these were the proper limits of the new standards and values.

But egalitarian ideas, once they had crept into the old heirarchical system, could slink beyond whatever pale the men of an older generation might try to raise against them. By the 1900s there were young Nairs prepared to flay their castemen who played and prospered in palace politics. There had been factions surrounding the palace before, but for the first time the rhetoric of the 'good of the people' and the 'will of the people' was introduced into their disputes. There were two reasons for this. First, bureaucratic principles and concepts of promotion by merit had begun to take hold in Travancore. These had undermined the traditional authority of the Maharaja and the 'acceptance of his right', in Weber's words, 'to confer grace on the basis of his personal pleasure or displeasure'.[3] When Mulam Tirunal chose to behave as traditional ruler and bestow his bounty on a particular faction, other factions had new weapons available to them: a body of western-inspired dogma exalting merit and qualification—and vernacular newspapers in which to hammer home their points to a wide audience. Second, there was a genuine concern among educated Nairs for the 'good of the people'—Nair people, at any rate. The economic changes of the late nineteenth century, and the straitjacket of the new legal system had ruined many taravads. There was growing evidence of a transfer of wealth from Nairs to Christians and even *avarna* Hindus. Such a transfer, coupled with the spread of egalitarian ideas among the same groups, posed a threat to the social position and local political dominance of Nairs which few could ignore.

V.P. Madhava Rao established the Sri Mulam Popular Assembly in an attempt to counteract the influence of the palace factions, which hitherto had provided the focus for the political activity of the first generation of college-educated Nairs. The aim was to give the Dewan 'popular support' against the favourites and to bring political problems and grievances into an open, formal arena, thus taking the edge off disputes conducted in the corridors of the palace or the columns of the vitriolic local press. The Assembly, however, represented another step away from the old system of society. Men were to be elected, supposedly on their merits, and Ezhavas might sit on equal terms with Nambudiris. The Assembly suggested a number of possibilities to educated Nairs. To some, it offered a way of outflanking the conservative palace faction, particularly on the question of radical reform of the taravad. Moreover, an Assembly chosen on the basis of landholding and education would be dominated by Nairs and if such an Assembly had real power, Nairs would lead as they had led in the past.

The structure of Travancore society, however, was decidedly different from that of other regions of India. To be sure, Nairs were a dominant rural group similar to the non-Brahmin castes of most Tamil Nadu districts, the Marathas of Maharashtra, the Patidars of Gujarat and the Jats of Punjab and the western United Provinces. To be sure, there was an important Brahmin element in the government service in Travancore and the ingredients of an anti-Brahmin movement. But Ezhavas were not the Adi-Dravidas of Tamil Nadu—Travancore had its own slave castes—and though Ezhavas might be oppressed in traditional society, they had useful resources for the period of change after 1850. Similarly, traditional discrimination set Syrian and other Christians clearly apart from Nairs, yet Christians possessed wealth, education and aspirations which demanded recognition in a changing society. The clear divisions in old society and the disabilities enforced against various groups provided the basis, and the grievances, for intense competition when the old social bonds were loosened.

In 1908 when the Marumakkattayam Committee delivered its report, Nairs still exerted widespread influence. But this influence, increasingly based on negotiation and competition, was very different from the power which Nairs wielded in 1847. Then, to be a Nair guaranteed a man's place in society and dictated his relations with other men. When the missionaries began their campaign against slavery, Nairs could maltreat and probably kill their slaves with impunity. They controlled most of the land and extracted deference and submission from *avarna* Hindus. They numerically dominated the sirkar service, and although non-Malayali Brahmins held some of the highest posts, Nairs were prepared to accept their ritual superiority, just as *avarna* Hindus were expected to accept the ritual superiority of Nairs. If Nairs left trade and commerce to Syrian Christains, Muslims, non-Malayali Brahmins, Tamil Sudras and Ezhavas, it mattered little, for trade was limited by sirkar monopolies, the difficulties of communication and the corruption and inefficiency of the government. In such activities there was little advantage.

In an economy in which cash was little used, Nairs could live untroubled—'the lords of the country'[4]—in the matrilineal joint-family.

Their position in 1908, however, had changed dramatically. Their numerical dominance of the sirkar service, which in 1847 was unchallenged, was being questioned almost daily—in newspaper articles, at public meetings, in petitions and pamphlets, and by deputations. Ritual purity was now a poor justification for such control. The new forms of protest, moreover, illustrated the striking social and political changes which had occurred in sixty years. Local leaders of the earlier period were typified by the Raja of Mavelikara with whom the Rev. Joseph Peet had clashed. The Raja, it will be remembered, never deigned to leave his great house and sent messengers to deal with Peet. But in 1908 for a man to be acknowledged as a leader, it was more and more necessary for him to have a university degree, a law practice or a position under government, to be a good public speaker, to be voted to the chair at public meetings and perhaps to be the elected president of some social or professional organisation. The movement towards achieved status was pronounced.

How different too were the ways in which support was rallied. The Raja of Mavelikara, one may assume, extracted perfect obedience from his Nair managers and tenants and from their Ezhava sub-tenants and slaves. The breastcloth disturbances in 1859 indicated the extent to which *savarna* landlords could control and dictate the actions of their *avarna* tenants, dependents and ex-slaves. The vast majority of *avarna* Hindus made no attempt to join or aid the Shanars and, indeed, may have helped to intimidate them. By 1908 such patronage and intimidation had by no means disappeared, but they co-existed with the methods of the western-educated elite.

In less than sixty years, the joking prophesy of the Rev. Oomen Mamen's friend had been fulfilled. In 1857 the Nair tahsildar had asked why someone would trouble to educate *avarna* Hindus. 'They are taught to be qualified to the place of Proverthcaren, Goomastan and Tahsildar', Mamen's friend had replied. In March 1908, M. Govindan, BA, BL, was made the first Ezhava munsiff in Travancore; two other Ezhavas were made sub-registrars.[5] The value of a high ritual status was now worth less to its possessors than the value of the rupee.

The heir to the *gaddi* who was born during the celebrations following the passage of the Marumakkattayam Regulation of 1912[6] was to be the last Maharaja of Travancore. A social system and a political order were passing. Few Nairs at the beginning of the twentieth century would have quarrelled with William Logan's appreciation of their former importance and the misfortune of its decline:

> I would more especially call attention to the central point of interest...in any descriptive and historical account of the Malayali race—the position, namely, which was occupied for centuries on centuries by the Nayar caste in the civil and military organisation of the province, — a position so unique and so lasting that but for *foreign* intervention there seems to be no reason why it should not have continued to endure for centuries on centuries to come. Their functions in the body politic have been tersely described in their own traditions as '*the eye*', '*the hand*', and '*the order*' and to the present day we find them spread throughout the length and breadth of the land, but no longer—and I could say, alas!— 'preventing the rights (of all classes) from being curtailed or suffered to fall into disuse'.[7]

The realities of the early twentieth century were decidedly different. 'Travelling from Kottayam to Muvattupuzha', a distinguished Nair lamented to the Marumakkattayam Committee:

> I was surprised, and not a little concerned, to observe that not a single patch of waste land was being cultivated by a Nair. From one end to the other, the hill-sides, from top to bottom, were all aglow with cultivation. But it was the hand of the industrious native Christian or Ezhava that was at work, and the Nair—he was nowhere. I was informed that all the land once belonged to him. But now it has flown out of his hands into those who deserve to keep it.
>
> ...unless prompt measures are at once set on foot to improve [Nairs'] present deplorable condition, they will

> be swamped by the more enterprising classes, such as the Ezhavas and the Native Christians...[8]

'The Nairs: Do They Rise or Sink?', the *Malabar Herald* asked in 1905.[9] Nairs did not plunge to the bottom of some social and political sea. But by the beginning of the twentieth century, it was apparent that they could no longer regard buoyancy as their birthright; in future, like Christians and *avarna* Hindus, they too would have to swim.

# Notes

## Chapter 1

1. Elamkulam P.N. Kunjan Pillai, *Studies in Kerala Histoy* (Kottayam: National Book Stall, 1970), p. 264. K.A. Nilakanta Sastri, *A History of Southern India* (Madras: Oxford University Press, 1958), pp. 156, 192 and 209-10, emphasises the obscurity of the history of this period.
2. A. Sreedhara Menon, *A Survey of Kerala History* (Kottayam: National Book Stall, 1967), pp. 188-207, discusses 32 rulerships. S.J. Shahani, 'A Comparative Study of Traditional Political Organization of Kerala and the Punjab', unpublished Ph. D. thesis in anthropology for the School of Oriental and African Studies, University of London, 1965, suggests 'at least ninety chiefdoms'. For the ritual promotion of successful Nair chiefs, see Louis Dumont, *'Les mariages Nair comme fait indiens', L'Homme*, Vol. I, No.1, 1961, p. 27, and Samuel Mateer, *The Land of Charity* (London: John Snow, 1870), p. 169.
3. For the peculiar geography of Kerala, see Joan P. Mencher, 'Kerala and Madras: A Comparative Study of Ecology and Social Structure', *Ethnology*, Vol. V, 1966, pp. 137-47. For Cheruman Perumal, the legendary last Chera emperor, see Sreedhara Menon, *Survey*, pp. 135-7.
4. Mencher, 'Kerala and Madras', pp. 143-4, deals with the difference between the *tara* and the *desam*. The *tara—kara* in Travancore— was essentially the local organization of Nair elders. The *desam* was the unit of military organization, and its area was determined by the number of soldiers it was required to provide. The *desam* was

smaller if the area was densely populated. See also William Logan, *Malabar*, Vol. I (Madras: Government Press, 1951; first published 1887), p. 89, L.K. Ananthakrishna Iyer, *The Cochin Tribes and Castes*, Vol. II (Madras: Higginbotham, 1912), pp. 57-8 and 60.

5. V. Nagam Aiya, *The Travancore State Manual*, Vol. I (Trivandrum: Government Press, 1906), p. 249.
6. For a discussion of the petty chiefs, see Lieutenants Ward and Conner, *Memoir of the Survey of the Travancore and Cochin States* (Trivandrum: Sirkar Press, 1863; reprinted 1898), pp. 94-6; K.P. Padmanabha Menon, *History of Kerala*, Vol. I (Ernakulam: Cochin Government Press, 1924), pp. 416-17. For the overturning of the old system by Martanda Varma of Travancore, see Memorandum by William Logan, *Report of the Malabar Land Tenures Committee*, Vol. II (Madras: Government Press, 1887), Appendix I, p. 7; K.M. Panikkar, *A History of Kerala 1498-1801* (Annamalainagar: Annamalai University, 1960), p. 307.
7. Logan, *Malabar*, Vol. I, p. 597.
8. Ibid., pp. 132-3.
9. Duarte Barbosa, *The Book of Duarte Barbosa*, Vol. II, trans. M.L. Dames (London: Hakluyt Society, 1921), p. 49. See also Luiz de Camoens, *The Lusiads*, trans. Leonard Bacon (New York: Hispanic Society of America, 1950), especially Book VII.
10. Nagam Aiya, *Manual*, Vol. I, pp. 336-8; Sreedhara Menon, *Survey*, pp. 274-6.
11. P. Shankunni Menon, *A History of Travancore* (Madras: Higginbotham, 1878), pp. 110-11; Sreedhara Menon, *Survey*, p. 282.
12. S. Ramanath Aiyar, *A History of Travancore* (Madras: Srinivasa Varadachari, 1938), p. 42; *Travancore Census Report,* 1881, pp. 193-4; Nagam Aiya, *Manual,* Vol. II, pp. 277-86. For the *uttupuras,* see V. [Krishna Rao] Kristno Row, *A Description of the Administrative System of Travancore in the Year 1844* (Trivandrum: Sirkar Press, 1860), pp. 19-23. For the dedication to the god Padmanabha, see Sreedhara Menon, *Survey*, p. 282.
13. Panikkar, *Kerala*, pp. 309-57. Panikkar's view is a

popular one. A Malayalam film, *Panchavankatu*, released in 1971, cast Martanda Varma as the villain and the executed Nair chiefs as patriots and martyrs.

14. Lewin B. Bowring. *Haidar Ali and Tipu Sultan* (Oxford: Clarendon Press, 1899), pp. 139-44; Nagam Aiya, *Manual*, Vol. I, p. 402, where the treaty is reproduced in full.
15. Macaulay was the brother of Zachary Macaulay and uncle of the historian. He was a vice-president of the Church Missionary Society from his retirement from Travancore until his death in 1836.
16. Kundara Proclamation, 16 Jan. 1809, quoted in Shankunni Menon, *Travancore,* p. 343. *Kali Yug* is the fourth and present age of the world. Since independence Velu Thampi has been rehabilitated. His statue now stands within the railings that surround the Secretariat in Trivandrum; it looks with disapproval at the statue of Sir T. Madhava Rao, unprotected against bill posters, across the road.
17. Col. James Welsh, *Military Reminiscences*, Vol. I (London: Smith, Elder, 1830), p. 293, writing of the forcing of the Aruvamozhi Pass near Nagercoil on 10 Feb. 1810. For the detailed proceedings of the 1800-10 period, see *Parliamentary Papers*, 1810, Vol. V, pp. 13ff and 1812-13, Vol. X, pp. 171ff.
18. B.N. Mehta, 'A Little Known Event in the History of Travancore', *Journal of Indian History*, Vol. XXIX, 1951, pp. 27-31. The deposed Nair Dewan unsuccessfully plotted to kill Munro in May 1812.
19. Shankunni Menon, *Travancore,* p. 384, for Reddy Rao's background. N. Nanu Pillai (Dewan, 1877-80) was the only Travancore Nair to hold the dewanship as a permanent appointment after 1817. M. Krishnan Nair (Dewan 1914-20) was from Malabar.
20. Letter by Munro, quoted in Ulloor S. Parameswara Aiyar, 'Colonel Munro', *Kerala Society Papers*, No. II Series 7, 1931, p. 47.
21. Shankunni Menon, *Travancore*, p. 372.
22. Letter by Munro, quoted in CMS *Annual Report*, Vol. V, 1817, p. 454. Munro to the Chief Secretary, Fort St. George, 30 March 1818, in CMS *Annual Report*, Vol. VIII, 1820, p. 336.

23. Letter by Munro, quoted in CMS *Annual Report*, Vol. V, 1817, pp. 454-5. See also *Missionary Register*, Nov. 1816, p. 453; CMS *Annual Report*, Vol. VII, 1819, p. 170.
24. Munro to the Rev. J. Wardlaw Thompson, 26 May 1818, quoted in CMS *Annual Report*, Vol. VII, 1819, p. 168.
25. Rev. Joseph Fenn, letter, quoted in CMS *Annual Report*, Vol. VII, 1819, p. 323.
26. Rev. Henry Baker, Sr. *A Sermon Preached at Christ Church, Kottayam, on the 9th November 1859* (Kottayam: CMS Press, 1860), p. 15.
27. This can only be a guess. It is based on an estimate of 25,000 Nair joint-families at this time and perhaps 8,000 Nair sirkar officials and petty officials.
28. Travancore and Its Land Tenure', *Calcutta Review*, Vol. CXII, Jan. 1901, p. 130, quoting 'an experienced Travancore officer'.
29. *Travancore Calendar*, 1851, pp. vi-x.
30. Madras Political Proceedings [hereafter MPP], 15 July 1862, Range 321, Vol. XLVI, pp. 256-7.
31. *Travancore Calendar*, 1851, pp. vi-x.
32. William Cullen, Resident, to the Chief Secretary to the Madras Government [hereafter Ch. Sec.], 15 March 1843: Madras Residency Records [hereafter MRR], Letters to the Madras Government [hereafter LMG], Vol. XIV.
33. *Travancore Calendar*, 1851, pp. vi-x.
34. Cullen to the Ch. Sec., 25 Jan. 1858: MPP, 9 Feb. 1858, Range 321, Vol. XXXIX, p. 237.
35. J.H. Hutton, *Caste in India* (Bombay: Oxford University Press, 1969; first published 1946), pp. 79-85, discusses pollution at some length and cites all his examples from Kerala and south Tamil Nadu.
36. A.H. [awksworth], *Day Dawn in Travancore* (Kottayam: CMS Press, 1860), pp. 8-9.
37. Hutton, *Caste*, pp. 79-80, gives a convenient digest.
38. 'Miss Baker's School at Kottayam', 1884, probably written by Mary Baker who was the daughter of the Rev. Henry Baker, Jr., Church Missionary Society Archives [hereafter CMSA], No. 38 of 1884.
39. Rev. Jacob Chandy, Sr., 'Journal', 15 Aug. 1855 and 25 Nov. 1856: CMSA, uncatalogued.

40. See Rev. Jacob Chandy, Sr, 'Journal', 7 July 1853, 15 June 1854; Rev. Oomen Mammen to the Secretary, CMS, 5 Jan. 1857, 31 Jan. 1866: CMSA, uncatalogued.
41. *Savarna* refers to high-caste Hindus; *avarna* to low castes.
42. *Census*, 1875, p. 191.
43. See the advertisement in the *Travancore Government Gazette* [hereafter *TGG*], Vol. XXXII, No. 45, 6 Nov. 1894, for a Nambudiri, aged 20 to 40, of 'unblemished character', to be priest of the main Badrinath temple in the Himalayas.
44. Nagam Aiya, *Manual*, Vol. II, pp. 286-8, for a discussion of the Pottis.
45. *Report of the Travancore Marumakkathayam Committee 1908* [hereafter *Maru. Report*], p. 13.
46. Fred. Fawcett, 'Notes on some of the people of Malabar', *Madras Government Museum Bulletin*, Vol. III, No. 1, 1900, p. 61. For a description of the elaborate trials for fornication staged by Nambudiris, see Logan, *Malabar*, Vol. I, pp. 122-6.
47. The major public appearance of the Malayali Brahmins was the sexennial *murajapam* ceremony when they went to Trivandrum to chant prayers and be feasted. One, Parameswaran Nambudiri, was chief justice of the Sadr Court for ten years in the 1840s and early 1850s, but his case was exceptional.
48. Rev. Samuel Mateer, *The Land of Charity* (London: John Snow, 1871), p. 29; Nagam Aiya, *Manual*, vol. II, p. 255; Fawcett, 'Notes', p. 85.
49. See Joan Mencher, 'The Namboodiri Brahmins of Kerala', *Journal of Asian and African Studies*, Vol. I, 1966, pp. 189-90, for a Nambudiri's explanation for their 'backwardness' in the twentieth century.
50. Ward and Conner, *Memoir*, p. 137.
51. Logan, *Malabar*, Vol. I, p. 129.
52. *Report of the Malabar Marriage Commission* [hereafter *Mal. Mar. Com.*], 1891, Appendix III, p. 4. 'Answers to Interrogatories' by C. Karunakara Menon, sub-editor, *The Hindu*.
53. Krishna Chaitanya, *A History of Malayalam Literature* (Bombay: Orient Longmans, 1971), pp. 120 and 122. Chaitanya's translation.

54. U. Balakrishna Nair, 'The Nairs: A Race of Hereditary Fighters', *Malabar Quarterly Review,* Vol. I, No. 2, June 1902, pp. 83-4. It should be noted that as late as 1902, after four fairly accurate censuses, Nairs were still describing themselves as 'the bulk' of the inhabitants.
55. Kathleen Gough, 'The Nayars and the Definition of Marriage', *Journal of the Royal Anthropological Institute*, Vol. LXXXIX, 1959, p. 24; Francis Buchanan, *A Journey from Madras*, Vol. II (Madras: Higginbotham, 1870), pp. 93-4; *Mal. Mar. Com.*, p. 6.
56. *Mal. Mar. Com.*, p. 6; *Census*, 1891, Vol. I, p. 761. It would be wrong to make too much of these menial Nairs. Their proportion of the Cochin 'Nair' population in 1891 was, for example, less than ten percent. *Cochin Census*, 1901, Vol. I, pp. 156 and 163.
57. Rev. Samuel Mateer, *Native Life in Travancore* (London: W.H. Allen, 1883), p. 111.
58. *Census*, 1875, pp. 197-8, gave thirty-five subdivisions of Nairs; *Census*, 1891, Vol. I, p. 761, seventy-four subdivisions; *Census*, 1901, Vol. I, 116 subdivisions. However, it is important to remember that the Illam (traditionally retainers of Nambudiris) and Swarupam (temple retainers) were by far the largest. In 1901, Illam (62 per cent) and Swarupam (19 per cent) Nairs comprised 81 per cent of all Nairs.
59. *Malayala Manorama*, 11 March 1899.
60. Nagam Aiya, *Manual*, Vol. II, pp. 350-51.
61. *Ibiid.*, pp. 277-9, gives a description of the Nair house. There is an elaborate model of an idealised taravad in the mus-eum in Trivandrum. See also M.S.A. Rao, *Social Change in Malabar* (Bombay: Popular Book Depot, 1957), p. 76.
62. The fear of incest in this situation was great. See Joan Mencher, 'Nayars of South Malabar', in M F Nimkoff (editor) *Comparative Family Systems* (Boston: 1965), p. 183; Kathleen Gough, 'Incest Prohibitions and Rules of Exogamy in Three Matrilineal Groups of the Malabar Coast', *International Archives of Ethnography*, Vol. XLVI, 1952, pp. 82-105; Samuel Mateer, 'Nepotism in Travancore', *Journal of the Anthropological Institute,* Vol. XII, 1882, p. 297.

63. For discussion of polyandry in old Cochin—the situation was similar in north Travancore—see Kathleen Gough, 'The Nayars and the Definition of Marriage', p. 26. See also Kathleen Gough, 'Cults of the Dead among the Nayars', in Milton Singer (editor), *Traditional India: Structure and Change* (Philadelphia: American Folklore Society, 1959), p. 240; F. Fawcett, 'Nayars of Malabar', *Madras Government Museum Bulletin*, Vol. III, No. 3, 1901, p. 241.

64. Whether *talikettukalyanam* was a real marriage has been a fruitful source of argument. See Louis Dumont, 'Les Marriages', p. 13 and also *Hierarchicus*, p. 162. For description of the ceremony, see Kathleen Gough, 'Female Initiation Rites in the Malabar Coast', *Journal of the Royal Anthropological Institute*, Vol. LXXXV, Part 2, 1955, pp. 45-80; Nagam Aiya, *Manual*, Vol. II, pp. 352-7; L.A. Krishna Iyer, *Social History of Kerala: The Dravidians*, Vol. II (Madras: Book Centre Publication, 1970), pp. 63-5.

65. See Kunjan Pillai, *Studies*, pp. 284-369, which emphasizes the effect of the military role on the family system. Mencher, 'Nayars of South Malabar', p. 176, seeks to minimize the influence of the military role: 'it cannot be stated that their occupation as soldiers was by itself a major factor in the weakness of marital ties'. Kathleen Gough, 'Changing Kinship Usages in the Setting of Political and Economic Change among the Nayars of Malabar', *Journal of the Royal Anthropological Institute*, Vol. LXXXI, 1952, p. 77, seems closer to Kunjan Pillai's view when she writes that the Nair system of marriage 'was consistent with a special type of military organisation'.

66. Lt. Col. E. Cadogan, Resident, to the Ch. Sec., 1832, quoted in T.K. Velu Pillai, *The Travancore State Manual*, Vol. II (Trivandrum: Government Press, 1940), p. 547.

67. See Appendix. Christians were underenumerated in 1854, as the figures for the 1875 census indicate. By 1875, too, many more converts had been made.

68. L.W. Brown, *The Indian Christians of St. Thomas* (Cambridge: University Press, 1956), pp. 49-51 and 59.

69. *Ibid.*, pp. 70-4. An elaboration of the story of Thomas of Cana credits Thomas with a west Asian wife who lived

south of the river at Cranganore and a Nair wife who lived to the north; thus, Nordists and Suddists. Rev. F.E. Keay, *A History of the Syrian Church in India* (Madras: SPCL in India, 1938), p. 20.

70. Brown, *Christians*, p. 92.
71. *Ibid.*, p. 100. S.G. Pothan, *The Syrian Christians of Kerala* (Bombay: Asia Publishing House, 1963), pp. 46-7.
72. Brown, *Christians*, pp. 109-31.
73. See P. Cheriyan, *The Malabar Syrians and the Church Missionary Society, 1816-40* (Kottayam: CMS Press, 1935), pp. 71-141. See also Munro to Rev. J. Wardlaw Thompson, 7 Aug. 1815, in CMS, *Annual Report*, Vol. V, 1817, p. 454.
74. The split resulted from resentment at the CMS agents' interference in the financial and ritual affairs of the Jacobite church. See Cheriyan, *Syrians*, pp. 223-48. It was four years before the break was complete and CMS evangelising began in earnest.
75. Brown, *Christians*, pp. 74-7, for a discussion of the ancient copperplate grants made to the Syrians.
76. L.K. Ananthakrishna Ayyar, *Anthropology of the Syrian Christians* (Ernakulam: Cochin Government Press, 1926), p. 56.
77. 'Brief Sketch of the History of the St. Thomas Christians', 1886, p. 7, handwritten manuscript in the library at the Mannanam Monastery, 2224/32/B/22. The anonymous author writes that Syrians in the days of the Chera Empire 'were looked upon as superior to the Nairs who held as they still do a high social position, and so the Syrians formed as a rule members of nobility [sic]'. LMS Travancore District Committee [hereafter TDC], *Annual Report*, 1866, p. 5, where the Rev. F. Wilkinson of Quilon wrote that the Syrians 'rank as Sudras in the estimation of the heathen'. Brown, *Christians*, pp. 169-71 and 173.
78. A. Aiyappan, 'Iravas and Culture Change', *Madras Government Museum Bulletin*, Vol. V, No. 1, 1943, p. 76, wrote that 'both Christians and Muslims do not observe pollution'. In the case of Syrian Christians this is incorrect. Syrians alive today say that as children they were told to bathe when touched by low castes. The difficulty of the CMS

in getting Syrians to sit with low castes in the same church illustrates the point. See, for example, Rev. K. Koshi, 'Journal', 11 Aug. 1857: CMSA, uncatalogued; Hodges to Wigram, 2 Dec. 1893: CMSA, No. 152 of 1893.

79. Abraham M. Nidhiry, *Father Nidhiry* (Kottayam: Deepika Press, 1971), p. 3; Rao, *Social Change*, p. 22.

80. The first book in Malayalam was said to have been printed by Portuguese Jusuits in Cochin about 1580 but printing in Malayalam died out until Rev. Benjamin Bailey cut his own type in Kottayam in the 1820s. Rev. T. Whitehouse, *Some Historical Notices of Cochin on the Malabar Coast* (Kottayam: CMS Press, 1859), p. 10

81. *Madras Mail*, 9 Oct. 1895; *Kerala Patrika*, 3 March 1894 in *Reports on Native Newspapers, Madras* [hereafter *RNNM*], Malayalam, fortnight ending 15 March 1894.

82. *Census*, 1891, Vol. II, p. 980, which lists seven subdivisions recognised by Ezhavas for purposes of marriage. Krishna Iyer, *Social History*, Vol. II, p. 57; C. Kesavan, *Jivitasamaram* (Kottayam: National Book Stall, 1965), p. 38.

83. *Census*, 1901, Vol. I, p. 279; Francis Day, *Land of the Perumals* (Madras: Gantz Brothers, 1863), p. 321; Ballard, Resident, to the Ch. Sec. 9 March 1870: MRR, MPP, 23 April 1870, G.O. No. 143.

84. A.H. [awksworth], *Day Dawn*, p. 8; Day, *Perumals*, p.321; Rev. J. Chandy, Sr., 'Journal', 15 Aug. 1855, 12 Feb. 1857: CMSA, uncatalogued, makes it clear that such prohibitions were strictly observed.

85. Day, *Perumals*, p. 321.

86. Good illustrations of Ezhava marriage and inheritance customs are Appeal Suits No. 144 of 1041 and No. 15 of 1042 in *TGG*, Vol. V, No. 48, 10 Dec. 1867.

87. *Census*, 1875, p. 190. The cocoanut palm was also easier to climb and tap. See Aiyappan, 'Iravas', p. 109.

88. Rev. John Abbs. *Twenty-Two Years' Missionary Experience in Travancore* (London: John Snow, 1870), p. 200.

89. *Census*, 1875, p. 229; Edgar Thurston, *Castes and Tribes of Southern India*, Vol. V. (Madras: Government Press, 1909), pp. 241 and 295. T. Ponnambalam Pillai, 'The Antiquity of Nanjinad and Shenkottah', *Malabar Quarterly Review*, Vol. III, No. 3, Sept. 1904, p. 281, for the customs

of Nanjanad Vellalas.

90. Rev. Dr. Charles Leitch to the Foreign Secretary, LMS. 1 Feb. 1854: CCWM, Travancore, Box 4, Folder 3, Jacket D.

91. Rev. Frederic Baylis, 'Report', 1857, in J.A. Jacob, 'History of the London Missionary Society in Travancore', manuscript, p. 102: United Theological College, Bangalore [hereafter UTC], No. 97. Baylis wrote that there were 14,673 adherents. See also William Robinson (ed.), *Ringeltaube, the Rishi* [Journals and Letters] (Sheffield: Independent Press, 1902).

92. *Census*, 1881, p. 177.

93. Rev. Samuel Mateer, 'The Pariah Caste in Travancore', *Journal of the Royal Asiatic Society*, New Series, Vol. XVI, 1884, pp. 192-5. T.K. Gopal Panikkar, *Malabar and Its Folk* (Madras: G.A. Natesan, third edition, 1929; first published, 1900), p. 133.

94. Abbs to the Foreign Secretary, LMS, 12 Sept. 1854: CCWM, Travancore, Box 4, Folder 3, Jacket D.

95. Mateer, 'Pariah', p. 191.

96. Cullen to the Ch. Sec., 10 Nov. 1854: MPP, 28 Nov. 1854, Range 321, Vol. XV, pp. 5053-55, reporting the results of a census of sirkar slaves.

97. Rev. Henry Baker, Jr. to the Secretary, CMS, 12 Oct. 1847: CMSA, No. 29 of 1847; Rev. George Matthen, quoted in the *Church Missionary Record*, Vol. XXIII, Aug. 1852, p. 184. Any caste could be sold into slavery.

98. Emily Gilchrist Hatch, *Travancore* (Madras: Oxford University Press, 1933), p. 221; Sreedhara Menon, *Survey*, pp. 268-9.

99. Cullen to V. Krishna Rao, Dewan, 25 May 1852: Travancore Government English Records [hereafter TGER], Cover No. 15540.

100. Aiyappan, 'Iravas', p. 111.

101. Hannyngton, Resident, to Rama Rao, Dewan, 24 June 1890: TGER, Cover No. 1739, referring to a petition about slave-holding; K.M. Panikkar, 'Some Aspects of Nayar Life', *Journal of the Royal Anthropological Institute*, Vol. XLVIII, 1918, pp. 285-6.

102. Travancore Tenures', pp. 130-1.

103. Nagam Aiya, *Manual*, Vol. III, pp. 311-14; Kunjan Pillai, 'The Evolution of the Janmi System in Kerala', *Studies*, pp. 324-69.
104. Note by T.V. Anantan Nair, *Report of the Malabar Land Tenures Committee*, 1887, Vol. I, p. 64.
105. By 1886 there were only fourteen pure janmis in Travancore. V. Ramiengar, 'Memorandum on the Revenue Survey and Settlement of Travancore', 14 April 1885, in S. Padmanabha Aiyar (ed.), *Report of the Revenue Settlement of Travancore, 1883-1911*, Vol. II (Trivandrum: Government Press, 1913), Appendix II, p. 143. In Malabar the British government re-established the janmis in the 1790s, and big absentee landlords continued to hold much of the land in Malabar until after independence in 1947. Varghese, *Agrarian Change*, p. 217, *Report of the Special Commission on Malabar Land Tenures*, Vol. I (Madras: 1882), p. 134.
106. This was in contrast to number of states in northern India where semi-autonomous local chiefs survived under the raja. Jaipur and Baroda are examples.
107. *Travancore Administration Report* [hereafter *TAR*], 1864-5, pp. 28-30. See also Varghese, *Change*, p. 30. In the 1830s, Travancore had an estimated 741 square miles (475,000 acres) in rice. W.G. Horsley, *Memoir of Travancore* (Trivandrum: Sirkar Press, 1863; first published, 1839), p. 1.
108. In 1913 after much simplification there were still 66 kinds of tenure and 387 permutations. Padmanabha Aiyer (ed.), *Settlement Report*, Vol. I, Appendix II, No. 3, pp. lxxvi-lxxvii. See also Ramiengar, 'Memorandum', p. 145.
109. Ward and Conner, *Memoir*, p. 72.
110. *Census*, 1875, pp. 261 and 266.
111. *Ibid.*, p. 267.
112. Horsley, *Memoir*, p. 1.
113. Welsh, *Reminiscences*, Vol. II, p. 107.
114. Ward and Conner, *Memoir*, p. 50.
115. Bailey, Baker and Fenn to Col. D. Newall, Resident, 18 March 1822, in CMS, *Annual Report*, Vol. X, 1823, p. 238.
116. Nidhiry, *Nidhiry*, p. 9; Diary of Fr. Mathew Palakkunnel, once held by the late of P.J. Sebastian, Perumpanachey, Kottayam District, who translated portions for me during

an interview on 8 August 1971; A.O. Mathai, 'Life of the Venerable Archdeacon Oomen Mamen, CMS', *Travancore and Cochin Diocesan Record*, Vol. XV, No. 1, Jan. 1905, p. 7. Matthai was Mamen's son. Rev. J. Chandy, Sr., 'Journal', 13 Dec. 1856: CMSA, uncatalogued.

117. Ward and Conner, *Memoir*, p. 72.
118. *The Regulations and Proclamations of Travancore*, Vol. V, p. 797, Regulation III of 1100.
119. Rev. J. Russel to the Foreign Secretary, LMS, 24 Jan. 1856: CCWM, Travancore, Box 4, Folder 4, Jacket B.
120. Logan, *Malabar*, Vol. I, pp. 245-9.
121. See Ashin Das Gupta, 'The Making of Travancore', *Bengal Past and Present*, Vol. LXXX, July-Dec. 1961, pp. 124-48 and Ashin Das Gupta, *Malabar in Asian Trade 1740-1800*. (Cambridge: University Press, 1967).
122. Krishna Rao, *Description*, p. 47.
123. Ward and Conner, *Memoir*, pp. 8-9 and 89.
124. Quoted in Rev. T. Whitehouse, *Lingerings of Light in a Dark Land* (London: Brown, 1873), p. 6n.
125. A.H. [awksworth], *Day Dawn*, p. 50.
126. Nidhiry, *Nidhiry*, p. 3; Rao, *Change*, p. 22.
127. C.P. Matthen, *I Have Borne Much* (Madras: Ampthill, 1951), p. 12. See also Aiyappan, 'Iravas', p. 41; K. Kuruvilla, *A History of the Mar Thoma Church and Its Doctrines* (Madras: Christian Literature Society for India, 1951), p. 41; Brown, *Christians*, p. 172; E.M. Philip, *The Indian Church of St. Thomas* (Nagercoil: LMS Press, 1950), p. 420.
128. Ward and Conner, *Memoir*, pp. 137-8.
129. Rev. J. Russel to the Foreign Secretary, LMS, 24 Jan. 1856: CCWM, Travancore, Box 4, Folder 4, Jacket D.
130. *Census*, 1875, p. 260
131. It would be wrong to overemphasise the demand for manufactured goods in Kerala. In 1901 Fawcett wrote that among Nairs 'a few houses' kept 'razors of English or German manufacture'. Scissors were regarded as 'new fangled'. Fred Fawcett, 'Nayars of Malabar', *Madras Government Museum Bulletin*, Vol. II, No. 3, 1901, pp. 194-5.

## Chapter 2

1. A. Aiyappan, *Social Revolution in a Kerala Village* (New York: Asia Publishing House, 1965), p. 35; Eric J. Miller, 'Caste and Territory in Malabar', *American Anthropologist*, Vol. LVI, 1954, p. 419. Samuel Mateer, *Native Life in Travancore* (London: W.H. Allen, 1883), p. 34.
2. Abbs to the Foreign Secretary, LMS, 1 Feb. 1855: CCWM, Travancore, Box 4, Folder 4, Jacket A.
3. Minutes of the CMS Travancore Conference, 17 Dec. 1857: UTC, No. 39.
4. Rev. Henry Baker, Jr. to the Secretary, CMS, 12 October 1847: CMSA, No. 30 of 1847; Rev. Dr. Charles Leitch to the Foreign Secretary, 1 Jan. 1853: CCWM, Travancore, Box 4, Folder 3, Jacket C; Rev. Ebenezer Lewis to the Foreign Secretary, LMS, 28 Jan. 1853: CCWM, Travancore, Box 4, Folder 3, Jacket C; Rev. J.O. Whitehouse to the Foreign Secretary, LMS, 2 Sept. 1853: CCWM, Travancore, Box 4, Folder 3, Jacket B.
5. Rev. Joseph Peet to the Secretary, CMS, 28 June 1861: CMSA, uncatalogued.
6. Rev. G.O. Newport, quoted in LMS, Travancore District Committee, *Annual Report* [hereafter LMS, TDC, *Report*], 1866, p. 7.
7. See the *Madras Athenaeum*, 2 Nov. 1848, 2 Jan 1855, 6 Dec. 1856. Krishna Rao, the Dewan, was said to provide the Resident with women. See also the Petition of Koratty Kara Swamyar to the Madras Government, 5 Nov. 1854: MPP, 6 Feb. 1855, Range 321, Vol. XVIII, p. 518, which accused Cullen of 'the ruin of many women of cast[e] and respectability'. Forty years later it was said of another Resident, J.D. Rees, that 'his behaviour quite recalled the days of General Cullen, only that in Cullen's time the ladies concerned received an adequate remuneration'. R.S. Lepper to Curzon, 29 June 1903, quoting 'a cultured Hindu official': IOR, Ampthill Papers, E/233/17.
8. [Vishakham Tirunal], 'A Native Statesman', *Calcutta Review*, Vol. LV, 1872, p. 229.

9. Rev. Joseph Peet to the Secretary, CMS, 5 May 1859: CMSA uncatalogued; Rev. Samuel Mateer, *The Land of Charity* (London: John Snow, 1871), p. 297; Abbs, *Experience*, p. 82.
10. Ainslie T. Embree, *Charles Grant and British Rule in India* (London: George Allen and Unwin, 1962), pp. 238-9.
11. Cullen to the Ch. Sec., n. d.: MPP, 24 June 1853, Range 321, Vol. III, p. 2156. Also Cullen to the Ch. Sec., 24 Aug. 1853: MPP, 14 Feb. 1854, Range 321, Vol. VII, pp. 527-8; Cullen to the Ch. Sec., n.d.: MPP, 5 June 1855, Range 321, Vol. XXI, pp. 2389-2403; Cullen to the Ch. Sec., 24 Sept. 1853: MPP, 24 Feb. 1854, Range 321, Vol. VII, p. 726.
12. See Cullen, 'Memorandum addressed to the Madras Government on the 5th Dec. 1843' (Trivandrum: 1849), and his article in Edward Balfour, *On the Influence exercised by Trees on the Climate of a Country* (London: 1849). Also A. Sreedhara Menon, *Kerala District Gazeteers: Quilon* (Trivandrum: Government Press, 1964), p. 12. Dawson, Acting Resident, to the Dewan, 18 June 1891: MRR, Letters to the Dewan, Vol. XXVI, describing Cullen's school for the children of the Residency staff. See also, Rev. J.O. Whitehouse to the Foreign Secretary, LMS, 7 Sept. 1852: CCWM, Travancore, Box 4, Folder 3, Jacket A, for a report of Cullen's 20-pound donation to the Nagercoil Seminary for 'philosophical apparatus'.
13. Cullen to the Dewan, 23 March 1859: MRR, LD, Vol. XI, Jan. 1857 to Dec. 1859, in which Cullen subscribed Rs. 1,000 for a bridge-building project. He owned considerable property in the state. His loneliness, however, seems to be indicated by his efforts to have a young relative appointed to his staff. He wrote that he felt 'very sensibly the loss of the only officer personally attached to me and living in my family...' Cullen to the Ch. Sec., 28 Dec. 1850: MRR, LMG, Vol. XV, Jan. 1848 to Dec. 1854.
14. Baylis to the Foreign Secretary, LMS, 12 Dec. 1854: CCWM, Travancore, Box 4, Folder 3, Jacket D; Petition to the Madras Government from John Cox, 12 Feb. 1855: MPP, 17 March 1855, Range 321, Vol. XIX, p. 1278.
15. See Robert E. Frykenberg, *Guntur District, 1788-1848*

(Oxford: Clarendon Press, 1965), especially Chapter V, for the corruption and mismanagement Krishna Rao would have witnessed.

16. Cullen to the Ch. Sec., 15 March 1843: MRR, LMG, Vol. XIV. All the preceding biographical information is taken from this letter.
17. See Nagam Aiya, *Manual*, Vol. I, p. 506; Shankunni Menon, *Travancore*, pp. 423-9. Cullen claimed the appointment was made 'without the slightest suggestion or communication from me'. Cullen to the Ch. Sec., 18 June 1842: MRR, LMG, Vol. XIV.
18. The full text of the letter, dated 21 Aug. 1843, is given in Ramanath Aiyar, *Travancore*, Appendix V.
19. Shankunni Menon, *Travancore*, p. 425; Cullen to the Ch. Sec., 18 June 1842: MRR, LMG, Vol. XIV.
20. For example, Cullen to Krishna Rao, 31 Oct. 1854, 12 Jan. 1857 and 6 March 1852: MRR, LD, Vols. IX, XI and VIII.
21. For examples, Cullen to Krishna Rao, 14 Oct. 1850, 27 March 1851, 31 March 1851, 17 June 1851, 16 July 1851: MRR, LD, Vol. VIII. For his comments on the misuse of elephants, Cullen to Krishna Rao, 22 Oct. 1852: MRR, LD, Vol. VIII.
22. Cullen to Krishna Rao, 25 May 1853: MRR, LD, Vol. IX.
23. Memorandum of Walter Elliott, n.d.: MPP, 15 March 1859, Range 321, Vol. XLII, p. 286.
24. [Vishakham Tirunal], 'Statesman', p. 229.
25. Krishna Rao to Cullen, 6 Oct. 1857: TGER, Cover No. 4660.
26. Cox complained to the Bishop of Madras about Peet's interference with LMS adherents at Quilon. Cox to the Foreign Secretary, LMS, 2 Dec. 1853: CCWM, Travancore, Box 4, Folder 3, Jacket C.
27. Travancore rulers are differentiated by the star under which they were born. Thus, Uttaram Tirunal—the person born under Uttaram.
28. Abbs, *Experience*, p. 88, describes Uttaram Tirunal and his easy manner with Europeans.
29. Petition, 19 March 1847, signed by Rev. Messrs. Mead,

Bailey, Baker, Sr., Mault, Thompson, Russel, Cox, Abbs, Hawksworth, Lewis, Whitehouse and Baker, Jr.: TGER, Cover No. 286.

30. V. Krishna Rao to Cullen, 1 June 1857: TGER, Cover No. 286.
31. Petition, March 1848: TGER, Cover No. 286. Benedicte Hjejle, *Slavery and Agricultural Bondage in South India in the Nineteenth Century* (Copenhagen: Scandinavian Institute of Asian Studies, 1967), p. 98, points out that the act had little effect.
32. Cullen to Krishna Rao, 15 Aug. 1848: TGER, Cover No. 286.
33. Memorandum by Cullen, 12 March 1849: TGER, Cover No. 286.
34. MPP, 26 July 1853, Range 321, Vol. IV, p. 2557.
35. Rev. Henry Baker, Jr. to the Secretary, CMS, 12 Oct. 1847: CMSA, No. 29 of 1847.
36. Rev. Charles Mault to the Foreign Secretary, LMS, 4 Feb. 1851: CCWM, Travancore, Box 4, Folder 2, Jacket B.
37. Rev. Henry Baker, Sr. to the Secretary, CMS, 14 July 1845, quoted in W.S. Hunt, *The Anglican Church in Travancore and Cochin, 1816-1916*, Vol. II (Kottayam: CMS Press, 1933), p. 57.
38. Rev. George Matthen, quoted in CMS, *Annual Report*, Vol. XXI, 1851-2, p. 145.
39. The identity of 'Not the Last' was a well-kept secret, but Cox's grandson, Charles H. Simpson, 'Blackrock Estate', said that it was always known in the family that Cox was 'Not the Last'. Interview, 13 Oct. 1971. For examples of the publicity, see the *Madras Athenaeum*, 2 Nov. 1851, 20 Sept. 1853, 18 Jan. 1855, 20 Jan. 1855, 13 March 1855, 6 Dec. 1856. *Madras Church Missionary Record*, Feb. 1854. *Church Missionary Intelligencer*, London, Jan. 1855.
40. Mault to Cullen, 23 Feb. 1852, Lewis to Cullen, 23 Feb. 1853,CCWM, Travancore, Box 4, Folder 3, Jacket B. The missionaries did not get satisfaction, although the case dragged on for six months.
41. Krishna Rao to the Tahsildar of Tiruvalla, Feb. 1851: MPP, 21 Jan. 1853, Range 320, Vol. LXXIV, p. 277. The Dewan

was paraphrasing the missionary's letter of complaint.

42. *Loc. cit.* Cullen questioned the missionaries' interpretation and ridiculed their use of 'edict'. Cullen to the Ch. Sec., 24 Aug. 1853: MPP, 14 Feb. 1854, Range 321, Vol. LXXVII, p. 515. The term 'mapilla' was applied to both Syrian Christians and Muslims in Travancore.
43. Krishna Rao to Cullen, 3 March 1853: TGER, Cover No. 215.
44. Cullen to the Ch. Sec., 24 Aug. 1853: MRR, LMG, Vol.XV.
45. Cullen to the Ch. Sec., 22 Sept. 1853: MPP, 28 March 1854, Range 321, Vol. VIII, p. 1157. The figures were collected in 1849 and Cullen rightly thought them too low. Cullen to the Ch. Sec., 10 Nov. 1854: MPP, 28 Nov. 1854, Range 321, Vol. XV, pp. 5053-55, communicated the results of a more recent and accurate slave census.
46. Proclamation, 14 Oct. 1853: MPP, 28 March 1854, Range 321, Vol. VIII, p. 1164.
47. The Governor, Major-General Sir Henry Pottinger, supported Cullen and blamed the missionaries for causing trouble. Walter Elliott, member of the council, agreed with Pottinger, although he did not condemn the missionaries. I.F. Thomas, the other member of the council, defended the missionaries and argued that the Madras Government should exert much greater pressure on Travancore. MPP, 28 March 1854, Range 321, Vol. VIII, pp. 1178-1203.
48. Cullen to Krishna Rao, 5 May 1854: MRR, LD, Vol. IX. Krishna Rao issued the proclamation before Cullen had time to read and comment on the draft.
49. Resolution No. 17, 14 Feb. 1854: MPP, 14 Feb. 1854, Range 321, Vol. VIII, p. 652. The 'edict' was allowed to stand, and the missionaries were forbidden to take up their converts' grievances. I.F. Thomas dissented and supported the missionaries.
50. *Madras Church Missionary Record,* Feb. 1854, reproduced in the *Church Missionary Intelligencer,* London, Vol. VI, Jan. 1855, p. 23.
51. Hjejle, *Slavery*, p. 109.
52. Resolution No. 371, 3 Oct. 1854: MPP, 3 Oct. 1854, Range 321, Vol. XIII, p. 3892.
53. Cullen to the Ch. Sec., 10 Nov. 1854: MPP, 28 Nov. 1854,

Range 321, Vol. XV, pp. 5053-5.

54. Cullen to Krishna Rao, 20 June 1855: MRR, LD, Vol. X.
55. Cullen to Krishna Rao, 1 Dec. 1855: MRR, LD, Vol X, quoted a letter from the Rev. Henry Baker, Sr. which claimed that the proclamation was scarcely publicised and constantly ignored. Cullen asked how many copies had been printed.
56. Rev. Henry Baker, Sr. to the Secretary, CMS, 1855, quoted in CMS *Annual Report*, Vol. XXIII, 1855-6, p. 131.
57. *Loc. cit.*
58. Peet to the Secretary, CMS, 2 Feb. 1858: CMSA, No. 206 of 1858.
59. Baylis to Cullen, 17 Jan 1859: TGER, Cover No. 2115.
60. Rev. Henry Baker, Sr. to the Secretary, CMS, 30 June 1855, quoted in CMS *Annual Report*, Vol. XXIII, p.132. See also Rev. Henry Baker, Sr. *A Sermon Preached at Christ Church, Cottayam on the 9th November 1859* (Kottayam: CMS Press, 1860), p. 18.
61. Minutes of the CMS Travancore District Conference, 16 Dec. 1857: UTC No. 39. The ever-calculating Peet made this suggestion which was resisted by the senior Baker. See Rev. Henry Baker, Sr. to the Secretary, CMS, 29 Aug. 1862: CMSA, No. 29 of 1862.
62. P.D. Devasagaim's obituary, *Travancore Times*, 1 Jan. 1885; Cullen to Krishna Rao, 3 July 1856: MRR, LD, Vol. X. Cullen was indignant at Russel's slight to Travancore.
63. Abbs, *Experience*, p. 215; Baylis to the Foreign Secretary, LMS, 30 June 1856: CCWM, Travancore, Box 4, Folder 4, Jacket D. A disaffected convert claimed that the panchayats were usurping the authority of the sirkar. Cullen reported this to the Madras Government which took no notice. Cullen to the Ch. Sec., 27 Sept. 1856: MPP, 24 Aug. 1858, Range 321, Vol. XLI, p. 231.
64. LMS, TDC, *Report*, c. 1870. [Title page of the copy in Scott Christian College, Nagercoil, is missing.]
65. See, for example, Rev. Jacob Chandy, Sr., 'Journal', 2 March 1853; Rev. K. Koshi, 'Journal', 18 March 1857; Rev. Oomen Mamen, 'Journal', 12 Feb. 1857: CMSA, uncatalogued.

66. Chandy, 'Journal', 13 June 1850 and 22 Dec. 1853; see also 18 May 1853 and 28 Jan. 1859: CMSA, uncatalogued.
67. Mamen, 'Journal', 21 Oct. 1857: CMSA, uncatalogued.
68. Mamen to the Secretary, CMS, Jan. 1861: CMSA, uncatalogued.
69. Rev. J.O. Whitehouse to the Foreign Secretary, LMS, 17 Aug. 1851: CCWM, Travancore, Box 4, Folder 2, Jacket C.
70. *Missionary Register*, Dec. 1827, p. 603.
71. Koshi, 'Journal', 18 March 1857: CMSA, uncatalogued.
72. Ecclesiastical Despatch to Madras, No. 9 of 1855, quoted in CMS *Annual Report*, Vol. XXIII, p. 131.
73. Abbs, *Experience*, p. 31.
74. Rev. Dr. Charles Leitch to Rev. John Cox, 7 April 1854 quoted in Cox's printed petition to the Madras Government, p. vi: MPP, 11 March 1856, Range 321, Vol. XXVIII, bound between pp. 774-5.
75. Cox to the Foreign Secretary, LMS, 7 April 1851: CCWM, Travancore, Box 4, Folder 2, Jacket D.
76. Peet to the Secretary, CMS, 19 Feb. 1861: CMSA, uncatalogued.
77. Cullen to Krishna Rao, 7 Feb. 1853: MRR, LD, Vol. VIII.
78. Peet to Cullen, 28 June 1851, quoted in Cullen to the Ch. Sec., 24 Aug. 1853: MRR, LMG, Vol. XV.
79. R. Ranga Rao to Gen. J.S. Fraser, 6 April 1838: TGER, Cover No. 16034.
80. Peet to Rev. Henry Baker, Sr., Dec. 1851, quoted in Hunt, *Anglican Church*, Vol. II, p. 137.
81. Cullen to Krishna Rao, 11 May, 1857: MRR, LD. Vol. XV.
82. *Census*, 1875, p. 228, draws the distinction between north and south Travancore. Until about 1920, women clothed above the waist could not enter temples in Cochin. J.A. Thorne, I.C.S. of Tellicherry, in Duarte Barbosa, *The Book of Duarte Barbosa*, trans. M.L. Dames, Vol. II (London: Hakluyt Society, 1921), p. 20n.
83. Venkata Rao, Dewan, to Col. Morrison, Resident, 11 May 1829: TGER, Cover No. 16443.
84. Proclamation of 3 Feb. 1829, quoted in MRR, MPP, 24 Aug. 1897, G.O. No. 565. For an account of the breast-cloth disturbances and their importance for Shanars, see

Robert L. Hardgrave, Jr., 'The Breast-Cloth Controversy: Caste Consciousness and Social Change in Southern Travancore', *Indian Economic and Social History Review,* Vol. V, No. 2, June 1968, pp. 171-87, and Hardgrave, *The Nadars of Tamilnad* (Berkeley: University of California Press, 1969), pp. 60-70.

85. Lewis to the Foreign Secretary, LMS, 20 Dec. 1854: CCWM, Travancore, Box 4, Folder 4, Jacket A.
86. Baylis to the Foreign Secretary, LMS, March 1856: CCWM, Travancore, Box 4, Folder 4, Jacket C.
87. Cullen to the Ch. Sec., 31 March 1855: MRR, LMG, Vol. XVI.
88. Cullen to the Rev. John Russel, 15 March 1858: TGER, Cover No. 2115. Christians, Cullen claimed, were flatly refusing to do *uriyam.*
89. Shankunni Menon to Madhava Rao, 3 Jan. 1859: TGER, Cover No. 2115.
90. Shankunni Menon to Madhava Rao, 4 Jan. 1859: TGER, Cover No. 2115. The notification had been issued in Trivandrum on 27 Dec., but it did not reach Nagercoil, according to Shankunni Menon, until the afternoon of 3 Jan.
91. See Hardgrave, 'Breast-Cloth Controversy', pp. 182-3. He accepts the missionary accounts and makes the disturbances sound rather like the relief of Lucknow.
92. Cullen to Madhava Rao, 14 Jan. 1859: MRR, LD, Vol. XI.
93. Cullen to the Ch. Sec., 16 Feb. 1859: MPP, 15 March 1859, Range 321, Vol. XLII, p.281.
94. Cullen to the Ch. Sec., 18 Jan. 1859: MRR, MPP, 1 Feb. 1859, G.O. No. 75; Hardgrave, 'Breast-Cloth Controversy', p.183
95. Madhava Rao to Cullen, 12 Feb. 1859: MPP, 15 March 1859, Range 321, Vol. XLII, p. 284; Cox to F.N. Maltby, Resident, 7 May 1860: TGER, Cover No. 2115. Cox wrote that eleven mission buildings had been damaged or destroyed. The sirkar later replaced the buildings. Maltby to Madhava Rao, 18 June 1860: MRR, LD, Vol. XII: Cullen to the Ch. Sec., 14 Jan. 1859: MRR, MPP, 1 Feb. 1859, G.O. No. 75.

96. Cullen to the Ch. Sec., 16 Feb. 1859: MPP, 15 March 1859, Range 321, Vol. XLII, pp. 281-6: Cullen to the Ch. Sec., 13 Jan. 1859: MPP, 1 Feb. 1859, Range 321, Vol. XLII, pp. 143-7.
97. Cullen to the Ch. Sec., n.d. [1853]: MPP, 1 April 1853, Range 321, Vol. II, p. 1162.
98. MPP, 17 Aug. 1852, Range 320, Vol. LXX, p. 2236.
99. R. Ranga Rao to Fraser, 6 April 1838: TGER, Cover No. 16034.
100. Cullen to Krishna Rao, 1 Dec. 1852: MRR, LD, Vol. VIII.
101. MPP, 24 Feb. 1854, Range 321, Vol. VIII, p. 737; Petition, 22 Oct. 1853: MPP, 29 Nov. 1853, Range 321, Vol. V, p. 3589.
102. Cullen to the Ch. Sec., 19 Feb. 1855: MPP, 6 March 1855, Range 321, Vol. XVIII, p. 918.
103. Cullen to Krishna Rao, 18 Dec. 1855: MRR, LD, Vol.X. See also Cullen to Krishna Rao, 25 Sept. 1850: MRR, LD. Vol. VIII.
104. F.N. Maltby, Resident, to the Ch. Sec., 20 Feb. 1860: MPP, 26 March 1860, Range 321, Vol XLIV, pp. 232-40.
105. Cullen to Krishna Rao, 20 Aug. 1855: MRR, LD, Vol. X; MPP, 31 May 1853, Range 321, Vol. III, p. 1963; Rev. John Cox, *Travancore Its Present Ruin...* (Nagercoil: London Mission Press, 1857), p. viii. Cox wrote that there was more smuggling than destroying. Cullen to Krishna Rao, 20 Aug. 1855: MRR, LD, Vol. X. See also MPP, 9 Oct, 1855, Range 321, Vol. XXIV, p. 4370.
106. Cullen to Krishna Rao, 25 Aug. 1855: MRR, LD, Vol. X.
107. Petition of Mr. Harris to the Governor-General, 8 March 1855: MPP, 12 June 1855, Range 321, Vol. XXI, p. 2473. Harris, a Eurasian, claimed that all tahsildarships were for sale and that one, sold for Rs. 7,000, brought its purchaser Rs. 60,000 in eighteen months, although a tashildar's pay was only Rs. 70 a month. The Madras Government concluded, however, that 'the character and position of Mr. Harris are not such as to give any weight to his assertions'.
108. Cullen to Krishna Rao, 18 April 1856; Cullen to Krishna Rao, 23 Feb. 1857: MRR, LD, Vol. X.

109. MPP, 14 Aug. 1855, Range 321, Vol. XXIII, pp. 3799-3800; Secretary to the Government of India to the Ch. Sec. to the Madras Government, 12 Oct. 1855: MPP, 27 Nov. 1855, Range 321, Vol. XXV, p. 5019.
110. MPP, 11 March 1856, Range 321, Vol. XXVIII, a printed petition inserted between pp. 774-5.
111. *Madras Athenaeum*, 25 Oct. 1856. The first part of the article was published on 23 Oct.
112. Baylis to Madhava Rao, 1 Jan. 1856, quoted in 'Raja Sir T. Madhava Rao', *Prominent Tanjoreans*, No. II (Tanjore: C.S. Maniya, 1915), p. 25.
113. Memorandum by Lord Harris: MPP, 15 March 1859, Range 321, Vol. XLII, p. 285. Walter Elliott concurred.
114. Political Despatch No. 4 of 31 March, No. 11 of 19 Aug., and No. 21 of 8 Dec. 1859: Political Despatches to Madras, Vol. I, 1858-69.
115. Petition, n.d., signed by Russel, Cox, Baylis, Denis, Mateer and Ashton: MPP, 2 Sept. 1859, Range 321, Vol. XLIII, pp. 126-46.
116. Trevelyan to Cullen, 6 May 1859: MPP, 10 May 1859, Range 321, Vol. XLII, pp. 87-8.
117. Trevelyan had long been a bitter critic of what he saw as the follies of Hinduism. See his article 'The Thugs: or Secret Murderers of India', *Edinburgh Review*, Vol. LXIV, Jan. 1837, pp. 357-95, especially pp. 393-4.
118. Rev. Charles Mead to Eusebius Mead, 24 Aug. 1860, quoted in Agur, *Church History*, p. 51.
119. Memorandum by F.N. Maltby, n.d.: MPP, 24 Dec. 1858, Range 321, Vol. XLIII, p. 243, Trevelyan's colleagues were indignant at his irregular transaction with Maltby and appalled at the mention of 'cold steel'. So was Sir Charles Wood, the Secretary of State. See his Minute, 12 June 1860, and Political Despatch No. 17 of 24 July 1860: Political Despatches to Madras, Vol. I, 1858-69.
120. Rev. John Hawksworth, quoted in CMS *Annual Report*, Vol. XXVI, 1860-1, p. 149.
121. Jacob, 'History', p. 141.

## Chapter 3

1. Bhupen Qanungo, 'British Relations with the Native States of India', *Journal of Asian Studies*, Vol. XXVI, No. 2, Feb. 1967, p. 265.
2. Quoted in M.P. Duraiswamy (ed.), 'Raja Sir T. Madhava Rao', *Prominent Tanjoreans*, No. II (Tanjore: G.S. Maniya, 1915), pp. 19-20. Powell was not a stranger to clever young men. Madhava Rao's contemporaries at the High School included Muthuswamy Aiyar, the first Indian to act as chief justice of Madras; Ranga Charlu, Dewan of Mysore after rendition; Rangananda Sastri, member of the Madras Legislative Council; Sadasiva Pillai, chief justice of Travancore; and Ramiengar and Sashiah Sastri, both Dewans of Travancore. See also G. Parameswaran Pillai, *Representative Men of Southern India*, (Madras: Price Current Press, 1896), p. xiv.
3. 'Testimonials Received by Sir Madhava Rao, 1867': MRR, MPP, 29 Jan. 1869, G.O. No. 20.
4. Cullen to the Ch. Sec., n.d: MPP, 24 Feb. 1854, Range 321, Vol. VIII, pp. 728-9. Uttaram Tirunal had four nephews: the first and third were retarded; Ayilyam and Vishakham were the second and fourth. Madhava Rao to Cullen, 27 Aug. 1853: MPP, 24 Feb. 1854, Range 321, Vol. VIII, p. 746.
5 Speech, 19 Oct. 1860, quoted in Maltby to the Ch. Sec. 22 Oct. 1860, MRR, MPP, 6 Nov. 1860, G.O. No. 656; Speech, 9 Dec. 1866: MPP, 20 Feb. 1867, Range 441, Vol. IV, p. 86.
6. Quoted in Nagam Aiya, *Manual*, Vol. I, p. 556.
7. Vishakham Tirunal] 'A Native Statesman', *Calcutta Review*, Vol. LV, 1872, p. 243. The authorship is identified in Ballard to the Acting Ch. Sec., 12 Jan. 1875: MRR, MPP, 28 Jan. 1875, G.O. No. 5. The article was written shortly after Madhava Rao's dismissal by Ayilyam Tirunal. Lady Denison's diary, 23 Oct. 1862, quoted in Sir William Denison, *Varieties of Viceregal Life*, Vol. II (London: Longmans, Green, 1870), p. 208.
8. [Rev. T. Pettigrew] 'A Retired Chaplain', *Episodes in the Life of an Indian Chaplain* (London: Sampson, Low, 1881),

p. 333; Hannyngton to the Ch. Sec., 3 Aug. 1885: MRR, MPP, 7 Sept. 1885, G.O. No. 625-B.

9. [Vishakham] 'Statesman', p. 251.
10. The story was told by A.J. Thampi, Vishakham's grandson. Vishakham's wife lived until 1909.
11. Ch. Sec. to the Madras Government to the Secretary to the Government of India, 23 March 1859: MPP, 28 March 1859, Range 321, Vol. XLII, p. 358. Peet to the Secretary, CMS, 19 Feb. 1861: CMSA uncatalogued. Madhava Rao's wealth in his early years is somewhat in doubt. See Shankunni Menon, *Travancore*, p. 458, which implies that he came to Travancore a poor man. The Madras police estimated that he was worth Rs. 12.5 lakhs by 1886. Col. T. Weldon, Commissioner of Police, Madras, to the Ch. Sec., 13 Sept. 1886: MRR, MPP, 15 Sept. 1885, G.O. No. 853.
12. Kathleen Gough, 'Literacy in Kerala', in Jack Goody (editor), *Literacy in Traditional Societies* (Cambridge: University Press, 1968), pp. 151, 146 and 155. The 1971 census showed Kerala with a literacy rate of about 60 per cent, twice as great as the all-India figure.Of the five most literate towns in India, four (Alleppey, 70.06 per cent; Nagercoil, 69.52 per cent; Trivandrum, 69.38 per cent; Quilon, 64.48 per cent) were in Travancore; the fifth was Cochin (69.30 per cent). See *The Hindu*, Madras, 10 July and 17 and 22 Aug. 1971.
13. *Census*, 1875, pp. 232-3 and 245-6.
14. *TARs*, 1866-7, p. 78 and 1902-3, p. 49. See Sreedhara Menon, *Survey*, pp. 155, 182-3 and 262 for accounts of the *kalari* in old Kerala.
15. *TAR*, 1872-3, pp. 128-9. For the harsh punishments and thunderous noise of a village school in the 1880s, see Mannath Padmanabhan [Pillai], *ente jivitasmaranakal* (Trivandrum: NSS Press, n.d. [c. 1957), pp. 5-7.
16. J. Broun, Acting Resident, to Suba Rao, Dewan, 10 Sept. 1840: TGER, Cover No. 15863.
17. Fraser to Suba Rao, 20 April 1836: TGER, Cover No. 14814.
18. Speech by Madhava Rao to the audience at the prize giving at the Maharaja's High School, 28 Dec. 1866, quoted in *TGG*, Vol. V, No. 2, 22 Jan. 1867.

19. Memorandum by Madhava Rao, n.d. [c. May 1866]: TGER, Cover No. 15982.
20. Speech by Ayilyam Tirunal, read by Madhava Rao at the laying of the foundation stone for the College, 30 Sept. 1869, quoted in *TGG*, Vol. VII, No. 39, 5 Oct. 1869.
21. Memorandum by William Fisher, Resident, 8 Aug. 1863: MRR, LD, Vol. XIII. *TAR*, 1868-9, p. 14.
22. The Madras Government forced some of the Dewan's relati-ves to resign. Fisher to Madhava Rao, 7 Aug. 1863: MRR, LD, Vol. XIII. The lack of educated Nairs in the 1860s was still being used to explain the large number of non-Malayai Brahmins in the administration in the 1890s. See the Counter-Memorial, *Madras Times*, 10 July 1891, p. 5.
23. *TARs*, 1860-1, p. 7 and 1861-2, p. 10.
24. Madhava Rao to Major Heber Drury, 7 Sept. 1859: MRR, MPP, 12 Nov. 1859, G.O. No. 665.
25. *TAR*, 1863-4, p. 21.
26. Nagam Aiya, *Manual*, Vol. II. p. 448; Fisher to Madhava Rao, 11 Feb. 1864: MRR, LD, Vol. XIII; *TGG*, Vol. V. No. 2, 22 Jan. 1867.
27. Mateer, *Charity*, p. 155; *TGG*, Vol. V, No 2, 22 Jan.1867.
28. Obituary of John Ross, *Madras Mail*, 10 April 1905, p. 3.
29. *TAR*s, 1862-3, p. 38; 1865-6, p. 50; 1866-7, p. 72; 1868-9, p. 55.
30. Rev. Henry Baker, Jr. to the Secretary, CMS, 1869, quoted in Hunt, *Anglican Church,* Vol. II, p. 133. See also CMS, *Annual Report*, Vol. XXX, 1869-70, p. 173.
31. From *Madras University Calendars*. The matriculates for 1870 are not available, but excluding that year, Travancore had produced 162 matriculates: seventy-one non-Malayali Brahmins, twenty-seven Nairs, twenty-seven Christians of all sects, but excluding Eurasians, and seventeen 'other Hindus' or Eurasians.
32. Madhava Rao to Drury, 24 Sept. 1859: TGER, Section Books, Letters to the Resident; *TGG*, Vol. I, No. 16, 13 May 1864; *TGG*, Vol. X, No. 32, 6 Aug. 1872.
33. Madhava Rao to Newill, 1 Oct. 1867: MRR, MPP, 26 Nov. 1867, G.O. No. 316.
34. Memorandum by Madhava Rao, n.d. [but about May 1866]:

TGER, Cover No. 15982.

35. Kerala Varma to Sashiah Sastri, 12 Aug. 1872: TGER, Cover No. 290; see also Sankara Subbaiyer, Director of Vernacular Education to Madhava Rao, 10 March 1867: TGER, Cover No. 16182.
36. *TGG*, Vol. VIII, No. 26, 12 July 1870.
37. Sankara Subbaiyer to Madhava Rao, 10 March 1869: TGER, Cover No. 290.
38. Sankara Subbaiyer to Madhava Rao, 24 Sept. 1869: TGER, Cover No. 290. Also *TGGs*, 23 April and 24 Dec. 1867.
39. *TGG*, Vol. VIII, No. 32, 23 Aug. 1870.
40. Sankara Subbaiyer to Madhava Rao, 31 Oct. 1870: TGER, Cover No. 15982.
41. Atholl MacGregor, Resident, to the Ch. Sec., 19 Sept. 1867: MRR, MPP, 16 Nov. 1876, G.O. No. 729, reviewing the Dewan's report for 1874-5; and J.C. Hannyngton, Resident, to the Officiating Ch. Sec, 5 July 1881: MRR, MPP, 29 Aug. 1881, G.O. No.429, reviewing the Dewan's report for 1879-80.
42. From *TARs*.
43. MPP, 26 Feb. 1872, Vol. CDX, pp. 28-35.
44. Rev. R. Baylis to Madhava Rao, 26 Sept. 1865: TGER Cover No. 135.
45. Rev. G.O. Newport to Madhava Rao, 18 Sept. 1865; TGER, Cover No. 135.
46. MRR, MPP, 23 April 1870, G.O. No. 143; *TAR*, 1866-7, pp. 82-3.
47. See Ballard to Sashiah Sastri, 1 May 1873: TGER, Cover No. 15817, forwarding suggestions of the Rev. Samuel Mateer (LMS) for grants-in-aid; and the Rev. J. Caley quoted in CMS *Report*, 1875-6, p. 149, for CMS apprehensions.
48. Peet to the Secretary, CMS, 19 Feb. 1861: CMSA, uncatalogued; Rev. J.M. Speechly to the Secretary, CMS, 16 March 1868: CMSA, uncatalogued.
49. *Travancore Almanack*, 1864, pp. 79-85.
50. Rev. R.H. Maddox to the Secretary, CMS, Dec. 1867: CMSA, uncatalogued.
51. Ballard to the Ch. Sec., 9 March 1870: MPP, 13 April 1870, Range 441, Vol. VIII, p. 132.
52. Newill to Madhava Rao, 17 May 1865: TGER, Cover No. 15901.

53. Rama Rao, dewan peshkar, Quilon, to Madhava Rao, 30 Sept. 1869: TGER, Cover No. 286.
54. *TGG*, Vol. III, No. 20, 1 Aug. 1865 and No. 22, 15 Aug. 1865; Newill to Madhava Rao, 28 July 1865: TGER Cover No. 16116; K.C. Velu Pillai, dewan peshkar, Trivandrum to Madhava Rao, 13 Oct. 1869: TGER, Cover No. 286.
55. Ballard's report of 9 March 1870 was taken up on 13 April.
56. Rama Rao to Madhava Rao, 9 Nov. 1869: TGER, Cover No. 286. The Resident also underestimated the total population and that of the low castes. He put their population at five lakhs out of twelve or thirteen; the 1875 census showed them at about twelve lakhs out of twenty-three. Ballard to the Ch. Sec., 9 March. 1870.
57. Madhava Rao to the Judges of the Sadr Court, 7 April 1870: MPP, 9 May 1870, Range 441, Vol. VIII, pp. 146-7.
58. MPP, 9 May 1870, G.O. No. 158, Range 441, Vol. VIII, p. 147.
59. *TGG*, Vol. XXII, No. 33, 12 Aug. 1884; see also R.W. Barlow, Acting Resident, to the Ch. Sec., 2 Aug. 1884: MPP, 23 Aug. 1884, Vol. 2401-A, p. 39.
60. *TGG*, Vol. VIII, No. 14, 19 April and No. 17, 10 May 1870.
61. Madhava Rao to Newill, 25 April 1865: TGER, Cover No. 228.
62. *Ibid.*, and *TAR*, 1864-5, pp. 28-30.
63. LMS Petition, n.d., Appendix K: MPP, 14 Aug. 1855, Range 321, Vol. XXIII, p. 3690.
64. Vishakham Tirunal, 'Memorandum: the Janmi and Kanam Rights in Travancore', 10 May 1881: TGER, Cover No. 4801. See also Memorandum by Madhava Rao in *Report of the Malabar Land Tenure Committee*, 1887, Vol. I, pp. 29-34.
65. Madhava Rao, 'Memorandum of Kanappattom Tenure', 11 June 1867: TGER, Cover No. 15128; Sadasiva Pillai, 'Memorandum Re: The Rights of Janmis and Tenants', 10 Feb. 1866: TGER, Cover No. 15128, which argued lengthily on the janmis' behalf: *TAR*, 1866-7, p.37.
66. One writer compares the reforms with those in Japan after the Meiji Restoration. K.N. Raj, in T.C. Varghese, *Agrarian Change and Economic Consequences* (Bombay: Allied Publishers, 1970), p. xi.

67. Sir Stafford Northcote, *Hansard*, 24 May 1867, Vol. CLXXXVII, p. 1068.
68. Memorandum by William Fisher, 8 Aug. 1863: MRR, LD, Vol. XIII. Fisher was paraphrasing a report from Barton.
69. Barton quoted in *TAR*, 1865-6, p. 91.
70. Fisher to Madhava Rao, 26 Oct. 1863: MRR, LD, Vol. XIII.
71. Barton, quoted in *TAR*, 1865-6, p. 93; *TGG*, Vol. VI No. 4, 4 Feb. 1868. The rate stayed roughly at four annas until the 1890s when a new planting boom forced it up to five annas. See *Madras Mail*, 30 June 1897, p. 7.
72. *Census*, 1875, p. 63. Mateer, *Native Life*, pp. 235-6 gives a similar account and attributes the increased cost of labour to the coffee estates and the P.W.D.
73. Caley to the Secretary, CMS, 21 Feb. 1876: CMSA, uncatalogued.
74. *Census*, 1875, p. 63; Newill to the Ch. Sec., 4 Dec. 1865: MRR, MPP, 20 Feb. 1866, G.O. No. 38; *TGG*, Vol. III, No. 21, 8 Aug. 1865.
75. *Census*, 1875, p. 266.
76. Barton, quoted in *TAR*, 1865-6, p. 91.
77. This was K.K. Kuruvila who began his course in 1873 and graduated from Madras University in 1877. He received a scholarship from the sirkar. J.E. Lafrenais, a Eurasian, had taken a BCE in 1875.
78. Memorandum by G.A. Ballard, 13 Aug. 1872: MRR, LD, Vol. XVIII.
79. See MPP, 12 Jan. 1858, 22 Jan. 1867 and 5 Dec. 1872.
80. Joan Mencher, 'Kerala and Madras: A Comparative Study of Ecology and Social Structure', *Ethnology*, Vol. V, No. 2, April 1966, p. 162. See also Eric J. Miller, 'Caste and Territory in Malabar', *American Anthropologist*, Vol. LVI, 1954, pp. 411-20, where he notes the importance, for the political and social structure, of the area's rivers.
81. Cullen to the Ch. Sec., 31 Dec. 1845: MRR, LMG, Vol. XIV.
82. Fraser to Venkata Rao, 19 Jan. and 26 Feb. 1838: TGER, Cover No. 14825.
83. John Cox, *Travancore, Its Present Ruin...* (Nagercoil: LMS Press, 1857).

84. For the uncertainty of water communication, see Memorandum by G.A. Ballard, 25 June 1876 [incorrectly dated; in fact, 1874]: TGER, Cover No. 16522.
85. Maltby to Madhava Rao, 12 April 1860; Memorandam by F.N. Maltby, 4 Nov. 1861 and 21 Feb. 1861: MRR, LD, Vol. XII.
86. *TARs*, 1865-6, p. 88; 1865-9, p. 85; 1871-2, p. 113.
87. *TAR*, 1871-2, pp. 108 and 113; Nagam Aiya, *Manual*, Vol. III, pp. 221-31. In the 1860s the P.W.D. also built the Victoria-Martanda Varma Canal to south Travancore and the Alleppey lighthouse and tramway. It dredged canals and backwaters and began work on the Varkkalla tunnel to connect the water communications of north and south Travancore.
88. Atholl MacGregor to the Ch. Sec., 19 April 1877: MRR, MPP, 30 April 1877.
89. Ballard to the Acting Ch. Sec., 13 Feb. 1874: MRR, MPP, 15 Aug. 1876, G.O. No. 508.
90. Nagam Aiya, *Travancore Manual*, Vol. I, p. 520; Vol. III, pp. 387 and 566; also *TARs*.
91. In line with its increasing importance, Alleppey got a new lighthouse in 1862 and a set of tram lines to connect the backwaters with the harbour. Memorandum by Maltby, 4 April 1862: MPP, 23 July 1862, Range 321, Vol. XLVI, p. 289.
92. Nagam Aiya, *Manual*, Vol. III, pp. 184-6.
93. Madhava Rao to Cullen, n.d.: MPP, 12 Aug. 1859, Range 321, Vol. XLIII, pp. 101-04.
94. MPP, 23 May 1861, Range 321, Vol. XLV, pp. 293-306.
95. *Loc. cit.* The loan was paid off by December 1862. Major Heber Drury, Acting Resident, to Madhava Rao, 9 Nov. 1859: MRR LD, Vol. XI.
96. James Forbes, *Oriental Memoirs*, Vol. 1 (London: Richard Bentley, 1834), pp. 200-01, wrote that there was a coffee plantation on an island near Tellichery in 1772. The East India Company started a plantation under Murdoch Brown at Anjarakandi near Cannanore at the turn of the eighteenth century. By 1859 there were said to be 80 planters in Malabar district of British India. Rev. Henry Baker, Sr.

to the Secretary, CMS, 18 Jan. 1858: CMSA, No. 30 of 1858.

97. Memorandum by J.S. Fraser, 13 Feb. 1838: TGER, Cover No. 14825. Also Covers Nos. 7253, 15630 and 15866.
98. Maltby to the Ch. Sec., 30 April 1862: MPP, 23 July 1862, Range 321, Vol. XLVI, p. 268: *TAR*, 1861-2, pp. 12-13; *Travancore Almanack,* 1864, p. xxii; *TARs*.
99. TGER, Cover No. 4485; Newill to the Ch. Sec., 31 Oct. 1867: MRR, MPP, 26 Nov. 1867, G.O. No. 316; Memorandum by Ballard, 24 Dec. 1869: MPP, 26 Jan. 1870, Range 441, Vol. VIII, pp. 64-7; Memorandum by Maltby, 25 Jan. 1862: MPP, 23 July 1862, Range 321, Vol. XLVI, pp. 273-8.
100. 'S.R.R.' in [Vishakham Tirunal], 'Industrial Status', pp. vi-vii. By the time Madhava Rao sold, the estate was planted in cardamoms. Col. T. Weldon, Commissioner of Police, Madras, to the Ch. Sec., 13 Sept. 1886: MRR, MPP, 15 Sept. 1886, G.O. No. 853.
101. Hay, Acting Resident, to the Ch. Sec., 19 June 1875: MRR, MPP, 2 July 1875, G.O. No. 416.
102. Travancore Coffee Planters' Memorial to the Madras Government, n.d.: MRR, MPP, 20 March 1879, G.O. No. 113.
103. 'Cotton Hill House' was Madhava Rao's; 'Hill View', Rama Rao's. For background on Trivandrum, see Horsley *Memoir*, p. 12; *TGG*, Vol. VIII, No. 27, 19 Sept. 1865, which gave the results by caste of a census taken in August. The population was put at 51,718. The public offices, college and hospital are still in use today.
104. Newill to Madhava Rao, 6 Dec. 1865: TGER, Cover No. 15249.
105. 'S.R.R.' [A member of the Benares bar'] in his preface to H.H. the First Prince of Travancore [Vishakham Tirunal]. *Our Industrial Status* (Benares: Benares Printing Press, 1880), p.v.
106. See *TGG*, Vol. IV, No. 14, 17 April 1866; *TGG*, Vol. V, No. 46, 26 Nov. 1867; Ballard to Nanu Pillai, dewan peshkar in charge, 10 April 1872: TGER, Cover No. 195; *TGG*, Vol. IV, No 46, 27 Nov. 1866 and *TAR*, 1865-6, p. 93; *TAR*, 1868-9, p.95.
107. *TAR*, 1868-9, p. 95.

## Chapter 4.

1. The situation is explained in Ballard to the Ch. Sec., 7 Feb. 1872: MRR, MPP, 20 March 1872.
2. *Census*, 1891, Vol. II, p. 964.
3. *Madras Mail*, 23 July 1890, p. 5. Mateer, *Native Life*, p. 218. Fr. Mathew Palakkunnel also noted a rise in the price of rice. He wrote in his diary for Sept. 1878 that ten paras of rice (1 para equals about 80 cubic inches) in 1846 sold for 20 chakrams (28 chakrams equals 1 rupee). In 1851 ten paras sold for 25 chakrams. But he had just sold ten paras for 140 chakrams, an increase of nearly six-fold in 27 years. It is important to note that the wealthy Romo-Syrian priest was selling, not buying. Fr. Mathew Palakkunnel, *nalagamam*, ed. by P.J. Sebastian (Changanacherry: Bastian's Publications, 1972), p. 248. As late as 1865 Travancore was still exporting rice. *Madras Mail*, 24 Feb. 1913, p. 3. The question was raised in the Assembly.
4. Mateer, *Native Life*, p. 218.
5. *Ibid.*, pp. 235-6.
6. *Cochin Census Report*, 1891, Vol. 1, p. 144.
7. *Ibid.*, p. 144.
8. *Ibid.*, p. 137.
9. Mannath Padmanabhan [Mannath Padmanabha Pillai], *ente jivitasmaranakal*, (Trivandrum: Nair Service Society Press, n.d. [1957?), pp. 1-2. Compare this experience with that of the warriors in Bisipara who also felt obligated to carry out ceremonies on the old scale. Bailey, *Economic Frontier*, pp. 9-10.
10. See for example the two partition deeds concluded by Nair families near Kottayam in the 1880s. CMSA, No. 187 of 1895, Appendices Ci and Cii.
11. *Travancore Almanack*, 1891, p. 165; *Madras Mail*, 21 June 1890, p. 3.
12. *TARs*, 1871-2 to 1890-1.
13. *TARs*, 1880-1, p. 61, and 1896-7, p. 101.
14. *Census*, 1875, p. 155, and 1891, Vol. I, p. 578.
15. H.N. Read, Principal, to T. Rama Rao, Dewan, 6 April 1891: TGER, Cover No. 1744.

16. Miller, 'Caste and Territory', p. 410.
17. *The Hindu*, 18 Aug. 1894, p. 4, leading article.
18. This was the *Malayala Manorama* newspaper, founded by Kandathil Varghese Mappillai. See *Travancore Almanack*, 1906, pp. 206-12, and *Story of Manorama* (Kottayam: Malayala Manorama, 1968), pp. 9-10, 13-14.
19. *Trivandrum Almanack*, 1873, pp. 51-64, shows non-Malayali Brahmins holding three of the five top executive posts, including the Dewanship. Of fourteen jobs in the huzur kutcherry, they had seven. They supplied one of the four Sadr Court judges (and 25 of that court's 37 licensed pleaders) and five of the eleven Zilla Court judges (and 50 out of 73 licensed pleaders). They held the headmastership of ten of seventeen district schools and seventeen out of 29 vernacular schools. In the palace they had seven out of fourteen posts, including that of tutor to the princes, which was held by R. Raghunatha Rao, who was married to Madhava Rao's first cousin. Europeans and Eurasians held more than a quarter of the highest paying posts.
20. *Paschima Taraka*, 1 Aug. 1873, in *RNNM*, Malayalam, fortnight ending 15 Aug. 1875.
21. *TAR*, 1868-9, p. 55. There were two Nairs, B. Govinda Pillai and P.K. Palpanabha Pillai. The latter had a sirkar scholarship to Presidency College, Madras, and became the first Travancore graduate in 1864.
22. *TAR*, 1868-9, p. 14.
23. *Madras University Calendars.* The 1880-9 returns exclude the year 1885 for which the *Calendar* in the Madras University Library is missing. H.N. Read, Principal, to Rama Rao, 6 April 1891: TGER, Cover No. 1744, wrote that the Maharaja's College had produced 112 non-Malayali Brahmin graduates.
24. *Travancore Almanack*, 1891, pp. 4-40.
25. *Kerala Mitram*, 1 April 1882, in *RNNM*, Malayalam, fortnight ending 15 April 1882. See also *Kerala Mitram*, *RNNM*, Malayalam, for 28 May 1881, Oct. 1882, April 1886 and June 1887.
26. *Census*, 1881, p. 195.
27. *Travancore Almanack*, 1881, pp. 98-100.
28. *Census*, 1881, p. 195.

29. I am indebted to my friend Dr. V. Ramaswamy formerly of the Physics Department, University of Victoria, Canada, for this account of his great-grandfather and for an introduction to his late grand-father in Alleppey.
30. Sankara Subbaiyer, Dewan, to the Superintendent of the Central Jail, 9 April 1897; TGER, Judicial Section Books, 2195/J520. See also Major A.F.F. Bloomfield, Acting Resident to the Ch. Sec., 21 Sept. 1874: MRR, MPP, 19 Oct. 1874, G.O. No. 428.
31. *Travancore Times*, 1 Jan. 1886 and 10 Dec. 1886; *Madras Standard*, 7 Dec. 1887, p. 2. See also K.P.S. Menon, *Many Worlds* (London: OUP, 1965), p. 24; Mateer, *Native Life*, p. 370.
32. Henry Bruce, *Letters from Malabar and on the Way* (London: Routledge, 1909), p. 100.
33. *Madras Mail*, 26 May 1909, p. 4, reported that 8,000 Brahmins were being fed daily. [Krishna Rao], *Description*, p. 21, wrote that twelve lakhs of meals were dispensed in the *uttupuras* in 1841-2. This is equivalent of feeding 1,600 people two meals a day. The cost of the *uttupuras* climbed to Rs. 4.39 lakhs annually by the end of the nineteenth century. *TAR*, 1899-1900, pp. 78-9.
34. One of the Malayali Sabha's abortive projects in the 1880s was a programme for hostels for Nair students. See C. Krishna Pillai to C.V. Raman Pillai, 17 Adi 1062 [1887], quoted in P.K. Parameswaran Nair, *si. vi. raman pilla* (Trivandrum: Kerala Sahitya Sahakarana Sangham Ltd., 1948; second edition, 1959), p. 72.
35. Hannyngton to the Ch. Sec., 26 Feb. 1887: MRR, MPP, 8 March 1887, G.O. No. 561.
36. Hannyngton to the Ch. Sec., 9 July 1888: MRR, MPP, 13 Aug. 1888, G.O. No. 184.
37. *Kerala Patrika*, 11 Aug. 1888, in *RNNM*, Malayalam, fortnight ending 14 Aug. 1888.
38. Parameswaran Nair, *raman pilla*, p. 209. The Nair favourite was T. Sankaran Thampi.
39. *Madras Standard*, 29 March 1886, p. 2, leading article.
40. James Thompson, Acting Governor of Madras, to Ampthill, Acting Viceroy, 18 May 1904: IOR, Ampthill Papers, E/233/34/1.

41. *Madras Mail*, 30 June 1882, p. 3; *Travancore Times*, 10 Sept. 1885.
42. *Travancore Times*, 21 June 1886. The lone Nair member was a Thampi, i.e. a Nair descended from Kshatriyas.
43. Raja Sir T. Madhava Rao, *Political Opinions*, ed. by S.C. Srinivasa Charier (Madras: Ripon Press, 1890), p. 114.
44. Sashiengar, *An Appeal to the Enlightened and Philanthropic Members of the Hindu Community of South India* (Nagercoil: LMS Press, 14 May 1872): MRR, MPP, 2 Feb. 1875.
45. LMS, TDC, *Report*, 1872, p. 7, quoting the Rev. J. Duthie of Nagercoil. The bridegroom later studied in the Nagercoil Seminary. Samuel Mateer, 'Nepotism in Travancore', *Journal of the Anthropological Institute*, Vol. XII, 1883, pp. 295-6.
46. Ballard to the Ch. Sec., 16 July 1872: MRR, MPP, 2 Feb. 1875.
47. Ballard to the Ch. Sec., 20 March 1874: MRR, MPP, 2 Feb. 1875. The story had a fairly happy ending. Although the girl's father was ostracised, the re-marriage was a success. The girl's brother S. Swami Aiyengar, was an early graduate of the Saidpet Agricultural College and became a wealthy contractor in Travancore. His daughters attended the women's college in Trivandrum. *Madras Mail*, 24 June 1904, p. 5; *Madras Times*, 9 Nov. 1904, p. 3.
48. Ballard to the Ch. Sec., 16 July and 15 Aug. 1872; MRR, MPP, 2 Feb. 1875.
49. Sashiah Sastri to the Ch. Sec., 1873, quoted in V. Kamesvara Aiyar, *Sir A. Sashiah Sastri. K.C.S.I.* (Madras: Srinivasa Varadachari, 1902), pp. 219-20.
50. V. Kamesvara Aiyar, 'Sir A. Sashiah Sastri: A Few Reminiscences', *Malabar Quarterly Review*, Vol. III, No. 2, June 1904, p. 117. Madhava Rao, *Opinions*, p. 34.
51. S. Ramanath Aiyar, *The Problem of Charity in Travancore* (Trivandrum: Malabar Mail Press, 1907), p. 13.
52. One must not ignore the rivalries among non-Malayali Brahmin officials. V. Nagam Aiya, for example, sought the Dewanship and was sometimes willing to fire a desultory salvo at K. Krishnaswami Rao and S. Sankara Subbaiyer,

both Travancore servants who had risen to be Dewan. See *Madras Mail*, 8 Feb. 1901, p. 5 and Ampthill to Curzon, 15 Sept. 1903: AP, E/233/8.

53. Rev. W.A. Richards to the Secretary, CMS, 15 Feb. 1881: CMSA, uncatalogued.
54. Brown, *Christians*, p. 141; Agur, *Church*, pp. 130-2 and 140. Joseph Peet, who was one of Athanasius's first teachers, thought him 'an artful, subtle, no principled man; up to most of the crooked movements in life'. But Peet was notoriously uncharitable in his judgements of Indians who were not willing to fall in with his plans. See the long letter, Peet to the Secretary, CMS, 10 Dec. 1859: CMSA, uncatalogued.
55. Ballard to the Ch. Sec., 16 Nov. 1869: MRR, LMG, Vol. XIX.
56. *Madras Church Missionary Record*, Vol. XLI, No. 11, Nov. 1874, pp. 324-8.
57. Acting Resident to Sashiah Sastri, 14 June 1875: TGER, Cover No. 10806. Rev. Henry Baker, Jr. to the Secretary, CMS, 1 Jan. 1878: CMSA, uncatalogued.
58. MacGregor to the Ch. Sec., 16 Aug. 1876: MRR, MPP, 29 Aug. 1876. *Travancore Times*, 10 March 1886, for Walker's obituary. Also 'Supplement to the *Western Star*', 3 Jan. 1905, in the possession of Thomas George, Pattom, Trivandrum.
59. H.M. Walker to Sashiah Sastri, 25 June 1875: TGER, Cover No. 10806.
60. Agur, *Church*, p. 150; Ballard to the Officiating Ch. Sec., 10 Oct. 1875: MRR, MPP, 23 Oct. 1875, G.O. No. 715.
61. Memorandum by Wolfe Hay, Acting Resident, 4 Sept. 1875: MRR, MPP, 2 Feb. 1876, G. O. No. 76; Agur, *Church*, p. 152.
62. Rev. J.M. Speechly to the Secretary, CMS, 22 May 1880: CMSA, uncatalogued.
63. See Jacob Chandy, Sr., 'Journal', 8 June 1856; Oomen Mamen, 'Journal', 23 May 1858: CMSA, uncatalogued. Rt. Rev. C.N. Hodges to the Secretary, CMS, 11 April 1891: CMSA, No. 69 of 1891.
64. Nidhiry, *Nidhiry*, pp. 149-50. Vicar Apostolic of Malabar, Circular, 28 March 1856, quoted in Whitehouse, *Lingerings*,

Appendix F, p. 310.

65. Nidhiry, *Nidhiry*, pp. 42-4. Rokos, a bishop from western Asia, claimed to have been sent by the Pope. He won over 144 of 154 Romo-Syrian parishes before he was exposed as a fraud and excommunicated.
66. *Ibid.*, pp. 80-8 and 130; *Madras Times*, 1 Dec. 1890, p.6.
67. A study of Syrian Christian factions in Kerala in the late nineteenth and twentieth centuries is still needed in 1993.
68. *TGG*, Vol. X, No. 32, 6 Aug. 1872; *Trivandrum Almanack*, 1872, pp. 51-64.
69. *Madras Mail*, 27 Nov. 1901, p. 5, obituary.
70. *Paschima Taraka and Keralapataka*, 15 Sept. 1875, in *RNNM*, Malayalam, fortnight ending 15 Sept. 1876.
71. Rev. Henry Baker, Sr. to the Secretary, CMS, 30 June 1855, quoted in CMS, *Annual Report*, Vol. XXIII, 1855-6, p.132.
72. *Jnana Nikshepam*, n.d., quoted in *Paschima Taraka and Keralapataka*, 15 Sept. 1876, in *RNNM*, Malayalam, fortnight ending 15 Sept. 1876.
73. *Paschima Taraka and Keralapataka*, 15 Sept. 1876, in *RNNM*, Malayalam, fortnight ending 15 Sept. 1876; Logan, *Malabar*, Vol. I, p. 210n; *Kerala Mitram*, 1 Feb. 1881, in *RNNM*, Malayalam, fortnight ending 14 Feb. 1882.
74. *Madras University Calendars*.
75. 'Annual Report of CMS College, 1889': CMSA, No. 27 of 1890. Enrolment was about equally divided between Anglican and Jacobite Syrians with a few dozen Hindus and a handful of Roman Catholics. See 'Annual Report of CMS College, 1882': CMSA, No. 31 of 1882.
76. 'Annual Report of CMS College, 1889'.
77. 'The Counter-Memorial', *Madras Times*, 10 July 1891.
78. MRR, MPP, 9 July 1880, G.O. No. 34, reviewing the Travancore administration report from 1878-9. *Travancore Almanack*, 1886, pp. 30-3; 1891, pp. 37-40; 1896, pp. 80-7.
79. Petition to Cardinal John Simeoni, Cardinal Prefect of Propaganda, 11 Nov. 1886: Mannanam Monastery Library [hereafter MML], 1539/32/B/50.
80. 'Brief Sketch of the History of the St. Thomas Christians',

11 June 1886, handwritten: MML, 2224/32/B/22.

81. *Bombay Catholic Examiner*, 19 June 1888: MML, 1539/32/B/50, p. 181.
82. 'Declaration of Objectives', n.d., quoted in *Nidhiry*, pp. 149-50.
83. Nidhiry, *Nidhiry*, p. 152.
84. Nidhiry to Dr. Bernard, Archbishop of Verapoly, 24 May 1899, in the diary of Fr. Nidhiry. This is in the possession of Abraham M. Nidhiry, Kuravilangad.
85. Nidhiry, *Nidhiry*, p. 177. Nidhiry to the Delegate Apostolic, 2 July 1889, in Fr. Nidhiry's diary. See also Rev. A.J. French Adams, Principal, CMS College, to the Secretary, CMS, 27 May 1891: CMSA, No. 94 of 1891, in which he outlines the difficulties of Mar Dionysius and Fr. Nidhiry.
86. See *Madras Mail*, 11 May 1916, p. 3, for 25th anniversary celebrations. St. Berchman's High School became a college in 1924. *Madras Mail*, 6 Dec. 1924, p. 4.
87. Both men died in March 1916. See *Madras Mail*, 29 March 1916, p. 3, for both obituaries.
88. F.G.R. [ichardson], Savernake, Pirmed, letter to the editor, *Madras Mail*, 29 April 1902, p. 5.
89. Rev. Henry Baker, Jr. to Madhava Rao, 22 Jan. 1863: TGER, Cover No. 4428. Eira Dalton, *The Baker Family in India* (Kottayam: CMS Press, 1963), p. 24. The Nair convert took the name of P. Varghese.
90. Rev. C.A. Neve to the Rt. Rev. J.M. Speechly, 23 Sept. 1886: CMSA, No. 90 of 1885.
91. J. Arklie, Revenue Surveyor, to the Dewan, 21 Nov. 1876: TGER, Cover No. 4486. See Mateer, *Native Life*, p. 236, who says few Syrians went into planting.
92. Ballard to the Ch. Sec., 16 Nov. 1874: MRR, MPP, 2 Dec. 1874.
93. Interview with P.C. Joseph, retired principal of CMS College and a friend of the late John Mathai. See also 'Annual Report of CMS College', 1882: CMSA, No. 31 of 1882.
94. MacGregor to Nanu Pillai, 25 July 1879: MRR, LD, Vol. XXI.
95. Note by F.G. Richardson, quoted in Nagam Aiya, *Manual*, Vol. III, p. 72. The Pirmed road was scarcely a grand-

trunk affair even by the 1890s, however. Mannath Padmanabhan, *jivitasmaranakal*, p. 11, writes that in the village on the Pirmed road where he had his first job as a teacher there was not a good house, public building or place to buy food and drink. Occasionally poor Christian women would sit by the roadside selling plantains and coffee to coolies going to the hills. This was about 1894.

96. Varghese, *Agrarian Change*, pp. 69-71.
97. There were four presses in Kottayam about 1896—one owned by each of the four Syrian sects, Romo-Syrian, Mar Thomite, Jacobite and Anglican. C. Govinda Pillai, 'Memo. of the Kottayam Taluk', n.d. [c. 1896]: TGER, Cover No. 11650.
98. 'Supplement to the *Western Star*', 3 Jan. 1905. *Madras Mail*, 2 March 1901, p. 5.
99. This was O. Philippose. See *Kerala Mitram*, 1 Feb. 1882, in *RNNM*, Malayalam, fortnight ending 14 Feb. 1882.
100. Chaitanya, *Literature*, pp. 259-60 and 173-4.
101. 'Devi Bhimji, pioneer in Malayalam journalism', *The Hindu*, 18 July 1971; *Madras Mail*, 3 Aug. 1904; Nidhiry, *Nidhiry*, p. 153n.
102. *TAR*, 1892-3, p. 163. These included the *Travancore Times* and *Travancore Abhimani* of Nagercoil.
103. *Paschima Taraka* and *Keralapataka*, 1 March 1877, in *RNNM*, Malayalam, fortnight ending 14 March 1877.
104. *TAR*, 1895, p. 143.
105. *Trivandrum Almanack*, 1876, pp. 72-7; *Census*, 1875, pp. 111, 160 and 252.
106. Madhava Rao to Newill, 5 Nov. 1868: MPP, 11 Sept. 1869, Range 441, Vol. VII, p. 433. The outburst was provoked by the case of the Rev. William Lee who was assaulted when he insisted on passing through a Brahmin street. The same incident produced 'The Good Sir Gammon Row', the verse by R.C. Caldwell, the son of Bishop Caldwell of Tinnevelly. See *Chutney Lyrics* (Madras: Higginbotham, second edition, 1889), pp. 23-9.
107. LMS, TDC, *Report*, 1866, pp. 20-2.
108. *Travancore Times*, 1 Jan. 1886. Jacob, 'History', pp. 160-1. Interview with J.B. Thanka Raj, Nagercoil, 14 Aug. 1971. Mr. Thanka Raj was the grand-nephew of Devasagaim and lived in the controversial two-storeyed house.

Devasagaim had no children.

109. Interview with C.H. Simpson, 13 Oct. 1971. Mr. Simpson was Cox's grandson and lived on Cox's 'Blackrock Estate'. See also Cox to Madhava Rao, 28 Jan. 1863: TGER, Cover No. 4456.
110. TGER, Cover No. 4475 and 4456.
111. Rev. F. Baylis and Rev. Samuel Jones to Madhava Rao, 16 Oct. 1871: TGER, Cover No. 14893; Rev. J. Duthie to the Acting Dewan, 29 May 1872: TGER, Cover No. 4436; V. Moses to Sashiah Sastri, 20 and 21 Oct. 1873: TGER, Covers No. 4427 and 4443.
112. See TGER, Covers No. 4415, 4431, 4430 and 4612.
113. Interview with J.B. Thanka Raj. Mateer, *Native Life*, pp. 18-19 and 225-31. Rev. Samuel Mateer, *The Gospel in South India* (London: Religious Tract Society, n.d. [c. 1882]), pp. 151-2.
114. LMS, TDC, *Report*, 1871, p. 5.
115. LMS, TDC, *Report*, 1874, p. 21.
116. See the commemorative advertisement in the *Indian Express* (Madura), 12 May 1971.
117. LMS, TDC, *Report*, 1882, pp. 24-5.
118. *Travancore, Times*, 21 Dec. 1885, 21 July 1884, 11 Oct. 1886, 2 May 1887.
119. Agur, *Church*, p. 903. [Vishakham Tirunal] Rama Varma, *Our Industrial Status* (Benares: Chhannulal, Benares Printing Press, 1880), p. 15. Vishakham Tirunal presented Devasagaim with a shawl, a ring and a watch. The last is still kept by the family.
120. LMS, TDC, *Report*, 1890. p. 6.
121. *Travancore Times,* quoted in the *Madras Times*, 4 Aug. 1890, p. 7.
122. *Census*, 1875, pp. 148-53.
123. *Census*, 1901, Vol. I, p. 337. Edgar Thurston, *The Castes and Tribes of South India*, Vol. V. (Madras: Government Press, 1909), p. 241.
124. *Travancore Almanack*, 1891, pp. 44-6.
125. Thompson to the Foreign Secretary, LMS, 7 Oct. 1888: CCWM, Travancore, Box 12, Folder 2, Jacket A.
126. Rev. Henry Baker, Sr. to the Secretary, CMS, 29 Aug. 1862: CMSA, No. 29 of 1862.

127. Rt. Rev. J.M. Speechly to the Secretary, CMS, 2 April 1881: CMSA, No. 19 of 1881.
128. Rt. Rev. E. H. Hodges to the Secretary, CMS, 2 Dec. 1892: CMSA, No. 152 of 1893.
129. See the printed appeal for funds for an industrial school for CMS Pulayas, dated 1892: CMSA, No. 136 of 1892.
130. Rev. Henry Baker, Jr. to the Secretary, CMS, 1867, quoted in Hunt, *Anglican Church*, Vol. II, p. 103.
131. Speechly to the Secretary, CMS, 22 May 1880: CMSA, No. 15 of 1880.
132. Speechly to the Secretary, CMS, 25 Sept. 1887: CMSA, No. 128 of 1887. Another convert, whose father came from the astrologer caste, was ordained at the same time and with similar secrecy about his background.
133. *Travancore Almanack*, 1891, p. 38.
134. *Census*, 1931, Vol. I, pp. 382-9, returned the caste of 77 per cent of Travancore's population of Christian converts. The figures showed 168,000 Shanar converts, 157,000 Pulaya converts and only 2,311 Ezhava converts. Undoubtedly, many Ezhava converts refused to give their old caste, but the figures are still striking.
135. Memorial of P. Palpu to Sankara Subbaiyer, Dewan, 13 May 1895: TGER, Cover No. 3234.
136 *TARs*, 1870-1 to 1891-2.
137. *TARs*, 1870-1 to 1891-2.
138. *TAR*, 1882-3, pp. 67-8.
139. *Madras Mail*, 8 May 1901, p. 6, and 23 May 1904. p. 3. 'The Dewan's Tour: Inspection Notes', by V.P. Madhava Rao, 16 May to 18 June 1904: TGER, Travancore Political Department [hereafter TPD], No. 97 of 1904.
140. The sirkar's revenue from the toddy and arrack trade in 1861-2 was Rs. 78,000; in 1880-1, it was Rs. 190,041. Mateer, *Native Life*, p. 281.
141. *Travancore Times*, 1 July 1885, reported that the wealthy Thavasimuttu Nadar bought the abkari rights for three-quarters of the taluks in Travancore. For the range of Thavasimuttu Nadar's interests, see his obituary in *The Hindu*, 7 March 1888, p. 4. See also TGER, Cover No. 10271.

142. Hannyngton, Resident, to Ramiengar, 16 Dec. 1886: TGER, Cover No. 10312.
143. LMS, TDC, *Report*, 1874, pp. 16-7.
144. Petition of Kumaraswamy Nadar, 11 July 1889: TGER, Cover No. 10312.
145. See the *Madras Standard*, 3 Feb. 1886, p.2, for the arrest of two Ezhavas who were smuggling toddy from the British enclave of Anjengo into Travancore. The position of Ezhavas is somewhat similar to that of the distiller castes in Bisipara. 'But the biggest gains [from the new economic opportunities available after 1855] went to the DISTILLER caste-groups, who profited from a monopoly arising out of caste-beliefs and Government support.' Bailey, *Economic Frontier* p. 173.
146. The father of the late R. Sankar, Chief Minister of Kerala, 1962-4, is said to have employed about 20 people in such a factory. *R. Sankar Shastiabdapurthi Commemoration Volume* (Quilon: 1969), p. 193. See also C. Kesavan, *jivitasamaram* (Kottayam: National Book Stall, 1968), pp. 39-40. Kesavan's mother employed other women to weave.
147. *Vivekodayam* [Malayalam], Vol. I, No. 1, 1903, pp. 2-3. I am indebted to K. Prabhakaran for making available to me his copies of the magazine and for translating much of it for me.
148. Petition of Kurikkacheril Mathavan, Kunju Raman and others of Shertallai to the Madras Government, 6 April 1884: MRR, MPP, 9 May 1889, G.O. No.321. A member of the Madras Council noted: 'A curious paper. We can do nothing, but such documents should be kept with care...' Why the petition took five years to come before the Council is unexplained. It was postmarked in Alleppey on 6 April 1884.
149. Ballard to the Ch. Sec., 9 March 1870: MRR, MPP, 13 April 1870, G.O. No. 143.
150. 'A Travancore Tiya' [P.Palpu], letter to the editor, *Madras Mail*, 19 Feb. 1891, p.6. Of the 36 successful candidates in the examination, there were 23 non-Malayali Brahmins, seven Nairs, four Vellalas, one Chetti and one Eurasian. *TGG*, Vol. III, No. 8, 9 May 1865.

151. Velayudhan Panikkassery, *da. palpu* (Trichur: Currrent Books, 1970), p. 14. Regional Records Survey Committee, *The History of the Freedom Movement in Kerala*, Vol. II (Trivandrum: Government Press, 1972), p. 457n.
152. Ballard to the Ch. Sec., 9 March 1870: MRR, MPP, 13 April 1870, G.O. No. 143.
153. Panikkassery, *palpu*, pp. 18-9.
154. *Malabar Herald*, 13 Jan. 1906; *Madras Mail*, 14 April 1909, p. 4, for Velayudhan's obituary.
155. P. Palpu to Madhava Rao, 2 Oct. 1886: TGER, Cover No. 841.
156. TGER, Cover No. 841.
157. LMS, TDC, *Report*, 1872, p. 18.
158. Minute Book, LMS, TDS meeting of 10 to 13 Aug. 1886: UTC, No. 79.
159. Evangelists' reports for 1891-2: CMSA, No. 11 of 1893. See also Rev. Oomen Mamen, 'Journal', 15 Aug. 1857: CMSA, uncatalogued, writing of an Ezhava who had met the missionaries. '[He] is a true missionary. He speaks to all whom he meets with. His brothers and neighbours are now desirous to be taught; he himself, though poor and a servant of a Syrian family, has learned to read since he began to care for his soul. He has now built a prayer room in his master's compound in which he and his party meet together every morning and evening for social prayer'.
160. 'A Travancorean', letter to the editor, *Madras Mail*, 16 Nov. 1896, p. 3.
161. LMS, TDC, *Report*, 1890, p. 18.
162. LMS, TDC, *Report*, 1865, p. 9. See also Rev. W.J. Richards to the Secretary, CMS, 18 Sept. 1885: CMSA, No. 87 of 1885, for the problems of Ezhava converts at Alleppey.
163. *Travancore Law Reports*, Vol. IV, Special Appeal Suit No. 221 of 1060, pp. 12-17. Special Committee to the Dewan, 13 March 1889: TGER, Cover No. 6154.
164. Rev. Jacob Chandy, Sr., 'Journal', 21 June 1852 and 4 Jan. 1856: CMSA, uncatalogued. See also Chandy, 'Journal', 29 April 1857, for a long discussion with an elderly Ezhava convert on the aspirations of converts and the dangers of converting Pulayas.

165. Dairy of Rev. A.F. Painter, 8 Sept. 1882: CMSA, No. 49 of 1882.
166. Nagam Aiya, *Manual*, Vol. II. p. 397, writes that cremation among Ezhavas was rare. Krishna Iyer, *Social History of Kerala*, Vol. II, p. 100, discusses the prestige value of cremation for Ezahvas.
167. Thurston, *Castes*, Vol. II. pp. 396-7.
168. *Ibid.*, p. 397. A. Sreedhara Menon, *Kerala District Gazetteers: Quilon* (Trivandrum: Government Press, 1964), p. 170.
169. LMS, TDC, *Report*, 1865, p. 9.
170. Thurston, *Castes*, Vol. II.p. 393. Sreedhara Menon, *Quilon*, p. 170. Aiyappan, 'Culture Change', p. 18. Barbosa, *Book*, Vol. II, p. 60. *Census*, 1901, Vol. I, p. 279. TGER, Cover No. 9047. A modern Ezhava account claims that before the Nambudiris came to Kerala all men were equal. Some Keralans collaborated with the invaders and became Nairs; others resisted and became Ezhavas.
171. *Travancore Law Reports*, Vol. IV, Appeal Suit No. 21 of 1062, 4 July 1887, pp. 70-2.
172. *Census*, 1875, pp. 245-6; 1891, Vol. I. p. 498. There were still only 187 'other Hindus', the euphemism for low castes, in government secondary schools in 1889. The total enrolment was about 3,000, two-thirds of which was Nair and non-Malayali Brahmin. MRR, MPP, 21 Aug. 1890, G.O. No. 404.
173. *Census*, 1875, p. 255.
174. *TARs*, 1868-9, p. 14; 1864-5, p. 1.
175. H.N. Read, Principal to Rama Rao, 6 April 1891: TGER, Cover No. 1744.
176. TGER, Cover No. 1744.
177. *TAR*, 1895-6
178. There is no way of knowing exactly the number of Nair matrilineal joint-families in Travancore in the 1890s, but 32,903 Nari families partitioned themselves in the five years after the reform regulation of 1925. *Census*, 1931, Vol. I, p. 168. Augusta Blandford, *The Land of the Conch-Shell* (London: CEZMS, n.d. [c. 1901]), p. 38, wrote that Nair families could consist of 'as many as 30 people living under the same roof'. She worked for forty years among

Nairs around Trivandrum; father north, travads may have been larger. Dividing the Nair population of 1891 by 20, one arrives at a figure of between 25,000 and 30,000 taravads.

179. *TAR*, 1889-90, p. 149.
180. Mannath Padmanabhan *jivitasmaranakal*, pp. 10-12
181. Sankara Subbaiyer, Director of Vernacular Education, to Madhava Rao, 10 March 1869: TGER, Cover No. 290. See also *TGG*, Vol. V. No. 33, 27 Aug. 1867. *TGG*, Vol. XXLL, no. 7, 12 Feb. 1884. Kerala Varma to Rama Rao, 20 July 1890: TGER, Cover No. 1361.
182. 'Anniversary of His Highness the Maharaja's College and High School, Trivandrum', 25 June 1881, bound with *TGG*, 9 Aug. 1881.
183. *The Hindu*, 15 May 1891, p. 4, reported that the Maharaja's College and High School alone had produced 786 matriculates since 1870. About 30 per cent of these were Nairs.
184. Rev. John Caley to the Secretary, CMS, 17 July 1889: CMSA, No. 97 of 1889. See also *Madras Mail*, 22 Sept. 1891, p. 3, for Read's retirement.
185. Blandford, *Conch-Shell*, p. 39. Painter to the Secretary, CMS, n.d. [received in London, Oct. 1895]: CMSA, No. 180 of 1895.
186. *Census*, 1875, p. 142.
187. See Kathleen Gough, 'Nayar: Central Kerala', in Schneider and Gough (eds.), *Matrilineal Kinship* (Berkeley: University of California Press, 1962), pp. 337-8. *Malabar Herald*, 11 Sept. 1909. LMS, TDC, *Report*, 1887, p. 23. *Paschima Taraka and Keralapataka*, 2 July 1877, in *RNNM*, Malayalam, fortnight ending 14 July 1877.
188. 'Notes by Henry Baker, Jr.' n.d. [c. 1875]: CMSA uncatalogued.
189. Ananthakrishna Iyer, *Cochin Tribes*, Vol. II, p. 22. *The Hindu*, 10 June 1887, p. 5.
190. Polyandry was still practised among some Nairs in the 1880s. See Rev. A.F. Painter,' On the Hill Arrians', *Journal of the Anthropological Society of Bombay*, Vol. II, 1887, p. 148, in an aside about Nairs. Rev. Samuel Mateer, 'Social Reforms Among the Nayars of Malabar', *Journal of the Anthropological Society of Bombay*, Vol. II. 1887, pp. 317-8.

191. *Kerala Mitram*, 11 March 1882, in *RNNM*, Malayalam, fortnight ending 15 March 1882.
192. Rev. Samuel Mateer, 'Nepotism in Travancore', *Journal of the Anthropological Institute*, Vol. XII, 1883, p. 297. Mateer cited a case for libel brought by a group of Nairs against G.K. Varma who had made the charge in a Malayalam book. See also *Madras Times*, 1 July 1891, p. 6.
193. A. Govinda Pillai, 'Essay on the Marumakathayam Marriage Questions', *Report of the Malabar Marriage Commission*, 1891, Appendix III. p. 6.
194. O. Chandu Menon, *Indulekha*, trans. W. Dumergue (Calicut: Mathrubhumi Publishing Co. Ltd., 1965; first published in English, 1890; in Malayalam, 1889), pp. xix and 4. The novel is set in British Malabar, but the remarks here apply equally to Travancore. See Chaitanya, *Literature*, pp. 261-5, for a discussion of *Indulekha*.
195. In 1885 a junior member of a taravad successfully sued his karanavan for the expenses of his education in English. *Kerala Patrika*, Nov. 1885, in *RNNM*, Malayalam, fortnight ending 30 Nov. 1885.
196. *TAR* 1865-6, pp. 11-2.
197. *TARs*, 1866-7 to 1871-2.
198. W.E. Ormsby, *Outlines of Marumakatayam Law* (Kottayam: CMS Press, 1884), p. iv.
199. *TARs*, 1872-3 to 1877-8.
200. *TARs*, 1880-1 to 1890-1.
201. *Census*, 1881, pp. 242-3.
202. H.B. Grigg to the Ch. Sec., 14 Aug. 1890: MRR, MPP, 9 Sept. 1890, G.O. No. 436.
203 *TGG*, Vol. XXII, No. 37, 9 Sept. 1884.
204. Complaints about the employment of 'foreigners' in the sirkar service were recurrent in the 1880s. See for example, *Kerala Mitram*, 28 May 1881, Oct. 1882, April 1886, June 1887, Nov. 1887, in *RNNM*, Malayalam.
205. S. Sankara Subbaiyer, C. Pacheappa Naicker, P. Thanu Pillai, 'Report of the Viruthi Committee', 12 June 1889, TGER, Cover No. 1664.
206. Pocock, *Kanbi and Patidar*, p. 52, makes the useful distinction between 'standing' within a caste and 'status' in the overall

social system. A man might have high standing within his caste, though it has low ritual status.

207. *Malabar Special Commission: Malabar Land Tenures. Report*, Vol. I (Madras: Government Press, 1882), pp. cvii-cviii.

## Chapter 5

1. *Paschima Taraka and Keralapataka*, 2 Feb. 1880, in *RNNM*, Malayalam, fortnight ending 14 Feb. 1880. The Brahmin was said to be T. Gopala Rao of Kumbakonam College.
2. Nanu Pillai's appointment as Dewan in 1877 resulted from the feud between the Maharaja, Ayilyam Tirunal, and his brother Vishakham Tirunal. Ayilyam chose Nanu Pillai to forestall the appointment of another of Vishakham's and Madhava Rao's friends. See MacGregor to the Ch. Sec., 6 March 1877: Political and Secret Letters from Madras, Vol. I, 1875-6, pp. 779-88.
3. Parameswaran Nair, *raman pilla*, p. 86. *Madras Mail*, 2 May 1902, p. 5.
4. Parameswaran Nair, *raman pilla*, p. 80. See *The Hindu*, 15 June 1887, p. 3, for the Malayali Sabha's farewell function for Harvey, and *Madras Mail*, 30 June 1882, p. 3, for a meeting at which V.I. Keshava Pillai read a paper on the 'Need of Certain Reforms in Travancore, Cochin and Malabar'. John Ross commented on the paper.
5. Parameswaran Nair, *raman pilla*, p. 81. See Biographical Notes.
6. Note by Thanu Pillai, 15 Aug. 1880, quoted in *ibid.*, pp. 64-5.
7. Thanu Pillai to C.V. Raman Pillai, 5 Jan 1881, quoted in *ibid.*, p. 93. All Thanu Pillai's correspondence was in English and was translated into Malayalam by Parameswaran Nair. The correspondence has been lost in the thirty years since Parameswaran Nair wrote *raman pilla*.
8. *Madras Standard*, 21 Dec. 1887, p.2. Parameswaran Nair, *raman pilla*, p. 64, says the Sabha was created in 1886, but this is clearly wrong.
9. *Travancore Times*, 20 Nov. 1885. The Brahmin was R. Raghunatha Rao, dewan peshkar of Padmanabhapuram, who was soon to emerge as a *bete noire* of the Sabha.
10. *Paschima Taraka and Keralapataka*, 2 July 1877, in *RNNM*, Malayalam, fortnight ending 14 July 1877.
11. Krishna Pillai to Raman Pillai, 11 Kanni 1062 [about 1 Oct. 1885], in Parameswaran Nair, *raman pilla*, p. 67.
12. *Travancore Times*, 20 Nov. 1885.
13. Parameswaran Nair, *raman pilla*, p. 69. Judges T.R.

Narayana Pillai, S. Kunhiraman Nair and A. Govinda Pillai chaired Sabha meetings at this time. Membership included a few Nambudiris, Ambalavasis and Nanjanad Vellalas, but was largely Nair.

14. *Travancore Times*, 10 Nov. 1886.
15. Hannyngton to Ramiengar, 27 Nov. 1886 and 16 March 1887: MRR, LD, Vol. XXIV.
16. Parameswaran Nair, *raman pilla*, p. 71; *Madras Standard*, 21 Dec. 1887, p. 2; *Travancore Almanack*, 1891, p. 30, showed the Malayali Sabha with fourteen schools receiving grants-in-aid.
17. G. Parameswaran Pillai, *Select Writings and Speeches*, edited by G.P. Sekhar (Trivandrum: Radh-Ind Publications, 1964), pp. 179-80.
18. The first of the *Standard's* attacks was published on 15 Aug. Krishna Pillai to Raman Pillai, 18 Karkatagam 1062 [early Aug. 1887] in Parameswaran Nair, *raman pilla*, p. 73, wrote of harassment of Sabha members. This letter, like many others, was in English but was translated into Malayalam. The original has been lost.
19. *Madras Standard*, 15 Aug. 1887, p. 2. Attacks followed in the issues of 24, 26, 29 and 31 Aug. and throughout September.
20. *Madras Standrd*, 23 Sept. 1887, p. 2.
21. *Madras Standard*, 26 Sept. 1887, p.2.
22. Regional Records Survey Committee, *The History of the Freedom Movement in Kerala*, Vol. II, (Trivandrum: Government Press, 1972), pp. 4-7. The Survey Committee quotes from the 'Open Letter', but I was unable to find a copy in London, Madras or Kerala.
23. *Madras Standard*, 3 Oct. 1887, p. 2.
24. Parameswaran Pillai, *Writings*, p. 175.
25. *Madras Standard*, 26 Sept 1887, p. 2.
26. *Madras Standard*, 24 Oct. 1887, p. 2.
27. J.D. Rees, *Narratives of Tours in India Made by His Excellency Lord Connemara*, 1886-1890 (Madras: Government Press, 1891), p. 56. Connemara to Lord Lansdowne, Viceroy, 29 March 1890: IOR, Lansdowne Papers, D/558/18. Hannyngton to the Ch. Sec., 22 Nov. 1890: MRR, LMG, Vol. XXIV. K.C.S.I. stands for Knight Commander

of the Order of the Star of India.

28. See for examples *Madras Standard*, 16 and 19 Sept., both p. 2, and 31 Oct., p. 2.

29. *Madras Standard*, 12, 21 and 30 Dec., all p. 2. A. Sitarama Aiyar was the grand-uncle of Sir C.P. Ramaswamy Aiyar, Dewan of Travancore from 1936 to 1947. P. Padmanabha Iyer, *Souvenir of the Sashtiabdapurti of Sachivothama Sir C.P. Ramaswami Aiyar* (Trivandrum: ARV Press, 1940), p. 213.

30. *Madras Standard*, 25 Jan. 1888, p. 2.

31. *Madras Standard*, 25 Jan. 1888, p. 2.

32. Thanu Pillai to Raman Pillai, 12 Alpashi 1061 [early 1887], in Parameswaran Nair, *raman pilla*, pp. 92-3. Thanu Pillai published a book in Malayalam in 1887 which outlined the membership and aims at the Sabha, but I have been unable to find a copy.

33. See *Madras Standard*, 30 Jan. 1888, p. 2, which began a series, 'The Autobiography of Saravanai' by 'A Lover of His Country'. Instalments of this heavy-handed satire appeared on 1,3,6,8,10,13,15,17,20,22,24 and 29 Feb. 1888 and on 2, 5 and 7 March. See also *RNNM*, Malayalam, for May and June 1888.

34. Fisher to the Ch. Sec., 25 Aug. 1863: MPP, 23 Sept. 1863, Range 321, Vol. XLVVI, pp. 313-5; Fisher to Madhava Rao, 7 Aug. 1863: MRR, LD, Vol. XIII.

35. Parameswaran Pillai, *Writings*, p. 172.

36. The *Travancore Almanack* in 1881 listed 438 sirkar jobs, about a third of which were held by Brahmins and the same number by Nairs. In the 1888 edition there are 617 jobs, and the shares remain roughly the same. The Brahmin share of tahsildarships and dewan peshkarships, however, had increased.

37. *Madras Standard*, 16 Sept. 1887, p. 2. See also 19 and 26 Sept. 1887, both p. 2.

38. Excerpt from 'Travancore for the Travancoreans' in Parameswaran Pillai, *Writings*, p. 102. I have been unable to find a copy of the pamphlet which was published about 1890. Parameswaran Pillai's four examples were Kesava Das, Velu Thampi, Aiyappan Marthandan and Chempakaraman, all Dewans of Travancore.

39. *Madras Standard*, 25 and 27 Feb. both p. 3, and 24 Sept. 1888, p. 2.
40. *Madras Standard*, 12 Sept. 1888, p. 2, 20 Feb. 1889, p.2, 31 Oct. 1888, p. 2, 10 June 1889, p. 2. The charge of assault drew a denial from the Maharaja's secretary, M.C. Neelakantha Pillai, but the *Standard* made no retraction. 'Travancore for the Travancoreans', in Parameswaran Pillai, *Writings*, pp. 101-2. The *Hindu* ignored the *Standard* and praised Rama Rao. See 25 April 1888, p. 4, and 3 Sept. 1889, p. 4.
41. *Madras Standard*, 22 Nov. 1889, p. 2. I have been unable to find a copy of the pamphlet.
42. C.V. Raman Pillai, *Marthanda Varma*, trans. B.K. Menon (Trivandrum: Kamalalaya Book Depot, 1936; first published in Malayalam, 1891). Chaitanya, *Literature*, pp. 266-7, discusses the book. He concludes (p. 269) that Raman Pillai's historical fiction has never been surpassed in Malayalam. Parameswaran Nair, *raman pilla*, pp. 132-144, discusses the writing and publishing of the novel.
43. *Madras Standard*, 14 Oct. 1889, p. 2.
44. *Madras Standard*, 30 Dec. 1887, p. 2.
45. Parameswaran Nair, *raman pilla*, p. 71.
46. The Palace to Rama Rao, 11 Jan. 1889: TGER, Cover No. 15319.
47. *Madras Standard*, 23 Sept. 1889, p. 1. See also Parameswaran Nair, *raman pilla*, p. 132.
48. See the note by K. Padmanabhan Thampi quoted in Parameswaran Nair, *raman pilla*, pp. 133-4n.
49. Parameswaran Pillai later edited the *Madras Standard* which one governor of Madras thought of as Norton's paper. See Lord Wenlock to Lord George Hamilton, Secretary of State for India, 28 Nov. 1895: IOR, Wenlock Papers, D. 592. Norton's divorce cases in 1894 and 1895 brought a temporary fall from favour. See the *Indian Social Reformer*, 18 May 1895, p. 289.
50. Parameswaran Nair, *raman pilla*, p. 174, writes that Raman Pillai composed most of the Memorial and that amendments were later made by Eardley Norton. In Parameswaran Pillai, *Writings*, p. 181, Parameswaran Pillai's son claims the drafting was done by his father. Regional Records

Survey Committee, *The History of the Freedom Movement in Kerala,* Vol. II (Trivandrum: Government Press, 1972), p. 8, bestows the credit on Sankara Menon, Parameswaran Pillai, P. Palpu, 'and others'. It seems likely, however, that C.V. Raman Pillai provided most of the statistics regardless of who drafted the Memorial.

51. 'G.P.', letter to the editor, *Madras Mail*, 20 Jan. 1891, p. 6.
52. Parameswaran Nair, *raman pilla*, p. 178.
53. *Ibid.*, p. 179, confuses the story and writes that when Fr. Nidhiry refused to sign, Raman Pillai recruited another Nidhiry, a vakil. In fact, Syriac Nidhiry, Fr. Nidhiry's brother, who was a landholder, was the signer. Nidhiry, *Nidhiry*, pp. 309-11.
54. Printed verston of the Memorial in MRR, MPP, 11 Feb. 1891, G.O. No. 87-A. It was claimed that leading Malayalis like Thanu Pillai, A. Govinda Pillai, M. Kunjukrishna Panikkar and M.C. Neelakantha Pillai (see Biographical Notes) had not signed the Memorial. 'A Hindu Liberal', letter to the editor, *The Hindu*, 6 Feb. 1891, p. 6. The reply was that only two of those mentioned were important, and they supported the Memorial. Their reason for not signing was 'an open secret in Travancore'. 'One of the Ten Thousand', letter to the editor, *The Hindu*, 20 Feb. 1891, p. 3.
55. *Madras Times,* 8 July 1891, p. 5, where the full text of the Memorial is printed and from which come subsequent references in this chapter.
56. Rama Rao was ill, and the Resident wanted him to retire. 'Though only 50 years of age he is past all power of quick and energetic work'. Hannyngton to the Ch. Sec., 17 June 1889: MRR, MPP, 12 July 1889, G.O. No. 364. Hannyngton's only advice about the Memorial was unimaginative. 'The receipt of the Petition should be acknowledged with a remark that the subject will be duly considered by His Highness's Government'. Hannyngton to the Ch. Sec., 20 Feb. 1891: MRR, MPP, 20 March 1891, G.O. No. 171.
57. Endorsement by Rama Rao, 21 April 1891: TGER, Cover No. 1744.
58. *Madras Times*, 10 July 1891, p. 5, where the full text of

the Counter-Memorial is printed.

59. Letter to the editor, *Madras Times*, 2 July 1891, p. 4.
60. 'A Christian Travancorean', letter to the editor, *Madras Mail*, 2 July 1891, p.5. The Palace to Rama Rao, 8 July 1891: TGER, Cover No. 1733, forwarded a petition, which has not survived, alleging that three Nagercoil officials, including the district judge, were working for the Counter-Memorial.
61. 'Proceedings of the Trivandrum Meeting of the Counter-Memorialists', 1 July 1891: TGER, Cover No. 1744, claimed the figure of 27,000. When the Counter-Memorialists met the Dewan, however, Ramanatha Rao said that their Petition was 'signed by 1,000'. *Madras Times*, 8 July 1891, p. 5. On 3 June the Counter-Memorialists were claiming 11,197 signatures. TGER, Cover No. 1744. In mid-June they claimed 15,000. *The Hindu*, 15 June 1891, p. 4.
62. *Madras Times*, 8 June 1891, p. 5.
63. *Madras Times*, 23 June 1891, p. 4.
64. *Madras Times*, 8 and 23 June and 4 and 7 July 1891.
65. 'Proceedings of the Alleppey Meeting of the Counter-Memorialists', 27 June 1891: TGER, Cover No. 1744. Although Mar Gregorious sided with the Counter-Memorialists, Jacobites were divided. E.M. Philip, a Jacobite stalwart, had participated in the Memorialists' meeting in Kottayam on 3 June. *Madras Times*, 8 June 1891, p. 5. *Malayala Manorama*, 4 July 1891, supported the Memorial.
66. 'Proceedings' of the Quilon Meeting of the Counter-Memorialists', 29 June 1891; 'Proceedings of the Nagercoil Meeting of the Counter-Memorialists', 29 June 1891; proceedings of the Trivandrum Meeting of the Counter-Memorialists, 1 July 1891: TGER, Cover No. 1744.
67. 'Quilon Counter-Memorial Meeting Proceedings'.
68. 'Nagercoil Counter-Memorial Meeting Proceedings'.
69. 'A Hindu Liberal', letter to the editor, *The Hindu*, 6 Feb. 1891, p. 6.
70. 'Trivandrum Counter-Memorial Meeting Proceedings'.
71. *Madras Mail*, 16 June 1891, p. 4.
72. *TGG*, Vol. XXIX, No. 26, 30 June 1891.
73. *Madras Times*, 8 July 1891, p. 5.
74. *Malayala Manorama*, 4 July 1891. Although *Manorama*

was owned by Jacobites, it supported the Memorial.

75. Parameswaran Nair, *raman pilla*, p. 179, writes that Krishna Pillai's rights were ignored by government and Raman Pillai was passed over.

76. 'A Travancoroean', letter to the editor, *Madras Mail*, 8 Dec. 1891, p. 6, saw a notification granting dismissed servants the right of appeal as a victory for the Memorialists.

77. *Madras Mail*, 16 Jan. 1891 and 16 June 1891, both p. 4. *The Hindu*, 20 Jan., 27 April and 3 May 1891, all p. 4.

78. 'A Travancorean', letter to the editor, *Madras Mail*, 16 Nov. 1896, p. 3. Other letters appearing at this time under the pseudonym, 'A Travancorean', were obviously from Palpu. See *Madras Mail*, 4 Dec. 1896, p. 5, for example. *Malayala Manorama*, 23 Oct. 1901; *Malabar Herald*, 8 April 1905.

## Chapter 6

1. Sankara Menon to Rama Rao, 15 June 1892: TGER, Cover No. 11208.
2. C.V. Raman Pillai, *Videshiya Medhavitvam,* quoted in Parameswaran Nair, *raman pilla,* p. 501. Raman Pillai first wrote this account in instalments for a newspaper, *Mitabhashi,* after T. Raghavayya, a Tamil Brahmin, succeeded M. Krishnan Nair as Dewan in 1920.
3. *Malayala Manorama,* 18 Sept. 1897.
4. *Dewan's Note dated 15 August 1912, on the Suppression of the Swadeshabhimani Newspaper* (Trivandrum: Government Press, 1912) p. 10.
5. C.V. Raman Pillai became High Court Manager in 1897; V.I. Keshava Pillai became a first-class magistrate in 1892 and a dewan peshkar in 1899; P. Ayyappan Pillai became headmaster of the Trivandrum High School, then a school inspector and ultimately, about 1903, Educational Secretary. All three had signed the Memorial. C.M. Madhavan Pillai, a Nanjanad Vellala and a member of the Malayali Sabha, rose to be huzur deputy peshkar. A. Govinda Pillai, an occasional chairman of Malayali Sabha meetings, whose claims had been asserted by the *Madras Standard,* was a dewan peshkar by 1895 and a High Court Judge by 1900. The fiery C. Krishna Pillai, however, was notably passed over.
6. Sankara Subbaiyer to the Chief Justice, 25 Feb. 1898: TGER, Judicial Section Books, n.n./J242-1/2. Parameswaran Pillai, *Writings,* p. 206.
7. *Malayala Manorama,* 19 Feb. 1898.
8. For the decline of the *Malayali,* see Parameswaran Nair, *raman pilla,* p. 179. The India Office Library's holdings of the *Madras Standard* end with 1889, and the Connemara Library, Madras, discarded its back numbers. The only issues still in existence for the 1890s seemed to be with Parameswaran Pillai's son, G.P. Sekhar, of Trivandrum, but I was not able to use them. The references here are from Parameswaran Pillai, *Writings,* p. 109.The book was compiled by Mr. Sekhar. In 1896 the *Standard* also commented on the unpopularity of the administration.

Quoted in *Madras Mail*, 24 Sept. 1896, p. 3.

9. See the letter of the Rev. John Knowles, LMS, *Madras Mail*, 30 Sept. 1896, p. 5, in which he said that harassment of Christian converts had come only after Sankara Subbaiyer became Dewan.

10. *Madras Standard*, 25 Feb. 1888, p. 3. It is fair to add that the *Standard*, 12 Oct. 1887, p. 2, had labelled Sankara Subbaiyer 'a despiser of the Sudras'.

11. Rev. A.F. Painter to the Secretary, CMS, 5 Jan. 1887 [incorrectly dated 1886] and 14 Jan. 1887: CMSA, Nos. 10 and 14 of 1887.

12. See Hodges to the Secretary, CMS, 29 Aug. 1894: CMSA, No. 128 of 1894. The Dewan's relative was working for the CMS in Travancore. Also, 'X', letter to the editor, *Madras Mail*, 8 June 1897, p. 5 for the marriage of Sankara Subbaiyer's granddaughter.

13. C.V. Raman Pillai provides perhaps the best example of the attachment which educated Nairs had for their glorified past. His biographer writes that Raman Pillai was a firm admirer of Nair strength, that he worshipped the benevolent lordship and love of country which was the essence of the old Nair taravad, and that he grieved that all this was passing. He blamed its passing on foreign rule. Parameswaram Nair, *raman pilla*, pp. 207-8; see also pp. 154 and 205.

14. Rev. Samuel Mateer, 'On Social Reforms Among the Nayars of Malabar', *Journal of the Anthropological Society of Bombay*, Vol. II, 1887, p. 319.

15. See *Travancore Law Reports*, Vol. II, A.S. No. 393 of 1057, 9 July 1883, pp. 3304, in which a karanavan tried unsuccessfully to assert his claims over a branch which had separated more than 40 years before; Vol. XIV, A.S. No. 123 of 1072, 16 July 1897, pp. 49-54, in which the court held that in some circumstances a detached branch of a taravad was responsible for debts incurred by the karanavan of the undivided travad; Vol. I, A.S. No. 99 of 1057, 13 July 1882, pp. 94-5, in which the court ruled that taravad property was inalienable except for taravad necessities and that any adult member could challenge alienations in the courts; Vol. V, Royal Court of Final Appeal, No. 2 of 1061, 1885, pp. 6-13, in which all sales

or gifts of taravad property made without the express or implied consent of *all* the adult members were held invalid; Vol. I, A.S. No. 72 of 1055, 20 Jan. 1881, in which the court ruled that members living outside the main taravad house without the karanavan's consent had no right to maintenance; Vol. I, A.S. No. 516 of 1055, 9 July 1881, pp. 63-4, in which a mortgage executed by junior members while the karanavan was in jail was held to be invalid because as long as the karanavan was alive he retained his exclusive powers; Vol. III, Special A.S. No. 167 of 1059, 21 May 1884, pp. 42-3, in which the court held that any debt contracted by a karanavan was presumed to be a taravad debt. Also *Madras Mail*, 28 Sept. 1893, p. 4, reporting a case in Malabar in which for the first time a non-Malayali Brahmin was ordered to pay maintenance for his child by a woman of a poor taravad.

16. W.E. Ormsby, *Outlines of Marumakatayam Law* (Kottayam: CMS Press, 1884), p. xvi.
17. *TARs*.
18. 'Bhagirath', letter to the editor, *Madras Mail*, 11 Feb. 1890, p. 5.
19. Parameswaran Pillai, *Writings*, p. 175.
20. 'Kartiyam', 'Beta', and 'P.C.', letters to the editor, *Madras Mail*, 11 Feb., 20 March and 20 Feb. 1890, all p. 5.
21. 'R', letter to the editor, *Madras Mail*, 4 March 1890, p. 6; Chandu Menon to Karunakaran Menon, *Madras Mail*, 29 Aug. 1890, p. 5; 'A Travancorean', letter to the editor, *Madras Mail*, 14 Oct. 1903, p. 5, in which he charged that the Memorial agitation had been directed partly against non-Malayali Brahmins who had sambandham with Nairs.
22. See *Report of the Malabar Marriage Commission* [hereafter *Mal. Mar. Com.*] (Madras: 1891). Also *Madras Times*, 5 May 1891, p. 3. The members were Muthuswami Aiyar; H.M. Winterbotham, collector of Malabar; Sankaran Nair; the Raja of Parapanad; O. Chandu Menon, the author of *Indulekha* and district munsiff of Calicut; and M. Mandappa Bangera, district munsiff of Mangalore.
23. Rama Rao to H.M. Winterbotham, 30 April 1891: *Mal. Mar. Com.*, Appendix III, p. 1; A. Govidha Pillai, 'Essay on the Marummakathayam Marriage Question', *Mal. Mar.*

*Com.*, Appendix III, pp. 10-11; T. Kunhi Raman Nair, 'Answers to Interrogatories', *Mal. Mar. Com.*, Appendix III, pp. 9-11.

24. *Madras Mail*, 18 June 1906, p. 4. Only one sambandham had been registered in each of the years 1904-5 and 1905-6. In the first 14 months of the act's operation, 51 sambandhams were registered, and after that interest rapidly declined. *Madras Mail*, 16 Sept. 1897, p. 3; 1 Sept. 1898, p. 3; *Madras Times*, 7 Aug. 1903, p. 3.
25. Parameswaran Nair, *raman pilla*, p. 180. T. Kunhi Raman Nair, 'Answers to Interrogatories', *Mal. Mar. Com.*, Appendix III, pp. 9-19.
26. *Report of the Special Commission on Malabar Land Tenures* (Madras: 1882), p. cviii.
27. Speech by Thanu Pillai, 'Abstract Proceedings of the Travancore Legislative Council' [hereafter 'TLC Proc.'] 20 June 1896: *TGG*, Vol. XXXIV, No. 25, 23 June 1896.
28. Parameswaran nair, *raman pilla*, p. 180.
29. 'TLC Proc.', 20 June 1896: *TGG*, Vol. XXXIV, No. 25, 23 June 1896.
30. *Madras Mail*, 16 Sept. 1896, p. 5. See also Parameswaran Nair, *raman pilla*, p. 180, and *TGGs*, 8 Sept. and 1 Dec. 1896, which record the receipt of 92 petitions and letters regarding the bill, most of them favouring it and most of them signed by more than 50 people.
31. 'TLC Proc.', n.d.: *TGG*, Vol. XXXV, No. 3, 19 Jan. 1897.
32. *Madras Standard*, 3 Oct. 1887, p. 2 and 29 Feb. 1858, p. 2. Also 25 Jan. 1888, p. 2 and 12 Sept. 1888, p. 2. The Resident, though not alluding to the Maharaja's private life, admitted that the palace was caught up in corruption and intrigue. Hannyngton to the Ch. Sec., 9 July 1888: MRR, MPP, G.O. No. 561, 13 Aug. 1888. However, Hannyngton earlier had described the Maharaja's moral character as 'exceedingly good'. Hannyngton to the Ch. Sec., 24 Aug. 1885: MRR, MPP, G.O. No. 625A-B, 7 Sept, 1885. The Maharaja's Nair wife had died in 1882.
33. *Madras Times*, 19 May 1903, p. 3. A pamphlet had been published in Trivandrum which condemned such nudity. This had been a recurring theme for 25 years. *RNNM*, Malayalam, 1 Sept. 1877, July 1887, 18 Feb. 1888. By

1905 women in the annual Arat procession in Trivandrum had begun covering their breasts. *The Hindu*, 4 Nov. 1905, p. 4.

34. F.A. Nicholson to the Ch. Sec., 28 May 1897: MRR, MPP, G.O. No. 426, 29 June 1897.
35. *TGGs*, 8 June and 21 Sept. 1897 for reports of the submission of more petitions regarding the bill.
36. Parameswaran Nair, *raman pilla*, p. 181; *Malayala Manorama*, 18 Nov. 1899.
37. Krishnaswami Rao to the Acting Resident, 25 Jan. 1899: TGER, Judicial Section Books, n.r./J105. 'TLC Proc.', 27 May 1899: *TGG*, Vol. XXXVII, No. 22, 30 May 1899. For the first discussions of the bill, see *TGG*, Vol. XXXV, No. 40, 5 Oct. 1897.
38. *Malayala Manorama*, quoted in the *Madras Mail*, 15 June 1899, p. 6.
39. Rev. John Knowles, letter to the editor, *Madras Mail*, 15 June 1899, p. 5.
40. Grigg to Rama Rao, 17 Sept. 1890: MRR, LD, Vol. XXV. See article, probably by Rev. Samuel Mateer, *Madras Mail*, 30 June 1890, p. 3.
41. *Malayala Manorama*, 12 May 1894, in *RNNM*, Malayalam, fortnight ending 31 May 1894.
42. *Travancore Law Reports*, Vol. IV, 1885, Special Appeal Suit, No. 221 of 1060, pp. 12-17.
43. Special Committee to Rama Rao, 13 March 1889: TGER, Cover No. 6154. See also Minutes of the Travancore CMS Conference, 18-20 Aug. 1858: United Theological College Archives, Bangalore, No. 40; Hannyngton to the Ch. Sec., 18 May 1889: MRR, LMG, Vol. XXIV; Rama Rao to the Rev. C.A. Neve, 2 July 1889: TGER, Judicial Section Books, 3228/J1204.
44. Minutes of the LMS Travancore District Committee Meeting, 5 Nov. 1889: CCWM, Travancore, Box 12, Folder 4, Jacket A; Minutes of the Travancore CMS Conference, 18-23 July 1891: UTC, No. 40.
45. Painter to the Secretary, CMS, 18 Nov. 1895: CMSA, No. 209 of 1895.
46. 'A.F.P.', Kottayam, letter to the editor, *Madras Mail*, 4 Aug. 1894, p. 7.

47. Petition to Lord Wenlock, July 1895: CMSA, No. 187 of 1895.
48. Sankara Subbaiyer to the Resident, 5 March 1898: TGER, Judicial Section Books, 1115/J288.
49. *Madras Mail*, 16 Jan. 1899, p. 6. South India Missionary Conference Memorial, 23 May 1900: Government of India, Foreign Department, Intl. B., Oct. 1900. Missionaries in Mysore at this time were also trying to win increased rights for their converts.
50. *Malayala Manorama*, 27 Jan. 1900.
51. *TAR*, 1892-3, p. 154.
52. Jacobites had about 90 schools in 1890 and more than 250 by 1907. See E.M. Philip, *The Indian Church of St. Thomas* (Nagercoil: LMS Press, 1950), p. 356.
53. *TGGs*, April 1897 to March 1898.
54. *Kerala Patrika*, 12 May 1888, in *RNNM*, Malayalam, May 1888.
55. 'Kerala Mitra', letter to the editor, *Madras Mail*, 15 Aug. 1894, p. 5. Also 'Education', letters to the editor, *Madras Mail*, 4 and 18 Aug. 1894.
56. 'Inops', letter to the editor, *Madras Mail*, 24 Nov. 1894, p. 5. For other pro-Christian letters, see the *Mail* for 14, 15, 18, 20, 27 and 28 Aug. 1894. The European missionaries involved were Painter and Palmer of the CMS and Hacker, Knowles and Duthie of the LMS.
57. *Madras Mail*, 3 Aug. 1894, p. 4. and letter to the editor, 31 Aug. 1894, p. 5.
58. 'Julian', letter to the editor, *Madras Mail*, 14 Aug. 1894, p. 5.
59. Rev. John Knowles, letter to the editor, *Madras Mail*, 24 Sept. 1895, p. 5.
60. Rev. I.H. Hacker, letters to the editor, *Madras Mail*, 18 Oct. p. 5, and 28 Oct. 1895, p. 6.
61. Rev. John Caley, letters to the editor, *Madras Mail*, 21 Sept., p. 5, and 20 Oct. 1896, p. 5. C. Sathianathum, letter to the editor, *Madras Mail*, 10 Oct. 1896, p. 5. Rev. C.A. Neve, letter to the editor, *Madras Mail*, 21 Oct. 1896, p. 7.
62. Rev. John Caley, letter to the editor, *Madras Mail*, 5 Oct. 1895, p. 7.

63. In twelve years the sirkar claimed that only five of 127 applications had been rejected, three of them as a result of the objection of other Christians. 'TLC Proc.', 20 June 1896: *TGG*, Vol. XXXIV, No. 25, 23 June 1896.
64. Rev. C.F. Breay, letter to the editor, *Madras Mail*, 12 Oct. 1895, p. 7. Father F. M. Victor, letter to the editor, *Madras Mail*, 19 Oct. 1895, p. 5. The missionaries were also attacked by other letter writers. See letters to the editor, *Madras Mail*, 18 and 19 Oct. 1895.
65. *Malayala Manorama*, quoted in *Madras Mail*, 1 Nov. 1895, p. 4. See also *Malayala Manorama*, quoted in 'Fair Play', letter to the editor, *Madras Mail*, 15 Oct. 1895, p. 6.
66. 'Travancorean', letter to the editor, *Madras Mail*, 15 Oct. 1895, p. 6.
67. Rev. John Caley, letter to the editor, *Madras Mail*, 25 Oct. 1895, p. 5.
68. *List of Public Servants of the Travanncore Government*, 1893-4.
69. 'Memorandum of the Kottayam Taluk', by C. Govinda Pillai, B.A., B.L., tahsildar, n.d. [about 1896]: TGER, Cover No. 11,650.
70. TGER, Cover No. 10,241.
71. *Malayala Manorama*, 16 Oct. 1897.
72. *Malayala Manorama*, 16 Oct. 1897.
73. *Malayala Manorama* 2 April 1898.
74. *Malayala Manorama*, 30 April 1898.
75. Nidhiry, *Nidhiry*, p. 271.
76. P.J. Itteyyerah, 'Gregorious Bar Ebraya and His Nomo Canon', *Malabar Quarterly Review*, Vol. I, No. 2, June 1902, p. 116. Also *Malayala Manorama*, 21 Aug. 1901 for an account of the efforts to reunite the Jacobites for the same reason.
77. *Madras Mail*, 13, 14 and 15 June and 21 July 1899.
78. See the *Malabar Herald*, 6 Oct. 1906; *The Hindu*, 20 May 1924, which laid responsibility for the strict and systematic exclusion of Ezhavas from environs of the Vaikam temple on Sankara Menon.
79. *Madras Mail*, 19 Oct. 1899, p. 5.
80. *Madras Mail*, 17 May 1898, p. 6.

81. *Madras Mail*, 27 Nov. 1901, p. 5. for T.C. Poonen's obituary. That his bank was unsuccessful I have on the authority of P.C. Joseph, former principal of CMS College, Kottayam, who was a colleague of one of Poonen's sons. M. Poulose of the Tiruvalla Bank was the father of C.P. Matthen, whose Travancore and Quilon National Bank was broken, he claimed, in 1938 by the actions of Sir C.P. Ramaswami Aiyar, the Dewan. C.P. Matthen, *I Have Borne Much* (Madras: Ampthill, 1951), p. 34.
82. *Travancore Almanack*, 1906, pp. 206-12.
83. *Madras Times*, 10 Oct. 1904, p. 3.
84. *Madras Mail*, 2 March 1901, p. 5, obituary of C. John, father of C.J. Curien of the *Western Star*.
85. *TAR*, 1902-3, p. 58.
86. The value of tea exported from Travancore went from Rs. 12.97 lakhs in 1892-3 to Rs. 31.49 lakhs in 1894-5. *TARs*. In 1896 the Finlay Muir Co. of Glasgow acquired the great Kannan Devan concession in the High Range and accelerated its development. See articles by J.B. Soutar and W.S.S. MacKay in *James Finlay and Co. House Magazine*, Spring 1972. F.G.R. [ichardson], letter to the editor, *Madras Mail*, 29 April 1902, p. 5. The school on Stagbrook Estate at Pirmed, as one example, was run by the Rev. Mr. Samuel and John Chacko. In 1898 a CMS agent reported 100 Europeans in the High Range 'with Malayalam writers and artisans (some of whom are C.M.S. Christians)'. He also warned that 'the Roman Catholics are already in the field'. 'Note on Mission on Kannan Devan', c. July 1898 [possibly by Rev. C.A. Neve]: CMSA, No. 124 of 1898. See *Census*, Vol. I, 1911, p. 35 for the flow of Kottayam people to the estates. Pepper, exports of which increased by 111 per cent between 1891 and 1901, was already a profitable cash crop for ryots by 1905. *Malabar Herald*, 17 June 1905; *Census*, Vol. I, p. 66.
87. *Madras Mail*, 3 Feb. 1903, p. 7.
88. *TAR*, 1888-9, p. 185; *TGG*, Vol. XXVIII, No. 28, 15 July 1890. The measures provided low-interest loans to cultivators and tax-free enjoyment of reclaimed land for five years.
89. *Madras Mail*, 3 Feb. 1903, p. 7. Varghese, *Agrarian Change*, p. 69.

90. *Madras Times*, 25 Oct. 1904, p. 6. V.R. Pillai and P.G.K. Panikkar, *Land Reclamation in Kerala* (Bombay: Asia Publishing House, 1965), p. 16.
91. *Madras Mail*, 9 Oct. 1901, p. 7.
92. 'Anon', *Madras Mail*, 9 Oct. 1901, p. 7. If 'Anon' was not a Syrian Christian, his impersonation was superb. Dr. E. Poonen, nephew of T.C. Poonen, also quoted Thanu Pillai's speech in an address to a Syrian audience in Trivandrum. *Malayala Manorama*, 9 Oct. 1901.
93. *Malayala Manorama*, 11 March 1899; *Madras Mail*, 11 March 1899, p. 7.
94. *Malayala Manorama*, 11 Feb. 1899.
95. *Malayala Manorama* 25 March 1899.
96. See *Malayala Manorama*, 18 March 1899; *Madras Mail*, 18 Oct. 1900, p. 5, where 'Fibbertigibbet' listed nine highly qualified Syrians 'in exile'; *Madras Mail*, 19 March 1901, p. 5. *Malayala Manorama*, 23 Oct. 1901.
97. *Friend of Malabar*, Vol. XI, 1901, pp. 18-20; *Madras Mail*, 24 Dec. 1900, p.7.
98. *Madras Times*, 11 July 1903, p. 3. *Malayala Manorama*, 12 Dec. 1903; Nidhiry, *Nidhiry*, p. 271.
99. Dewan Peshkar to Madhava Rao, 28 Sept. 1904: TGER, Travancore Political Department [hereafter TPD], File 113A of 1904.
100. *Madras Mail*, 5 Jan. 1905, p. 3. This included four English and one or two Tamil.
101. For example, see *Malayala Manorama*, 25 Nov. 1903 for K. Kuruvila's speech at the Mar Dionysius Seminary, and *Madras Times*, 16 Oct. 1903, p. 2 for M. LaBouchardiere's speech at College Day in Trivandrum.
102. LMS, TDC, *Report*, 1897, pp. 8-9, quoting Rev. W.D. Osbourne.
103. P. Palpu to Sankara Subbaiyer, 13 May 1895: TGER, Cover No. 3234. Shankara Subbaiyer's reply, if there was a written one, has not been preserved here.
104. Velayudhan Panikkassery, *da. palpu* (Trichur: Current Books, 1970), pp. 76-7. See pp. 114-6 for the letters of the Ezhava applicants. One of the latter was M. Govindan who became the first Ezhava munsiff in 1908. *Madras Mail*, 14 March 1908, p. 5. See also the letter from 'A

Travancorean', probably Palpu, in the *Madras Mail*, 15 Oct. 1896, p. 5. and *Madras Mail*, 13 Dec. 1895, p.4.

105. Panikkassery, *palpu*, pp. 77-8.

106. *Madras Mail*, 6 Oct. 1896, p. 3, printed the Memorial in full. The copy in TGER, Cover No. 1231 is in Malayalam.

107. Endorsement, 3 Oct. 1896: TGER, Cover No. 1231. *Madras Mail*, 5 Nov. 1896, p. 5.

108. *Madras Mail*, 15 Oct. 1896, p. 5.

109. *Madras Mail*, 4 Dec. 1896, p. 5.

110. For his speech in 1895 and one of the *Standard's* editorials in November 1896, see Parameswaran Pillai, *Writings*, pp. 111-8. In 1898, however, he was convicted of plagiarism and in 1899 of defamation. See the *Madras Mail*, 19 Nov. 1898, p. 6 and 7 July 1899, p. 6, Much of *Representative Indians*, the book on which much of his fame today rests, appears to have been written by others.

111. Panikkassery, *palpu*, p. 93.

112. Narayana's obscure early life has been further blurred by hagiography. *Census*, 1931, Vol. I, p. 353, says he was born in August 1856 (the Malabar year ends in mid-August). A. Aiyappan, 'Iravas and Culture Change', p. 151, gives 1854. Nataraja Guru, *The Word of the Guru* (Ernakulam: Paico Publishing House, 1968; first published 1952), p. 254, estimates 1854, though agreeing that the exact date is uncertain. I have generally accepted the account of Narayana's life which Kumaran Asan gave to a meeting of the S.N.D.P. Yogam in 1903 and which was published in the S.N.D.P. magazine, *Vivekodayam*, Vol. I, No.1, 1904, pp. 2-3. I am indebted to K. Prabhakaran, Asan's son, for making the magazine available and translating the article for me. See also Daniel Thomas, *Sree Narayana Guru* (Bangalore: Christian Institute for the Study of Religion and Society, 1965), pp. 7-10, and C.O. Kesavan, *kumaran asan mahakavi* (Trivandrum: Chandra Mohan Press, 1958), pp. 52-3. K.P.K. Menon, *Chattambi Swamigal* (Trivandrum: P.G. Narayana Pillai, 1967), p. 3, says that Narayana learned yoga from the Nair sanyasi, Chattambi, among whose followers was P. Parameswaran. See Nataraja Guru, *Word*, pp. 258-60, for Narayana and Chattambi.

113. LMS, TDC, *Report*, 1896, p. 7, quoting K.P. Thomas.

114. This paragraph is based chiefly on, and quotations are from, Asan's handwritten 'Biographical Note', prepared in 1922 when he was decorated by the Prince of Wales. It is in the Asan Museum at Tonnaykkal, a few miles north of Trivandrum. See also Kesavan, *asan*, pp. 43, 61-5 and 73.
115. *Vivekodoyam*, Vol. I, No. 1, 1904, pp. 22-3.
116. P. Parameswaran to Krishnaswami Rao, 8 Jan. 1903: TGER, Cover No. 8338. The bye-laws are in the same file.
117. *Vivekodayam*, Vol. I, No. 1, 1904, p. 3.
118. *Madras Mail*, 4 June 1904, p.5, and 21 Nov. 1904, p. 5.
119. *Madras Mail*, 7 Feb. 1905, p.3.
120. *Madras Mail*, 8 May 1901, p. 6, and 23 May 1904, p. 3, for accounts of Ezhava commercial enterprise.
121. C. Kesavan, *jivitasamaram* (Kottayam: National Book Stall, 1968), pp. 40 and 42.
122. *Ibid*, pp. 40 and 42.
123. *Madras Mail*, 8 Feb. 1905, p. 3.
124. *Travancore Times*, 1 Feb. 1887.
125. LMS, TDC, *Report*, 1892, p. 8, quoting a catechist, V. Charles Victor.
126. *TAR*, 1895-6, p. 143.
127. *Madras Mail*, 24 April 1900, p. 3.
128. LMS, TDC, *Report*, 1900, p. 16, quoting Rev. W.D. Osbourne.
129. Rev. John Caley to the Secretary, CMS, 29 May 1900: CMSA No. 69 of 1900.
130. Rt. Rev. N. Hodges to the Secretary, CMS, 7 May 1900: CMSA, No. 67 of 1900; Minutes of the Travancore and Cochin CMS Missionary Conference, Kottayam, 27 Feb.-5 March 1900: CMSA, No. 44 of 1900.

## Chapter 7

1. James Thompson, Acting Governor of Madras, to Lord Ampthill, Acting Viceroy, 6 June 1904: India Office Records, Ampthill Papers [hereafter AP], E/233/34/1.
2. R.S. Lepper, Professor of History in the Maharaja's College, to Curzon, 29 June 1903: AP, E/233/17. Lepper claimed that Krishnaswami Rao told friends that he hoped 'for his reward in the next world because he has always hated Europeans'.
3. Ampthill to Curzon, 20 July 1903, quoting a letter from the Resident, G.T. Mackenzie: AP, E/253/8.
4. See the *Malabar Herald*, 12 Jan. and 13 April 1907.
5. Parameswaran Nair, *raman pilla*, pp. 209 and 213.
6. H.B. Grigg, Resident, to the Ch. Sec., 14 Aug. 1890: MRR, MPP, 9 Sept. 1890, G.O. No. 436.
7. Ampthill to Curzon, 15 Sept. 1903: AP, E/233/8. In the same letter, Ampthill ruled out any suggestion that the Maharaja was homosexual.
8. See the *Malabar Herald*, 15 June 1907, for the extravagant marriage ceremonies of Saravanai's granddaughter. The *Herald* claimed he was worth 80 lakhs of rupees, but that seems an exaggeration. For Sankaran Thampi, see the *Madras Mail*, 11 Aug. 1920, p. 6, which reported that he was establishing scholarships valued at Rs.50,000 to celebrate his 60th birthday.
9. Hodges to the Secretary, CMS, 22 Nov. 1902: CMSA, No. 139 of 1902.
10. See the *Madras Mail*, 22 May 1902, p. 4. Ampthill to Lord George Hamilton, Secretary of State for India, 10 Dec. 1902: AP, E/233/7/1.
11. Ampthill to Curzon, 27 Feb. 1902 [in fact, 1903]: AP, E/233/8.
12. Lepper to Curzon, 29 June 1903: AP, E/233/17. The quotations which follow are from this letter.
13. Ampthill to Hamilton, 26 Aug. 1903: AP, E/233/7/2.
14. *oc. clt.*
15. Ampthill to Curzon, 20 July 1903: AP, E/233/8.
16. Ampthill to Curzon, 29 Aug. 1903: AP, E/233/8.

17. Thompson to Ampthill, 20 Oct. 1904: AP, E/233/34/2.
18. Ampthill to Curzon, 21 Feb. 1904: AP, E/233/8.
19. *Loc. cit.*
20. Ampthill to Curzon, 13 March 1904: AP, E/233/8.
21. Maconachie, private secretary to the Maharaja of Mysore, to V.P. Madhava Rao, n.d. [February 1904], published in the *Madras Mail*, 15 March 1906, p. 6. Madhava Rao was angry at the publication of this confidential correspondence. See the *Madras Mail*, 20 March 1906, p. 4. The correspondence does not seem to have survived elsewhere.
22. Parameswaran Nair, *raman pilla*, pp. 213 and 204.
23. *Ibid.*, pp. 213-14. Madhava Rao was said to have been prevented from entering the temple because he was wearing a singlet. He saw Sankaran Thampi's influence behind this humiliation. It is worth pointing out, however, that men are expected to be bare from the waist up to enter the Padmanabhaswami Temple even today. The story seems to survive only in Raman Pillai's biography.
24. *Ibid.*, p. 214.
25. Ampthill to St. John Brodrick, Secretary of State for India, 9 March 1905: AP, E/233/7/2.
26. Madhava Rao to Sir James Bourdillon, Resident in Mysore, 11 July 1904: AP, E/233/34/1.
27. Ampthill to Bourdillon, 24 July 1904: AP, E/233/40.
28. Thompson to Ampthill, 20 Oct. 1904, quoting a letter from the Maharaja: AP, E/233/34/2.
29. The judgement was published in the *Madras Mail*, 1 March 1906, p. 3, which heartily approved of Sadasiva Aiyar's courage. For other examples of the favourites' influence, see P. Thandu Iyer (ed.), *Select Unreported Decisions* (Trivandrum: Subhodini Press, 1913), pp. 316-41. *Madras Mail*, 30 Nov. 1904, p. 3 and 18 May 1905, p. 5. *Malabar Herald*, 26 Aug. 1905 and 9 June 1906.
30. R.C.C. Carr, Acting Resident, 27 Feb. 1907, 'Confidential Report to Accompany the Review of the Travancore Administration Report in M[alabar] E[ra] 1081 (1905-06)': IOR, Crown Representative Records [hereafter CRR], R/1/21/26. At least one of Sankaran Thampi's ploys for 'vengeance' was rather transparent. His brother attacked the High Court in the Popular Assembly in January 1907. *Malabar*

*Herald*, 12 Jan. 1907.

31. Carr, 27 Feb. 1907: CRR, R/1/21/26.
32. Parameswaran Nair, *raman pilla*, p. 377.
33. *Malabar Herald*, 15 June 1907.
34. 'A Syrio-Nair Voice', 'Travancore Politics and Mr. V.P. Madhava Rao', *Madras Review*, Vol. X, 1904, p. 268. The names of the other members of the delegation have not survived. The device of claiming to represent numerous interests recalled the Malayali Memorial.
35. Parameswaran Nair, *raman pilla*, pp. 301-2. Mallur K. Govinda Pillai had just begun to practise law in Trivandrum. See *Nair Service Society Golden Book* (Kottayam: India Press, 1964), pp. 583-4.
36. *Madras Mail*, 29 July 1904, p. 5. The meeting was on 28 July. *Madras Times*, 6 Aug. 1904, p. 3.
37. Madhava Rao to the Dewan Peshkars, 26 Aug. 1904: TGER, TPD, File 113A of 1904.
38. *Madras Times*, 20 Sept. 1904, p. 3.
39. 'A.G.M.', letter to the editor, *Madras Mail*, 13 Sept. 1904, p. 5. 'X', letter to the editor, *Madras Mail*, 21 Sept. 1904, p. 5. A correspondent of *The Hindu*, 4 Nov. 1905, p. 3, thought that the Assembly was creating 'a spirit of patriotism', and helping to 'cement society'.
40. Madhava Rao, Alwaye, to the Ch. Sec., Trivandrum, 2 Oct. 1904[Telegram]: TGER, TPD, File 113A of 1904.
41. TGER, TPD, File 133 of 1904.
42. TGER, TPD, File 133A of 1904. C.V. Raman Pillai was assigned to look after Nair delegates. There were others in charge of the reception of Brahmins; Christians and Muslims; Europeans; and Ezhavas.
43. *Madras Times*, 24 Oct. 1904, p. 7. See also *Madras Times*, 9 Nov. 1904, p. 3.
44. *Madras Mail*, 4 June 1904, p. 5. *Vivekodayam*, Vol. II, 1905. See Nos. 1, 2, 4 and 6 for Vivekananda's speeches and writing translated into Malayalam.
45. *Madras Mail*, 21 Nov. 1904, p. 5.
46. C. Kesavan, *jivitasamaram* (Kottayam: National Book Stall, 1968), pp. 407-11. Kesavan (1891-1969) was Chief Minister of Travancore-Cochin state in 1951-2.
47. *Ibid.*, pp. 409-10.

48. *Ibid*, p. 407,
49. In Malabar the caste which cared for the cocoanut palm was known as Tiyyas. According to Thurston, *Castes*, Vol. VII, pp. 38-40, they claimed higher status than Ezhavas, but in pre-British times, it is unlikely that *avarna* Hindus from Travancore and Malabar often met.
50. *Madras Times*, 11 Jan. 1905, p. 3. *Madras Mail*, 11 and 13 Jan. 1905, both p. 5.
51. *Malayala Manorama*, 21 Jan. 1905.
52. Submission, 26 May 1905: TGER, Travancore Judicial Department [hereafter TJD], File No. 115 of 1905. *Madras Mail*, 7 Feb. 1905, p.3.
53. *Madras Mail*, 4 June 1904, p. 5. Submission, 26 May 1905. *Travancore and Cochin Diocesan Record*, Vol. XV, No. 6, Nov. 1905, p. 90, quoting Rev. W.A. Stephens: CMSA, No. 139 of 1905. N. Rajaram Rao, Acting District Magistrate, Quilon, to the Dewan, 29 Jan. 1905: TGER, TJD, File No. 115 of 1905.
54. *Madras Mail*, 8 Feb. 1905, p. 3, reported that the school boys had been bloodily beaten. The police in Trivandrum received similar accounts from Ezhavas, but the superintendent who saw the boys wrote that their injuries had been grossly exaggerated. Bensley to the Ch. Sec., Trivandrum, 28 Jan. 1905: TGER, TJD, File No. 115 of 1905. Government received the first protest from Ezhavas in a petition from Komathu Kunju Panikkan, the secretary of the Kartigapalli Irava association, received 25 Jan. 1905. A telegram from Kochu Kunju Channar, complaining of the assault on the boys, was received the same day. TGER, TJD, File No. 115 of 1905.
55. Nagam Aiya to Keshava Pillai, 9 Feb. 1905: TGER, TJD, No. 115 of 1905.
56. Madhava Rao to Keshava Pillai, 23 Feb. 1905: TGER, TJD, File No. 115 of 1905.
57. *Madras Mail*, 21 Feb. 1905, p. 3. *Madras Times*, 28 Feb. 1905, p. 3.
58. *Malabar Herald*, 11 March 1905, wrote that Ezhavas had acted 'very injudiciously'. This newspaper was owned by Romo-Syrians and published from Cochin.
59. *Madras Times*, 17 March 1905, p. 3.

60. Kumaran Asan to Madhava Rao, 9 March 1905: TGER, TJD, File No. 115 of 1905.
61. *Satyavadi*, 22 March 1905, in *RNNM*, Malayalam, fortnight ending 31 March 1905. Also, Submissions, 26 May 1905.
62. Quoted in *Madras Mail*, 9 March 1905, p. 3.
63. Editor, *Sujanandhini*, to Madhava Rao, 11 March 1905 [telegram]: TGER, TJD, File No. 115 of 1905. 'Sujanandhini office was burnt by Nairs previous night beg protection [sic]'.
64. Madhava Rao, 'The Dewan's Tour: Inspection Notes', 15 and 16 March 1905: TGER, TPD, File No. 71 of 1905.
65. *Madras Mail*, 21 March 1905, p. 5. The other resolutions proclaimed that 'reports about inter-racial animosity are quite unfounded', that the two communities could improve themselves without harming each other, and that pending cases should be settled out of court. See also the *Malabar Herald*, 25 March 1905.
66. Bensley to Madhava Rao, 3 April 1905: TGER, TJD, File No. 115 of 1905.
67. *Madras Times*, 21 March 1905, p. 3. The cry of anti-Brahmin arson had gone up, along with a number of Brahmin houses, in most hot weathers since the Malayali Memorial. See for example the *Madras Mail*, 19 March 1892, p. 7, 28 April 1894, p. 5, and 23 April 1897, p. 5.
68. *Madras Mail*, 20 March 1905, p. 5.
69. Petition, received 29 April 1905: TGER, Travancore Educational Department [hereafter TED], File No. 255 of 1907. *Malabar Herald*, 22 July 1905. In August, Ezhavas were admitted to the Changanacherry middle school. G.O. 21 Aug. 1905: TGER, TED, File No. 255 of 1907.
70. *Madras Mail*, 8 April 1905, p. 5.
71. *Madras Mail*, 1 July 1905, p. 5. C.O. Kesavan, *asan*, p. 331. Regional Records, *Freedom Movement*, Vol. II, p. 462n.
72. *Travancore Almanack*, 1896, pp. 85-7.
73. *Madras Mail*, 2 Oct. 1901, p.7. 19 Oct. 1904, p. 3 and 10 Oct. 1905, p.5.
74. Raman Pillai's biographer writes that both Krishna Pillai and Raman Pillai had quick tempers and that there were many differences of opinion. Parameswaran Nair, *raman*

*pilla*, p. 74. The *Malabar Herald*, 1 April 1905, saw the 'educated section' of Nairs 'split up into two parties. The so-called stronger section consists of the few officers that grace the higher grades of the Sircar service'. The *Herald* was firm in its support for Krishna Pillai who was said to lead the 'popular' section.

75. Mannath Padmanabhan [Mannath Padmanabha Pillai], *ente jivitasmaranakal*, p. 20.
76. K.C. Kesavan Pillai to M.C. Govinda Pillai, 16 Dhanu 1079 [January 1904], quoted in K.N. Gopala Pillai, 'Kuraccu parayakaryannal' in *Nair Service Society Golden Book*, p. 247.
77. For Ramakrishna Pillai's view of the deportation, see his *ente natukatattal* (Kottayam: Good Shepherd Press, 1948; first published 1910).
78. For translated excerpts from *Swadeshabhimani*, see *Dewan's Note Dated 15th August 1912, on the Suppression of the Swadeshabhimani Newspaper* (Trivandrum: Government Press, 1912), Appendix IV.
79. *Dewan's Note*, p. 4.
80. *Swadeshabhimani*, 5 Nov. 1909 and 2, 4, 7 and 16 March 1910, in *Dewan's Note*, Appendix IV.
81. Parameswaran Nair, *raman pilla*, p. 366. O.M. Thomas, *Under the Knife* (Allahabad: New Book Syndicate, third edition, 1970; first published about 1925), p. 92.
82. *Madras Mail*, 24 Oct. 1906, p. 3. *Malabar Herald*, 3 Nov. 1906. Chaitanya, *Literature*, p. 269. Chaitanya writes that *Parapuram* was published in the 1890s, but the *Herald* was explicit in 1906 that the book had just appeared. It attributed the authorship to Ramakrishna Pillai.
83. *Swadeshabhimani*, 3 and 24 July and 7 and 14 Aug. 1907 in *Dewan's Note*, Appendix IV.
84. *Dewan's Note*, p. 11.
85. *Swadeshabhimani*, 26 Nov. 1909, in *Dewan's Note*, Appendix IV.
86. *Swadeshabhimani*, 2 March 1910, in *Dewan's Note*, Appendix IV.
87. For numerous examples, see *Dewan's Note*, Appendix IV. He charged P. Rajagopalachari with staring at the Maharaja's wife from across a street. *Swadeshabhimani*, 24 Aug. 1910, in *Dewan's Note*, Appendix IV. At the same time,

however, Rajagopalachari's passions seem to have been notorious. See K.P.S. Menon, *Many Worlds* (London: Oxford University Press, 1965), p. 13, for the story of the Dewan, the Brahmin tahsildar's wife and the Syrian prostitute.

88. This was B. Kalyani Amma who edited *Sarada*, the first women's magazine in Malayalam. See the *Madras Times*, 31 Jan. 1905, p. 3. *Madras Mail*, 8 Feb. 1906 and 23 Feb. 1907, both p. 5.
89. *Swadeshabhimani*, 14 June 1909, in *Dewans's Note*, Appendix IV.
90. Mannath Padmanabhan [Pillai], *jivitasmaranakal*, pp. 1-3 and 7-8.
91. *Ibid.*, p. 46. Parameswaran Nair, *raman pilla*, p. 374.
92. *Nair Service Society Golden Book*, pp, 453-5.
93. *Malabar Herald*, 25 March 1905 and 12 Jan. 1907. The Dewan, S. Gopalachari, prevented Changanacherry from speaking on marumakkattayam.
94. [Changanacherry] K. Parameswaran Pillai, 'A plea for Partition in Marumakkathayam Tarawads', *Malabar Quarterly Review*, Vol. VI, No. 2. Sept. 1907, p. 91.
95. *Loc. cit.*
96. *Madras Mail*, 14 Oct. 1903, p. 5.
97. K. Kannan Nair, letter to the editor, *Madras Mail*, 29 Oct. 1903, p. 4. See also Mannath Padmanabhan [Pillai], *jivitasmaranakal*, p. 19.
98. *Malabar Herald*, 28 April 1906, gives an account of Krishna Pillai's efforts.
99. Mannath Padmanabhan [Pillai], *jivitasmaranakal*, p. 19.
100. Parameswaran Nair, *raman pilla*, p. 217. Parameswaran Nair says that the agreement was made in the Malayalam month of Makaram (January-February).
101. *Madras Mail*, 10 Oct. 1905, p. 5, gives an account of the speech, but it was *The Hindu*, 17 Oct. 1905, p. 3, which took exception to the attack on Brahmins.
102. *Malabar Herald*, 14 Oct. 1905.
103. *Malabar Herald*, 4 Nov. 1905. The officers of the united association were all associates of C.V. Raman Pillai.
104. *Malayala Manorama*, 23 Oct. 1905. *Madras Mail*, 6 Nov. 1905, p. 5. *Malabar Herald*, 28 Oct. 1905, found 'in some instances [the session] was pretty nauseating ...'
105. *Malabar Herald*, 5 May 1906.

106. See the *Madras Mail*, 30 Aug. 1906, p. 3. *Malayala Manorama*, 19 Sep. 1906. *Malabar Herald*, 7, 22 and 29 Sept. 1906. The chairman of the Trivandrum meeting was a Syrian Christian vakil, but all the speakers were Nairs.
107. *Malabar Herald*, 24 Nov. 1906.
108. *Madras Mail*, 17 Nov. 1906, p. 5. *Malabar Herald*, 22 Dec. 1906.
109. *Madras Mail*, 21 July 1899, p. 5. Dewan Peshkar, Trivandrum, to the Dewan, 14 Aug. 1900: TGER, Cover No. 7189. *Travancore Almanack*, 1906, pp. 184-5. The Union Club had a few Malayali Kshatriyas, Tamil Sudras and Eurasians.
110. Quoted in the *Madras Mail*, 14 Oct. 1903, p. 5.
111. *Madras Mail*, 2 March 1905, p. 5.
112. *Madras Times*, 21 March 1905, p. 3. *Malayala Manorama*, 8 Nov. 1905. *Madras Mail*, 24 Nov. 1905, p. 3.
113. *Madras Mail*, 24 Nov. 1905, p. 3.
114. R.C.C. Carr, 'Confidential Report', 27 Feb. 1907: CRR, R/1/21/26.
115. *Malabar Herald*, 12 and 19 Jan. 1907. See also the *Madras Mail*, 14 Jan. 1907, p. 3.
116. *Malabar Herald*, 12 Jan. 1907.
117. *Malabar Herald*, 26 Jan. 1907.
118. *Madras Mail*, 17 Oct. 1907, p. 3.
119. Mallur K. Govinda Pillai, one of C.V. Raman Pillai's proteges, spoke in support of the first resolution, and P.K. Keshava Pillai supported the resolution on sambandham and moved the resolution on village associations.
120. *Madras Mail*, 19 Oct. 1907, p. 5.
121. Parameswaran Nair, *raman pilla*, pp. 503-4.
122. *Report of the Marumakathayam Commtitee, Travancore* [hereafter *Maru. Report*] (Trivandrum: Government Press, 1908), p. 1.
123. *Maru. Report*, pp. 1-70, for the recommendations in detail.
124. *Maru. Report*, p. 57. *Madras Mail*, 9 July 1908, p. 3.
125. See Parameswaran Nair, *raman pilla*, pp. 207-8.
126. *Madras Mail*, 15 April 1908, p. 3.
127. 'Travancorean', letter to the editor, *Madras Mail*, 21 Dec. 1907, p. 7.
128. *Maru. Report*, pp. 57 and 59.

129. K. Parameswaran Pillai, 'Plea for Partition', pp. 84-5.
130. *Maru. Report*, p. 25.
131. *Maru. Report*, p. 58, quoting K.G. Parameswaran Menon, B.A., B.L., High Court vakil. For a taravad murder case, see the *Madras Mail*, 23 Nov. 1907, p. 5. Members of a taravad in Quilon district allegedly beat to death another member who persistently demanded partition. Mannath Padmanabhan [Pillai], *jivitasmaranakal*, pp. 93-4, melodramatically describes the murder of two Karanavans. For a suit between nephews and a karanavan in Kottayam district over possession of an elephant, see *Malabar Herald*, 29 April 1905.
132. See the table in Chapter 7 showing the caste of the 361 landholders in Kottayam division paying more than Rs. 100 a year in land tax; 154 were Nairs, and this was the division where Syrian Christians were most numerous. Dewan Peshkar to V.P. Madhava Rao, 28 Sept. 1904: TGER, TPD, File 113A of 1904.
133. *Census*, 1901, Vol. I, p. 208. There were 3,058 Nairs literate in English and 2,638 non-Malayali Brahmins. Christians of all sects had the most English literates (5,529), but many of these were Protestant converts for whom English was sometimes their only valuable resource.
134. In 1909 C. Krishna Pillai brought the interdining question to a head when he demanded that the Thampis, Nairs descended from Kshatriyas, eat with humbler Nairs like himself at a palace feast. The Thampis refused, and Krishna Pillai and his supporters left. *Madras Mail*, 12 Feb. 1909, p. 6. For similar reasons K. Ramakrishna Pillai urged Nairs not to eat at the marriage ceremony of the Maharaja's daughter in 1910. *Swadeshabhimani*, 21, 23 and 26 March 1910, in *Dewan's Note*, Appendix IV.
135. For the split in the Keraliya Nair Samaj, see the *Madras Mail*, 19 Nov. 1915, p. 3.

## Epilogue

1. These were M. Madhavan Thampi, a vakil, P.K. Keshava Pillai of the C.V. Raman Pillai circle, and A. Sri Narayana Thampi, the son of the late Maharaja, Vishakham Tirunal. For their campagin against the partition clause, see the *Madras Mail*, 7 Nov. 1910, p. 3, 7 March 1911, p. 3, 10 April 1911, p. 5, and 9 Feb. 1912, p. 3. Mannath Padmanabhan [Pillai], *jivitasamaranakal*, p. 91, has harsh words for those who successfully opposed the partition clause.
2. Regulartion I of 1088, *Regulations and Proclamations of Travancore,* Vol. V, p. 820.
3. K. Kannan Nayar, 'The Path of the Nayar Society to the "Family Stage",' *Malabar Quarterly Review*, Vol. IV, No. 2, June 1905, pp. 110-1.
4. *Madras Mail,* 18 Feb. 1913, p. 5.
5. *Madras Mail,* 4 May 1914, p. 6.
6. *Madras Mail,* 12 Feb. 1909, p. 6.
7. Mannath Padmanabhan [Pillai], *jivitasmaranakal*, pp. 20-1.
8. K.K. Nair, letter to the editor, *Madras Mail*, 24 Aug. 1922, p. 10. *Census*, 1931, Vol. I, p. 364, noted that only two subdivisions of Nairs were returned in 1931.
9. *Madras Mail*, 19 Nov. 1915, p. 3. Mannath Padmanabhan [Pillai], *jivitasmaranakal*, p. 46. Parameswaran Nair, *raman pilla*, p. 373.
10. *Madras Mail*, 15 May 1916, p. 3.
11. *Madras Mail*, 28 Sept. 1916, p. 3.
12. *Madras Mail*, 18 Aug. 1917, p. 3 and 19 Dec. 1919, p. 6.
13. *Madras Mail*, 3 Nov. 1920, p. 6. Mannath Padmanabhan [Pillai] *jivitasmaranakal*, pp. 97-8.
14. *Madras Mail*, 13 July 1920, p. 6; 20 and 21 April 1923, both p. 4; 18 May 1923, p. 4; 1 Oct. 1924, p. 3; 8 Oct. 1924, p. 8. Mannath Padmanabhan [Pillai], *jivitasmaranakal*, p. 99-102.
15. Regulation II of 1100, especially para. 33, *Regulations and Proclamations of Travancore*, Vol. V, pp. 611-770. Ezhava

and Nanjanad Vellala regulations followed. Similar legislation was passed for Malabar district of British India in 1933. Cochin had passed an act for branch partition in 1920. *Madras Mail*, 11 June 1920, p. 6.

16. *Census*, 1931, Vol. I, pp. 472-3.
17. *Ibid.*, p. 488.
18. See the statistics for alienation of land by Nairs in four taluks of Travancore for four years after the Regulation of 1924, in *channanasseri samelana ripporttu* (Trivandrum: NSS Press, 1930) pp. 192-5. I am indebted to Dr. R.L. Rooksby for pointing out this reference and making his copy of the report available to me.
19. R. Ramakrishnan Nair, *Constitutional Experiments in Kerala* (Trivandrum : Kerala Academy of Political Science, 1964), pp. 17-19.
20. Mannath Padmanabhan [Pillai], *jivitasmaranakal*, p. 37.
21. *Madras Mail*, 5 June 1916, p. 3. Diary of Kumaran Asan, Asan Memorial Museum, Tonnaykkal, Trivandrum district, entry for 14 Feb. 1913.
22. Diary of Kumaran Asan for 11 Oct. 1911, 16 Nov. 1911, 10 Oct. 1912, 16 Feb. 1913, 21 June 1913, 24 June 1913, 19 Jan. 1914.
23. See the *Madras Mail*, 23 May 1910, p. 3; 14 Feb. 1911, p. 6; 30 Dec. 1911, p. 10; 2 Jan. 1912, p. 6; 16 April 1914, p. 3; 24 Feb. 1915, p. 5; 26 May 1916, p. 3; 5 March 1919, p. 6; 7 March 1922, p. 4; 15 Dec. 1922, p. 10.
24. *Madras Mail*, 2 April 1919, p. 3; 8 April 1919, p. 3; 1 March 1920, p. 7. Regional Records, *Freedom Movement*, Vol. II, pp. 279-89.
25. *Madras Mail*, 15 April 1919, p. 4; 7 May 1919, p. 5.
26. *Madras Mail*, 23 Sept. 1921, p. 6. Regional Records, *Freedom Movement*, Vol. II, p. 288.
27. *Madras Mail*, 10 May 1925, p. 6.
28. *Madras Mail*, 21 July 1921, p. 6.
29. Regional Records, *Freedom Movement*, Vol. II, pp. 105-15. *Madras Mail*, 30 Aug. 1921, p. 6; 7 Sept. 1921, p. 6; 15 Sept. 1921, p. 3; 21 Sept. 1921, p. 6; 24 Sept. 1921, p. 7; 26 Sept. 1921, p. 6; 6 Oct. 1921, p. 3; 7 Oct. 1921, p. 3; 19 June 1922, p. 4.
30. *Madras Mail*, 28 Dec. 1921, p. 5.
31. Thomas, *Knife*, pp. 48-54.

32. T. Howard Somervell, *Knife and Life in India* (London: Livingstone Press, 1955; first published 1940), p. 135 for example.
33. *The Hindu*, 31 March 1924. This is in a file of clippings relating to Vaikam which was in the Kerala Secretariat, Trivandrum. Mulam Tirunal died at the height of the campaign in August 1924.
34. *The Hindu*, 20 June 1921, p. 7; 23 June 1921, p. 6.
35. Ramakrishnan Nair, *Experiments*, pp. 17-19.
36. Regional Records, *Freedom Movement*, Vol. II, pp. 354-5.
37. See, for example, *Weekly Secret Bulletin*, Vol. I, No. 14, 31 March 1934, for K. Aiyappan's speech to a meeting at Alleppey. The *Secret Bulletins* were held in the Kerala State Archives, The Fort, Trivandrum, in 1971.
38. Regional Records, *Freedom Movement*, Vol. II, pp. 368-72.
39. *Abstract of Intelligence*, Vol. VI, No. 48, 9 Dec. 1939. The *Abstracts* were held in the Kerala State Archives, the Fort, Trivandrum, in 1971.
40. Changanacherry K. Parameswaran Pillai, 'Plea for Partition', p. 87.
41. See *Census*, 1941.
42. Travancore Unemployment Enquiry Commission, *Report*, 1926, p. 48.
43. Regional Records, *Freedom Movement*, Vol. II, pp. 405-14. Sreedhara Menon, *Survey*, pp. 352-3.
44. T.V. Krishnan, *Kerala's First Communist* (New Delhi: Communist Parrty of India, 1971), pp. 4-5.
45. *The Hindu*, 4 Dec. 1946, p. 7.
46. *The Hindu*, 15 Nov. 1946, p. 6.
47. *The Hindu*, Kerala edition, 10 July 1971; 17 and 23 Aug. 1971.
48. K.R. Krishna Pillai, in *Pattam Thanu Pillai Smaraka Souvenir* (Trivandrum: S.M. Basheer, 1971), p. 27.
49. T.V. Ananthan Nair, 'Some Distinctive Features of Malabar Sociology and their Effects', *Malabar Quarterly Review*, Vol. I, No. 2, June 1902, p. 101.

## Conclusion

1. The evidence suggests that by about 1200 A.D. some groups in Kerala society had become matrilineal and the caste system as it prevailed until the nineteenth century had become established. Kunjan Pillai, *Studies*, pp. 217-66, 284-91, 292-323, 324-69.
2. Uttaram Tirunal to Lord Harris, 21 April 1856: NAI, Government of India, Foreign Department, Foreign Consultations, 4 July 1856, No. 53.
3. Max Weber, *The Theory of Social and Economic Organizations*, ed. Talcott Parsons (New York: The Free Press, 1947), p. 342.
4. U. Balakrishna Nair, 'The Nairs: A Race of Hereditary Fighters', *Malabar Quarterly Review*, Vol. I, No. 2, June 1902, p. 83.
5. *Madras Mail*, 14 March and 9 April 1908, both p. 5.
6. *Madras Mail*, 14 Nov. 1912, p. 3. This was Chitra Tirunal who was invested with ruling powers in 1931. He became Raj Pramukh, or governor, when the state of Travancore-Cochin was formed in 1949. He died in 1991.
7. Logan, *Malabar*, Vol. I, pp. v-vi.
8. Memorandum by K.P. Padmanabha Menon, *Maru. Report*, p. lxv.
9. *Malabar Herald*, 1 April 1905.

*Appendix*

*Travancore population by social categories, 1816-1901.*

| Category | 1816 | % of total pop. | 1836 | % of total pop. | 1854 | % of total pop. | 1875 | % of total pop. | 1891 | % of total pop. | 1901 | % of total pop. |
|---|---|---|---|---|---|---|---|---|---|---|---|---|
| Nambudiris and Pottis | 12,240 | 1.35 | 9,843 | 0.77 | 10,238 | 0.81 | 10,762 | 0.47 | 7,201 | 0.24 | 9,475 | 0.33 |
| Non-Malayali Brahmins | 17,750 | 1.96 | 18,751 | 1.46 | 24,409 | 1.15 | 27,672 | 1.20 | 28,100 | 1.10 | 33,307 | 1.13 |
| Kshatriyas | 5,612 | 0.62 | 1,319 | 0.10 | 1,855 | 0.15 | 1,456 | 0.06 | - | - | 1,575 | 0.05 |
| Ambalavasis | 14,734 | 1.62 | 27,231 | 2.13 | 18,870 | 1.49 | 7,078* | 0.29* | 6,953 | 0.27 | 6,853 | 0.24 |
| Nayars | 274,885 | 30.32 | 365,470 | 28.54 | 384,242 | 30.43 | 440,932 | 19.10 | 483,725 | 18.92 | 520,941 | 17.65 |
| Muslims | 42,058 | 3.54 | 60.291 | 4.71 | 61,861 | 4.90 | 139,905 | 6.06 | 158,823 | 6.21 | 190,566 | 6.46 |
| Christians | 112,158 | 12.37 | 174,566 | 13.64 | 191,009 | 15.13 | 468,518 | 20.29 | 526,019 | 20.60 | 697,387 | 23.62 |
| Artisan and Service Castes | 63,688 | 7.01 | 104,195 | 8.14 | 88,264 | 7.02 | - | - | - | - | - | - |
| Shanars | n.a. | n.a. | 108,515 | 8.47 | 82,861 | 6.56 | 97,730 | 4.23 | 136,611 | 5.34 | 155,864 | 5.28 |
| Iravas | 164,229 | 18.10 | 180,956 | 14.04 | 168,866 | 13.37 | 383,017 | 16.59 | 414,217 | 16.20 | 491,774 | 16.66 |
| Pariahs | 21,532 | 2.38 | 38,625 | 3.02 | 41,360 | 3.28 | 63,688 | 2.76 | 71,786 | 2.80 | 69,974 | 2.37 |
| Slaves | 98,974 | 10.92 | - | - | - | - | - | - | - | - | - | - |
| Pulayas | - | - | 90,598 | 7.08 | 98,766 | 7.82 | 188,916 | 8.18 | 202,616 | 7.92 | 206,503 | 6.99 |
| Total of categories in table | 827,860 | - | 1,180,360 | - | 1,172,601 | - | 1,829,674 | - | 2,036,051 | - | 2,384,219 | - |
| Total pop. | 906,587 | - | 1,280,668 | - | 1,262,647 | - | 2,311,379 | - | 2,557,736 | - | 2,952,157 | - |
| %age literate | - | - | - | - | - | - | 5.74 | - | 10.97 | - | 12.40 | - |

*Figures and percentage are from the 1881 census.

Sources: Ward and Conner, pp.128-9: Horsley, pp. 54-5 and 60-1: *Travancore Census Reports*, 1875, 1891, 1901

# *Glossary*

**Abkari.** *abkari.* The business of making and selling intoxicating drinks and the excise charged thereon.

**Ambalavasi.** *ampalavasi.* A caste of temple servants ranking above Nairs.

**Anandaravan.** *anantaravan.* Male member of a taravad who is not the karanavan. Literally, 'a successor, one who is next of kin or succession'.

**Asan.** *asan.* A village schoolmaster.

**Aurat.** *arattu.* The ceremony in which a temple idol is taken in procession and bathed in a river or at the sea.

**Avarna.** *avaranam.* Used to designate polluting castes including, and below, Ezhavas.

**Ayilyam.** *ayilyam.* The ninth lunar cluster of stars, under which sign Maharaja Rama Varma, who ruled from 1860 to 1880, was born.

**Ayurveda.** *ayurveda.* A system of traditional Hindu medicine.

**Chogan, Chovan, Chegavan.** *cakan, covan, cakavan.* A name by which Ezhavas were known in north Travancore and Cochin.

**Coir.** The fibre of the coconut husk used for making ropes and matting because of its resistance to rot. The word is derived from the Malayalam, *kayaru*, a rope or line.

**Copra.** The dried kernel of the coconut which is pressed to extract oil.

**Desam.** *desam.* A village or small subdivision of the country, ruled in pre-British times by a *desavari, desavali.*

**Devasam.** *devasvam.* Religious endowments and property belonging to temples.

**Dewan.** The chief executive minister of the Maharaja. The term was first used in Travancore in the late eighteenth century. Also spelled 'Diwan', though in Travancore the usual spelling was 'Dewan'.

**Dewan Peshkar.** An officer directly below the Dewan in rank. From 1854, usually a divisional officer.

**Dharma.** *dharmmám.* Virtue; moral and religious merit; duty; charity. In Travancore, the sense of 'charity' was given great emphasis.

**Division.** The largest administrative unit in Travancore, usually presided over by a dewan peshkar. There were four divisions in the latter part of the nineteenth century: Padmanabhapuram, Trivandrum, Quilon and Kottayam.

**Huzur kutcherry.** The Dewan's office.

**Elaya Raja.** *ilaya raja.* The junior raja or heir to the throne.

**Gaddi.** The throne. Literally, a cushion on which the ruler sat.

**Illam.** *illam.* The house of a Nambudiri.

**Ezhava.** *ilavan.* One of the names given to the Malayalam-speaking caste, traditionally concerned with the cultivation of the cocoanut palm. Also known as Chogans in north Travancore and Cochin, and as Tiyyas in British Malabar.

**Jacobite.** A sect of Syrian Christians recognizing, in theory, the authority of one of the West-Asian patriarchs. The name comes from Jacob Baradaeus, a Syrian, whose heresy spread in the eastern Churches in the sixth and seventh centuries.

**Janmam.** *janmam.* A type of land ownership, said to have been created by Parasurama, the legendary founder of Kerala, which conferred absolute tax-free proprietorship on the holder who was usually a Nambudiri Brahmin.

**Janmi.** *janmi.* One who holds *janmam* land.

**Kaliyuga.** According to traditional Hindu reckoning, the fourth and present age of the world.

**Kara.** *kara.* Traditionally, the local organization of Nairs in Travancore; the same as *tara* in northern Kerala. After the imposition of British rule, *kara* came to be used interchangeably with *tara* and *desam* to mean a village.

**Karanavan.** *karanavan.* The eldest male member and manager of a taravad.

**Kathanar.** *kattanar.* A Syrian priest or cleric.

**Kerala.** *keralam.* The Malayalam-speaking region on the South-Western coast of India, separated from Tamil Nadu by the Western Ghats, and made up in British times of Travancore and Cochin states, the British district of Malabar and the southernmost portion of the British district of South Kanara.

**Kudumi** *kutumi.* The tuft of hair worn on the head by Hindus. Malayalis wore it at the front of the head and were thus easily distinguished from Tamils who wore it at the back.

**Kuppayam.** *kuppayam.* A jacket or short smock, the right to wear which was granted to Christian Shanar women in south Travancore in 1829.

**Kutcherry.** A government office.

**Malabar Era (M.E.).** The Kerala system of reckoning the years, which begins in 825 A.D. of the Christian calendar. It is said to be calculated either from the date of the founding of the town of Quilon or the departure for Mecca of the last Perumal emperor of Kerala.

**Mar Thomite.** Name applied to those Syrians who remained with Mar Thomas Athanasius after his defeat in the civil suit over Jacobite property in 1889. The members of this sect had fairly close relations with the agents of the Church Missionary Society.

**Makkattayam.** *makkattayam.* System of inheritance and descent through the male line.

**Marumakkattayam.** *marumakkattayam.* System of inheritance and descent through the female line, a man's legal heirs being the children of his sisters.

**Masnad.** *masnad.* The throne. Literally, the cushion on which the ruler sat.

**Mulam.** *mulam.* The nineteenth cluster of lunar stars, under which sign Maharaja Rama Varma, who ruled from 1885 to 1924, was born.

**Munsiff's Court.** The lowest civil court, presided over by a munsiff.

**Murajapam.** *murajapam.* Literally, 'prayer by regular arrangement'. The sexennial feasting of the Malayali Brahmins in Trivandrum, begun in the eighteenth century by Maharaja Martanda Verma to win over the disaffected Nambudiris. In return for fifty-six days of feasting, tthe Nambudiris offered prayers for the State.

**Nad.** *natu.* The territory of a Nair chief, which was made up of a number of *desams*, in pre-British Kerala.

**Nambudiri.** *namputiri.* A caste of Malayali Brahmins concentrated in north Travancore, Cochin and Malabar District.

**Nambudiripad.** *namputirippatu.* A particularly exalted section of Nambudiris.

**Nair** *nayar.* *Savarna* Hindus who constituted the warriors, landed gentry and yeomen of pre-British Kerala.

**Onam** *onam.* The most important Malayali festival, celebrating the annual return to Kerala of the legendary king, Mahabali, in August-September.

**Para.** *para.* A measure of quantity, or area, of rice. Fixed by the survey and settlement begun in 1883 at 80 cubic inches in capacity, or .14 acres in area.

**Paripalana.** *paripalanam.* Protection, propagation, fostering care. Thus, the Sri Narayana Dharma Paripalana Yogam.

**Pattar.** *pattar.* The name given by Malayalis to non-Malayali Brahmins, especially Smartas.

**Pravratti.** *pravratti.* One or more villages administered by a subordinate government officer called a *pravrattikaran.*

**Samanta.** *samanta.* Small matrilineal caste, claiming higher rank than Nairs but held to be inferior to Kshatriyas. Found in north Travancore, Cochin and Malabar.

**Sambandham.** *sambandham,* Literally, 'connection'. The simple Nair marriage ceremony involving the presentation of a cloth by the man to the woman. In old Kerala it appears that both men and women could have sambandham with more than one person at the same time.

**Savarna.** *savarnnam.* Caste Hindus.

**Shanar.** *cannan.* Tamil-speaking tappers of the palmyra palm in south Travancore, many of whom were converted to Christiianity.

**Sirkar.** *sarkkar* The government.

**Sirkar Pattam.** *sarkkar pattam.* Lands owned by the government and leased out under an irksome tenure. In 1865 absolute ownership was conferred on tenants of sirkar pattam land.

**Tahsildar.** An executive officer presiding over a taluk. The title dated from Munro's Dewanship.

**Tali.** *tali.* The small gold pendant tied by the bridegroom round the neck of the bride at the time of marriage. Both Nairs and Syrians tied the tali. Traditionally, among Nairs the tali-tying was a pre-puberty ceremony or 'mock-marriage'.

**Talikettukalyanam.** *talikkettukkalyanam.* Literally, 'tali tying marriage'. The costly pre-puberty 'mock-marriage' usually performed on a number of Nair girls at the same time. The tali was sometimes tied by a non-Malayali Brahmin. It is disputed whether the man who tied the tali was permitted to consummate the 'marriage'; in most cases, he probably was not.

**Taluk.** The administrative unit beneath a division, presided over by a tahsildar. There were about thirty in Travancore.

**Tara.** *tara.* The local organisation of Nair families in traditional times. The word seems to belong to north Kerala and to equate with *kara* in Travancore.

**Taravad.** *taravatu.* The Nair joint-family; also the house in which it lived.

**Terundakuli.** *teruntakuli.* The ceremony performed on the occasion of a Nair girl's first menses.

**Tirunal.** *tirunal.* The birthday of any person of rank. Thus, Mulam Tirunal—the birthday of the important person born under the sign of Mulam.

**Uriyam.** *uliyam.* Forced labour demanded by the sirkar.

**Uttupura.** *uttupura.* Free feeding houses for Brahmins. The sirkar maintained about 40 of these throughout Travancore.

**Valiya Koil Tampuran.** *valiya kovil tampuran.* The husband of the Senior Maharani of Travancore. Literally, 'elder Kshatriya prince'.

**Viruthi,** *virutti.* Land granted at concessionary rent or tax in return for the performance of certain services.

**Vishakham.** *visakham.* The sixteenth lunar cluster of stars. Thus, Vishakham Tirunal, who was born under that sign, Maharaja from 1880 to 1885.

# *Bibliography*

---


**A. Manuscript Sources**

1. India Office Records, London
   (a) Government Reccords
      Crown Representative Records.
      Madras Political Proceedings.
      Political Despatches from Madras.
   (b) Private Papers.
      Ampthill Papers.
      Curzon Papers.
      Sir Arthur Havelock Papers.
      Lansdowne Papers.
      Wenlock Papers.

2. National Archives of India, New Delhi
   (a) Government of India
      Foreign Consultations.
   (b) Madras Residency Records
      Files.
      Letter Books, Resident to the Dewan, 1840-92.
      Letter Books, Resident to the Madras Government. 1840-92.

3. Kerala Secretariat, Trivandrum
   Travancore Government English Records
      Cover Files, 1820-1905.
      Educational Department Files from 1904.
      General Department Files from 1904.

Judicial Department Files from 1904.
Political Department Files from 1900.
Section Books of Judicial Letters, 1881-1902.
Vaikam Satyagraha Files.

4. Kerala State Archives, The Fort, Trivandrum
   *Weekly Secret Bulletins* and *Intelligence Abstracts*, 1934-40.

5. Congregational Council for World Mission Archives, London.
   London Missionary Society's agents' letters from Travancore.
   Parker Papers, notes intended for use in writing history of the LMS.

6. Church Missionary Society Archives, London
   Agents' letters from Travancore.

7. United Theological College, Bangalore
   CMS, Minutes of Travancore Conferences, No. 39, 1857-66.
   J.A. Jacob, manuscript history of the LMS in Travancore, No. 97.
   LMS, Travancore District Committee, Correspondence, 4 Vols., Nos. 63-6, 1873-1903.

8. Mannanam Monastery Library, near Kottayam, Kerala State
   Manuscript histories.
   Copies of petitions.

9. Diaries
   Diary of N. Kumaran Asan, in the Asan Museum, Tonnaykkal, Trivandrum, Kerala.
   Diary of Fr. Emmanuel Nidhiry, in the possession of Abraham M. Nidhiry, Kuravilangad, Kerala.

## B. Official Publications and Printed Reports

1. British Government
Parliamentry Papers
1810, Vol. V, pp. 13ff.
1812-3, Vol. X, pp. 171ff.
1831-2, Vol. XIV, pp. 1ff.
1859-II, Vol. XXV, pp. 353ff.
1873, Vol. XII, pp. 19ff.

2. Government of India
*Census Report,* 1901.

3. Madras Government
*Census Report*, 1901
*Correspondence Concerning a Riot at Tinnevelly*, 1859
*Madras University Calendars*, 1859-92
*Malabar Special Commission, Malabar Land Tenures, Reports and Appendices*, 3 vols., 1882
*Minute on the Draft Bill Relating to Malabar Land Tenures by Sir Charles A. Turner*, 1885
*Report with Appendices of the Malabar Land Tenures Committee*, 3 vols., 1887
*Report of the Malabar Marriage Commission*, 1891
*Reports on Native Newspapers, Madras*, 1872-1910

4. Travancore Government
*Census Reports*, 1875, 1881, 1891, 1901, 1911, 1921, 1931, 1941.
*Dewan's Note dated 15th August 1912, on the Suppression of the Swadeshabhimani Newspaper*, with appendices, 1912.
*List of Public Servants of the Travancore Government*, 1870-1, 1872-3 and 1893-4.
*Proceedings of the Conference of Peishkars on State Charities, Devaswoms and Purificatory*

*Ceremonies (10th to 14th August 1908)*, n.d. [c. 1912].

(i) *Miscellaneous Papers Relating to Devaswoms and State Charities*, n.d. [c. 1912].

(ii) *Appendix to the Report on State Charities, Exhibits*, n.d. [c. 1912].

*Regulations and Proclamations of Travancore*, 5 vols., 1800-1929.

*Report the of Marumakkathayam Committee, Travancore*, 1908.

*Report of the Revenue Settlement of Travancore, 1883-1911*, 14 vols., compiled by S. Padmanabha Aiyar, 1913.

*Travancore Administration Reports*, 1854-5 to 1908-9.

*Travancore Almanack*, 1851-1910 [originally the *Travancore Calendar;* from 1863, the *Trevandrum Almanack;* from 1881, the *Travancore Almanack*].

*Travancore Government Gazette*, 1863-1905.

*The Travancore Land Revenue Manual*, 5 vols, 1915.

*The Travancore Law Reports*, ed. by P. Thandu Aiyar, Vols. I to XIV, 1880-1900.

5. Cochin Government

*Census Reports*, 1891, 1901.

6. Missionary Societies

CMS, *Annual Report* 1817-75.

LMS, Travancore District Committee, *Annual Report*, 1859-1900.

**C. Newspapers and Perriodicals**

*Friend of Malabar*, 1890-1905.

*The Hindu*, 1887-1908.

*Indian Social Reformer*, 1894-8.

*Indian Statesman*, 1859 and 1861.

*Kerala Society Papers*, 1928-32.

*Madras Athenaeum*, 1848-62.

*Madras Mail*, 1890-1925.

*Madras Standard*, 1886-9.

*Madras Times*, 1889-92, 1903-8.

*Malabar Herald*, 1905-10.
*Malabar Quarterly Review*, 1902-15.
*Malayala Manorama*, 1889-1908.
*Missionary Register*, 1847-59.
*Nasrani Deepika*, 1887-95.
*Travancore and Cochin Diocesan Record*, 1905-10.
*Travancore Times*, 1884-7.
*Vivekodayam*, 1904-10.

## D. Secondary Works

### *1. Manuals, Handbooks and Gazetteers*

**Ananthakrishna Iyer, L.K.** *The Cochin Tribes and Castes*, 2 vols., (Madras: Higginbotham, 1909 and 1912).

**Krishna Aiyer, L.A.** [son of the above] *The Travancore Tribes and Castes*, 3 vols. (Trivandrum: Government Press, 1937-41).

**Innes, C.A.** *Malabar and Anjengo* (Madras: Government Press, 1915).

**Logan, William.** *Malabar*, 2 vols. (Madras: Government Press, 1951; first published 1887).

— *A Collection of Treaties, Engagements and Other Papers of Importance Relating to British Affairs in Malabar* (Madras: Government Press, 1951; reprint of second edition of 1889).

**Nagam Aiya, V.** *The Travancore State Manual*, 3 vols. (Trivandrum: Government Press, 1906).

**Sreedhara Menon, A.** *Trivandrum, Kerala District Gazetteers* (Trivandrum: Government Press, 1962).

— *Quilon, Kerala District Gazetteers* (Trivandrum; Government Press, 1964).

**Thurston, Edgar.** *Castes and Tribes of Southern India*, 7 vols. (Madras: Government Press, 1909).

**Velu Pillai, T.K.** *The Travancore State Manual*, 4 vols. (Trivandrum: Government Press, 1940).

## 2. *Contemporary Books and Articles*

**Abbs, John.** *Twenty-Two Years' Missionary Experience in Travancore* (London: John Snow, 1870).

**Agur, C.M.** *Church History of Travancore* (Madras: S.P.S. [G?] Press, 1903).

**Ananthan Nayar, T.V.** 'Some Distinctive Features of Malabar Sociology and their Effects', *Malabar Quarterly Review*, Vol. I, Nos. 1 and 2, 1902, pp. 76-82, and 98-106.

*Anniversary of His Highness the Maha Rajah's College and High School, Trivandrum, 17th October 1891* (Trivandrum: Government Press, 1891).

**Appadorai Iyer, S.** 'The Nambutiris', *Calcutta Review*, Vol. CVIII, Jan. 1899, pp. 139-47.

— 'The Cherumars of Malabar', *Calcutta Review*, Vol. CX, April 1900, pp. 365-70.

'A Syrio-Nair Voice', 'Travancore Politics and Mr. V.P. Madhava Rao', *Madras Review*, Vol. X, 1904, pp. 256-76.

**Baker, Rev. Henry, Sr.** *A Sermon Preached at Christ Church Cottayam, on the 9th November 1859* (Kottayam: CMS Press, 1860).

**Balakrishnan Nair U.** 'The Nair as Warrior'. *Calcutta Review*, Vol. C, 1895, pp. 375-82.

— 'The Sterner Aspects of Nair Life', *Calcutta Review*, Vol. CIV, 1897, pp. 272-6.

— 'The Origin of the Malabar Nairs', *Calcutta Review*, Vol. CVII, 1898, pp. 111-20.

— 'The Malabar Tenantry and the Improvements Bill. From the Tenants' Point of View', *Calcutta Review*, Vol. CIX, 1899, pp. 123-6.

— 'The First Great Malayalam Novel', *Calcutta Review* Vol. CIX, 1899, pp. 2443-61.

— 'A Travancore State Ceremony', *Calcutta Review*, Vol. CXI, 1900, pp. 330-42.

— 'A Travancore Magician', *Calcutta Review*, Vol. CXIV, 1902, pp. 65-9 and 289-90.

— 'The Nairs: A Race of Hereditary Fighters', *Malabar Quarterly Review*, Vol. I, No. 2, June 1902, pp. 83-97.

**Balfour, Edward.** *On the Influence Exercised by Trees on the Climate of a Country* (London: 1849) [contribution by William Cullen].

**Barbosa, Duarte.** *The Book of Duarte Barbosa*, Vol. II, trans.

M.L. Dames (London: The Hakluyt Society, 1921).

**Blandford, Augusta M.** *The Land of the Conch Shell* (London: Church of England Zenana Missionary Society, n.d. [c. 1901].

**Blunt W.S.** 'Ideas about India', *Fortnightly Review*, Vol. XLIII, Feb. 1885, pp. 234-48.

**Bruce, Henry.** *Letters from Malabar and on the Way* (London: George Routledge and Sons, 1901).

**Buchanan, Francis.** *A Journey from Madras through the Countries of Mysore, Canara and Malabar*, Vol. II (Madras: Higginbotham, 1870).

**Buckland, C.E.** *Dictionary of Indian Biography* (London: Swan, Sonnenschein, 1906).

**Caldwell Rev. R.** *The Tinnevelly Shanars* (London: SPCK, 1850).

**[Caldwell R.C.]** *Chutney Lyrics* (Madras: Higginbotham, 1871).

**Chandu Menon, O.** *Indulekha*, trans. W. Dumergue (Calicut: Mathrubhumi Printing and Publishing Co. Ltd., 1965; first published in English, 1890).

**Chettur K.N.** 'The Nambudiri Brahmins of Kerala', *Calcutta Review*, Vol. CXIII, July 1901, pp. 121-36.

*Copyright Case, The.* (Madras: Lawrence Asylum Press, 1898).

**Cox, John.** *Travancore, Its Present Ruin Shown and the remedy sought in a correspondence with the Government of Madras in the years, 1855-1857* (Nagercoil: LMS Press, 1857).

**Cullen, Lt. Gen. William.** *Napoleon III's Works: Manuel d'artillerie* [from the manuscript of Lt. Gen. W. Cullen] (St. Thomas Mount: Artillery Depot Press, 1853).

— *Memorandum Addressed to the Madras Government on the 5th December 1843* (Trivandrum: 1849).

**Day, Francis.** *The Land of the Perumals, or Cochin, Its Past and Present* (Madras: Gantz Brothers, 1863).

**de Camoens, Luiz.** *The Lusiads*, trans. Leonard Bacon (New York: Hispanic Society of America, 1950).

**Denison, Sir William.** *Varieties of Viceregal Life*, 2 vols (London: Longmans, Green, 1870).

**Drury, Capt. Heber.** 'Notes on an Excursion along the Travancore Backwater', *Madras Journal of Literature and Science*, Vol. III, New Series, Oct.-Dec. 1857, pp. 203-19.

— *Reminiscences of Life and Sports in Southern India* (London: W.H. Allen, 1890).

**Duraiswamy Aiyar, M.P.** 'Raja Sir T. Madhava Rao', *Prominent Tanjoreans,* No. II (Tanjore: G.S. Maniya, 1915).

*An Essay on the Nayar System of Gallantry and Inheritance...* (London: J. Ridgeway, n.d. [c. 1800]).

**Evans, Florence.** 'Mala Vedars of Travancore', *Madras Government Museum Bulletin,* Vol. III, No. 1, 1900, pp. 86-8.

**Fawcett, Fred.** 'Notes on Some of the People of Malabar', *Madras Government Museum Bulletin,* Vol. III, No. 1, 1900, pp, 1-85.

— 'Nayars of Malabar', *Madras Government Museum Bulletin,* Vol. III, No. 3, 1901, pp. 185-322.

**Forbes, James.** *Oriental Memoirs,* 2 vols. (London: Richard Bentley, 1834).

**Gibb, H.A.R. ed.** *Ibn Battuta, Travels in Asia and Africa, 1325-1354* (London: Routledge and Kegan Paul, 1953).

**Gopal Panikkar, T.K.** *Malabar and its Folk* (Madras: Natesan and Co., 1900).

— *Storm and Sunshine. A Novel Illustrative of Malayalee Domestic Life* (Calicut: Norman Printing Bureau, 1916).

**Grant Duff, Sir M.E.** *Notes From a Diary Kept Chiefly in Southern India, 1881-1886,* 2 vols. (London: John Murray, 1899).

**Griffin, Lepel.** 'Indian Princes at Home', *Fortnightly Review,* Vol. XL, Oct. 1883, pp. 482-96.

**Hacker, Rev. I.H.** *A Hundred Years in Travancore* (London: H.R. Allenson, 1908).

— *Kerala, the Land of Palms* (London: London Missionary Society, 1912).

**Harvey, Dr. R.** 'Travancore', *The Indian Magazine and Review,* No. 262, Oct. 1892, pp. 499-506.

**H [awksworth], A.** *Day Dawn in Travancore* (Kottayam: CMS Press, 1860).

**Horsley, W.H.** *Memoir of Travancore* (Trivandrum: Sirkar Press, 1863; first published 1839).

*Indian Statesmen: Dewans and Prime Ministers of Native States* (Madras: G.A. Natesan, 1939).

**Itteyyerah, P.J.** 'Gregorious Bar Ebraya and His Nomo-Canon', *Malabar Quarterly Review,* Vol. I, No. 2, June 1902, pp. 116-23.

**Johnston, Rev. James.** *A Reply to a Letter Addressed by His Highness the Maharaja of Travancore to His Excellency* *the Right Honourable M.E. Grant Duff, Governor of Madras* (London: 7 Adam Street, Strand, 1882).

**Kalyanakrishna Aiyar, T.K.** 'Marriage among the Malayalis', *Malabar Quarterly Review*, Vol. I, Nos. 1 and 2, March and June 1902, pp. 62-74 and 152-67, and Vol. II, No. 4, Dec. 1903, pp. 326-37.

**Kamesvara Aiyar, V.** *Sir A. Sashiah Sastri, K.C.S.I.* (Madras: Srinivasa Varadachari, 1902).

— 'Sir A Sashiah Sastri: A Few Reminiscences', *Malabar Quarterly Review*, Vol. III, No. 2, June 1904, pp. 113ff.

**Kannan Nayar, K.** 'The Nayars', *Malabar Quarterly Review*, Vol. I, No. 2, June 1902, pp. 229-45.

— 'The Nayar Tarwad', *Malabar Quarterly Review*, Vol. I, No. 4, Dec. 1902, pp. 308-16.

— 'The Path of the Nayar Society to the "Family Stage",' *Malabar Quarterly Review*, Vol. IV, No. 2, June 1905, pp. 110-16.

**Karunakara Menon, C.** *A Critical Essay on Sir A. Seshia Sastri K.C.S.I.* (Madras: Thompson and Co., 1903).

**Kelvo Nair, Kookel.** 'Memorandum on the Syrian and Jewish Copper Plates of Malabar', *Madras Journal of Literature and Science*, Vol. IX, New Series, April-Sept. 1859, pp. 30-55.

**Knowles, Rev. John.** 'The Phonetic Alphabet and Vernacular Education', *Calcutta Review*, Vol. LXXIX, 1884, pp. 184-206.

**Kristno Row [Krishna Rao], V.** *A Description of the Administrative System of Travancore in the Year 1844* (Trivandrum: Sirkar Press, 1860).

**Lear, E.** *Indian Journal*, ed. by Ray Murphy (London: Jarrolds, 1955).

**Loti, Pierre.** *India*, trans. G.A.F. Inman (London: T. Werner Laurie, 1913; first published 1906).

**Mackenzie, G.T.** *Christianity in Travancore* (Trivandrum: Government Press, 1901).

**Madhava Rao, Raja Sir T.** *A Conversation on Female Education* (Madras: Ripon Press, 1890).

— *Political Opinions*, ed. by S.C. Srinivasa Charier (Madras: Ripon Press, 1890).

— *Notes on Hindu Astrology* (Trichinopoly: Indian Catholic Truth Centre, 1922; first published 1887).

'The Malabar Onam Festival', *Calcutta Review*, Vol. CIX, Oct. 1899, pp. 19-31.

**Maltby, F.N.** 'Public Works in Travancore', *Madras Journal of Literature and Science*, Vol. VI, New Series, 1860-1, pp. 127-38.

'Mappila Faith and Fanaticism', *Calcutta Review*, Vol. CV, 1897, pp. 212-20.

**Markham, C.R.** 'On the Inland Navigation of Travancore', *Journal of the Royal Geographical Society*, Vol. XXXVI, 1866, pp. 195ff.

'The Marriage System in Malabar', *Calcutta Review*, Vol. XCIX, 1894, pp. 385-98.

**Mateer, Rev. Samuel.** *The Land of Charity* (London: John Snow, 1871).

— *The Gospel in South India* (London: Religious Tract Society, n.d. [c. 1882]).

— *Native Life in Travancore* (London: W.H. Allen, 1883).

— 'Nepotism in Travancore', *Journal of the Anthropological Institute*, Vol. XII, 1883, pp. 288-306.

— 'The Pariah Caste in Travancore', *Journal of the Royal Asiatic Society*, Vol. XVI, New Series, 1884, pp. 180-95.

— 'On Social Reforms among the Nayars of Malabar', *Journal of the Anthropoological Society of Bombay*, Vol. II, 1887, pp. 317-20.

— 'Coinage of Travancore', *Madras Journal of Literature and Science*, Vol. XCIV, 1889, pp. 49-67.

**Moore, Lewis.** *Malabar Law and Custom* (Madras: Higginbotham, 1905).

**Nagam Aiya, V.** *A. Seshia Sastri, 1872-1894. Commemoration Day Celebrations, 1913* (Madras: Law Printing House, 1913).

**Ormsby, W.E.** *Outline of Marumakatayam Law* (Kottayam: CMS Press, 1884).

**Padmanabha Iyer, A.** 'Cultivation of Tapioca in Travancore', *Tropical Agriculturalist*, Vol. XLVII, 1916, pp. 360-2.

**Padmanabha Menon, K.P.** *History of Kerala*, 4 vols. (Ernakulam: Cochin Government Press, 1924-37).

**Padmanabhan Tampi, K.** 'Quilon, an Indian Port of Former Days', *Calcutta Review*, Vol. CXII, April 1901, pp. 201-12.

**Painter Rev. A.W. [F.]** 'On the Hill Arrians', *Journal of the*

*Anthropological Society of Bombay*, Vol. II. 1887, pp. 146-55.

**Parameswaran Pillai, G.** *Representative Men of Southern India* (Madras: Price Current Press, 1896).

— *Representative Indians* (London: Routledge, 1897).

— *London and Paris through Indian Spectacles* (Madras: Vaijayanti Press, 1897).

— *Representative Indians* (London: Thacker, 1902).

— 'A Trip to Travancore: or Dan and I,' *Malabar Quarterly Review*, Vol. II, No. 1, March 1903, pp. 27-40.

**Parameswaran Pillai, [Changanacherry] K.** 'A Plea for Partition in Marumakkathayam Tarawads', *Malabar Quarterly Review*, Vol. VI, Nos. 1 and 2, June and Sept. 1907, pp. 15-29 and 83-91.

**[Pettigrew, Rev. T.]** 'A Retired Chaplain', *Episodes in the Life of an Indian Chaplain* (London: Sampson, Low, Marston, Searle and Rivington, 1882).

**Pharoah and Co.** *A Gazetteer of Southern India* (Madras: Pharoah and Co., 1855).

**Philip E.M.** *A Letter to the Secretary to the Corresponding Committee of the C.M.S., Madras, Re the Syrian Church Endowment* (Kottayam: Malayala Manorama Press, 1902).

— *The Indian Church of St. Thomas* (Nagercoil: London Mission Press, 1950 [written in 1907])

**Ponnambalam Pillai, T.** 'The Morality of the Ramayana', *Malabar Quarterly Review,* Vol. VIII, No. 2, June 1909, pp. 83-7.

*Proceeding of the Trivandrum Museum Society* (Trivandrum: Sirkar Press, 1856).

**Rae, George Milne.** *The Syrian Church in India* (Edinburgh: William Blackwood and Sons, 1892).

**Raman Menon, K.** 'The Scythian Origin of the Nairs', *Malabar Quarterly Review,* Vol. I, No. 2, June 1902, pp. 143-52.

**Raman Pillai, C.V.** *Marthanda Varma (A Historical Romance)*, trans. B.K. Menon (Trivandrum: Kamalalaya Book Depot, 1936).

**Ramanath Aiyar, S.** *Brief Sketch of Travancore, The Model State of India* (Trivandrum: Western Star Press, 1903).

— *The Royal House of Travancore, with a Brief Memoir of H.H. the Maharaja* (Trivandrum: Malabar Mail Press, [1904]).

— *The Problem of Charity in Travancore* (Trivandrum: Malabar Mail Press, 1907).

— *Travancore of Today* (Madras: Oriental Encyclopaedic Publishing Co., 1920).

— *Diwan T. Rama Row* (Trivandrum: Anantha Rama Varma Press, 1926).

— *A History of Travancore* (Madras: Srinivasa Varadachari, 1938).

**Rees, J.D.** 'Prince Albert Victor in Travancore', *Macmillan's Magazine*, May 1890, pp. 71-80.

— *Narratives of Tours in India Made by His Excellency Lord Connemara, 1886-1890* (Madras: Government Press, 1891).

— 'The Daily Life of an Indian Prince', *Macmillan's Magazine*, July 1906, pp. 711-20.

**Richards, Rev. W.J.** 'Notes on the Tandu Palayans of Travancore', *Indian Antiquary*, Vol. IX, 1880, p. 120.

— *The Indian Christians of St. Thomas* (London: Bemrose and Sons, 1908).

**Robinson, William, ed.** *Ringeltaube the Rishi* [letters and journals] (Sheffield: Sheffield Independent Press, 1902).

**Sadasiva Aiyar, T.** '"The Morality of the Ramayana"— A Review', *Malabar Quarterly Review*, Vol. VIII, No. 3, Sept. 1909, pp. 208-15.

**Sankara Menon, K.P.** 'On the Castes of Malabar', *Madras Journal of Literature and Science*, 1878, pp. 172-87.

**Sawyer, A.M.** 'Tapioca Cultivation in Travancore', *Indian Forester*, Vol. XXI, 1895, pp. 290-6.

**Seshagiri Prabhu, M.** 'A Note on the Word Nayar', *Malabar Quarterly Review*, Vol. I, No. 4, Dec. 1902, pp. 347-9.

**Shungoony Menon P.** *A History of Travancore from the Earliest Times* (Madras: Higginbotham, 1878).

**Singh, Prithipal.** 'Raja Sir T. Madhava Rao, K.C.S.I.', *East and West*, Vol. V, April 1906, pp. 366-73.

*Some Noted Indians of Modern Times* (Madras: Christian Literature Society, 1892).

**Sundaram Pillai, P.** *Some Early Sovereigns of Travancore* (Madras: Addison, 1894).

**Thurston, Edgar** 'Miscellania', *Madras Government Museum Bulletin*, Vol. III, No. 1, 1900, pp. 89-92.

'Travancore', *Native States,* No. 1 (n.p., n.d.).

'Travancore and Its Land Tenures', *Calcutta Review*, Vol. CXII, Jan. 1901, pp. 125-35.

*The Travancore Memorials and Counter Memorials* (Madras: Madras Times Press, 1891).

**[Trevelyan, Sir Charles].** 'The Thugs; or, Secret Murderers of India', *Edinburgh Review*, Vol. LXIV, Jan. 1837, pp.357-95.

**[Vishakham Tirunal].** 'A Native Statesman', *Calcutta Review,* Vol. LV, 1872, pp. 225-63.

— *Our Industrial Status* (Benares: Chhannulal, Benares Printing Press, 1880).

— *Observations on Higher Education and the Education of the Masses in India. A Letter Addressed to H.E. the Right Honourable M. E. Grant Duff, Governor of Madras* (Madras: Addison, 1882).

— *A Cursory Notice of Certain Statements in the Rev. J. Johnston's Reply* (Madras: Addison, 1882).

— *Addresses Presented to and Replies Given by His Highness the Maharaja of Travancore during his Tour to Madras in 1883* (Trivandrum: Government Press, 1883).

**Visscher, Jacob Canter.** *Letters from Malabar* (Madras: Gantz Brothers, 1882).

*V.P. Madhava Rao* (Madras: G.A. Natesan, 1918).

**Ward and Conner, Lieutenants.** *Memoir of the Survey of the Travanccore and Cochin States* (Trivandrum: Sirkar Press, 1863; reprinted, 1898).

**Welsh, Colonel James.** *Military Reminiscences*, 2 vols. (London: Smith, Elder, 1830).

**Whitehouse, Rev. T.** *Some Historical Notices of Cochin on the Malabar Coast* (Kottayam: CMS Press, 1859).

— *Lingerings of Light in a Dark Land* (London: Brown and Co., 1873).

**Wyndham Quin, Lady Eva.** 'A Trip to Travancore', *The Nineteenth Century*, Vol. XXXI, Feb. 1892, pp. 255-62.

### *3. Anthropology and Sociology since 1910*

**Abraham C.M.** 'Social Change among the Nairs of Kerala', *Journal of Social Research,* Vol. VIII, 1965, pp. 25-34.

**Aiyappan, A.** 'Nayar Polyandry', *Man,* Vol. XXXII, 1932, No. 99, pp. 78-9.

— 'Polyandry', *Man*, Vol. XXXII, 1932, No. 337, p. 288.

— 'Fraternal Polyandry in Malabar', *Man in India*, Vol. XV, 1935, pp. 109-18.

— 'Iravas and Culture Change', *Madras Government Museum Bulletin*, Vol. V, No. 1, 1943.

— *Social Revolution in a Kerala Village* (New York: Asia Publishing House, 1965).

**Alexander, K. C.** *Social Mobility in Kerala* (Poona: Deccan College Postgraduate and Research Institute, 1968).

**Anantakrishna Ayyar, L.K.** *Anthropology of the Syrian Christians* (Ernakulam: Cochin Government Press, 1926).

— 'Nayar Polyandry', *Man*, Vol. XXXII, 1932, No. 320, pp. 269-70.

**Bailey, F.G.** *Caste and the Economic Frontier* (Manchester: Manchester University Press, 1957).

— *Tribe, Caste and Nation* (Manchester: Manchester University Press, 1960).

— 'Closed Social Stratification in India', *European Journal of Sociology*, Vol. IV, No. 1, 1963, pp. 107-24.

**Bala Ratnam, L.K., ed.** *Anthropology on the March* (Madras: 1963).

**Beteille, Andre.** *Caste, Class and Power* (Berkeley: University of California Press, 1965).

— *Castes, Old and New* (Bombay: Asia Publishing House, 1969).

**Dube S.C.** 'Caste Dominance and Factionalism', *Contributions to Indian Sociology,* New Series, No. II, Dec. 1968, pp. 58-81.

**Dumont, Louis,** 'Marriage in India', *Contributions to Indian Sociology*, No. V, 1961, pp. 75-95.

— 'Les marriages Nayars comme fait indiens', *L'Homme*, Vol. I, No. 1, 1961, pp. 11-36.

— 'Marriage and Status, Nayar and Newar', *Contributions to Indian Sociology*, No. VII, 1964, pp. 80-98.

— *Homo Hierarchicus* (London: Paladin, 1972).

**Elliott, Carolyn M.** 'Caste and Faction among the Dominant Caste: Reddis and Kammas of Andhra', in Rajni Kothari, ed., *Caste in Indian Politics* (Bombay: Orient Longmans, 1970), pp. 129-71.

**Epstein, T. Scarlett.** *Economic Development and Social Change in South India* (Manchester: Manchester University Press, 1962).

**Evans-Pritchard, E.E. and Fortes, M., eds.** *African Political Systems* (Oxford: Oxford University Press, 1962). pp. 272-96.

**Gardner, Peter M.** 'Dominance in India: A Reappraisal', *Contributions to Indian Sociology*, New Series, No. II, Dec. 1968, pp. 82-97.

**Ghurye, G.S.** *Caste and Class in India* (Bombay: Popular Book Depot, 1950).

**Gough, Kathleen.** 'Changing Kinship Usages in the Setting of Political and Economic Change among the Nayars of Malabar', *Journal of the Royal Anthropological Institute*, Vol. LXXXI, 1952, pp. 71-88.

— 'Incest Prohibitions and Rules of Exogamy in Three Matrilineal Groups of the Malabar Coast', *International Archive of Ethnography*, Vol. XLVI, 1952, pp. 82-105.

— 'Female Initiation Rites in the Malabar Coast' *Journal of the Royal Anthropological Institute*, Vol. LXXXV, Part 2, 1955, pp. 45-80.

— 'Criteria of Caste Ranking in South India', *Man in India*, Vol. XXXIX, No. 2, April-June 1959, pp. 115-26.

— 'Cults of the Dead among the Nayars', in Milton Singer, ed., *Traditional India: Structure and Change* (Philadelphia: Folklore Society, 1959).

— 'The Nayars and the Definition of Marriage', *Journal of the Royal Anthropological Institute*, Vol. LXXXIX, 1959, pp. 23-34.

— 'The Hindu Jajmani System', *Economic Development and Cultural Change*, Vol. IX, No. 1, Oct. 1960, pp. 83-91.

— 'Indian Nationalism and Ethnic Freedom', in D. Bidney, ed., *Concept of Freedom in Anthropology* (The Hague: Mouton, 1963). pp. 170-207.

— 'Village Politics in Kerala', *Economic Weekly*, 20 and 27 Feb. 1965, pp. 363-72 and 413-20.

— 'Kerala Politics and the 1965 Elections', *The International Journal of Comparative Sociology*, Vol. VIII, 1967, pp. 55-88.

— 'Literacy in Kerala', in Jack Goody, ed., *Literacy in Traditional Societies* (Cambridge: Cambridge University Press, 1968), pp. 132-60.

— 'Political Party Conflict in a Kerala Village', in Pradhan et al., eds., *Anthropology and Archaeology* (London: Oxford University Press, 1969), pp. 127-41.

**Hutton, J.H.** *Caste in India* (Bombay: Oxford University Press, 1969; first published 1946).

**Kapadia, K.M.** *Marriage and Family in India* (Calcutta: Oxford University Press, 1955).

**Klausen, Arne Martin.** *Kerala Fishermen and the Indo-Norwegian Project* (London: Allen and Unwin, 1956).

**Koshy, Ninan.** *Caste in the Kerala Churches* (Bangalore: Christian Institute for the Study of Religion and Society, 1968).

**Krishna Iyer, L.A.** *Social History of Kerala*, 2 vols. (Madras: Book Centre Publications, 1970).

**Luiz, A.A.D.** *Tribes of Kerala* (New Delhi: Bharatiya Adimjati Sevak Sangh, 1962).

**Marriott, McKim.** 'International and Attributional Theories of Caste Ranking', *Man in India*, Vol. XXXIX, No. 2, 1959, pp. 92-107.

**Mayer, Adrian C.** *Land and Society in Malabar* (Bombay: Oxford University Press, 1952).

— 'The Dominant Caste in a Region of Central India', *Southwestern Journal of Anthropology*, Vol. XIV, 1958, pp. 407-27.

**Mencher, Joan P.** 'Changing Familial Roles among South Malabar Nayars', *Southwestern Journal of Anthropology*, Vol. XVIII, 1962, pp. 230-45.

— 'Growing Up in South Malabar', *Human Organization*, Vol. XXII, 1963, pp. 54-65.

— 'The Nayars of South Malabar', in M.F. Nimkoff, ed., *Comparative Family Systems* (Boston: 1965), pp. 163-91.

— 'Namboodiri Brahmins: An Analysis of a Traditional Elite in Kerala', *Journal of Asian and African Studies*, Vol. I, 1966, pp. 183-96.

— 'Kerala and Madras: A Comparative Study of Ecology and Social Structure', *Ethnology*, Vol. V, No. 2, April 1966, pp. 135-71.

— 'The Namboodiri Brahmins of Kerala', *Natural History*, Vol. LXXV, May 1966, pp. 14-21.

**Mencher, Joan P. and Goldberg, Helen.** 'Kinship and Marriage Regulations among the Namboodiri Brahmins of Kerala',

*Man*, New Series, Vol. II, No. 1, March 1967, pp. 87-106.

**Miller, Eric J.** 'Caste and Territory in Malabar', *American Anthropologist*, Vol. LVI, 1954, pp. 410-20.

— 'Village Structure in North Kerala', in M.N. Srinivas, ed., *India's Villages* (London: Asia Publishing House, 1960), pp. 42-55.

**Oomen T.K.** 'The Concept of Dominant Caste: Some Queries', *Contributions to Indian Sociology*, New Series, No. IV, Dec. 1970, pp. 73-83.

**Orenstein, Henry.** 'Caste and the Concept, "Mahratta", in Maharashtra', *Eastern Anthropologist*, Vol. XVI, 1963, pp. 1-9.

**Panikkar, K.M.** 'Some Aspects of Nair Life', *Journal of the Royal Anthropological Institute*, Vol. XLVIII, 1918, pp. 254-93.

**Rao, M.S.A.** 'Caste in Kerala', *Sociological Bulletin*, Vol. IV, No. 2, 1955, pp. 122-9.

— *Social Change in Malabar* (Bombay: Popular Book Depot, 1957).

**Srinivas, M.N.** 'The Social System of a Mysore Village', in McKim Marriot, ed., *Village India* (Chicago: University of Chicago Press, 1955), pp. 1-36.

— 'The Dominant Caste in Rampura', *American Anthropologist*, Vol. LXI, 1959, pp. 1-16.

— *Caste in Modern India* (Bombay: Asia Publishing House, 1962).

**Yalman, Nur** 'On the Purity of Women in the Castes of Ceylon and Malabar', *Journal of Royal Anthropological Institute*, Vol. XCIII, Part 1, Jan-June 1963, pp. 25-58.

### *4. Writings on Post-Independence Kerala Politics*

**Ahmed, Bashiruddin.** 'Communist and Congress Prospects in Kerala', *Asian Survey*, Vol. VI, July 1966, pp. 393-5.

**Bhagat, K.P.** *The Kerala Mid-Term Election of 1960* (Bombay: Popular Book Depot, 1960).

**Fic, Victor M.** *Kerala: Yenan of India* (Bombay: Nachiketa Publications, 1970).

**Gnanadason, Jonathan N.** 'The Nagercoil By-Election, January 1969. A Study of the Congress Campaign', *Economic and Political Weekly,* 16 Aug. 1969, pp. 1337-40.

**Hardgrave, Robert L.** 'Caste in Kerala: A Preface to the Elections', *Economic Weekly,* 21 Nov. 1964, pp. 1841-7.

— 'Caste and the Kerala Elections', *Economic Weekly,* 17 April 1965, pp. 669-72.

**Hunter, Thelma.** 'Indian Communism and the Kerala Experience of Coalition Government, 1967-69', *Journal of Commonwealth Political Studies,* Vol. X, No. I, 1972, pp. 45-70.

**Julien, Francois.** 'Strategies communistes au Kerala', *France-Asie,* No. 1, 1968, pp. 59-82.

**Klatt Werner.** 'Caste, Class and Communism in Kerala', *Asian Affairs,* Oct. 1972, pp. 275-87.

**Mankekar, D.R.** *The Red Riddle of Kerala* (Bombay: Manaktalas, 1965).

**Ramakrishan Nair, R.** *How Communists Came to Power in Kerala* (Trivandrum: Kerala Academy of Political Science, 1965).

**Ramakrishnan Nair, R. and Nossiter, T.J.** 'The Rules of the Electoral Game: Kerala 1970', *South Asian Review,* Vol. IV, No. 3, 1971, pp. 202-12.

**Turlach, Manfred.** *Kerala* [in German with a 4-page English summary] (Wiesbaden: Otto Harrassowitz, 1970).

**Velayudhan, R.** *Kerala: The Red Rain Land* (New Delhi: Indian Institute of Social Affairs, 1958).

**Zinkin, Taya** *Reporting India* (London: Chatto and Windus, 1962), pp. 148-203.

## 5. *Other Works in English*

**Asher, R.E.** 'Three Novelists of Kerala', in T.W. Clark, ed., *The Novel in India* (London: George Allen and Unwin, 1970), pp. 205-34.

— 'The Beginnings of the Tamil Novel', in T.W. Clark, ed., *The Novel in India* (London: George Allen and Unwin, 1970), pp. 179-204.

*Baker Memorial Girls' High School 150th Anniversary Souvenir, February* 1971 (Kottayam: CMS Press, 1971).

**Bernstorff, Dagmar.** 'Eclipse of "Reddy-Raj"? The Attempted Restructuring of the Congress Party Leadership in Andhra Pradesh', *Asian Survey*, Vol. XIII, No. 10, Oct. 1973, pp. 959-79.

**Bowring, Lewin B.** *Haidar Ali and Tipu Sultan* (Oxford: Clarendon Press, 1899).

**Brown, L.W.** *The Indian Christians of St. Thomas* (Cambridge: Cambridge University Press, 1956).

**Chacko, K.C.** *Father Kuriackos Elias Chavara* (Mannanam: Vice-Postulator, Cause of Fr. Kuriackos Elias, 1968).

**Chandrasekhara, N.S.** *Dewan Rangacharlu* (New Delhi: Publications Division, 1968).

**Cheriyan, P.** *The Malabar Syrians and the Church Missionary Society, 1816-1840* (Kottayam: CMS Press, 1935).

**Chettur, Usha.** 'Nayars', *Illustrated Weekly of India*, 20 Dec. 1970, pp. 8-15.

**Chidambara Aiyar, K.** *Martanda Varma* (no place of publication, 1914).

**Cowen, D.V.** *Flowering Trees and Shrubs in India* (Bombay: Thacker, 1952).

**Crowley, Eileen.** *Champion of the Outcaste. Lester Hooper of Travancore* (London: Highway Press, 1941).

**Dalton, Eira.** *Who Thee By Faith. The Biography of Bishop Jacob* (Kottayam: CMS Press, 1962).

— *The Baker Family in India* (Kottayam: CMS Press, 1963).

— *Fellow Workers with God* (Kottayam: CMS Press, 1966).

**Das Gupta, Ashin.** 'The Makings of Travancore', *Bengal Past and Present*, Vol. LXXX, July-Dec. 1961, pp. 124-48.

— *Malabar in Asian Trade, 1740-1800* (Cambridge: Cambridge University Press, 1967).

**Derrett, J.D.M.** *Introduction to Modern Hindu Law* (Bombay: Oxford University Press, 1963).

**Embree, Ainslie T.** *Charles Grant and British Rule in India* (London: George Allen and Unwin, 1962).

**Executive Committee,** The All-Travancore Joint Political Congress. *Travancore: The Present Political Problem* (Calicut: Empire Press, 1934).

**Frykenberg, Robert E.** *Guntur District, 1788-1848* (Oxford: Clarendon Press, 1965).

**George, Grace.** 'Missionary Activity and the Syrian Christians in Kerala', in Brian Holmes, ed., *Educational Policy and the Mission Schools* (London: Routledge and Kegan Paul, 1967).

**George, K.M.** *A Survey of Malayalam Literature* (London: Asia Publishing House, 1968).

**George, T.J.S.** *Krishna Menon* (London: Jonathan Cape, 1964).

**Gopalan, A.K.** *Kerala, Past and Present* (London: Lawrence and Wishart, 1959).

**Gopala Pillai, N.** *Kerala Pratiba. Sanskrit Renderings of Some Malayalam Poems* [with English notes on poets] (Trivandrum: Government Press, 1965).

**Hardgrave, Robert L. Jr.** 'The Breast-Cloth Controversy: Caste Consciousness and Social Change in Southern Travancore', *Indian Economic and Social History Review*, Vol. V, No. 2, June 1968, pp. 171-87.

— *The Nadars of Tamilnad* (Berkeley: University of California Press, 1969).

**Hatch, Emily Gilchrist.** *Travancore* (Madras: Oxford University Press, 1933).

**Hjejle, Benedicte.** *Slavery and Agricultural Bondage in South India in the Nineteenth Century* (Copenhagen: Scandinavian Institute of Asian Studies, 1967).

**Hunt, W.S.** *The Anglican Church in Travancore and Cochin*, 2 vols. (Kottayam: CMS Press, 1920 and 1933).

**Ittiavira, Verghese.** *Social Novels in Malayalam* (Bangalore: Christian Institute for the Study of Religion and Society, 1968).

**Jayaraman, R.** 'Indian Emigration to Ceylon: Some Aspects of the Historical and Social Background of the Emigrants', *Indian Economic and Social History Review*, Vol. IV, 1967, pp. 319-59.

*A Judicial History of Travancore* (Trivandrum: V.V. Press Branch, 1932).

**Keay, Rev. F.E.** *A History of the Syrian Church in India* (Madras: SPCK in India, 1938).

**Kershaw, K.L.** 'Mundakayam', in *United Planters' Association of South India Commemoration Volume* (Coonoor: UPASI, 1951) pp. 210-28.

**Koshy, M.J.** 'Genesis of Political Consciousness in Travancore', *Journal of Indian History*, Vol. L, Part 1, April 1972, pp. 173-83.

**Krishna Ayyar, K.V.** *The Zamorins of Calicut* (Calicut: Norman Printing Bureau, 1938).

**Krishnamurti, N.** 'The Ruler of Travancore', *Asiatic Review*, Vol. XXVIII, 1932, pp. 129-32.

**Krishnan, T.V.** *'Sakhavu' Krishna Pillai–Kerala's First Communist* (New Delhi: Communist Party Publications, 1971).

**Kumar, Dharma.** *Land and Caste in South India* (Cambridge: Cambridge University Press, 1965).

**Kunjan Pillai, Elamkulam P.N.** *Studies in Kerala History* (Kottayam: National Book Stall, 1970).

**Kuruvilla, K.K.** *A History of the Mar Thoma Church and its Doctrines* (Madras: Christian Literature Society for India, 1951).

**Langley, W.K.M., ed.** *Century in 'Malabar. The History of Peirce Leslie and Co. Ltd.* (Madras: Madras Advertising Company, 1962).

**Lengyel, Emil.** *Krishna Menon* (New York: Walker and Company, 1962).

**Leonard, John G.** 'Politics and Social Change in South India: A Study of the Andhra Movement', *Journal of Commonwealth Political Studies*, Vol. V, No. 1, March 1967, pp. 60-77.

**Madhavan Nair, K.** *The Malabar Law Digest (1862-1941) and Acts* (Calicut: Vilasam Press, 1941).

*Mannath Padmanabhan: Creator of Miracles.* (Changancherry: Nair Service Society, 1966).

*Manufacturer and East India Merchant, 1750-1950* [history of James Finlay, Co.]. (Glasgow: Jackson Son and Co., 1951).

**Mathew, I.** 'Travancore a Hundred Years Ago: The Times of the Ranees and Colonel Munro', *Kerala Society Papers*, No. II. Series 8, Nov. 1931, pp. 123-33.

**Matthen, C.P.** *I Have Borne Much* (Madras: Ampthill, 1951).

**Mehta, B.N.** 'A Little Known Event in the History of Travancore', *Journal of Indian History*, Vol. XXIX, 1951, pp. 27-31.

**Menon, K.P.K.** *Chattambi Swamigal: The Great Scholar-Saint of Kerala* (Trivandrum: P.G. Narayana Pillai, 1967).

**Menon, K.P.S.** *Many Worlds* (London: Oxford University Press, 1965).

— *C. Sankaran Nair* (New Delhi: Publications Division, 1967).

**Namboodiripad, E.M.S.** *Kerala : Yesterday, Today and Tomorrow* (Calcutta: National Book Agency, 1967).

**Nair, Balakrishna N.** *The Dynamic Brahmin* (Bombay: Popular Book Depot, 1959).

**Narayanan, Kattumadan.** 'Nambudiris', *Illustrated Weekly of India*, 5 March 1972, pp. 8-15.

**Natarajan, Dr. P.** *The Way of the Guru* (Geneva: Sufi Publishing Association, 1931).

— [Nataraja Guru] *The Word of the Guru* (Ernakulam: Paico Publishing House, 1968; first published, 1952).

**Nidhiry, Abraham M.** *Father Nidhiry* (Kottayam: Deepika Press, 1971).

**Nightingale, Pamela.** *Trade and Empire in Western India* (Cambridge: Cambridge University Press, 1970).

**Nilakanta Sastri, K.A.** *A History of South India* (Madras: Oxford University Press, 1958).

**Noble, Willian A., ed.** *Kerala State, India: Bibliography* [European languages] (Columbus, Mo.: Geography Department, University of Missouri, 1970).

**Padmanabha Iyer, A., ed.** *Souvenir of the Sashtiabdapurti of Sachivothama Sir C.P. Ramaswami Aiyar K.C.I.E. Ll. D., Dewan of Travancore* (Trivandrum: ARV Press, 1940).

**Pakenham-Walsh, Herbert.** 'The Christa Sishya Sanga', *East and West Review*, Vol. III, 1937, pp. 277-38.

**Panikkar, K.M.** *Indian States and the Government of India* (London: Martin Hopkinson, 1932).

— *A History of Kerala, 1498-1801* (Annamalainagar: Annamalai University, 1960).

**Parameswara Aiyer, Ulloor S.** 'Colonel Munro', *Kerala Society Papers*, No. II, Series 7, 1931, pp. 41-70.

**Parameswaran Nair, P.K.** *History of Malayalam Literature*, trans. E.M. Venniyoor (New Delhi: Sahitya Academy, 1967).

**Patterson, Maureen L.P.** 'Caste and Political Leadership in Maharashtra. A Review and Current Appraisal', *Economic Weekly*, 25 Sept. 1954, pp. 1065-7.

**Perumal, Nilkan.** *A Hindu Reformation* (Madras: R.J. Ram and Company, 1937).

**Placid, Rev. Fr. and Job, K.E.** *The Syrian Church of Malabar* (Changanacherry: St. Joseph's Orphanage Press, 1938).

**Pillai, M.R.G.** 'Some Eminent Nayars', *Illustrated Weekly of India*, 20 Dec. 1970, pp. 24-7.

**Pillai, V.R. and Panikkar, P.G.K.** *Land Reclamation in Kerala* (Bombay: Asia Publishing House, 1965).

**Podipara, P.J.** *The St. Thomas Christians* (London: Darton, Longman and Todd, 1970).

**Pothan, S.G.** *The Syrian Christians of Kerala* (Bombay: Asia Publishing House, 1963).

**Qanungo, Bhupen.** 'A Study of British Relations with the Native States of India', *Journal of Asian Studies*, Vol. XXVI, No. 2, Feb. 1967, pp. 251-65.

**Raja, P.K.S.** *Medieval Kerala* (Annamalainagar: Annamalai University Historical Series, 1953).

**Rajaraja Varma Raja, M.** *A Tribute to a Great Soul. Being a Pen Picture of Professor A.R. Rajaraja Varma, M.A.* (Trivandrum: Reddiar Press, 1935).

**Rajayyan, K.** 'Kerala Varma and the Malabar Rebellion', *Journal of Indian History*, Vol. XLVII, Part II, Dec. 1969, pp. 549-57.

**Rajkumar, N.V.** *Evolution and Working of the Government in Travancore* (Cochin: Gosri Scout Printing Service, 1940).

**Ramakrishnan Nair, R.** *Constitutional Experiments in Kerala* (Trivandrum: Kerala Academy of Political Science, 1964).

**Ramaswami Aiyar, Sir C.P.** *Pen-Portraits, Essays and Addresses* (Bombay: Hind Kitabs Limited, 1948).

**Ravindran, T.K.** *Cornwallis System in Malabar* (Calicut: Paraspara-sahayi Co-op Printing and Publishing Works, 1969).

**Regional Records Survey Committee.** *The History of the Freedom Movement in Kerala*, 2 vols. (Trivandrum: Government Press, 1970 and 1972).

**Rudolph, Lloyd I. and Susan Hoeber.** 'Rajputana under British Paramountcy: The Failure of Indirect Rule', *Journal of Modern History*, Vol. XXXVIII, No. 2, June 1966, pp. 138-60.

— *The Modernity of Tradition* (Chicago: University of Chicago Press, 1967).

— 'The Political Modernization of an Indian Feudal Order: an Analysis of Rajput Adaptation in Rajasthan', *Journal of Social Issues*, Vol. XXIV, No. 4, 1968, pp. 93-127.

*[R.]Sankar Shashtiabdapurthi Commemoration Volume.* (Quilon: R. Sankar Shashtiabadapurthi Celebrations Souvenir Committee, 1969).

**Sergeant, Philip W.** *The Ruler of Baroda* (London: John Murray, 1928).

**Shea, T., Jr.** 'Barriers to Economic Development in Traditional Society: Malabar, A Case Study', *Journal of Economic History*, Vol. IX, 1958, pp. 504-22.

**Slater, Gilbert, ed.** *Some South Indian Villages* (London: Oxford University Press, 1918).

*S.N.D.P. Yogam Golden Jubilee Souvcnir.* (Quilon: S.N.D.P. Yogam, 1953).

**Somasundaram Pillai, S.A.** *Dr. T.M. Nair, M.D.* (Madras: 1920).

**Somervell, T. Howard.** *Knife and Life in India* (London: Livingstone Press, 1955; first published, 1940).

**Sreedhara Menon, A.** *A Survey of Kerala History* (Kottayam: National Book Stall, 1967).

**Sreedhara Variar, K.** *Marumakkathayam and Allied Systems of Law in the Kerala State* (Cochin: The Author, 1969).

**Stephen, P.L.** *Bishop Alexander Chulaparambil* (Kottayam: Catholic Mission Press, 1969).

*Story of Manorama.* (Kottayam: Malayala Manorama, 1968).

**Stuart Smith, T.G.** 'The Ezhava Movement in Travancore', *East and West Review,* Vol. II, 1936, pp. 333-40.

**Subramanian, K.R.** *The Maratha Rajas of Tanjore* (Madras: Huxley Press, 1928).

**Subramania Sastri, K.R.** *The Domestic Law of Kerala* (Madras: Tata Printing Works, 1921).

**Suntharalingam, R.** 'The Madras Native Association: A Study of an Early Indian Political Organization,' *Indian Economic and Social History Review*, Vol. IV, No. 3, Sept. 1967, pp. 233-53.

— 'The "Hindu" and the Genesis of Nationalist Politics in South India, 1878-1985', *South Asia,* No. 2, Aug. 1972, pp. 64-80.

**Tandon, Prakash.** *Punjabi Century* (Berkeley: University of California Press, 1968).

**Thandu Iyer, P. ed.** *Select and Unreported Decisions* (Trivandrum: Subhodini Press, 1913).

**Thomas, Daniel.** *Sree Narayana Guru* (Bangalore: Christian Institute for the Study of Religion and Society, 1965).

**Thomas. O.M.** *Under the Knife* (Allahabad: New Book Syndicate, revised edition, 1970).

**Tisserant, Eugene.** *Eastern Christianity in India,* trans. E.R. Hambye (London: Green, 1957).

**Trevelyan, Humphrey.** *The India We Left* (London: Macmillan, 1973).

**Varghese, T.C.** *Agrarian Change and Economic Consequences* (Bombay: Allied Publishers, 1970).

**Velu Pillai, T.K.** *A History of Travancore* (Trivandrum: Ananta Rama Varma Press, 1935).

**Watts, M.E.** 'Travancore', *Asiatic Review,* Vol. XXVI, 1930, pp. 228-32, 591-8 and 725-40.

**Weber, Max.** *The Theory of Social and Economic Organization,* ed. Talcott Parsons (New York: The Free Press, 1947).

**Woodcock, George.** *Kerala* (London: Faber & Faber, 1967).

**Working Committee of the Travancore State Congress.** *Travancore Today; Her Struggle for Freedom* (Cochin: Union Press, 1938).

## *6. Manuscripts and Theses*

**Buehner, Andrew John.** 'An Enquiry into Some Major Factors of European Efficiency in the Tropics with Special Reference to Missionaries in the Travancore-Cochin State', Ph. D. thesis in sociology for the University of Travancore, 1950.

**Copland, Ian F.S.** 'Imperial Authority in the Indian States: 1858-1921', M.A. thesis in history for the University of Western Australia, 1966.

**George, Dr. K.M.** 'Asan', manuscript.

**Gustafson, Donald Rudolph.** 'Mysore: 1881-1902, The Making of a Model State', Ph.D. thesis history for the University of Wisconsin, 1969.

**Rooksby, R.L.** 'Tribe, Caste and Association in India', mimeographed paper for the Seminar on South Asian Politics and History, Australian National University, n.d.

**Shahani, Savitri Jivatram.** 'A Comparative Study of Traditional Political Organization of Kerala and Punjab', Ph.D. thesis in anthropology for the School of Oriental and African Studies, University of London, 1965.

**Taylor, Dorothy.** 'The Story of the Fort Girls' Mission High School, Trivandrum, Kerala State, India', manuscript, 1964.

## *7. Malayalam*

**Bailey, Rev. Benjamin.** *Malayalam-English Dictionary* (Kottayam: Gurunadhan Press, 1970; first published, 1846).

**Balakrishna Pillai, U., ed.** *Nair Service Society Golden Book* (Kottayam: India Press, 1964).

*cannanaseri: sammelanaripporttu.* (Trivandrum: NSS Press, 1930).

**Gopala Pillai, K.N.** '*kuraccu palayakaryannal*', in *Nair Service Society Golden Book* (Kottayam: India Press, 1964), pp. 247-50.

**Gundert, Rev. H.** *guntartt nighantu* (Kottayam: Vidyarti Mitram Press, 1972; first published, 1872).

**Kesavan, C.** *jivitasamaram* (Kottayam: National Book Stall, 1968).

**Kesavan, C.O.** *mahakavi kumaran asan* (Trivandrum: Chandra Mohan Press, 1958).

**Padmanabhan [Pillai], Mannath.** *ente jivitasmaranakal* (Trivandrum: NSS Press, n.d. [c. 1957])

**Palakkunnel, Fr. Mathew.** *nalagamam,* ed. P.J. Sebastian (Changanacherry: Bastian's Publications, 1972).

**Panikkassery, Velayudhan.** *da.palpu* (Trichur: Current Books, 1970).

**Parameswaran Nair, P.K.** *si. vi. raman pilla* (Kottayam: National Book Stall, 1959; first published, 1948).

*Pattam Thanu Pillai Smaraka Souvenir.* (Trivandrum: S.M. Basheer, 1971).

**Ramakrishna Pillai, K.** *ente natukatattal* (Kottayam: Good Shepherd Press, 1948; first published, 1910).

# *Biographical Notes*

---

**Asan, N. Kumaran** (1873-1924). Ezhava. Father was a trader. Studied in village schools and later learned Sanskrit. Accountant for a merchant. Spent two years with Sri Narayana Guru, q.v., at Aruvipuram, 1892-4. Studied Sanskrit in Bangalore, Calcutta and Madras under sponsorship of Dr. Palpu, q.v., 1895-9. Secretary, S.N.D.P. Yogam, 1903-19. Married a cousin of Palpu, 1918. Member of Popular Assembly, 1911. Perhaps the greatest modern Malayalam poet. Drowned in a boat accident.

**Athanasius, Mar** (1818-77). For a time the supreme authority over the Jacobite Syrians, and, in effect, the founder of the Mar Thomites. Educated at CMS College, Kottayam, where he learned English, and at Bishop Corrie's School, Madras. Won encouragement from CMS by presenting himself as a reformer. To Antioch in 1843 and claimed to have been consecrated bishop by the Patriarch. Recognised by the Travancore sirkar as supreme head of Travancore Jacobites, 1852. Opposition arose around Mar Dionysius, q.v., who was consecrated by the Patriarch of Mardin, 1865. Sirkar withdrew recognition of Athanasius, 1876, and told parties to go to the courts. Athanasius was succeeded by his cousin, Mar Thomas Athanasius, who founded the Mar Thomite Church after losing civil suits with Mar Dionysius, 1889. Thomas Athanasius died in 1893 and was succeeded by his brother, Mar Titus.

**Ayyappan Pillai, P.** (c. 1857-1907), Nair. Born at Trivandrum. Educated Maharaja's College and High School; FA, 1974; BA, 1880. Teacher; assistant professor in Maharaja's College; headmaster of Trivandrum Vernacular High School; inspector of schools; Educational Secretary, about 1903. Ayyappan Pillai's Trivandrum home provided a meeting place for young educated Nairs in the 1870s and 1880s. Published a pamphlet, 'Raja Keshava Dass and His Times', in 1889 in which he glorified the eighteenth century Nair Dewan. Member of the Malayali Social Union and the Malayali Sabha. Signed the Malayali Memorial. Presided over the meeting of the Keraliya Nair Samaj in Trivandrum during the Assembly session in October 1905.

**Bailey, Rev. Benjamin** (1791-1871). Yorskhire woolstapler. Ordained in Church of England, 1815. To Travancore, 1816. Established a press and cast his own Malayalam type in the 1820s. Compiled and published the first Malayalam-English dictionary, 1846. Retired from Travancore, 1850. Brother, Joseph (d. 1840), was a CMS missionary in Ceylon.

**Baker Family.** CMS missionaries. Rev. Henry Baker, Sr. (1793-1866) came to Travancore in 1818 as a member of 'mission of help' to the Syrian Christians. Wife started girls' schools. Six sons and five daughters, many of whom remained in south India. George and William became planters in Travancore. Rev. Henry Baker, Jr. (1819-78), the eldest son, was also a missionary in Travancore, working chiefly among the hill tribes east of Kottayam. His only son, H.W. Baker (d. 1899), was a planter in Travancore, and his three daughters, Mary (d. 1901), Annie (d. 1912) and the redoubtable Isabel (d. 1939 at 92), carried on the girls' schools established by their grand-mother and mother.

**Chandy, Rev. Jacob, Sr.** (c. 1825-70). CMS Syrian. Educated CMS College, Kottayam. Catechist; deacon, 1847; first CMS Syrian to be ordained, 1851. His diaries, 1850-9, in the CMSA, London, describe his travels and give an almost unique view of Travancore society. Father of Rev. Jacob Chandy, Jr., who became an archdeacon in 1906.

**Chattambi Swami** (1853-1924). Nair. Father a non-Malayali Brahmin. Ascetic and holyman who tried to break the Brahmin hold on the performance of religious ceremonies. Attacked caste and associated with Ezhavas, including Palpu's brother, P. Parameswaran. Said to have taught yoga to Sri Narayana Guru, q.v. Claims about the relative merits of the two men have often led to acrimony between Nairs and Ezhavas.

**Cox, Rev. John** (1811-95). LMS missionary. To Travancore, 1837. Most aggresssive of the later LMS agents. Campaigened for converts' rights in the 1850s and dabbled freely in local politics. Attacked the Travancore sirkar in *Madras Athenaeum* under the pseudonym 'Not the Last'. First wife died, 1857; he retired from the mission when he married a Shanar convert in 1861 and raised another family. Became a planter and started 'Black Rock Estate' in the hills behind Nagercoil where one of his descendants was living in 1975. Employed Christians on his estates. Joined the Salvation Army, 1890, and went to Ceylon; thrown from his horse and forced to return to 'Black Rock'.

**Cullen, Lieutenant-General William** (c. 1787-1862). A Scot. Commissioned in the artillery, 1804; to India, 1805. Never returned to Britain. Commissary-General, about 1835. Resident in Travancore, 1840-60. Retired in Travancore, 1860. His amours were notorious. Buried in Alleppey.

**Devasagaim, P.D.** (1822-84). Second generation LMS Shanar convert. Born Nagercoil and educated in Nagercoil Seminary. To Ceylon briefly, 1842, and again, 1850, for nine years. Became wealthy as manager of coffee estates. Opened his own estate in Travancore, 1859. Supervised Madhava Rao's and Vishakham Tirunal's estate. Church benefactor, and while coffee flourished, probably the wealthiest LMS adherent. Built the first two-storey Christian house in Nagercoil. His wife's nephew, P.C. Joseph, founded the *Travancore Times*.

**Dionysius, Mar** (1832-1909). Educated at home. Sent to Mardin, 1862, to be consecrated in oppossition to Mar Athanasius, q.v. Consecrated by Patriarch of Mardin,

1865, and returned to compete with Mar Athanasius for control of the Jacobite church. Won civil suit against Athanasius's successor, 1889, and took control of churches and endowments. Romo-Syrians hoped that he would eventually bring his followers into communion with Rome, but it was the Anglican bishop whom he saw most frequently before his death.

**Gopalachari, S.** (c. 1850-?). Vaishnavite Brahmin. Vakil in Madura. Sub-judge, Madura, 1885; later district judge of Tinnevelly, whence he came to Travancore as Dewan, 1906-7. His choice showed the difficulty in finding able Indians willing to risk their careers in Travancore. The course proved too rough for him, and he resigned prematurely.

**Govinda Pillai, A.** (1849-1924). Nair. Born at Trivandrum. Matriculation, High School, Trivandrum, 1866; FA, 1867; BA, Presidency College, Madras, 1869. Teacher in Maharaja's College and High School, Trivandrum, where he taught Thanu Pillai, Raman Pillai, K.K. Kuruvila, q.v., and others. BL, 1874. Munsiff and district judge in Nagercoil, 1870s and early 1880s. High court judge temporarily, 1889. Dewan peshkar, Padmanabhapuram, about 1893. High Court judge, about 1898. Acting chief justice, 1905. Retired, 1908. Presided over Malayali Sabha meetings, but was careful not to identify himself too closely with the Sabha. President of the Marumakkattayam Committee, 1908. Dewan Bahadur, about 1910. Legislative Council, 1904-8.

**Gregorious, Mar** (1847-1902). Jacobite Bishop of Niranam and advocate of western-style education for Jacobites. Regarded as the most likely successor to Mar Dionysius whom he predeceased. Presided over Counter-Memorial meeting at Alleppey in June 1891.

**Hannyngton J.C.** (c. 1837-95). Last class from Haileybury; to India, 1857. Judge of Salem. Resident in Travancore for a total of about ten years between 1878 and 1892. Settled the Travancore-Cochin boundary, 1886. According to a Governor of Madras, Lord Wenlock, he was a good hunter and fisherman. According to a collector of Malabar, William Dumergue, he was a bad Resident.

**Kerala Varma,** Valia Koil Tampuran (1845-1914). Kshatriya. Married to the Senior Rani, 1859; no children. Chairman of the Book Committee, 1867-72, and again in late 1880s and 1890s. Imprisoned at Alleppey, 1875-80, for writing scurrilous letters to Ayilyam Tirunal. Released by Vishakham Tirunal, 1880. While in prison, wrote his most famous Malayalam poem, 'The Peacock Messenger'. A leading member of the Bhasha Poshini Sabha which encouraged Malayalam literature; sometimes referred to as 'the father of modern Malayalam prose'. Member of Legislative Council, 1891-4. Guardian of the adopted Ranis, about 1900.

**Keshava Pillai, V.I.** (c. 1858-1908). Nair. Educated at Maharaja's College and High School, Trivandrum; BA, 1879. Teacher; head clerk in the palace office; tahsildar and magistrate; assistant to the dewan peshkar, Trivandrum, 1892; dewan peshkar, 1899. Agent for a number of the Maharaja's trips outside Travancore. Six years on the Legislative Council. Member of Malayali Sabha; signed Malayali Memorial. Implicated in the bribery case of 1906, but not so deeply as C.M. Madhavan Pillai, q.v.

**Koshi, Archdeacon K.** (1825-99). CMS Syrian. Deacon, 1856; ordained, 1859; archdeacon, 1885, first Indian archdeacon in Anglican Church; honorary doctor of divinity, 1891. Revised the Malayalam translation of the New Testament. Translated *Pilgrim's Progress* and *Holy War* into Malayalam. Author of Malayalam tracts and stories.

**Krishna Pillai, C.** (1852-1916). Nair. Born at Trivandrum. Educated Maharaja's College and High School; BA, 1875. Teacher and headmaster, Trivandrum. School inspector, about 1882; transferred to central and northern range of schools, 1887, allegedly because of his strong views about Brahmin dominance of the sirkar service. Moving spirit of the Malayali Sabha which he tried to popularise during his itinerancies; collected signatures for the Malayali Memorial in the same way; signed the Memorial. Tried to maintain the Malayali Sabha in the 1890s; founded Travancore Nair Samaj, a collection of mofussil organisations, 1903. This became the Keraliya

Nair Samaj, 1905, but split in November 1915, ostensibly over the question of taravad partition. He campaigned for inter-dining among Nairs and abolition of subcaste distinctions. Patronised Mannath Padmanabha Pillai, Changanacherry K. Parameswaran Pillai and K. Ramakrishna Pillai, q.v.

**Krishna Rao V.** (1811-57). Brahmin. Born Masulipatam. Partly educated, and later employed, by missionaries. Hired by Cullen, q.v., then Commissary General, 1835. Accompanied Cullen to Travancore, 1840, but dismissed at Maharaja's insistence. Reappointed Dewan at Cullen's urging, 1847, and held the post until his death. Continuously attacked by the missionaries for inefficiency, corruption and oppression, but invariably received Cullen's public support, although in private Cullen chided him.

**Krishnaswami Rao, K.** (1845-1923). Desastha Brahmin. Matriculate. In British service in Nellore, 1864; sheristadar, 1867; disttrict munsiff, 1870; sub-judge of Kakinada, 1883. Chief Justice of Travancore, 1884-98. Dewan, 1898-1904. Retired to Madras.

**Kunchukrishna Panikkar, M.** (c. 1857-1903). Nair. Educated Maharaja's College and High School, Trivandrum; BA, 1879; BL; sirkar service. Member of the Malayali Social Union and the Malayali Sabha. Assistant to the dewan peshkar, Kottayam, 1900; district judge, 1903.

**Kunhi Raman Nair, T.** (c. 1850-1903). Nair. BA, BL. From a Malabar taravad near Cannanore. First-grade munsiff in British service; came to Travancore about 1883. Member of the Malayali Sabha; admirer of Sankara Subbaiyer's dewanship. High Court judge, about 1885. Brother of T.V. Anantan Nair, munsiff of Calicut.

**Kuruvila. K.K.** (c. 1855-1916). Jacobite Syrian whose parents had some contact with CMS. Wealthy, landowning family. Matriculation, CMS College, Kottayam, 1872; FA, Maharaja's College, Trivandrum, 1873; Bachelor of Civil Engineering, Madras, 1877. In Travancore public works department. Active in Travancore and Cochin Christian Association from 1898. First Syrian member of Legislative Council, about 1897. Father of K.K.

Lukose, High Court judge, who married Mary Poonen, q.v.

**Logan, William** (1841-1914). A Scot. To India, 1861. Collector of Malabar for many years. Acting Resident in Travancore, 1883-4. Resigned, 1888. Wrote the 2-volume manual, *Malabar*. Perhaps the greatest of the British antiquarians interested in Kerala.

**Macaulay, Colonel Colin** (1759-1836). A Scot. Brother of Zachary Macaulay. To India, 1775. Four years a prisoner of Tipu Sultan in Seringapatnam. Resident in Travancore 1800-9. A vice-president of the CMS until his death. M.P. for Saltast, 1828-30.

**Mackenzie, G.T.** (c. 1849-?). Judge of Coimbatore. Resident in Travancore, 1899-1904. A Protestant who converted to Catholicism while in India. Regarded by Curzon and Ampthill as most inept. Wrote *Christianity in Travancore*, a monograph which was incorporated into the *Travancore State Manual*.

**Madhava Rao, Raja Sir T.** (1828-91). Desastha Brahmin. Born Kumbakonam. Father, Ranga Rao, and uncle, Venkata Rao, were Dewans of Travancore. Educated in Madras High School under E.B. Powell, 1841-6. To Travancore as tutor to the princes, 1849. Deputy peshkar, 1853. Acting Dewan on death of Krishna Rao, q.v., 1857; confirmed, 1858; resigned, 1872. Knighted, 1866. Dewan of Indore, 1873-5; Baroda, 1875-82. Refused appointments to the Viceroy's Legislative Council at least twice. First cousin, T. Rama Rao, q.v., Dewan of Travancore, 1887-92. Died in Madras.

**Madhava Rao, V.P.** (1850-1934). Desastha Brahmin. Born Tanjore. Not related to Raja Sir T. Madhava Rao. Educated at Kumbakonam College under W.A. Porter; BA, 1869. Mysore service, 1870; headmaster of royal school; collector of Shimoga; inspector-general of police, 1892; revenue commissioner and member of council, 1902-4. Dewan of Travancore, 1904-6, a post he took to oblige the Madras government. Established Sri Mulam Popular Assembly. Opened many schools to Ezhavas. Dewan of Mysore, 1906-9; Baroda, 1914-6.

**Madhavan Pillai, C.M.** (c. 1858-1904). Nanjanad Vellala. Born Vaikam. Educated partly at the Ernakulam College; completed his studies at the Maharaja's College, Trivandrum; BA, 1879. Member of the Malayali Social Union. Attache in huzur cutcherry, 1880; palace office; assistant to the dewan peshkar, Padmanabhapuram, 1890; huzur deputy peshkar, 1900; dewan peshkar of Kottayam at his death. Member of Malayali Sabha; signed Malayali Memorial. Bribery case in the Travancore High Court in 1906 revealed him to have been closely involved with T. Sankaran Thampi, q.v., in some shady dealings.

**Mamen, Archdeacon Oomen** (1830-1904). CMS Syrian. Educated in Rev. Joseph Peet's English School, Mavelikara, from 1839; CMS College, Kottayam, 1847. Itinerant evangelist, 1852; ordained, 1856; archdeacon, 1902, succeeding K. Koshi, q.v. Also a landholder.

**Mead, Rev. Charles** (1792-1873). LMS missionary. Trained as a printer. Ordained, 1816, as a Methodist after an Anglican upbringing. In Travancore, 1817, at Kolachel. Aggressively championed Shanar converts in 1820s. To England, 1836-8, and returned with five new missionaries, among them Rev. John Cox, q.v. Feuded with Latin Catholics and the sirkar, 1840s. Married a 19-year-old Paraya convert as his third wife in 1851 and was forced to resign by the other missionaries. To Trivandrum where Cullen made him manager of the government press and supervisor of schools. Retired, 1870, and died in Trivandrum. Fathered 21 children, founded the Nagercoil Seminary and established the first press in Travancore, 1820.

**Munro, Colonel John** (c. 1770-1858). A Scot. To India, 1790. Resident in Travancore, 1810-9; Dewan, 1811-4. Patron of the CMS from 1820 until his death. Encouraged the missionaries in Travancore. His son, U. V. Munro (d. 1844) was in Travancore service, as was his grandson, J.D. Munro (d. 1895) who helped to open the hills east of Kottayam for planting.

**Nagam Aiya, V.** (1850-1917). Smartha Brahmin. 'A courtly old gentleman who probably never did an honest day's work in his life', according to one Resident. Born Tinnevelly and brought to Trivandrum as a child. Family had moved in and out of Travancore since eighteenth century; one forbear said to have been murdered by Velu Thampi. Matriculation, 1866; FA, 1867; BA, 1870; all from Maharaja's College and High School, Trivandrum; first student to do full BA course in Trivandrum. In Dewan's office, 1870; teacher; tahsildar. Conducted censuses of 1875, 1881 and 1891. Deputy peshkar, 1880; dewan peshkar of Trivandrum, 1883: later, of Quilon. In charge of revenue survey and settlement, 1892. On deputation to write *Travancore State Manual*, 1903. Member of Legislative Council, 1892-9; 1905-8. Six times acting Dewan, and Mulam Tirunal's choice for the Dewanship in 1904. Retired, 1908.

**Nanu Pillai, N.** (1827-86). Nair. Born at Neyyoor in what is now Tamil Nadu. Father a Nair. Educated at Neyyoor mission school, Nagercoil Seminary, and Free School, Trivandrum. Clerk in Resident's office until about 1861 when he entered sirkar service as assistant police sheristadar. Dewan peshkar, about 1865. Acting Dewan, 1872. Appointed Dewan at Ayilyam Tirunal's insistence, 1877, and asked to resign by Vishakham Tirunal within months of his becoming Maharaja in 1880. Died in Trivandrum. Two of his brothers were in sirkar service, and his son, N. Raman Pillai, who was later excise commissioner and secretary to the Marumakkattayam Committee, was expelled with G. Parameswaran Pillai, q.v., in 1882.

**Narayana Guru, Sri** (c. 1855-1928). Ezhava. Born near Trivandrum. Learned Malayalam, Tamil and Sanskrit in a village school. Studied in a Sanskrit school, about 1877-81. Was married against his will, but eventually left his wife. Parents died, 1884, and he wandered as a sanyasi. Started temple at Aruvipuram, near Neyyattinkara, 1887. The temple acquired property, 1893. Arranged with Palpu, q.v., for education of Kumaran Asan, q.v., 1894. Aruvipuram Temple Yogam established, 1899; S.N.D.P. Yogam, 1903, with Sri Narayana as president. Travelled extensively in Kerala to found temples. Recommended emphasis on education for Yogam, 1917. Took no part in Vaikam satyagraha, 1924-5, but lent encouragement.

**Neelacunda Pillai, Kavalam** (c. 1855-1905). Nair. Wealthy landlord. Vakil, but retired early. Gave financial backing to Malayali Memorial; member of Malayali Sabha. President of Travancore Nair Samaj of C. Krishna Pillai, q.v., 1903. Presided over reconciliation meeting between Nairs and Ezhavas in Quilon, 1905. Financed reclamation of land around Vembanad Lake. Legislative Council, 1888-91.

**Nidhiry, Father Emmanuel** (1842-1904). Romo-Syrian. Learned English at a school sponsored by his father in their village, Kuravilangad, near Kottayam. Wealthy landowning family with a tradition of providing priests. Also studied at CMS College, Kottayam; knew Malayalam, Tamil, Sanskrit, Syriac and English. Deacon, 1861, Secretary to the administrator of the Cranganore and Cochin dioceses, 1861-73. Ordained, 1875. Campaigned against schismatics, 1876-82. Tried to win over Jacobites to Rome, 1886-9. Founded and edited *Nasrani Deepika*. 1887. On friendly terms with Hindus and Protestants. Agitated for Indian bishops for Romo-Syrian dioceses. Member of Bhasha Poshini Sabha. Advocate of English education. Vicar-General, Kottayam diocese, 1889; resigned, 1892, over disputes with European hierarchy, which forced him to withdraw from Travancore and Cochin Christian Association, 1903. Wrote Malayalam poetry; widely esteemed as an ayurvedist. Supported the Malayali Memorial but did not sign it; his brother was a member of the delegation which met the Dewan.

**Padmanabha Menon, K.P.** (1857-1917). Nair. Matriculation, Ernakulam High School and Maharaja's College, Trivandrum, 1874; eventually, BA and BL. Son of P. Shankunni Menon, q.v., and brother of K.P. Sankara Menon, q.v. Madras High Court vakil. Signed Malayali Memorial. Returned to Travancore, 1890s, as a vakil. Member of Marumakkattayam Committee, 1908. Author of *History of Kerala*, 4 vols.

**Padmanabha Pillai, Mannath** ['Mannam'] (1878-1970). Nair. Born Changanacherry in a poor taravad; father a Nambudiri. Educated in village school and up to lower examination in sirkar vernacular schools. Appointed schoolmaster in 1893-4, by C. Krishna Pillai, q.v. Teacher-training course, Trivandrum, 1900. Left teaching and passed vakil examination, 1905. Follower of C. Krishna Pillai, in Keraliya Nair Samaj. Founded Nair Service Society, 1914, and became full-time organizer, 1915. General Secretary of N.S.S. for nearly 50 years. Joined Travancore State Congress, May 1947. Led 'liberation struggle' against Communist government of Kerala, 1959. Dropped 'Pillai' caste name in 1950s and became Mannath Padmanabhan.

**Parameswaran Pillai, Changanacherry K.** (1877-1940). Nair. Father a Nair. Orphaned at about twelve. Matriculated in Trivandrum, 1892; FA and BA, and taught in Fort Vernacular School; Helped by C. Krishna Pillai, q.v. BL. Delegate to Popular Assembly, 1907. Published 'A Plea for Partition in Marumakkathayam Tarawads', 1907. Follower of C. Krishna Pillai in contests with C.V. Raman Pillai. President of Nair Service Society after K. Kelappan Nair. Judge of Travancore High Court, 1927. In Travancore State Congress 1938-9 and briefly lost his government pension. Leading advocate of partition and piloted Nair Act of 1924 through Legislative Council.

**Parameswaran Pillai G.** (1864-1903). Nair. Father a non-Malayali Brahmin. Forced to flee Travancore, 1882, for writing anonymous articles in the *Cochin Argus* attacking the Dewan. BA, Presidency College, Madras, 1888. Attacked T. Rama Rao, the Dewan, q.v., in the *Madras Standard*, 1887-90. Translator, Madras High Court. Helped organize Malayali Memorial. Editor, *Madras Standard*, 1890s. In England with Dr. T.M. Nair, 1897. Lost suit brought against him for plagiarism, 1898; convicted of defamation, 1899. Publicised Ezhava grievances, 1894-7. Secretary for the Madras session of the Congress, 1894. Temperance worker. In England, 1899-1902; called to the bar. Died of tuberculosis in Quilon. Said to have been offered a judgeship by the sirkar when he returned to Travancore shortly before his death. Sometimes referred to as 'the father of political agitation in Travancore'.

**Palpu Dr. P.** (1863-1950). Ezhava. Born at Trivandrum. Father learned English from missionaries; one branch of the family converted to Christianity. P. Velayudhan, Palpu's elder brother, first Ezhava admitted to Maharaja's College, Trivandrum, about 1873. Palpu matriculated there, about 1883. Was refused admission to the medical class in Trivandrum; studied medicine in Madras. Rejected for employment in Travancore; in British service about 1890 and Mysore service, 1891. Signed Malayali Memorial. Organised Ezhava petitions to the Travancore sirkar, 1895 and 1896. Sponsored education of Kumaran Asan, q.v. Helped found SNDP Yogam, 1903, and was leading supporter for many years after.

**Parapanad, Raja of** (?-1900). Kshatriya. Born and raised in Travancore but lived most of his life on family property in Malabar. Member of the Malabar Marriage Commission, 1891. Member of Travancore Legislative Council, 1894-7. Member of committee set up to study Thanu Pillai's marriage bill, 1896. Opposed a marriage law, although in 1891 he had appeared to favour one when on the Malabar Marriage Commission.

**Peet, Rev. Joseph** (1802-65). CMS missionary. Ordained 1832. In Travancore, 1833. Most belligerent of CMS agents. Aimed at conversion of Ezhavas, Nairs and Brahmins, and did not encourage accessions from the slave castes. His most celebrated Brahmin convert, Justus Joseph, later led the heretical Six Years' Movement. Deeply involved in local politics, Peet's goal was 'delivering my people from political bondage'. He felt that 'Hinduism, like its sire Buddhism and its own child Popery, carries within itself the elements of its own destruction'. His intolerance helped to provoke the break with the Syrians which began in 1836 and which gentler spirits, like Henry Baker, Sr. and Bailey, would have gladly avoided.

**Poonen Dr. E.** (c. 1859-1916). CMS Syrian. Nephew of T.C. Poonen, q.v., and father of Mary Poonen, (Lukose), q.v. Partly educated at CMS College, Kottayam. Medical degree from Aberdeen, 1880s. In Travancore Medical Department. Surgeon at Alleppey, 1885; later, in charge of General Hospital, Trivandrum. Retired, 1914.

**Poonen (Lukose), Mary** (1886-1976). Daughter of Dr. E. Poonen. First Malayali woman graduate, 1909; first Malayali woman to study in Britain where she did medical degrees in London and Dublin, 1909-16. Married K.K. Lukose, son of K.K. Kuruvila, q.v., 1917. Director of Travancore Medical Department, 1924, and member of Legislative Council.

**Poonen T.C.** (1847-1901). CMS Syrian. Matriculation, CMS College, Kottayam, and Government Provincial School Calicut, 1864; FA, Presidency College, 1866; BA, 1869. In England, 1869-72; called to bar from Inner Temple; first Malayali to study in England. Failed to get work in Travancore. Vakil, Tellicherry. District judge, Cochin, about 1876-94. Retired to Kottayam and started a bank which failed. President of Travancore and Cochin Christian Association, 1898. Legislative Council, 1899-1901.

**Rajagopalachari, Sir P.** (c. 1860-c. 1925). Vaishnavite Brahmin. Born Chingleput district. BA, Presidency College, first place in the first class, 1880; MA, 1882; BL, 1884. High Court Vakil, 1885. Statutory Civil Service 1886; deputy collector; first grade collector; Dewan of Cochin 1896-1901. Registrar of Co-operative Societies, Madras, 1902-7. Dewan of Travancore, 1908-14. Minister of Local and Municipal Self-Government, Madras; Speaker of the Madras Legislative Council.

**Rajaram Rao, T.** (1844-1907). Desastha Brahmin. Educated at Free School, Trivandrum and Presidency College, Madras; BA, 1866. Clerk in the Dewan's Office; cashier of the Dewan's office, 1869-80; assistant to the Dewan; dewan peshkar, Kottayam, about 1888, and of Quilon, about 1894; in charge of the revenue survey and settlement, 1903; acting Dewan, 1906. Master of the Trivandrum Masonic Lodge, 1902. Elder brother, Hari Rao, was a tahsildar.

**Ramakrishna Pillai, K.** (1877-1916) Nair. Father a Potti Brahmin. Born Neyyattinkara taluk. BA, 1906. Journalist. Edited a number of newspapers, including the second incarnation of the *Malayali* and his most famous, *Swadeshabhimani*. For his attacks in the latter on P. Rajagopalachari, q.v, he was expelled from Travancore in 1910. Found a patron in Dr. T.M. Nair in Madras. Published a Malayalam biography of Marx, 1914. Married B. Kalyani Amma, first Nair woman graduate, in 1905.

**Rama Rao, T.** (1830-95). Desastha Brahmin. Born at Trivandrum. Father, who was a brother of Dewans Venkata Rao and Ranga Rao, was a Travancore judge. Educated at the Nagercoil Seminary and Free School, Trivandrum. Clerk in the huzur English office, 1851. Translator in British service in Calicut, 1855. T. Madhava Rao, his first cousin, brought him back to Travancore to be tahsildar in Padmanabhapuram division, 1856. Police sheristadar, 1858; head sheristadar, 1862; dewan peshkar, 1865, Dewan, 1887. Bitterly attacked in *Madras Standard*; received Malayali Memorial, 1891. Retired, 1892. Good relations with Christians. Died in Trivandrum.

**Raman Pillai, C.V.** (1858-1922). Nair. Father a Nair. Born at Trivandrum. Educated at Maharaja's College and High School, Trivandrum; FA, 1875; BA, 1881. Clerk in the High Court. Leading figure in Malayali Social Union; friend of P. Thanu Pillai, q.v. Secretary of the Malayali Sabha; editor of the first *Malayali*. In Madras 1889 and made arrangements with Nairs there for the Malayali Memorial campaign. Signed Memorial and did much of the organization. Published *Martanda Varma*, the first historical novel in Malayalam, 1891. High Court manager, 1897. Opposed taravad partition before Marumakkattayam Committee, 1908. Published two other historical novels, *Dharmaraja*, 1913, and *Rama Raja Bahadur*, 2 vols., 1917 and 1920.

**Ramiengar, V.** (1826-87). Vaishnavite Brahmin. Born at Madras. Educated at Madras High School. British service, 1845-80. Additional member of council, 1868-80. Madras municipal commissioner, 1872-80. To Travancore as Dewan, 1880, at Vishakham Tirunal's request. Accused of importing many non-Malayali Brahmins into the sirkar service; expelled G. Parameswaran Pillai, q.v., from the state, 1882. Retired after disputes with the Resident and Mulam Tirunal, 1887.

**Ramier, E.** (?-?). Smarta Brahmin from Shenkotta. Vakil, said to be the wealthiest and most successful in Travancore. Organized Counter-Memorial. Member of Legislative Council, 1891-4, 1897-1900, 1904-6. Hurriedly appointed to the first session of the Popular Assembly in 1904 when it was discovered he had been omitted.

**Ross, John** (1883-1905). Edinburgh graduate. Principal of the Maharaja's College and High School, Trivandrum, 1866-84. He and his colleague and successor, Robert Harvey (principal, 1884-90), another Scot, encouraged societies such as the Malayali Social Union and are said to have helped G. Parameswaran Pillai, q.v., when he fled to Madras. They also encouraged a number of Malayalis to go to Scottish universities. They were succeeded by two other Edinburgh men, H.N. Read (principal, 1890-2) and A. Crichton Mitchell (principal, 1892-1909).

**Sankara Menon, K.P.** (c. 1855-1911), Nair. Son of P. Shankunni Menon and brother of K.P. Padmanabha Menon, q.v. Educated at Maharaja's College and High School, Trivandrum; FA, 1875; later, BA, BL. Madras High Court vakil, 1880s. Titular leader of the Malayali Memorial. Retired as a vakil, 1897, and returned to Travancore where Sankara Subbayier, q.v, appointed him a district judge, 1898; dewan peshkar, about 1903; High Court judge, 1908. Member of Legislative Council, 1908-10. Retired, 1911.

**Sankara Subbaiyer, S.** (1836-1904). Smarta Brahmin. Born at Trivandrum. Educated at the Free School, Trivandrum. Teacher, 1859. Sheristadar in huzur cutcherry, 1863. Patronised by T. Madhava Rao who made him a deputy peshkar, about 1868. Director of vernacular education, 1867-72. Dewan peshkar, 1874; divisional officer of Padmanabhapuram, then Quilon. In charge of revenue survey and settlement, 1883-92. Dewan, 1892-8. Cordial relations with leading Nair officials; disliked by Christians. Legislative Council, 1888-98. Madras Legislative Council, 1898-1900. Died in Trivandrum.

**Sankaran Thampi, T.** (c. 1857-1930). Nair. Originally, simply Sankaran Pillai, but given the title 'Thampi' by Mulam Tirunal. The latter married Sankaran Thampi's first wife, and Sankaran Thampi himself married his ex-wife's sister. The family lived in the palace precincts, and Sankaran Thampi became the leading favourite of the Maharaja about 1900. Palace manager. Closely associated with C.V. Raman Pillai, q.v., and others of the old Malayali Sabha. Two of his brothers were tahsildars. His activities were exposed in a bribery case in the Travancore High Court in 1906, but this did little to lessen his influence. He survived the Dewanship of V.P. Madhava Rao, who tried to displace him, and appears to have remained powerful until Mulam Tirunal's death in 1924.

**Saravanai Ananda Narayana Aiyar** (c. 1857-c. 1920). Smartha Brahmin, Mulam Tirunal's favourite who rose from scullion to holder of high-paying sinecures. The emergence of Sankaran Thampi, q.v., about 1900 limited Saravanai's influence, but the latter remained close to the Maharaja.

**Sashiah Sastri, Sir A.** (1828-1903). Smarta Brahmin. Born in Tanjore district. Educated in Madras High School, 1842-8. In British revenue service. Head sheristadar of the Madras revenue board, 1869-72. Dewan of Travancore, 1872-7. Member of Madras Legislative Council, 1878; declined seat in Viceroy's council, 1879. Dewan of Pudukotta, 1878-94. Retired to Kumbakonam.

**Shankunni Menon P.** (1815-80). Nair. Father of K.P. Sankara Menon and K.P. Padmanabha Menon, q.v., continued it in Tellicherry, Calicut and finally the Free School, Trivandrum. Clerk in huzur cutcherry, about 1844. Superintendent of Police; dewan peshkar, Padmanabhapuram, 1857; later of Kottayam. Retired, 1879. Wrote *A History of Travancore*.

**Sivan Pillai, P.S.** (?-1904). Nanjanad Vellala. Wealthy landlord. Supported the Malayali Memorial. Member of Malayali Sabha. Legislative Council, 1888-91.

**Sundaram Pillai, P.S.** (1855-97). Vellala. Matriculation, District School, Alleppey and High School, Trivandrum,

1891; BA, Maharaja's College, Trivandrum, 1876; MA, private study, 1880. Teacher; professor in the College, Trivandrum, from 1880 until his death. Translated many ancient inscriptions and at his death was establishing an archaeological department. Held the view that the *Ramayana* was an Aryan tale used to enslave the Dravidians. Does not appear to have been associated with the Malayali Social Union or the Malayali Memorial.

**Thanu Pillai, P.** (1854-1902). Nair. Born near Malagamud in what is now Tamil Nadu. Early education at Takkalay English school; FA, Maharaja's College, Trivandrum, 1874; BA, 1877; MA, private study, 1880. Teacher in the College, where he taught C.V. Raman Pillai, q.v., and others. Manager of the Dewan's office, 1880, under Nanu Pillai. Assistant first-class magistrate, Quilon, 1883; huzur deputy peshkar, about 1889; chief secretary, 1895. Advised the Malayali Sabha but stayed clear of the Malayali Memorial. Legislative Council, 1891-1902. Introduced a bill to regulate Nair marriage, 1896. Was the Nair hope for the Dewanship.

# Index


Abbs, Rev. John, 35, 50
Abkari, 183, 188, 192, 242; Ezhavas and, 128
Adi-Dravidas, 244
Administration: in 1840s, 7; pre-British, 1-2
Agur, C. M., 122
Alamuttu Channar, 192
All-Kerala Nair Samaj, 233
Alleppey, 20, 30, 57, 84, 87-8, 100, 114, 120, 126, 148, 157, 183, 202, 238
Alwaye, 144
Ambalavasi, 8, 18, 153; position in caste system, 13; temple servants, 2
America, United States of, 20, 32, 89, 126, 192
Ampthill, Lord, 197-200
Anjengo, 131-2
Annexation, danger of, 59-60
Antioch, Patriarch of, 106
Arianayagam Pillai, 175
Aruvamozhi Pass, 1, 84
Aruvipuram, 189-91, 210
Ashambu Hills, 89, 119
Assembly, Sri Mulam Popular, 183, 185, 194, 196, 211, 215, 217-22, 231, 234, 236, 243-4; competition to enter, 218-19; composition of 204-05; inaugurated, 202-06; Nairs and, 218-19; Nair aims in, 228-9
Athanasius, Mar, 106-08
Attingal, 193
*Avarna*, 18, 235-7, 242-7
Ayilyam Tirunal, Maharaja Rama Varma, 60, 65, 69, 75, 89-90; attitudes of 66; becomes Maharaja, 64; conservatism of, 79; dismisses Madhava Rao, 93
Ayurveda, 188, 191; doctors in SNDP Yogam, 128
Ayyappan Pillai, P , 75, 143, 149, 153, 189, 213, 216-17

Bailey, Rev. Benjamin, 47; Malayalam-English dictionary, 38
Baker, Rev. Henry, Jr., 23, 35, 71, 114; aids slaves, 41;

defends Nair morals, 137

Baker, Rev. Henry, Sr., 42, 47, 114; opinion of low-caste conversion, 124; welcomes emancipation of slaves, 45

Ballard, G. A., 107, 129

Bangalore, 131, 190

Banks, 182

Barbosa, Duarte, 3

Barton, William, 82-3

Baylis, Rev. Frederic: analyses advantages of conversion, 46; encourages wearing of breastcloth, 54

Blandford, Augusta M., 136

Bourdillon, Sir James, 207

Bourdillon, T. F., 207

Brahmins, 18, 22, 31, 95, 124, 142, 178, 180, 184-5, 193-4; attacked by CMS agents, 48; in schools, 70; mobility of, 12; opposed to Christian conversion, 35

Desastha, 6-7

'Foreign', 103

Malayali, 4, 10-12, 24, 26-7, 29, 32-3

Nambudiri, 25, 28, 70, 126, 137, 153, 156, 172, 204, 213-14, 217, 234, 243; discussed, 10-12; distance pollution and, 9; learn English, 12; liaisons with Nair women, 167-8; relations with Nairs, 14

Non-Malayali, 24, 26, 31-33, 64, 69-70, 84, 87, 92, 95, 97-106, 137, 139-41, 143, 146-8, 153, 158, 172, 219, 229, 234, 242, 244; Dewans for 80 years, 152; discussed, 12-13; graduates, 135; in government service, 96, 99-100; liaisons with Nair women, 167-8; Malayali feeling against, 99-100; merchants, 30; Nair view of, 12; social reform among, 103-06

Potti, 10-12, 25, 137, 172, 213

Smarta, 7, 95

Tamil, 4, 49, 53, 161, 217; administrators, 3

Breastcloth: all castes get right to wear, 77-8; disturbances over, 53-6; outcome of disturbances, 60-2

British Cochin, 58, 87

Buchanan, Dr Francis, 31

Buddhism, 236

Caley, Rev. John, 179

Calicut, 30, 110, 115, 177

Cannanore, 207

Cape Comorin, 4

Cardamom, 89

Cash economy, 80-2, 92, 97, 192, 265; *see also* wages

Census:

1875: 26, 78, 83, 133, 136; literacy statistics, 68

1891: 133, 188

Ceylon, 46-7, 58, 119

Chandu Menon, O., 137
Chandy, Rev. Jacob, Sr., 48, 132; cites examples of distance pollution, 9; land and, 29
Changanacherry, 109, 113, 211, 213, 215-16, 232
Chengannur, 209
Chera Empire, 1
*Cheri*, 2
Chetti, 18, 30
Christians, 26-7, 30-1, 64, 84, 92, 97-8, 105-06, 152-3, 157, 209, 234, 236-7, 242-3, 247; exempted from forced labour, 52; in Joint Political Congress, 236; in Malayali Memorial, 153-4; in Munro's time, 6-7; in schools, 70; interests in education, 176-8; jobs in government service, 109-10, 179-83; land and, 28, 226-7, 233; literacy of in 1941, 238; Rama Rao said to favour, 149; tensions with sirkar, 173-86; *see also* Church Missionary Society, London Missionary Society, Syrian Christians
Church Missionary Society, 9, 17, 21, 23, 29, 31, 35-6, 117; begins to proselytize, 109; converts of, 124-5; Ezhavas and, 193-4; John Munro vice-patron of, 7; low castes use, 110, 113-14
CMS College, Kottayam, 47, 49, 109, 124, 136; matriculates from, 110
Churches: right to build, 174, 178
Civic Rights League, 234
'Civil rights', 75-9; missionaries strive for, 49-56
Cochin, 3-4, 16, 87, 94, 107, 109, 114, 126, 151, 210-11, 219, 221-2, 239-40; emancipates slaves, 45; employment opportunities in, 47; Raja of, 91
*Cochin Argus*, 145
Cocoanut palm: and Ezhavas, 19
Cocoanut products, 32, 96, 242; increase in export of, 126
Coffee: fails, 115; growth of, 89-90; missionary interest in 121-2
Coir, 126-7, 192
Commercial treaties, 87
Communist Party, 238
Connemara, Lord, 145, 147
Conversion to Christianity: increase in after breastcloth disturbances, 62; Ezhavas threaten, 210, 235; of slave castes, 23; reasons for, 35-6
Converts to Christianity, 117-25; CMS baptizes Pulaya, 43; Ezhava ordained, 125; facilities gained from LMS, 47-8; number of LMS, 118; LMS support Counter-Memorial, 155; marumakkattayam have not right to family support, 175-6; missionaries work for 'civil rights' of, 49-56; Nair, 175-6; planting and, 119; Pulaya,

180; Syrian Christian objections to, 47, 124; wish to wear breastcloth, 53-4
Coonen Cross, 16, 108
Cost of living, 94
Counter-Memorial, 155-8, 203
Cox, Rev. John, 50, 90, 120; attacks Travancore government, 42; estimates damage in breastcloth disturbances, 55; marries convert, 120; on state of roads, 85; publishes correspondence with Madras Government, 58
Cranganore, 211
Cumbum Valley, 86
Cullen, Lt-Gen. William, 37, 42-4, 51-2, 56, 59-60, 64-5, 67-8; attitude to breastcloth disturbances, 55; attitude to missionaries, 38, 43; employs Krishna Rao, 39; frustrations with Travancore government, 58; laments bad roads, 84; protects Krishna Rao, 58; relationship with Krishna Rao, 38-9; resignation of, 60-1; wants partial abolition of slavery, 40-1
'Cultivators', 28-9; in 1875 census, 27
Curien, C., 107
Curzon, Lord, 195, 197-8

da Gama, Vasco, 16, 30
Dalhousie, Marquis of: refuses to interfere in Travancore, 59
Darragh, James, 113
de Lannoy, Eustace, 3
*Desam*, 2, 96
Devasagaim, P. D., 47, 90, 119-20, 122
Devasam department, 234, 237
Dewan, 32, 37; choice of, 195, 199, 218; performs work in Marathi, 7
Dionysius, Mar, 112-13, 174; career of, 107-08; wins control of Jacobite churches, 108
Directors, Court of: inquiry into slavery in Travancore, 41; inquiry into Travancore affairs, 59; recognizes missionaries' rights, 49
Disturbances: breastcloth, *see* breastcloth; Nair-Ezhava, 208-12
Dress: restrictions on, 53
Duthie, Rev. James, 119

East India Company, 17, 38
Education, 92; advantages of, 116-17, 119; affects taravad, 136-8; among Syrian Christians, 110-11, 117; awakens aspirations, 74-5, 95, 139; books used in vernacular, 71, 135-6; Christian interest in, 74, 176-7; English-style, 24; expenditure on, 73; government schools closed to low castes, 73; government service and, 67-75; grant-in-aid code, 73-4, 177; growth in number of vernacular

schools, 72; Ezhavas and, 193; linked to government service, 68-9; Maharaja's aims in encouraging, 65; Nairs and, 134-5; promotes mobility, 136; vernacular, 71-2
Edwardes, Herbert, 38
Emlyn, Rev. James, 119
Exports: rise in value of, 87; *see also* trade
Ezhava Sabha, 187
Ezhavas, 9, 21, 24, 27, 33, 35, 64, 91-2, 95-7, 106, 117-34, 139, 141, 153, 159-61, 184, 186-94, 195-6, 201, 229, 234-5, 237, 243-4, 247; association with missionaries, 130-1; ayurvedists, 128; Christian converts, 43, 125; common grievances, 233; disabilities of, 128-9, 232; discussed, 19-20; distance pollution and, 9; disturbances with Nairs, 208-10; dress, 19; educated in English, 96; few become Christians, 125-6, 131-2; first munsiff, 245; imitate Nairs, 132-3; in Assembly, 204; in Joint Political Congress, 236; in Malayali Memorial, 153-4; land and, 26, 29, 224-5; literacy among, 133, 235; non-cooperation and, 235; right to cover breasts denied, 61; right to wear breastcloth, 77-8; schools closed to 129; threaten conversion to Christianity, 118; traders, 31; work for public works department, 82-3

Feedinghouses, *see uttupura*
Forced labour, 51-2; *see also uriyam*
Fort Reading Club, 103
Francis Xavier, 16
Free School, Raja's, 68-9
*Friend of India*, 42

Gandhi, M. K., 235
Gopalachari, S., 218, 220
Government: caste composition of, 7
Government service: caste Hindus control, 186; Christian converts excluded from, 117; expansion of, 95; Ezhavas and, 188; incompetence of, 57-8; jobs held by Christians, 109, 179-80; Nairs dominate, 138-9; reasons for caste Hindu hold of, 110
Govinda Pillai, A., 75, 168, 173, 223
Govinda Pillai, Mallur K., 202
Govinda Pillai, P. G., 231
Govindan, M. 245
Graduates, 99
*Gramam*, 2
Gregorious, Mar, 157

Haripad, 208
Harris, Lord, 45, 55, 59-60
Harvey, Dr Robert, 70, 143
Hawksworth, Rev. John, 31
High School and College,

Maharaja's, 70, 74, 99, 111, 134, 136, 144, 161, 198, 234; admits Ezhavas, 129
Hill tribes, 22
*Hindu, The*, 95, 159, 235
Huxham, William, 89
Hyderabad, 59, 65

Ignatius, Patriarch, 106-07
*Illam*, 12
Indian National Congress, 152, 235
*Indulekha*, 137
Islam, 236

Jacobites, *see* Syrian Christians
Janmis, 80-1, 204; powers of, limited, 81; *see also* land
Jats, 244
Jews, 30, 153
*Jnana Nikshepam*, 110
Joint Political Congress, 236
Joint-stock companies, 96, 183
Joseph, P. C., 119, 158

Kakinada, 235
Kanyakumari, 4, 123
*Kara*, 2
Karamanai, 90, 219
Karanavan, 15-16, 137, 156, 166, 170, 222; abuses power, 231; criticized, 137; duties of, 165; litigation and, 227-8; powers curtailed, 230
*Karayogam*, 222, 232
Kartigappalli, 209
Karunagappalli, 189, 209
Kerala, 25, 30, 37, 84, 88, 91, 109, 239; literacy in, 68; location of, 1; state in Indian Union, 239
*Kerala Mitram*, 116
*Kerala Patrika*, 102, 177
Kerala Provincial Congress Committee, 235, 238
Kerala Varma, Valia Koil Tampuran, 72, 168, 171-2
Keraliya Nair Samaj, 215-18, 221, 232-3
Kesavan, C., 192, 207, 237; recalls 1905 exhibition, 207-08
Keshava Das, Raja, 4
Keshava Pillai, K. C., 156
Keshava Pillai, P. K., 224
Keshava Pillai, V. I., 142, 201, 209, 213
Kolachel, 3
Konkanis, 18, 30
Koshi, Rev. K. 48-9
Kottar, 55
Kottarakara, 191
Kottayam, 85-6, 89, 110, 114-16, 133, 149, 156, 179, 182-4, 202, 234, 246
Kottayam Traders' Association, 183
Krishna Pandalai, K., 223
Krishna Pillai, C., 143-4, 146-7, 150-1, 164, 173, 212-17, 219, 233
Krishna Pillai, M., 223
Krishna Pillai, P., 238
Krishna Rao, V. 37, 40-1, 43-5, 49, 54, 58-60, 82, 84, 89;

background of, 38-40; Dewan, 8; his government's deficits, 56-8; relations with Cullen, 38-9; 'Tiruvalla Edict' and, 43
Krishnan Nair, M., 221, 232-3
Krishnaswami Rao, K., 171, 173, 175, 185, 195, 197-99
Kshatriyas, 2, 24-5, 29, 32, 34, 137, 168, 171-2, 204, 217, 232; liaisons with Nair women, 167-8; position in caste system, 13
*Kudumi*, 14
Kumaran Asan, N., 190, 207, 210, 234; accepts medal from Prince of Wales, 235; background of, 190
Kumbakonam College, 199
Kunchukrishna Panikkar, M., 143
Kunhi Raman Nair, T., 168-9, 171, 175
Kunjan Nambiar, 12
*Kuppayam*, 54
Kuravas, 22, 234
Kuravilangad, 109
Kuruvila, K. K., 114, 171, 181
Kuthirapalli, 109

Labour: on estates, 90, 183
'Labourers', 29; 1875 census, 26-7
Land, 32, 80-2; discussed, 25-9; Ezhavas and, 192; increased value of, 97; janmam tenure, 25; made alienable, 81; sirkar pattam tenure, 25-6; small holders in Travancore, 81-2; Syrians acquire, 184; taken up near roads, 86, 115; transfers of, 225
Landlords: analysis of, in Kottayam division, 185-6
Latin Catholics, 91, 177-8, 234; in Assembly, 204
Law: applied rigidly, 81; *see also* litigation
Lee, Rev. William, 119
Legislative Council, Travancore, 170, 173-4, 181, 202, 230-4, 236
Leitch, Rev. Dr. Charles, 36
Lepper, R. S.: charges against government, 198
Lewis, Rev. Ebenezer, 36, 53; pollutes idol procession, 42
Liquor trade: *see* abkari
Literacy: 1941, 238; 1971, 239; among Ezhavas, 133, 235; among Nairs, 68; in Kerala, 68; in southern division, 118; value of, 47; *see also* education
Litigation, 225-7; following Pattam Proclamation, 138; taravad and, 166-7; *see also* law
Lloyd, T. F., 157
Logan, William, 169; analyses Nairs' predicament, 141; appreciation of Nairs, 246; description of Nairs, 2
London Missionary Society, 21, 23-4, 36, 117; caste of its converts, 35; coffee planting and, 90; contributions to, 123;

encourages adherents to go abroad, 47; Ezhavas and, 193; facilities for converts, 48-9; relations with sirkar, 193
Low castes: banned from roads and buildings, 78; disabilities of, 76-7; improvement in conditions of, 75; *see also* *avarna*
Lubbays, 30

Mackenzie, G. T. 198
Macaulay, Major Colin, 5
Madhava Rao, Sir T., 52, 55, 58, 66-7, 71, 73, 78, 81, 84, 87, 89-92, 95, 97, 103-04, 109, 117-18, 123, 130-1, 134-5, 138, 155, 162-4, 199; ambitions of, 67; background, 60, 65; becomes Dewan, 60; combats corruption, 77; education policy of, 71, 73; budget surpluses, 87-8; helps Ezhava student, 130-1; interest in coffee estate, 89; laments lack of educated Nairs, 70, 90; leaves Travancore, 93; opens buildings to low castes, 78; plans road system, 85; reforms in Travancore, 64; relatives in government service, 69, 148; tutors princes, 65
Madhava Rao, V. P., 200-02, 205, 209-11, 213, 243; becomes Dewan, 199; resigns, 218
Madhavan, T. K., 235
Madhavan Pillai, C. M., 143, 198, 200
Madras, 47, 57, 190; Malayalis in, 151
*Madras Athenaeum*, 37, 59; missionaries in, 42
*Madras Church Missionary Record*, 44
Madras Government, 23, 34, 37-40, 49, 64, 74, 88, 90, 104, 148, 197-9, 241; calls for emancipation of slaves, 44; complaints to, 43; considers missionary petitions, 43, 176; disturbed at Travancore mismanagement, 56-61; supports Patriarch Ignatius, 107
Madras High School, 65, 67, 93
*Madras Mail*, 131, 156, 158-9, 174-7, 182-3, 188, 193, 203, 209, 224
*Madras Standard*, 103, 145-51, 159, 163, 172, 189
*Madras Times*, 205, 209
Madura, 30, 85, 115, 190
Maharajas, 34, 241; *see also* Ayilyam, Mulam, Swati, Uttaram and Vishakham Tirunal
Makkattayam, 153; *see also* marumakkattayam
Malabar, 18, 31, 151, 177, 188, 191, 207, 221, 232, 235, 238, 240; pepper in, 57
*Malabar Herald*, 160, 211, 217, 220, 247
*Malabar Mail*, 200
Malabar Marriage Bill and Act, 168-9, 176

Malabar Marriage Commission, 168-9, 176

*Malayala Manorama,* 116, 158, 160, 162, 172, 174, 176, 178, 180-1, 183, 185, 208

Malayalam: books in 72, 136; biography of Marx in, 214

*Malayali,* 143-4, 148, 163, 213, 219

Malayali Memorial, 133, 141, 161-2, 165, 168-9, 180-1, 187, 193, 201, 203-04, 212, 218, 223, 234, 237; demands of, 155; discussed, 151-60; grievances of, 153; signatories, 153

Malayali Sabha, 139, 141-64, 168-9, 172-3, 195-6, 201, 211-12, 216-18

Malayali Social Union, 142-3, 162

Maltby, Francis N., 64, 75, 85, 87, 89; becomes Resident, 61

Mamen, Rev. Oomen, 48-9, 245; lands of, 29

Mannam, *see* Padmanabha Pillai, Mannath

Marathas, 244

Marathi: work performed in, 7

Maravars, 209

Mardin, 107

Marriage bill, Thanu Pillai's 169-73

Martanda Varma, Maharaja, 4, 7, 12, 30, 81, 165; builds Travancore, 3; confiscates land, 25

Marumakkattayam, 24, 132, 153, 169, 173-6, 215, 239; system described, 14; *see also* matrilineal joint-family; matrilineal system; taravad

Marumakkattayam Committee, 221-30, 244, 246

Marumakkattayam Regulation, 246

Marx, Karl, 215, 236

Masulipatam, 37

Mateer, Rev. Samuel, 22, 119, 131-4, 137, 175

Matrilineal joint-family, 92, 94, 161, 165, 212, 215, 218, 228-9, 233, 242, 245; connections with sirkar service, 7; Ezhavas and, 192; partition of, 237; problems in, 97; *see also* marumakkattayam; matrilineal system; taravad

Matrilineal system, 32, 132, 138; criticized, 136-7

Matthai, John, 114

Matthai, Thomas, 114

Mault, Rev. Charles: aids slaves, 41; pollutes idol procession, 42

Mavelikara, 49, 150, 191, 245

Mead, Rev. Charles, 21, 47, 52-3; marries convert, 122

Merchants, 100

Misgovernment, 56-8

Missionaries, 28, 32, 34, 241, 244; aid low-caste converts, 36; build community among converts, 123; claim to be persecuted, 177-8; efforts to clothe women, 53-4; influence on high castes, 49; low castes seek, 34-5, 41, 46, 62; low castes suspicious of, 49-50; offer benefits, 124-5; oppose sirkar schools for low castes, 73; petition against slavery, 40; petition Madras Government, 56, 58, 60, 176; planting and, 119; 'political', 50-1; sirkar conciliates, 77; view of Cullen, 38; *see also* Church Missionary Society, London Missionary Society; converts to Christianity

'Mock-marriage', 15; *see also talikettukalyanam*

'Model Native State', 82, 93

Monopolies: pepper, 57-8, 87; tobacco, 87

Mulam Tirunal, Maharaja Rama Varma, 158-9, 172, 196, 243; his favourite, 103

Mundakayam, 85

Munro, Major John, 7-8, 47, 52, 110, 181; becomes Resident, 6; encourages missionaries, 17; reforms of, 6-7

*Murajapam*, 4, 8, 52, 57, 172

Muslims, 18, 31, 70, 87, 153, 156, 158-9, 183, 234, 244; in Joint Political Congress, 236; merchants, 30

Muthuswami Aiyar, Sir T., 168

Muvattupuzha, 246

Mysore, 131, 180, 187, 189, 196, 199, 207, 210-11

*Nad*, 2

*Naduvari*, 2

Nagam Aiya, V., 75, 99-101, 136, 199, 209; graduates, 99; on Nambudiris, 11

Nagercoil, 4, 21, 54-5, 85, 89, 104, 157-8, 163, 202

Nagercoil Seminary, 47, 49, 119, 120-2, 136

Nair Brigade, 7, 91; breastcloth disturbances and, 55

Nair Service Society, 215-16, 239; founded, 232

Nairs, 18, 22, 24-9, 32-3, 53, 64, 68, 92, 95, 97, 100-01, 124, 126, 133-4, 142, 148, 155, 159, 177, 180, 186, 192-6, 201, 211, 228, 230-3, 236-7, 240, 242-7; accosted by CMS, 48; as Dewans, 6; Assembly and, 204, 218-19; attitude during breastcloth disturbances, 54-5; Christian converts from, 35; compose army, 5; dilemmas of, 164-5, 184-5, 230; discussed, 13-16, 134-41; distance pollution and 8; disturbances with Ezhavas, 208-11; divisions among, 13, 157; dominate government service, 7, 96, 138; dress, 14; education among, 96; embarrassed by marriage customs, 95, 105; graduates, 134-5; imitate Christians, 49; in Malayali Memorial, 152-3; in Malayali Sabha, 143-4; in schools, 69; Kiriathu, 14; land and, 25,

80-2, 123, 225-6, 233; largest social category, 13; less warlike, 15-16; literacy among, 68, 96, 238; maintain caste disabilities, 75; marriage, 15-16; morals, 136; position in pre-British society, 2; recognized as Sudras, 2; right to kill low castes, 3; *Standard* exhorts, 149-50; women created for high castes, 11, 172
Namboodiripad, E. M. S., 239
Nambudiris, *see* Brahmins
Nanjanad Vellalas, 21, 143, 156-7; land in south Travancore, 123
Nanu Pillai, N., 49, 91, 122, 142, 151, 223
Narayana Guru, Sri, 191, 208; background of, 189-90
Narayana Kurukkal, K., 214
Narayana Tampi, K., 156
*Nasrani Deepika*, 116
National Club, 164, 219
National Social Conference, 189
*Nayar, The*, 216
Neelakanta Pillai, K., 153, 156, 158, 184, 211, 216
Newspapers, 187; attitude to Nair-Ezhava riots, 208; first Malayalam, 116; Syrian Christians and, 116, 184
Neyyattinkara, 190-1, 213
Nicholson, John, 38
Nidhiry, Father Emmanuel, 109, 113, 181, 185; family's land, 28-9; Malayali Memorial and, 152
Nidhiry, Syriac, 158
Non-cooperation, 234; Ezhavas and, 235
Norton, Eardley, 151

Ochterlony, David, 38

Padmanabha Menon, K. P., 223
Padmanabha Pillai, Mannath, 213-15, 232, 234, 239; describes his first school, 135
Padmanabha, Sri, 4, 34
Padmanabhapuram, 122, 203
Padmanabhaswami Temple, 88, 90, 200
Painter, Rev. Arthur F., 136, 176
Palace politics, 196-201, 212-13, 243
Palakunnel, Father Mathew, 29, 109
Palghat, 1
Palmyra palm, 20
Palpanabha Pillai, P. K., 158; first Travancore graduate, 71
Palpu, Dr P. 79, 126, 129-30, 133, 159, 190-1, 205-07, 209, 211; early life, 129-30; meets Sri Narayana, 190; petitions sirkar, 188-9; recruited for Malayali Memorial, 152
Parameswaran, P. 190
Paramaswaran Nambudiri, K., 81
Parameswaran Pillai, Changanacherry K., 213, 215-16, 220, 223, 233; estimates cost of litigation, 227; pleads for

taravad partition, 232
Parameswaran Pillai, G., 145-6, 148-9, 163, 167, 187, 223; flees to Madras, 145-6; offered judgeship, 162; supports Ezhavas, 189
Parapanad, Raja of, 168, 171
*Parapuram*, 213
Parsurama, 2, 11, 25
Paravur, 78, 193, 210
Parayas, 22, 35, 55, 62, 118, 122, 213; distance pollution and, 9; *see also* slave castes
Parsees, 30
Parur, 57
*Paschima Taraka*, 110, 116
Patidars, 244
Pattam Proclamation, 138
Pattars, 12, 167; *see also* Brahmins: 'Foreign', Smarta, Tamil
Peet, Rev. Joseph, 17, 36, 51, 76, 175, 245; clashes with Mavelikara Raja, 51; on low-caste conversion, 124; on Madhava Rao, 67, 74; view of missionary role, 46
Pepper, 89; exports of, 87; monopoly, 30
Perunna, 232
Pettah, 91, 129
Picchu Aiyar, 100
Pirmed, 86, 89, 114, 183
Planting, 89-90, 94; benefits Christians, 119-20; rubber, 183; sirkar held to, 89; Syrian Christians and, 114-15, 183; tea, 183; *see also* coffee
Political organization: pre-British, 1-3
Pollution: distance, 9-10, 22, 77; Ezhavas and, 18-19; missionaries pollute procession, 42
Poonen, Dr E. 114
Poonen, T. C., 110, 181-2
Population, 239; density, 93; increases, 93, 238
Porter, W. A., 199
Portuguese, 16
Pottinger, Sir Henry, 43-4, 49
Pottis, *see* Brahmins
Pouloose, M. 182
Powell, E. B., 65, 93, 199
Pravrattis, 7
President's rule, 239
Public works department, 82-6, 91-2, 182, 188; ends forced labour, 51; introduces salaried jobs, 82; established, 82
Pulayas, 22-3, 27, 29, 35-6, 79, 124-5, 132, 180, 213, 234; abduct high-caste women, 23; Christian converts, 43; distance pollution and, 9; *see also* slave castes
Punnapra-Vayalar rebellion, 238

Quilon, 30, 57, 68, 84-9, 103, 117, 122, 124, 148, 151, 156-7, 159, 189, 191, 193-4, 202-03, 207-11, 215, 218-20; Ezhava social system south of, 20

Raghunatha Rao, R., 148

Railway: Maharaja opposed to, 103
Rajagopalachari, P., 213, 234; background of, 222
Rama Aiyar, 3-4
Rama Rao, T., 49, 99, 121-3, 148-9, 153, 155-6, 158, 163, 168, 184, 187; retires, 162; said to favour Christians, 149
Rama Varma, Maharaja: 18th-century ruler, 5
Ramakrishna Pillai, K., 213-15
Raman Pillai, C. V., 143, 147-8, 150-3, 159, 161-3, 170, 172, 181, 194, 196, 200-01, 205, 212-13, 216-17, 221, 231-2, 242; opposes taravad partition, 223-4; praises Sankara Subbaiyer's administration, 162
Raman Pillai, N., 151, 223
Ramanatha Rao, R., 155
Ramaswami Aiyar, Sir C. P., 236, 238-9
Ramiengar, V., 103, 105, 130, 148-9
Ramier, E., 155, 157-8, 203, 205
Ranga Charlu, V. C., 199
Ranga Rao, T., 60
'Rank and property': men of, 27
Read, H. N., 136
Reddy Rao, 148; becomes Dewan, 6
Responsible government, 235-6, 239
Rice, 138, 140-1, 242; low castes can afford, 94; Travancore deficient in, 94
Richardson, F. G., 114-15, 183
Ringletaube, Rev. Tobias, 21
Roads: absence of 84-5; government's reluctance to build, 57; in Trivandrum, 91; Kottayam-Madura, 115, 184; mileage of, 85-6, 95; need for, 51-2; opened to low castes, 78
Roman Catholic Church: controls Syrian Christian churches, 16; *see also* Syrian Christians
Ross, John, 130, 143, 164; principal of High School and College, 70
Rubber, 115, 183; *see also* planting
Russel, Rev. John, 49

Sadasiva Aiyar, T., 200
St Berchman's High School, 113
Salar Jung, 59, 65
Salt, 30
Samantas, 2, 222, 226
Sambandham, 137, 167, 169, 172, 222-3; recognized as legal marriage, 230; registration of, 168
Sankara Menon, K. P., 151, 155-6, 158, 162, 182, 223; becomes judge, 162
Sankara Subbaiyer, S., 155, 161-3, 170, 173-4, 176, 180-1, 187-8, 194, 212; background of, 163-4; hostility to Christians, 173; Nairs praise, 162; Syrian Christians criticize, 163
Sankaracharya, 11

Sankaran Nair, C. 168-9, 176
Sankaran Thampi, T., 198-201, 212-13, 220, 229; background of, 196
Saravanai Ananda Narayana Aiyar, 102, 145-6, 148-9, 172, 196, 199, 201, 213; Maharaja's favourite, 102
Sashiah Sastri, A., 104, 108; becomes Dewan, 93
*Savarna*, 10, 237, 242, 245
Schisms: among Romo-Syrians, 109
Scots: in Kerala, 37
Seshadri Aiyar, Sir K., 199
Shanars, 8, 21, 24, 27, 33, 35, 46-7, 53-4, 56, 91, 118, 128, 131, 174, 209, 245; breastcloth disturbances and, 54, 60-1; convert to Christianity, 62; discussed, 22-3; in Assembly, 204; land and, 29, 225-6; traders, 33
Shankunni Menon, P., 39, 151, 223; breastcloth disturbances and, 54
Shanmadi Vilasa Sabha, 103
Shenkotta, 1, 85, 103, 155, 183
Sitarama Aiyar, A., 147
Sivan Pillai, P., 157-8
Slavery, 40-6; abolished, 62
Slaves, 29, 245; partial emancipation of 43-4; emancipated, 44; turn to missionaries, 62
Slave castes, 19; discussed, 21-5; work for public works department, 82; *see also* Parayas, Pulayas
Smiles, Samuel: students urged to read, 136
'Social civil war', 219
Special Commission on Malabar Land Tenures, 169
Sri Narayana Dharma Paripalana (SNDP) Yogam, 128, 209, 211, 235-6; founded, 191; industrial exhibition, 191-2, 194, 207-08; membership of, 208; role in Nair-Ezhava riots, 209-10
*Subhashini*, 200
Suchindram, 42, 57, 123, 190
Subcaste fusion, 232
*Sudharma*, 219
Sudras, 46; Nairs classed as, 2; Tamil, 70, 84, 244
*Sujanandhini*, 210
*Swadeshabhimani*, 213-14
Swati Tirunal, Maharaja Rama Varma, 39-40
Syrian Christians, 14, 24, 29, 31, 37, 86-7, 95-6, 106-17, 126, 128, 140, 159-60, 163, 186-7, 194-6, 201, 234, 237, 242, 244; acquire land, 184; advantages from Pattam Proclamation, 80; antagonisms with caste Hindus, 179-82; cleanse polluted objects, 31; commercial interests of, 114; conflicts among, 106-09, 182; described, 16-18; displaced from administration, 7; distance pollution and, 8; district officer from, 258;

dress, 17; education among, 109-10; find jobs outside government, 110; form association, 181-2; in Assembly, 204; increasing economic power of, 183; interests in newspapers, 116; John Munro's view of, 6-7; land and, 26, 28; merchants, 29; 'mission of help' to, 16; monopolize CMS College, 47; planting and, 116; resist convertss, 47, 132; sects among, 116; status of, 17, 51
Anglican, 17, 193
Jacobite, 16-17, 107-08, 113, 157, 174, 178; break with CMS, 41-2, 61, 124
Mar Thomite, 157, 174, 178, 237
Nordist, 16
Romo, 16-17, 28, 96, 160, 177, 185; conflicts among, 109; slow start in education, 113
Suddist, 16
*Syrian Evangelist*, 183
Syrian National Union Associatioon, 113

*Talikettukalyanam*, 15, 81, 94, 232; *see also* 'mock-marriage'
Tamil areas, 21, 239, 244
Tanjore, 47, 199
Tapioca, 89
*Tara*, 2
Taravad, 15, 26, 33, 81, 136, 138, 156, 159, 161, 167, 171, 173, 175, 194, 204, 212, 214, 216, 219, 220-2, 238; affected by education, 136-7; calls for reform of, 221-2; control of land and, 26; discussed in Assembly, 219-20; hypothetical example of a, 166-7; litigation and 138-9, 167-8; Madhava Rao criticizes, 134; missionaries and, 176; partition legislation for, 233; partition of, 222-5, 227, 230-1; problems of, 96-7, 137, 164-7; *see also* marumakkattayam; matrilineal joint-family; matrilineal system
Tea, 115, 183; *see also* planting
Teachers: education of, 72; first rung of government service, 75
Tellicherry, 110
Temple entry, 236-7
Temple Entry Proclamation, 125, 236
Temple servants, *see* Ambalavasis
Tenures: sirkar pattam, 25-6, 80-2, 138; viruthi, 139; *see also* land
*Terundakuli*, 94
Thanu Pillai, P., 75, 142-3, 147-8, 150, 164, 171, 187, 192, 197, 212, 218, 223; advances under Sankara Subbaiyer, 162; dies, 172; marriage bill of, 169-73, 231; on Nairs' dilemma, 184-5
Thanu Pillai, Pattam A., 237-9
Thomas, A. V., 120

Thomas, St, the Apostle, 16
Thomas Athanasius, Mar, 108, 112, 156
Thomas of Cana, 16-17
Thompson, Dr Alfred, 123
Tinnevelly, 30, 47, 55, 70, 100, 190, 209, 218, 235
Tipu Sultan, 5
'Tiruvalla Edict', 43-4, 49
Tiyyas, 188
Tobacco, 30, 87; *see also* monopolies
Torture Commission, 59
Trade, 30-3, 87-8; *see also* coffee; coir; copra; etc.
*Travancore Almanack*, 100
Travancore and Cochin Christian Association, 181, 185
'Travancore for the Travancoreans', 149
Travancore Nair Samaj, 216
Travancore State Congress, 236, 238
*Travancore Times*, 101, 119, 122, 144, 158, 193
Travancore Unemployment Enquiry Committee, 238
Travancore Wills Act, 173
Trevelyan, Sir Charles, 61, 64
Trivandrum, 4, 8, 22, 39, 50, 57, 68-74, 84-5, 99, 101, 116, 122, 128, 131, 136, 150, 155, 157-8, 161, 164, 178, 184, 187, 189, 191, 193, 202-03, 205, 209, 212, 214-15, 217, 219, 221, 232-3, 239-40; modernization of, 90-2
Tweeddale, Marquis of, 39

Union Club, 164, 219
*Uriyam*, 51-2, 82; *see also* forced labour
Uttaram Tirunal, Maharaja Martanda Varma, 39-40, 67; dies, 64
*Uttupuras*, 4, 57, 99-101, 103, 105, 179; cost of, 99

Vaikam, 193
Vaikam satyagraha, 235
Vaisyas: Syrian Christians seen as, 31
Varghese, M. M., 183
Varghese, T. M., 237
Varghese Mappillai, K. I., 116
Velayudhan, P., 129, 133, 152
Vellalas, 18, 156, 158; attitude to breastcloth disturbances, 55; *see also* Nanjanad Vellalas; Sudras
Vellore mutiny, 38
Velu Pillai, T. K., 233
Velu Thampi, 5-6, 84
Venkata Rao, T., 60
*Videshiya Medhavitvam*, 162
Vidhya Abhivardana Sabha, 212, 217
Vishakham Tirunal, Maharaja Rama Varma, 65-6, 103, 119, 122, 136, 180, 232; attitudes of, 66; interest in coffee estate, 89; opinion of Krishna Rao, 40; writes in *Madras Athenaeum*, 59

Vivekananda, 189, 207
*Vivekodayam*, 207

Wages, 139-40, 242; rise in, 82-3, 94-5
Ward and Conner, Lieutenants, 26, 28, 31
Walker, H. M., 107
Weber, Max, 243
Welsh, James, 6
Wenlock, Lord, 176
West Asia, 16, 30
Western Ghats, 1, 3, 12, 84, 89, 101, 179
*Western Star*, 107, 116, 183
Whitehouse, Rev. J. O., 36
Women: breastcloth and, 53-6, 77-8; Nair, 53, 172, 214; Syrian Christian, 53
Woodland Estate, 113